Ninth Edition

PARAGRAPHS & ESSAYS
A WORKTEXT WITH READINGS

Custom Version for Bucks County Community College

LEE BRANDON
Mt. San Antonio College

HOUGHTON MIFFLIN COMPANY
Boston   New York

Publisher: Patricia A. Coryell
Development Editor: Kellie Cardone
Editorial Assistant: Peter Mooney
Associate Project Editor: Shelley Dickerson
Manufacturing Manager: Florence Cadran
Marketing Manager: Annamarie Rice

Text credits appear on page 548, which constitutes an extension of the copyright page.

Custom Publishing Editor: Dee Renfrow
Custom Publishing Production Manager: Kathleen McCourt
Project Coordinator: Anisha Sandhu

Cover Design: Majel Peters
Cover Image: PhotoDisc

This book contains select works from existing Houghton Mifflin Company resources and was produced by Houghton Mifflin Custom Publishing for collegiate use. As such, those adopting and/or contributing to this work are responsible for editorial content, accuracy, continuity and completeness.

Printed in the United States of America.

ISBN: 0-618-53516-0
N03797

1 2 3 4 5 6 7 8 9 – CCI – 06 05 04

Houghton Mifflin
Custom Publishing

222 Berkeley Street • Boston, MA 02116

Address all correspondence and order information to the above address.

Contents

Preface   *xxi*

 Student Overview   **1**

 The Flow of Writing: Icon and Theme   2
 Practice with Principles   2
 Strategies for Self-Improvement   3
 Writing Process Worksheet   6

Part I: Linking Reading and Writing   7

Chapter 1: Reading-Related Writing   9

 Reading for Writing   10
  Underlining   10
  Annotating   11
  Outlining   12
 Types of Reading-Related Writing   14
  Writing a Summary   15
  Writing a Reaction   16
  Writing a Two-Part Response   17
 Journal Writing   18
 Cross-Curricular and Career-Related Writing   18
 Supporting Ideas with Quotations and References   18
 Basic Documentation   19
 Documentation in Action   20
 Essays and Applications   20
  Elizabeth Wong, "The Struggle to Be an All-American Girl"   20

   I had tried to disassociate myself from the nagging loud
   voice that followed me wherever I wandered in the nearby
   American supermarket outside Chinatown.

  Lee Little Soldier, "Native American Core Values and
   Cooperative Learning"   23

   Because traditionally they come from extended families,
   Native American children tend to be group-centered rather
   than self-centered.

  Writer's Guidelines   *25*

Part II: The Writing Process   27

Chapter 2: The Writing Process: Stage One
Exploring / Experimenting / Gathering Information   **29**
The Writing Process Defined   30
The Writing Process Worksheet   30
The Assignment   30
Your Audience   31
Stage One Strategies   31
Freewriting   31
Brainstorming   34
Clustering   36
Gathering Information   37
Writer's Guidelines   **37**

Chapter 3: The Writing Process: Stage Two
*Writing the Controlling Idea / Organizing
and Developing Support*   **39**
Defining the Controlling Idea   40
Writing the Controlling Idea as a Topic Sentence or Thesis   40
Organizing Support   44
Listing   45
Clustering   45
Outlining   45
Writer's Guidelines   **50**

Chapter 4: The Writing Process: Stage Three
Writing / Revising / Editing   **52**
Writing the First Draft   53
Revising   54
Coherence   54
Language   56
Unity   58
Emphasis   59
Support   60
Sentences   61
Editing   63
Student Demonstration of All Stages of the Writing Process   64
Writing Process Worksheet   64
Writer's Guidelines   **70**

Chapter 5: Writing the Paragraph   **71**
The Paragraph Defined   72
Basic Paragraph Patterns   72
The Writing Process and the Paragraph   75
Student Demonstration of All Stages of the Writing Process   76
Writing Process Worksheet   76
Writer's Guidelines   **80**

Chapter 6: Writing the Essay   **82**

    The Essay Defined in Relation to the Developmental Paragraph   83

    Special Paragraphs Within the Essay   85

      Introductions   85

      Conclusions   87

    Student Demonstration of All Stages of the Writing Process   88

      Writing Process Worksheet   89

    Writer's Guidelines   **96**

Part III: Writing Paragraphs and Essays:
Instruction, with Reading Selections   **99**

Chapter 7: Narration: Moving Through Time   **101**

    Writing Narration   102

      The Narrative Defined   102

      Basic Patterns   102

      Verb Tense   103

      Point of View   103

      Description   104

      Dialogue   104

    Practicing Narrative Patterns   105

    Connecting Reading and Writing   107

    PROFESSIONAL WRITERS   107

      Helen Keller, "W-A-T-E-R"   107

      *I knew then that "w-a-t-e-r" meant the wonderful cool
something that was flowing over my hand.*

      Andrea Lee, "B. B. King Live!"   108

      *King teases his audiences, urging them to clap along, to
whistle, to hoot their appreciation.*

      Gina Greenlee, "No Tears for Frankie"   109

      *Quite accommodatingly, he lay in a casket later that year. I
didn't shed a tear.*

      Lesley Hazelton, "Assembly Line Adventure"   111

      *My ears were ringing, my mind was reeling, and my hands
had never felt clumsier. I began to fumble the screws. . . .*

    STUDENT WRITERS   115

      Karen Bradley, "A Moment in the Sun" (demonstration
with stages)   117

      *After their first two batters made outs, the next one, a
speedy, little second baseman named Toni, walked. Everyone
knew she would try to steal second.*

      Jeanne Sewell, "From Survival to Living"   118

      *My husband and I made eye contact, and he smiled slightly.
His gaze shifted to Dr. Morton, and he said, "I married
Jeanne, not a pair of breasts."*

    Topics for Writing Narration   121

      Reading-Related Topics   121

General Topics   122
Cross-Curricular Topics   123
Career-Related Topics   123
Writer's Guidelines   **123**

Chapter 8: Description: Moving Through Space   **125**
Writing Description   126
Types of Description   126
Techniques of Descriptive Writing   127
Practicing Descriptive Patterns   130
Connecting Reading and Writing   134
PROFESSIONAL WRITERS   134
Craig Finley, "The Mousetrap"   134

*Also attached to the center kill bar is a bait pad, a little
rectangular piece of flat metal with a grooved edge extending
up from one side to hold the trigger rod.*

Amy Tan, "The Alley"   135

*The best playground, however, was the dark alley itself. It
was crammed with daily mysteries and adventures.*

Judith Ortiz Cofer, "More"   136

*Instead, I see [my grandmother's] room as a queen's chamber
where a small woman loomed large, a throne-room with a
massive four-poster bed in its center. . . .*

William Least Heat-Moon, "In the Land of 'Coke Cola'"   138

*Thirty or so people, black and white, sat around tables
almost foundering under piled platters of food.*

STUDENT WRITERS   141
Mike Kavanagh, "The Drag" (demonstration with stages)   143

*With the push of a button, I feel the rumble of the motor,
hear the scream of the blower, and smell the distinctive odor
of nitro in the air.*

Chanya Werner, "My Aircraft Carrier 'Bedroom'"   144

*The ships made for combat operations did not have the
luxury of cruise ships, nor did the Tarawa. All enlisted
females, regardless of rank, were assigned to sleep in the
same area called "berthing."*

Topics for Writing Description   146
Reading-Related Topics   146
General Topics   147
Cross-Curricular Topics   147
Career-Related Topics   148
Writer's Guidelines   **148**

Chapter 9: Exemplification: Writing with Examples   **149**
Surveying Exposition   150
Writing Paragraphs and Essays of Exemplification   150
Characteristics of Good Examples   150
Techniques for Finding Examples: Listing and Clustering   151
Number and Order of Examples   152

Practicing Patterns of Exemplification   152
Connecting Reading and Writing   153
PROFESSIONAL WRITERS   153

Wayne D. Hoyer and Deborah J. MacInnis, "Novelty Sells"   153
A perfume company is attracting attention with novel perfume fragrances—one labeled Dirt smells like potting soil. . . .

Eric Schlosser, "Colorado Springs—Every Which Way"   154
Colorado Springs has twenty-eight Charismatic Christian churches and almost twice as many pawnbrokers. . . .

Gregory Moorhead and Ricky W. Griffin, "Working in a Chicken-Processing Plant"   155
Some workers, for example, have to fight the live birds when they are first hung on the chains. These workers are routinely scratched and pecked by the chickens.

Deborah Kong, "Spanglish Creeps into Mainstream"   157
"Que beautiful it is to do nada, and then descansar despues". . . . "How beautiful it is to do nothing, and then rest afterward."

STUDENT WRITERS   159

Lara Olivas, "Cheating Is Not Worth the Bother"(demonstration with stages)   161
She was sitting next to me, so I could see everything she did. She kept her cheat cards in her bra.

Garabed Yegavian, "Traveling the World at Home"   162
In miles I hadn't gone far, but who needs to travel the world when one lives in Southern California?

Topics for Writing Exemplification   164
Reading-Related Topics   164
General Topics   165
Cross-Curricular Topics   165
Career-Related Topics   166
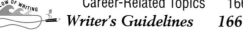 *Writer's Guidelines*   166

Chapter 10: Analysis by Division: Examining the Parts   167
Writing Instruction   168
Procedure   168
Organization   168
Sequence of Parts   168
Practicing Patterns of Analysis by Division   169
Connecting Reading and Writing   170
PROFESSIONAL WRITERS   170

Ian Robertson, "The Family and Its Parts"   170
What characteristics, then, are common to all family forms?

Leonard Engel, "The Zones of the Sea"   171
The life of the ocean is divided into distinct realms, each with its own group of creatures that feed upon each other and depend on each other in different ways.

Katherine S. Newman, "Low Wages, High Skills" 172

As entry-level employment, fast food jobs provide the worker with experience and knowledge that ought to be useful as a platform for advancement in the work world.

Kesaya E. Noda, "Growing Up Asian in America" 177

I am my mother's daughter. And I am myself. I am a Japanese-American woman.

STUDENT WRITERS 182

Selin Simon, "Skin" (demonstration with stages) 184

Skin is technically an organ because it is composed of several kinds of tissues that are structurally arranged to function together.

Allison Udell, "Ben Franklin, Renaissance Man" 185

Anyone who doesn't know the definition of Renaissance man *would do well to study Benjamin Franklin.*

Topics for Writing Analysis by Division 186
Reading-Related Topics 186
General Topics 187
Cross-Curricular Topics 188
Career-Related Topics 188
Writer's Guidelines 188

Chapter 11: Process Analysis: Writing About Doing **190**
Writing Process Analysis 191
Two Types of Process Analysis: Directive and Informative 191
Working with Stages 191
Basic Forms 192
Combined Forms 193
Useful Prewriting Procedure 193
Practicing Patterns of Process Analysis 193
Connecting Reading and Writing 196
PROFESSIONAL WRITERS 196

Rachel Carson, "The Birth of an Island" 196

The birth of a volcanic island is an event marked by prolonged and violent travail.

Will Brock, "Zen and the Art of Pomegranate Eating" 197

At your best, in your most reflective, patient mood, you will likely eat the fruit one grain at a time, savoring the experience by prolonging it.

Sharon S. Brehm, Saul M. Kassin, and Steven Fein, "How Low-Balling Works on Your Mind" 199

Salespeople who use this tactic are betting that you'll go ahead with the purchase despite the added cost.

Preston Gralla, "Fast, Sleek, and Shiny: Using the Internet to Help Buy New Cars" 201

Whether or not you plan to buy your new car over the Internet, make sure to do your prepurchase research online.

STUDENT WRITERS   203

    Maysim Mondegaran, "Sabzi Polo Mahi" (demonstration with stages)   206

In order to make this special dish, one must first know how to pick the right fish, rice, vegetables, and seasoning.

    Chanya Werner, "What's Behind a Brilliant Smile"   207

When everything is dried up, an arch wire will be placed on the brackets, inserted into the bands, and held in place by pieces of elastics.

Topics for Writing Process Analysis   209
    Reading-Related Topics   209
    General Topics   209
    Cross-Curricular Topics   210
    Career-Related Topics   210

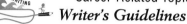 *Writer's Guidelines*   **210**

Chapter 12: Cause and Effect: Determining Reasons and Outcomes   **212**
Writing Cause and Effect   213
    Exploring and Organizing   213
    Composing a Topic Sentence or a Thesis   213
    Writing an Outline   214
    Considering Kinds of Causes and Effects   214
    Evaluating the Importance of Sequence   215
    Introducing Ideas and Working with Patterns   215
Practicing Patterns of Cause and Effect   216
Connecting Reading and Writing   218
PROFESSIONAL WRITERS   218

    Anastasia Toufexis, "What Happens to Steroid Studs?"   218

Steroids can cause temporary acne and balding, upset hormonal production, and damage the heart and kidneys.

    Marian Wright Edelman, "Family Heroes and Role Models"   219

The legacies that parents and church and teachers left to my generation of Black children were priceless but not material.

    Phyllis Rose, "The Purposes of Shopping"   220

It is a misunderstanding of the American retail store to think we go there necessarily to buy. Some of us shop.

    Dayana Yochim, "Living in Sin"   221

Forgive us for interrupting your giddy state of unwedded bliss with a dose of relationship reality. However, there are some things to consider if you and your love muffin share a roof.

    Alan Thein Durning, "The Seven Sustainable Wonders of the World"   226

To me, the real wonders are all the little things—little things that work, especially when they do it without hurting the earth.

STUDENT WRITERS   228

Richard Blaylock, "More Than the Classroom" (demonstration with stages)   230

Then I had no interest in going to college. Now I did, and one thing led to another.

Sergio Ramos, "Getting High and Living Low"   230

Once when we were in the eighth grade, we decided that we were going to smoke a marijuana cigarette with two girls from school.

Topics for Writing Cause and Effect   232
  Reading-Related Topics   232
  General Topics   233
  Cross-Curricular Topics   234
  Career-Related Topics   234
Writer's Guidelines   **234**

Chapter 13: Classification: Establishing Groups   236
  Writing Classification   237
    Selecting a Subject   237
    Using a Principle to Avoid Overlapping   237
    Establishing Classes   237
    Using Simple and Complex Forms   238
  Practicing Patterns of Classification   241
  Connecting Reading and Writing   242
    PROFESSIONAL WRITERS   242

William M. Pride, Robert J. Hughes, and Jack R. Kapoor, "Styles of Leadership"   242

In the last few decades, several styles of leadership have been identified: authoritarian, laissez-faire, and democratic.

T. Walter Wallbank, "Nobles, Peasants, and Clergy"   244

Though at times there was considerable social mobility, medieval society conventionally consisted of three classes.

Ron Geraci, "Which Stooge Are You?"   245

We're all variations of Moe, Larry, or Curly, and our lives are often short subjects filled with cosmic slapstick.

Sara Gilbert, "The Different Ways of Being Smart"   249

Book smarts, art smarts, body smarts, street smarts, and people smarts: These . . . labels . . . describe the various forms of intelligence and their use.

Donna Brown Hogarty, "How to Deal with a Difficult Boss"   253

Most bosses were promoted to management because they excelled at earlier jobs—not because they have experience motivating others.

STUDENT WRITERS   257

Boris Belinsky, "Doctors Have Their Symptoms, Too" (demonstration with stages)   259

I can figure out doctors' motives [for becoming doctors] by their symptoms, by which I mean behavior.

Annie Chen, "Types of Hepatitis"   260

Hepatitis is not a single disease coming from the same source: instead, it mainly takes three different forms. . . .

Topics for Writing Classification   261
    Reading-Related Topics   261
    General Topics   263
    Cross-Curricular Topics   263
    Career-Related Topics   263
Writer's Guidelines   264

Chapter 14: Comparison and Contrast:
    Showing Similarities and Differences   **265**
    Comparison and Contrast Defined   266
    Generating Topics and Working with the 4 *Ps*   266
        Purpose   266
        Points   267
        Patterns   268
        Presentation   269
    Analogy   271
    Practicing Patterns of Comparison and Contrast   271
    Connecting Reading and Writing   274
        PROFESSIONAL WRITERS   274
        Robert McGarvey, "Business Battle Tactics"   274

The same kind of thinking that enables a person to function in the chaos and confusion of war will help a businessperson make good decisions in a turbulent business economy.

        Alison Lurie, "Pink Kittens and Blue Spaceships"   276

Sex-typing in dress begins at birth with the assignment of pale-pink layettes, toys, bedding, and furniture to girl babies, and pale-blue ones to boy babies.

        Craig Calhoun, "The Small Town and the Big City"   277

In almost every way, Diagonal [Iowa] and the Upper West Side of Manhattan appear to be opposites.

        Luis Torres, "Los Chinos Discover el Barrio"   278

Two signs hang side by side behind the counter announcing in Spanish and in Chinese that cakes are made to order for all occasions.

        Paired Essays on Orderly and Disorderly People   281
        Suzanne Britt, "Neat People vs. Sloppy People"   282

I've finally figured out the difference between neat people and sloppy people. The distinction is, as always, moral. Neat people are lazier and meaner than sloppy people.

        Joyce Gallagher, "The Messy Are in Denial"   284

If they [messy people] are so contented, then why are so many of them latching onto and becoming entirely dependent on those of us who are organized?

        STUDENT WRITERS   287

Omar Zayas, "Disneyland or Magic Mountain: Fantasy or Thrills?" (demonstration with stages)   289

Once inside [Magic Mountain], the attractions may seem similar [to those of Disneyland], but overall the differences are as noticeable as Mickey's ears.

Brittany Markovic, "The Piper Cherokee and the Cessna 172"   290

Although either can be used for training, I believe that certain features make the Cessna 172 the better aircraft for the student [pilot].

Topics for Writing Comparison and Contrast   291
Reading-Related Topics   291
General Topics   293
Cross-Curricular Topics   294
Career-Related Topics   294
Writer's Guidelines   294

Chapter 15: Definition: Clarifying Terms   296
Writing Definition   297
Techniques for Writing Simple Definitions   297
Techniques for Writing Extended Definitions   300
Practicing Patterns of Definition   302
Connecting Reading and Writing   305
PROFESSIONAL WRITERS   305
Gregory Moorhead and Ricky W. Griffin, "Burnout"   305

Burnout is a general feeling of exhaustion that develops when a person simultaneously experiences too much pressure and has too few sources of satisfaction.

Ray Jenkins, "Georgia on My Mind"   306

Unless a man has . . . learned at least a few chords on a fiddle and guitar; has eaten sardines out of a can with a stick; . . . has been cheated by someone he worked hard for, . . . then he cannot understand what it was like in my South.

José Antonio Burciaga, "Tortillas"   307

While the tortilla may be a lowly corn cake, when the necessity arises, it can reach unexpected distinction.

Ellen Goodman, "A Working Community"   308

As more of our neighbors work away from home, the workplace becomes our neighborhood.

Ellen Bravo and Ellen Cassedy, "Is It Sexual Harassment?"   311

MYTH: You can't blame a guy for looking. Women invite attention by the way they dress.
FACT: If a woman's clothes are truly inappropriate for the job, management should tell her so.

STUDENT WRITERS   315
Linda Wong, "Going Too Far" (demonstration with stages)   317

People who love well may be tender and sensitive and attentive, but extremists are possessive or smothering.

Louise Rubec, "Prison Slang"   318
[Slang words] are part of prison life. All female convicts learn them—or else.

Topics for Writing Definition   319
Reading-Related Topics   319
General Topics   321
Cross-Curricular Topics   321
Career-Related Topics   321
Writer's Guidelines   **322**

Part V: Handbook   403

Handbook: Writing Effective Sentences   **405**
Subjects and Verbs   406
Subjects   406
Nouns   406
Pronouns   406
Compound Subjects   407
Implied Subjects   407
Trouble Spot: Prepositional Phrases   407
Trouble Spot: The Words Here *and* There   *408*
Verbs   408
Types of Verbs   408
Verb Phrases   408
Trouble Spot: Words Such as Never, Not, *and* Hardly   *408*
Compound Verbs   409
Trouble Spot: Verbals   409
Location of Subjects and Verbs   409
Kinds of Sentences   413
Clauses   413
Independent Clauses   413
Dependent Clauses   413
Relative Clauses   413
Trouble Spot: Phrases   414
Types of Sentences   414
Simple Sentences   414
Compound Sentences   415
Complex Sentences   417
Compound-Complex Sentences   418

Combining Sentences   422

Coordination: The Compound Sentence   422

Punctuation with Coordinating Conjunctions   423

Semicolons and Conjunctive Adverbs   423

Punctuation with Semicolons and Conjunctive Adverbs   424

Subordination: The Complex Sentence   424

Subordinating Conjunctions   425

Punctuation with Subordinating Conjunctions   426

Punctuation and Relative Pronouns   426

Coordination and Subordination: The Compound-Complex Sentence   426

Punctuation of Complicated Compound or Compound-Complex Sentences   427

Other Ways to Combine Ideas   427

Omissions   431

Variety in Sentence Types, Order, Length, Beginnings   432

Type   432

Order   433

Length   433

Beginnings   433

Correcting Fragments, Comma Splices, and Run-Ons   434

Fragments   434

Acceptable Fragments   434

Dependent Clauses as Fragments: Clauses with Subordinating Conjunctions   435

Dependent Clauses as Fragments: Clauses with Relative Pronouns   435

Phrases as Fragments   435

Fragments as Word Groups Without Subjects or Without Verbs   436

Comma Splices and Run-Ons   437

Four Ways to Correct Comma Splices and Run-Ons   437

Techniques for Spotting Problem Sentences   438

Verbs   444

Regular and Irregular Verbs   444

Regular Verbs   444

Irregular Verbs   446

"Problem" Verbs   449

The Twelve Verb Tenses   452

Simple Tenses   452

Perfect Tenses   452

Progressive Tenses   452

Perfect Progressive Tenses   452

Subject-Verb Agreement   455

Consistency in Tense   460

Active and Passive Voice   463

Strong Verbs   465

Subjunctive Mood   466

Pronouns   467

Pronoun Case   467

Subjective Case   467

Objective Case   468

Techniques for Determining Case   469

Pronoun-Antecedent Agreement   472

Agreement in Person   472

Agreement in Number   474

Agreement in Gender   475

Pronoun Reference   478

Adjectives and Adverbs   481

Selecting Adjectives and Adverbs   481

Comparative and Superlative Forms   483

Adjectives   483

Adverbs   484

Using Adjectives and Adverbs Correctly   485

Dangling and Misplaced Modifiers   488

Balancing Sentence Parts   491

Basic Principles of Parallelism   491

Signal Words   492

Combination Signal Words   492

Punctuation and Capitalization   496

End Punctuation   496

Periods   496

Question Marks   497

Exclamation Points   497

Commas   497

Commas to Separate   497

Commas to Set Off   498

Semicolons   502

Quotation Marks   505

Punctuation with Quotation Marks   506

Italics   507

Dashes   507

Colons   508

Parentheses   508

Brackets   509

Apostrophes   509

Hyphens   510

Capitalization   510

Spelling   514

Spelling Tips   514

Frequently Misspelled Words   516

Confused Spelling and Confusing Words   517

Your Spell Checker   519

Wordy Phrases   519

Brief Guide for ESL Students   521

Using Articles in Relation to Nouns   521

Articles   521

Nouns   521

Rules   521

Sentence Patterns   522
Verb Endings   522
Idioms   523
More Suggestions for ESL Writers   523

Appendixes   525
Appendix A: Parts of Speech   526
Appendix B: Taking Tests   535
Appendix C: Writing a Job Application Letter and a Résumé   537

Answer Key   540
Text Credits   548
Author and Title Index   549
Subject Index   553

Preface

The phrase "flow of writing" has always been prominent in the previous eight editions of *Paragraphs and Essays*. In this ninth edition, it takes shape as a unifying and reinforcing icon, demonstrating with coastal waves and a merry surf writer on a pencil that writing is cyclical, moving forward and backward and forward again. The surf writer will always be searching for the "perfect wave," meaning the best possible expression. That recursive movement, or revision, is the essence of good writing. Instruction in this book—comprehensive, flexible, relevant, and stimulating—is predicated on systematic, relentless revision.

Time-Tested Techniques

Written for either developmental or freshman composition writing courses, the ninth edition continues to feature highly accessible, easily remembered techniques that will enable students initially to survive and then to thrive. For example, the acronym **CLUESS** is a memory aid, with the letters representing key parts of rewriting: Coherence, Language, Unity, Emphasis, Support, and Sentences. Inexperienced writers can easily remember **CLUESS** and use it as a checklist. Another acronym (**COPS**—Capitalization, Omissions, Punctuation, and Spelling) is used for editing.

Student Demonstrations

All writers—beginners and professionals—depend on examples when confronted with new writing tasks. We are likely to say, "Show me what one looks like." Instruction in *Paragraphs and Essays* does just that. It also shows examples in each of eleven chapters of how students just like those using the book have begun with assignments and ended with compositions, detailing the pertinent stages of writing, as the writing flowed. These are real student products, not those that should be nominated for Pulitzer Prizes but those that did enable students to express themselves with satisfaction.

Integrated Writing and Reading

Paragraphs and Essays begins with a chapter on reading-related writing, offering instruction on basic reading techniques and common forms of writing about reading (summary, reaction, and two-part response). Useful for introductory assignments and ice-breaking discussions, it offers convenient material for diagnostic writing often used at the outset in writing classes.

Elsewhere, readings are presented within chapters that integrate instruction, demonstration, and content. Abundant readings from both professional and student writers have been selected as models of exemplary writing on stimulating topics. Readings are culturally diverse and varied in subject material, so they will appeal to students of different backgrounds—generational, ethnic, gender, and regional— while stressing the commonality of experience. Featured readings include mainly paragraphs and essays but also short stories, poems, and even a song.

Guide questions following the selections direct students to analyze the readings for form and to react to the content. Reading-related writing suggestions cover students' parallel experiences, evaluations, and analyses. Writing instruction includes explanations, examples, and exercises at the sentence, paragraph, and essay levels. Instruction for the paragraph and the essay is presented separately in Chapters 5 and 6. Thereafter, it pertains to both through eleven chapters of forms of discourse, with occasional separate and specific annotations or instructions. Forms of discourse are exemplified by both paragraph and essay reading selections. This arrangement allows instructors to choose an emphasis of either the paragraph or the essay, or a combined approach, perhaps beginning with paragraphs and culminating with essays. It even permits the instructor teaching students with disparate writing abilities to mix lengths and complexities of assignments within a class, without giving separate reading assignments or using different schedules.

Topic suggestions at the end of chapters include reading-related, general, cross-curricular, and career-related lists so instructors can specify one type or mix types for class assignments.

Chapter 18, Writing the Research Paper, includes forms of documentation as well as a discussion of libraries, online searching, plagiarism, and other research-related topics.

The Handbook presents explanations, examples, and exercises. Half of the exercises have answers in the Answer Key at the end of the book, allowing for both class work and independent work.

Changes and Special Features in the Ninth Edition

- More than 60 percent new professional essays
- More than 40 percent new content for Handbook exercises
- More than 90 percent new cartoons that make instructional points
- New feature on cross-curricular writing topics
- New feature in sentence variety
- New feature in word omissions
- New feature in word choice
- Additional career-related writing topics
- Additional emphasis on organization and revision
- Updated chapter on the research paper with a systematic ten-step approach
- Revised, more systematic approach to writing about literature
- Refined Writing Process Worksheet suitable for photocopying and designed to provide guidance for students and save time and effort for instructors
- Streamlined Self-Evaluation Chart to help students track their needs and goals and to promote self-reliance
- Additional computer-related writing tips incorporated into the text

Support Material for Instructors

The Instructor's Annotated Edition (IAE) contains immediate answers for exercises and activities, along with the following support:

- Instructor's Guide (all parts included in IAE)
- Diagnostic tests and sentence-writing quizzes
- Reproducible quizzes for Part III of the text
- Suggestions for effective and time-saving approaches to instruction
- Sample syllabi
- Reproducible quizzes for selected readings in Part III

Web Resources

Paragraphs and Essays offers instructors and students more opportunities to explore writing through the student and instructor websites.

Instructor Website

- Tips for new instructors on how to approach the text
- Sample syllabi
- Information on how to integrate ESL instruction into the classroom and how to work with basic writers
- PowerPoint slides that can be downloaded and used to enhance classroom instruction
- Dolphinville: an online writing community for any level writer
- Reproducible quizzes for selected readings in Part III
- Reproducible quizzes for Part V

Student Website

- Additional exercises and readings
- Dolphinville: an online writing community for any level writer
- A brief guide to APA style
- Additional instruction in writing résumés

Acknowledgments

I am profoundly indebted to the following instructors who have reviewed this textbook: Sally C. Hall of Honolulu Community College; Tammy Frankland of Casper College; Jill A. Lahnstein of Cape Fear Community College; Jude Roy of Madisonville Community College; Linda Caywood-Farrell, Piedmont Community College; Craig Frischkorn, Jamestown Community College; Thomas Beery, Lima Technical College; David Throne, Community College of Aurora; Cheryl West, Brewton Parker College; Dorothy Brown, Iowa Western Community College; William Gilbert, University of Houston—Downtown; Diane Dowdey, Sam Houston State University; Carol S. Hamm, Seminole State College; Herbert Karl Green, Jr., Camden County College; Ida R. Page, Durham Technical Community College; Elisabeth Leyson, Fullerton College; Joseph Szabo, Mercer County Community College; and Daniel E. M. Landau, Santa Monica College. Thanks also to the faculty members at Mt. San Antonio College.

I deeply appreciate the work of freelance editors Ann Marie Radaskiewicz, Robin Hogan, Mary Dalton-Hoffman, Nancy Benjamin of Books By Design, as well as my colleagues at Houghton Mifflin: Pat Coryell, Kellie Cardone, Peter Mooney, Annamarie Rice, Laura Hemrika, and Shelley Dickerson.

I am especially grateful to my family of wife, children and their spouses, and grandchildren for their cheerful, inspiring support: Sharon, Kelly, Erin, Michael, Shane, Lauren, Jarrett, and Matthew.

—Lee Brandon

Paragraphs and Essays

Student Overview

FLOW OF WRITING

The Flow of Writing: Icon and Theme   2
Practice with Principles   2
Strategies for Self-Improvement   3
Writing Process Worksheet   6

"Every sentence, paragraph, and essay begins with a single word."

A VARIATION ON A FAMILIAR SAYING
(LEE BRANDON)

© John Callahan, courtesy Levin Represents.

The Flow of Writing: Icon and Theme

You will see this icon frequently in *Paragraphs and Essays:*

Follow the line from top left over the waves, then down and around to the pencil with the little surf writer getting ready to hang ten.

Like the surf writer, you follow that pattern in writing, the pattern of the tide near the shore. In flowing cycles, the tide advances and withdraws, then regroups and proceeds again. The tide doesn't merely rush forward at one time and be done with it. Writing also moves in cycles with a rhythmic flow. You don't just write your message and walk away. Instead, you write—and, for revision and editing—back up, and rewrite, following that pattern until you're through. In writing, the back-and-forth movement is called *recursive*. It is the essence of the writing process.

In the coming pages, the icon will identify features that enable your own flow of writing and remind you of the importance of rewriting.

Paragraphs and Essays shows how to proceed from fragmented ideas to effective expression by blending instruction, examples, and practice. Like the surf writer going back again and again in quest of that perfect wave, you as a writer will go back again and again looking for that perfect composition.

Practice with Principles

Some will tell you that to become a better writer you should practice. Others will say that to become a better writer you should learn the principles of writing.

Each view is a half-truth. If you practice without knowing what to do, you'll get better only within your own limitations; any bad habits are likely to become more ingrained. If you're playing the piano with two fingers and you practice a lot, you may learn to play a great "Chopsticks," but Beethoven's "Moonlight Sonata" will remain beyond your reach.

However, if you learn the principles of writing and do not practice them, they will never become a functioning part of your skills. The solution is in your hands. You are now gazing at a book with a well-rounded approach, one that combines sound techniques and ample writing practice. It is designed for use both in class and on your own.

Each chapter in this book begins with a list of chapter topics.

Chapter 1 links reading and writing.
Chapters 2 through 4 explain the three stages of the writing process.
Chapters 5 and 6 present forms of writing and support: Chapter 5, the paragraph; Chapter 6, the essay.

Chapters 7 through 17 focus on forms of discourse, commonly called *patterns of development*: narration, description, exemplification (explaining), analysis by division, process analysis, cause and effect, classification, comparison and contrast, definition, and argument.

Chapter 18 discusses the research paper.

The Handbook, Part V, offers instruction in fundamentals and sentence writing. It also includes a brief guide for ESL students.

The three Appendixes include the following: (A) Parts of Speech, (B) Taking Tests, and (C) Writing a Job Application Letter and a Résumé.

A Self-Evaluation Chart appears on the inside front cover of this book (see page 4 for more information), and a Correction Chart appears on the inside back cover.

Strategies for Self-Improvement

Here are some strategies you can follow to make the best use of this book and to jump-start the improvement in your writing skills.

1. *Be active and systematic in learning.* Take advantage of your instructor's expertise by being an active class member—one who takes notes, asks questions, and contributes to discussion. Become dedicated to systematic learning: Determine your needs, decide what to do, and do it. Make learning a part of your everyday thinking and behavior.

2. *Read widely.* Samuel Johnson, a great English scholar, once said he didn't want to read anything by people who had written more than they had read. William Faulkner, a Nobel Prize winner in literature, said, "Read, read, read. Read everything—trash, classics, good and bad, and see how writers do it." Read to learn technique, to acquire ideas, and to be stimulated to write. Especially read to satisfy your curiosity and to receive pleasure. If reading is a main component of your course, approach it as systematically as you do writing.

3. *Keep a journal.* Keep a journal, even though it may not be required in your particular class. It is a good practice to jot down your observations in a notebook. Here are some topics for daily, or almost daily, journal writing:

   • Summarize, evaluate, or react to reading assignments.
   • Summarize, evaluate, or react to what you see on television and in movies, and to what you read in newspapers and in magazines.
   • Describe and narrate situations or events you experience.
   • Write about career-related matters you encounter in other courses or on the job.

   Your journal entries may read like an intellectual diary, a record of what you are thinking about at certain times. Keeping a journal will help you to understand reading material better, to develop more language skills, and to think more clearly—as well as to become more confident and to write more easily so that writing becomes a comfortable, everyday activity. Your entries may also provide subject material for longer, more carefully crafted pieces. The most important thing is to get into the habit of writing something each day.

4. *Evaluate your writing skills.* Use the Self-Evaluation Chart on the inside front cover of this book to assess your writing skills by listing problem areas you need to work on. You may be adding to these lists throughout the entire term. Drawing on your instructor's comments, make notes on matters such as organization,

development, content, spelling, vocabulary, diction, grammar, sentence structure, punctuation, and capitalization. Use this chart for self-motivated study assignments and as a checklist in all stages of writing. As you master each problem area, you can erase it or cross it out.

Most of the elements you record in your Self-Evaluation Chart are covered in *Paragraphs and Essays*. The table of contents, the index, and the Correction Chart on the inside back cover of the book will direct you to the additional instruction you decide you need.

- *Organization/Development/Content:* List aspects of your writing, including the techniques of all stages of the writing process, such as freewriting, brainstorming, and clustering; the phrasing of a good topic sentence or thesis; and the design, growth, and refinement of your ideas.
- *Spelling/Vocabulary/Diction:* List common spelling words marked as incorrect on your college assignments. Here, *common* means words that you use often. If you are misspelling these words now, you may have been doing so for years. Look at your list. Is there a pattern to your misspellings? Consult the Spelling section in the Handbook, Part V, for a set of useful rules. Whatever it takes, master the words on your list. Continue to add troublesome words as you accumulate assignments. If your vocabulary is imprecise or your diction is inappropriate (if you use slang, trite expressions, or words that are too informal), note those problems as well.
- *Grammar/Sentence Structure:* List recurring problems in your grammar or sentence structure. Use the symbols and page references listed on the Correction Chart (inside back cover of this book) or look up the problem in the index.
- *Punctuation/Capitalization:* Treat these problems the same way you treat grammar problems. Note that the Punctuation and Capitalization section in the Handbook numbers some rules; therefore, you can often give exact locations of the remedies for your problems.

Here is an example of how your chart might be used.

Self-Evaluation Chart

Organization/ Development/ Content	Spelling/ Vocabulary/ Diction	Grammar/ Sentence Structure	Punctuation/ Capitalization
needs more specific support such as examples, 60	avoid slang, 56	fragments, 434	difference between semicolons and commas, 502
refine outline, 45	avoid clichés such as "be there for me," 58	subject-verb agreement, 453	comma after long introductory modifier, 497
use clear topic sentence, 40	it's, its, 518	comma splice, 437	
	you're, your, 519	vary sentence patterns, 61	comma in compound sentence, 497
	receive, rule on, 515		

5. *Use the Writing Process Worksheet.* Record details about each of your assignments, such as the due date, topic, length, and form. The worksheet will also remind you of the stages of the writing process: explore, organize, and write. A blank Writing Process Worksheet for you to photocopy for assignments appears on page 6. Discussed in Chapter 2, it guides student work in almost every chapter. Your instructor may ask you to complete the form and submit it with your assignments.

6. *Take full advantage of technology.* Although using a word processor will not by itself make you a better writer, it will enable you to write and revise more swiftly as you move, alter, and delete material with a few keystrokes. Devices such as the thesaurus, spell checker, grammar checker, and style checker will help you revise and edit. Many colleges have writing labs with good instruction and facilities for networking and researching complicated topics. Used wisely, the Internet can provide resource material for compositions.

7. *Be positive.* To improve your English skills, write with freedom, but revise and edit with rigor. Work with your instructor to set attainable goals, and proceed at a reasonable pace. Soon, seeing what you have mastered and checked off your list will give you a sense of accomplishment.

   While you progress in your English course, notice how you are getting better at content, organization, and mechanics as you read, think, and write.

   Consequently, you can expect writing to become a highly satisfying pleasure. After all, once you learn to write well, writing can be just as enjoyable as talking.

   Finally, don't compare yourself with others. Compare yourself with yourself and, as you improve, consider yourself what you are—a student on the path toward more effective writing, a student on the path toward success.

It is appropriate to end this overview with the same quotation that introduced it.

   Every sentence, paragraph, and essay begins with a single word.

Let a word fall like thunder or a snowflake, to carry your thought.

FLOW OF WRITING

Writing Process Worksheet

Title _____

Name _____ Due Date _____

ASSIGNMENT In the space below, write whatever you need to know about your assignment, including information about the topic, audience, pattern of writing, length, whether to include a rough draft or revised drafts, and whether your paper must be typed.

STAGE ONE Explore Freewrite, brainstorm (list), cluster, or take notes as directed by your instructor. Use the back of this page or separate paper if you need more space.

STAGE TWO Organize Write a topic sentence or thesis; label the subject and the treatment parts.

Write an outline or an outline alternative.

STAGE THREE Write On separate paper, write and then revise your paragraph or essay as many times as necessary for **c**oherence, **l**anguage (usage, tone, and diction), **u**nity, **e**mphasis, **s**upport, and **s**entences (**CLUESS**). Read your work aloud to hear and correct any grammatical errors or awkward-sounding sentences.

Edit any problems in fundamentals, such as **c**apitalization, **o**missions, **p**unctuation, and **s**pelling (**COPS**).

Linking Reading and Writing

In college you write to be read, and you read to write. In your reading you will find not only ideas to ponder and discuss but also structures and skills to admire and emulate. The key to good writing is knowing what to do. The key to good reading is knowing what to look for. Those two keys are on the same chain. Or, for simplicity, you can use the third key—the one embracing the two and marked "Master Key."

Chapter 1

Reading-Related Writing

Reading for Writing   10
   Underlining   10
   Annotating   11
   Outlining   12
Types of Reading-Related Writing   14
   Writing a Summary   15
   Writing a Reaction   16
   Writing a Two-Part Response   17
Journal Writing   18
Cross-Curricular and Career-Related
   Writing   18
Supporting Ideas with Quotations
   and References   18
Basic Documentation   19
Documentation in Action   20
Essays and Applications   20
   "The Struggle to Be an All-American Girl"   20
   "Native American Core Values and Cooperative
      Learning"   23
Writer's Guidelines   25

"If you do not read more than you write, Samuel Johnson [see page 3] will not want to read your compositions."

LEE BRANDON

B. Hickerson, copyright Los Angeles Times Syndicate. Reprinted by permission.

Reading for Writing

Whether on campus or at the workplace, your skill in identifying main ideas and their support through reading and then commenting on them in writing will serve you well. The writing you will do in this chapter is commonly called *reading-related writing*. It includes

- reading effectively (which may include underlining, annotating, and outlining).
- writing a **summary** (main ideas in your own words).
- writing a **reaction** (usually a statement of how the reading relates specifically to you, your experiences, and your attitudes but also often a critique, involving the worth and logic of a piece).
- writing a **two-part response** (both a summary and a reaction, although they are separate).
- documenting (giving credit to sources you use).

These kinds of writing have certain points in common; they all

- originate as a response to something you have read.
- indicate, to some degree, content from that piece.
- demonstrate a knowledge of the piece of writing.

Underlining, annotating, and outlining will give you practice in reading analytically and in recording the main ideas and their support in a clear, direct manner.

Underlining

Imagine you are reading a chapter of several pages and you decide to underline and write in the margins. Immediately, the underlining takes you out of the passive, television-watching frame of mind. You are involved. You are participating. It is now necessary for you to discriminate, to distinguish more important from less important ideas. Perhaps you have thought of underlining as a method designed only to help you with reviewing. That is, when you study the material the next time, you won't have to reread all of it; instead, you can review only the most important, underlined parts. However, even while you are underlining, you are benefiting from an imposed concentration, because this procedure forces you to think, to focus. Consider the following guidelines for underlining:

1. Underline the main ideas in paragraphs. The most important statement, the topic sentence, is likely to be at the beginning of the paragraph.

2. Underline the support for those main ideas.

3. Underline answers to questions that you bring to the reading assignment. These questions may have come from the end of the chapter, from subheadings that you turn into questions, or from your independent concerns about the topic.

4. Underline only the key words. You would seldom underline all the words in a sentence and almost never a whole paragraph.

Does that fit your approach to underlining? Possibly not. Most students, in their enthusiasm to do a good job, overdo underlining.

The trick is to figure out what to underline. You would seldom underline more than about 30 percent of a passage, although the amount would depend on your purpose and the nature of the material. Following the preceding four suggestions will be useful. Learning more about the principles of sentence, paragraph, and essay organization in the following chapters will also be helpful.

Annotating

Annotating, writing notes in the margins, is a practice related to underlining. You can do it independently, although it usually appears in conjunction with underlining to record your understanding and to extend your involvement in your reading.

Writing in the margins represents intense involvement because it turns a reader into a writer. If you read material and write something in the margin as a reaction to it, then in a way you have had a conversation with the author. The author has made a statement and you have responded. In fact, you may have added something to the text; therefore, for your purposes, you have become a co-author or collaborator. The comments you make in the margin are of your own choosing according to your interests and the purpose you bring to the reading assignment. Your response in the margin may merely echo the author's ideas, it may question them critically, it may relate them to something else, or it may add to them.

The comments and marks on the following essay will help you understand the connection between writing and reading. Both techniques—underlining to indicate main and supporting ideas and annotating to indicate their importance and relevance to the task at hand—will enhance thinking, reading, and writing.

Total Institutions
Seymour Feshbach and Bernard Weiner

Total institution encompasses individual (thesis)   1

A <u>total institution</u> completely <u>encompasses</u> the <u>individual</u>, forming a barrier to the types of social intercourse that occur outside such a setting. Monasteries, jails, homes for the aged, boarding schools, and military academies are a few examples of total institutions.

1. Individual activities in same setting   2

<u>Total institutions</u> have certain <u>common characteristics</u>. <u>First,</u> the <u>individuals</u> in such environments must <u>sleep,</u> <u>play,</u> and <u>work</u> within the <u>same setting</u>. These are generally segmented spheres of activity in the lives of most individuals, but within a total institution one sphere of activity overlaps with others.

2. All life within group

<u>Second, each phase of life</u> takes place in the <u>company</u> of a <u>large group</u> of others. Frequently, sleeping is done in a barracks, food is served in a cafeteria, and so on. In such activities everyone is treated alike and must perform certain essential tasks.

3. Activities tightly scheduled

<u>Third, activities</u> in an institution are <u>tightly scheduled</u> according to a <u>master plan</u>, with set times to rise, to eat, to exercise, and to sleep. These institutional characteristics result in a <u>bureaucratic society</u>, which requires the hiring of other people for surveillance. What often results is a split in the groups within an institution into a large, managed group (inmates) and a small supervisory staff.

Managed groups and staff at distance

There tends to be <u>great social distance between</u> the <u>groups,</u> who <u>perceive each other according to stereotypes</u> and <u>have</u> severely <u>restricted communications</u>.

3

Two worlds—inside and outside

The <u>world of</u> the <u>inmate</u> <u>differs</u> greatly <u>from</u> the <u>outside world</u>. When one enters a total institution, all <u>previous roles</u>, such as father or husband, are <u>disrupted</u>. The <u>individual</u> is further <u>depersonalized</u> by the issuance of a

Personality altered

uniform, confiscation of belongings, and gathering of personal informa-tion, as well as by more subtle touches like doorless toilets, record keeping, and bedchecks. The <u>effects</u> of an institutional setting are so <u>all-encompassing</u> that one can meaningfully speak of an "<u>institutional personality</u>": a persis-tent manner of <u>behaving compliantly</u> and <u>without emotional involvement</u>.

4

Becomes psychotic, childlike, or depressive

Of course, there are <u>individual differences in adaptation</u> to the situation. They can be as extreme as <u>psychosis</u>, <u>childlike regression</u>, and <u>depression</u> or as mild as resigned compliance. <u>Most individuals do adjust</u> and build up a system of satisfactions, such as close friendships and cliques.

5

Individuals adjust but have trouble later on street

But because of these bonds and the fact that the habits needed to func-tion in the outside world have been lost, <u>inmates face</u> great <u>problems</u> upon <u>leaving an institution</u>. A <u>shift from</u> the <u>top of</u> a <u>small society</u> to the <u>bottom of</u> a <u>larger one</u> may be <u>further demoralizing</u>.

Outlining

After reading, underlining, and annotating the piece, the next step could be outlin-ing. If the piece is well organized, you should be able to reduce it to a simple outline so that you can, at a glance, see the relationship of ideas (sequence, relative impor-tance, and interdependence).

The essay on total institutions can be outlined very easily:

Total Institutions
  I. Common characteristics
     A. All activities in the same setting
     B. All phases of life within a larger group
     C. Activities scheduled according to a master plan
        1. Bureaucratic society
        2. Social distance between inmates and staff
 II. Adjusting to the world inside
     A. Individual depersonalized
        1. Wears uniform
        2. No personal belongings
        3. No privacy
     B. Adaptation
        1. Negative
           a. Psychosis
           b. Regression
           c. Depression
        2. Positive
III. Problems upon release outside
     A. Adjusting to a different system
     B. Encountering shock of going to the bottom of a new order

EXERCISE 1

Underlining, Annotating, and Outlining

Underline and annotate this passage. Then complete the outline that follows.

Effective E-Mail Practices

Use short lines and short paragraphs. A short line length (perhaps 50 to 60 characters) is much easier to read than the 80-character line of most text editors. Similarly, short paragraphs (especially the first and last paragraph) are more inviting to read. Avoid formatting a long message as one solid paragraph.

Don't shout. Use all-capital letters only for emphasis or to substitute for italicized text (such as book titles). Do NOT type your entire message in all capitals: It is a text-based form of *shouting* at your reader and is considered rude (not to mention being more difficult to read).

Proofread your message before sending it. Don't let the speed and convenience of e-mail lull you into being careless. While an occasional typo or other surface error will probably be overlooked by the reader, excessive errors or sloppy language creates an unprofessional image of the sender.

Append previous messages appropriately. Most e-mail systems allow you to append the original message to your reply. Use this feature judiciously. Occasionally, it may be helpful for the reader to see his or her entire message replayed. More often, however, you can save the reader time by establishing the context of the original message in your reply. If necessary, quote pertinent parts of the original message. If the entire original message is needed, treat it as an appendix and insert it at the *end* of your reply—not at the beginning.

Use a direct style of writing and think twice; write once. Put your major idea in the first sentence or two. If the message is so sensitive or emotionally laden that a more indirect organization would be appropriate, you should reconsider whether e-mail is the most effective medium for the message. Because it is so easy to respond immediately to a message, you might be tempted to let your emotions take over. Such behavior is called "flaming" and should be avoided. Always assume the message you send will never be destroyed but will be saved permanently in somebody's computer file.

Don't neglect your greeting and closing. Downplay the seeming impersonality of computerized mail by starting your message with a friendly salutation, such as "Hi, Amos" or "Dear Mr. Fisher."

An effective closing is equally important. Some e-mail programs identify only the e-mail address (for example, "70511.753 @compuserve.com") in the message header they transmit. Don't take a chance that your reader won't recognize you. Include your name, e-mail address, and any other appropriate identifying information at the end of your message.

Adapted from Scot Ober, Contemporary Business Communication

I. Short lines; short paragraphs

    A. _____

    B. _____

II. No shouting

    A. No entire message in capital letters

B. Causes problems

  1. _____

  2. _____

III. Proofread message before sending

  A. Resist temptation to send without checking

  B. Errors create unprofessional image

IV. Append messages appropriately

  A. _____

  B. Often better to establish context in your message

  C. _____

V. Direct style with deliberation

  A. _____

  B. _____

VI. Greetings and closings

  A. _____

  B. Provide necessary information in closing

    1. _____

    2. _____

    3. _____

Types of Reading-Related Writing

Much of the writing you will consider in this book, in both the student examples and your assignments, will be of a personal nature. The content will derive from direct and indirect experience (reading and listening), and will often involve opinion. Mastering this kind of writing is important, because you do have something to say. Many college writing tasks, however, will require you to evaluate and reflect on what you read rather than write about personal experience. You will be expected to read, think, and write. Your reading-related writing assignment may ask you to write summaries and reaction statements.

Writing a Summary

A **summary** is a rewritten, shortened version of a piece of writing in which you use your own wording to express the main ideas. Learning to summarize effectively will help you in many ways. Summary writing reinforces comprehension skills in reading. It requires you to discriminate among the ideas in the target reading passage. Summaries are usually written in the form of a well-designed paragraph or set of paragraphs. Frequently, they are used in collecting material for research papers and in writing conclusions to essays.

The following rules will guide you in writing effective summaries.

1. Cite the author and title of the text.

2. Reduce the length of the original by about two-thirds, although the exact reduction will vary, depending on the content of the original.

3. Concentrate on the main ideas and include details only infrequently.

4. Change the original wording without changing the idea.

5. Do not evaluate the content or give an opinion in any way (even if you see an error in logic or fact).

6. Do not add ideas (even if you have an abundance of related information).

7. Do not include any personal comments (that is, do not use *I,* referring to self).

8. Seldom use quotations. (If you do use quotations, however, enclose them in quotation marks.)

9. Use some author tags ("says York," "according to York," or "the author explains") to remind the reader(s) that you are summarizing the material of another author.

EXERCISE 2

Evaluating a Summary

Apply the rules of summary writing to the following summary of "Total Institutions," p. 11. Mark the instances of poor summary writing by using rule numbers from the preceding list.

Total Institutions

A total institution completely encompasses the individual. Total institutions have certain common characteristics. Institutions provide the setting for all rest, recreation, and labor. Residents function only within the group. And residents are directed by a highly organized schedule, which, I think, is what they need or they wouldn't be there. There residents are depersonalized by being required to wear a uniform, abandon personal items, and give up privacy. Some adapt in a negative way by developing psychological problems, but most adapt in a positive way by forming

relationships with other residents. Several popular movies, such as The *Shawshank*

Redemption, show how prison society works, to use one example. Once outside the

total institution, individuals must deal with the problem of relearning old coping

habits. They must also withstand the shock of going from the top of a small society

to the bottom of a larger one. Society needs these total institutions, especially

the jails.

The following is an example of an effective summary.

A Summary of "Total Institutions"
Michael Balleau

In "Total Institutions" Seymour Feshbach and Bernard Weiner explain that a total institution encompasses the lives of its residents, who share three common traits: The residents must do everything in the same place, must do things together, and must do things according to the institution's schedule. The institution takes away the residents' roles they had in society, takes away their appearance by issuing uniforms, takes away their personal property by confiscation, and takes away their privacy by making life communal. The authors say that some residents adapt negatively by developing psychological problems, but most form relationships and new roles within the institution. Upon release, these residents must learn to function in the free world all over again, as they start at the bottom of society. This shift "may be further demoralizing."

Writing a Reaction

The reaction statement is another kind of reading-related writing, one in which you incorporate your views. Some reactions require evaluation with a critical-thinking emphasis. Some focus on simple discussion of the content presented in the reading and include summary material. Others concentrate on the writer's experiences as related to the content of the passage.

The following paragraph is student Tanya Morris's reaction statement to "Total Institutions." She could have expanded her ideas to write an essay.

Institutions Always Win
Tanya Morris

The short essay "Total Institutions," by Seymour Feshbach and Bernard Weiner, is a study of conflicts in different settings. The common characteristics of such an institution are in personal combat with the individual, in which the resident is stripped of his or her choices and left to participate in all activities in the same setting, with no opportunity for a sanctuary. Further, the resident who tries to assert his or her uniqueness is controlled by a master plan. That plan is enforced by police personnel, who become the masters, set up social barriers, and maintain control over their underlings. Cut off from the free world, the resident is in conflict with significant matters of newness—clothes, facilities, regulations, and roles. The authors explain that inexorably the institution wins, converting the resident into a disturbed person or an amiable robot among others who are similarly institutionalized. But at that moment of conversion, the now-depersonalized individual may be thrust back into society to try to reclaim old roles and behaviors in another cycle of conflicts. The authors of this essay are very clear in showing just how comprehensive these institutions are in waging their war, for good or bad, against individuality. After all, they are "total."

Writing a Two-Part Response

As you have seen, the reaction response includes a partial summary or is written with the assumption that readers have read the original piece. However, your instructor may prefer that you separate each form—for example, by presenting a clear, concise summary followed by a reaction response. This format is especially useful for critical examination of a text or for problem-solving assignments, because it requires you to understand and repeat another's views or experiences before responding. The two-part approach also helps you avoid the common problem of writing only a summary of the text when your instructor wants you to both summarize and evaluate or otherwise react. In writing a summary and a reaction it is a good idea to ask your instructor if you should separate your summary from your response.

Total Institutions: A Summary and a Reaction
Michael Balleau

Part I: Summary

In "Total Institutions" Seymour Feshbach and Bernard Weiner explain that a total institution encompasses the lives of its residents, who share three common traits: The residents must do everything in the same place, must do things together, and must do things according to the institution's schedule. The institution takes away the residents' roles they had in society, takes away their appearance by issuing uniforms, takes away their personal property by confiscation, and takes away their privacy by making life communal. The authors say that some residents adapt negatively by developing psychological problems, but most form relationships and new roles within the institution. Upon release, these residents must learn to function in the free world all over again as they start at the bottom of society. This shift "may be further demoralizing."

Part 2: Reaction

The basic ideas in "Total Institutions" gave me an insight into the behavior of my cousin. Let's call him George. He spent almost five years in prison for white collar crime at the bank where he worked. When George was incarcerated, he was an individual, almost to the extreme of being a rebel. When he got out, he was clearly an institutionalized person. Cut off from the consumer society, George was reluctant to enter stores and go through checkout lines. He was fearful of being left alone. Because his prison setting was very noisy, silence made him uncomfortable, and he wanted a radio or television on all the time. Accustomed to being around people in the institution, George couldn't stand being alone, and he depended on others to suggest times for meals and chores. Of course, his new reputation and behavior now set him apart from his former roles. It took him almost three years to readjust.

Journal Writing

Your journal entries are likely to be concerned primarily with the relationship between the reading material and you—your life experiences, your views, your imagination. The reading material will give you something of substance to write about, but you will be writing especially for yourself, developing confidence and ease in writing, so that writing becomes a comfortable part of your everyday activities, as speaking already is.

These journal entries will be part of your intellectual diary, recording what you are thinking about a certain issue. They will help you understand the reading material; help you develop your writing skills, in uncovering ideas that can be used on other assignments; and help you think more clearly and imaginatively. Because these entries are of a more spontaneous nature than the more structured writing assignments, organization and editing are likely to be of less concern.

Each journal entry should be clearly dated and, if reading related, should specify the title and author of the original piece.

Even if your instructor wants you to concentrate on what you read for your journal writing, he or she might not want you to be restricted to the material in this text. Fortunately, you are surrounded by reading material in newspapers, magazines, and, of course, textbooks from other courses. These topics can serve you well, especially if you want to begin your journal writing now.

Cross-Curricular and Career-Related Writing

This textbook includes cross-curricular and career-related writing topics at the end of Chapters 7 through 17. These suggestions offer a wide range of subject material to those of you who would like to write about subjects you have encountered across campus, at work, and in your search for a career. Some of that writing may include ideas coming directly from your reading. Those ideas can be documented with a listing of the source, which usually includes the name of the author, title of the work, place of publication, publisher, date, and page numbers. The citations for quotations or specific references can be made in the same fashion as the ones for textbook sources (see the following three sections in this chapter).

Supporting Ideas with Quotations and References

In your reading-related writing assignments, you are likely to use three methods in developing your ideas: explanation, direct reference to the reading selection, and quotation from the reading. The explanations can take different forms, such as causes and effects, comparison, definition, or exemplification. These forms are explored later in this book. The references point the reader directly toward the reading selection. The more specific the reference—including even the page number—the more helpful it is to your readers. As for quotations, remember that the words are borrowed. They can be very effective as support, but you must give credit to the original writer.

These concepts are quite important in all reading-related writing but especially in the writing that you will be doing in Chapters 7 through 17 of this textbook. Your references should be very clear and direct. Your quotations should be exact and should always appear within quotation marks to indicate that you have borrowed words. The form for quotations is presented below.

In addition to these few requirements for reading-related writing based on material in this text, your instructor may also expect you to document your ideas. This means that you must indicate the sources of all the original ideas you have borrowed, even when you have changed the words.

Basic Documentation

Borrowing words or ideas without giving credit to the originators is called **plagiarism,** a kind of intellectual theft. Therefore, your instructor may ask you to document your reading-related writing.

Documenting sources for papers based on written material is usually quite simple. One documentation method is MLA (Modern Language Association) style. See Chapter 18, "Writing the Research Paper," for more explanation. Here are the most common principles of documentation that can be used for textbook or other restricted sources, with some examples.

- If you use material from a source you have read, identify that source so that the reader will recognize it or be able to find it.
- Document any original idea borrowed, whether it is quoted, paraphrased (written in your words but not shorter), or summarized (written in your words and shorter). Basic situations include the following:

   Normally, give only the author's name and a page number: (Rivera 45).
   If you state the author's name in introducing the quotation or idea, then usually give only the page number: (45).
   If the author has written more than one piece in the book, include a title or shortened form of the title: (Rivera, *The Land* 45).

Here is an example of documenting a quotation by an author represented only once in a textbook.

- **Using the author's name to introduce:** Suzanne Britt says that "neat people are bums and clods at heart" (255).

Following is an example of documenting an idea borrowed from an author but not quoted.

- **Using the author's name to introduce:** Suzanne Britt believes that neat people are weak in character (255).
- **Not using the author's name to introduce:** Music often helps Alzheimer's patients think more clearly (Weiss 112).

Documentation in Action

Your paragraph or essay may include ideas from newspapers, magazines, or books. To make classwork simpler for you, most of the reading-related assignments in this book are based on selections included in this book. When you are writing about something you have read, just write as you usually would, but bring in ideas and quotations from that source. You may also want to refer to more than one source. You may even use ideas from other sources to contrast with your own. For example, you may say, "Unlike Fred M. Hechlinger in 'The First Step in Improving Sex Education: Remove the Hellfire' (351), I believe that public schools should not offer sex education." Do not feel that each point you make must be directly related to sources.

Here is a paragraph illustrating how to incorporate ideas and document them:

Jackie Malone, "Sexist Men as Victims"

Sexist men are victims of their own bias against females. Because they cannot accept women as full human beings, they themselves are smaller in dimension. In Irwin Shaw's "The Girls in Their Summer Dresses," Michael looks at his wife, but he doesn't see a full human being; he just sees a sexual object: "what a pretty girl, what nice legs" (314). Because he sees her and other women that way, he cannot ever have the relationship with her that she deserves and that he would find fulfilling. Of course, thinking of women as just soft and cuddly has its effects on men in other ways. The man as father who thinks that way may very well regard his own daughter as one limited in her ranges of activities and limited in her potential. He may be one of those fathers who immediately stereotype their daughters as headed for a "life of the affections," not like a son's, "earning a living" (Lurie 249). Unfortunately, these men cannot accept females as their equals in any important respect, and, in doing so, they deprive themselves, as well as others.

Essays and Applications

The following essays demonstrate many of the elements of good writing that we have been exploring. To help you evaluate and write in response to those selections, each essay is accompanied first by a set of discussion and critical thinking questions and then by several reading-related writing suggestions. As you read, underline and annotate the material.

The Struggle to Be an All-American Girl

ELIZABETH WONG

The title of the reading may suggest that Elizabeth Wong would experience success if she became an "all-American girl." But then the question is, Would she enjoy as an adult what she had wanted as a child? Another question comes to mind: Must one relinquish one's own cultural identity to assume another cultural identity?

1   It's still there, the Chinese school on Yale Street where my brother and I used to go. Despite the new coat of paint and the high wire fence, the school I knew ten years ago remains remarkably, stoically the same.

2   Every day at 5 P.M., instead of playing with our fourth- and fifth-grade friends or sneaking out to the empty lot to hunt ghosts and animal bones, my brother and I had to go to Chinese school. No amount of kicking, screaming, or pleading could dissuade my mother, who was solidly determined to have us learn the language of our heritage.

3   Forcibly, she walked us the seven long, hilly blocks from our home to school, depositing our defiant tearful faces before the stern principal. My only memory of him is that he swayed on his heels like a palm tree, and he always clasped his impatient twitching hands behind his back. I recognized him as a repressed maniacal child killer, and knew that if we ever saw his hands we'd be in big trouble.

4   We all sat in little chairs in an empty auditorium. The room smelled like Chinese medicine and imported faraway mustiness. Like ancient mothballs or dirty closets. I hated that smell. I favored crisp new scents. Like the soft French perfume that my American teacher wore in public school.

5   Although the emphasis at the school was mainly language—speaking, reading, writing—the lessons always began with an exercise in politeness. With the entrance of the teacher, the best student would tap a bell and everyone would get up, kowtow, and chant, *"sing san ho,"* the phonetic for "How are you, teacher?"

6   Being ten years old, I had better things to learn than ideographs copied painstakingly in lines that ran right to left from the tip of a *moc but,* a real ink pen that had to be held in an awkward way if blotches were to be avoided. After all, I could do the multiplication tables, name the satellites of Mars, and write reports on *Little Women* and *Black Beauty.* Nancy Drew, my favorite book heroine, never spoke Chinese.

7   The language was a source of embarrassment. More times than not, I had tried to disassociate myself from the nagging loud voice that followed me wherever I wandered in the nearby American supermarket outside Chinatown. The voice belonged to my grandmother, a fragile woman in her seventies who could outshout the best of the street vendors. Her humor was raunchy, her Chinese rhythmless, patternless. It was quick, it was loud, it was unbeautiful. It was not like the quiet, lilting romance of French or the gentle refinement of the American South. Chinese sounded pedestrian. Public.

8   In Chinatown, the comings and goings of hundreds of Chinese on their daily tasks sounded chaotic and frenzied. I did not want to be thought of as mad, as talking gibberish. When I spoke English, people nodded at me, smiled sweetly, said encouraging words. Even the people in my culture would cluck and say that I'd do well in life. "My, doesn't she move her lips fast," they would say, meaning that I'd be able to keep up with the world outside Chinatown.

9   My brother was even more fanatical than I about speaking English. He was especially hard on my mother, criticizing her, often cruelly, for her pidgin speech—smatterings of Chinese scattered like chop suey in her conversation. "It's not 'What it is,' Mom," he'd say in exasperation. "It's 'What *is* it; what *is* it, what *is* it!'" Sometimes Mom might leave out an occasional "the" or "a," or perhaps a verb of being. He would stop her in mid-sentences: "Say it again, Mom. Say it right." When he tripped over his own tongue, he'd blame it on her: "See, Mom, it's all your fault. You set a bad example."

10   After two years of writing with a *moc but* and reciting words with multiples of meanings, I finally was granted a cultural divorce. I was permitted to stop Chinese school.

11   I thought of myself as multicultural. I preferred tacos to egg rolls; I enjoyed Cinco de Mayo more than Chinese New Year.

12   At last, I was one of you; I wasn't one of them.

13   Sadly, I still am.

EXERCISE 3

Discussion and Critical Thinking

1. By what steps is Wong transformed into an "all-American girl"?

2. Who or what influenced her the most?

3. How does she feel about her transformation?

4. Why can't Wong do anything about her transformation?

5. What advice would you give to her?

6. What advice do you think the author would give to her daughter?

EXERCISE 4

Suggestions for Reading-Related Writing

On separate paper, complete one of the following reading-related responses.

1. Write a summary.

2. Write a two-part piece composed of labeled summary and reaction parts.

3. Analyze the essay as a transformation that Wong experienced. Concentrate on stages of her change, using time as the principle for order. As you emphasize stages, resist any temptation to write only a summary.

4. Discuss how different parts of society—school, neighborhood, and family—influenced Wong. Use references to her essay and quotations from it.

Native American Core Values and Cooperative Learning

LEE LITTLE SOLDIER

As a professor of education at Texas Tech University, Lee Little Soldier has made a specific study of ways of learning in relation to cultural needs and values. For Native Americans, she matches core values with learning styles and concludes that cooperative learning is especially effective. This excerpt is from "Cooperative Learning and the Native American Student," first published in Phi Delta Kappan.

1   It is a truism that education must have personal meaning for students. Thus educators must begin where the students are, with material that is relevant to their culture. Yet if education is to provide students with an array of life choices, then mastery of basic skills is also essential. Bridging the gap between the Indian and non-Indian worlds is crucial to the success of schooling for Native Americans.

2   Despite vast differences among Native American tribes, certain core values characterize these diverse cultures. For example, Native Americans respect and value the dignity of the individual, and children are afforded the same respect as adults. Although outsiders may view Native American parents as too permissive, nonetheless they teach their children to seek the wisdom and counsel of their elders. At the same time, traditional Indian families encourage children to develop independence, to make wise decisions, and to abide by them. Thus the locus of control of Indian children is internal, rather than external, and they are not accustomed to viewing adults as authorities who impose their will on others. Native American students entering school for the first time may respond with confusion and passivity to an authoritarian teacher who places many external controls on them.

3   Other core values of Native Americans include cooperation and sharing. The idea of personal property may be foreign. Because traditionally they come from extended families, Native American children tend to be group-centered rather than self-centered. They are accustomed to sharing whatever they have with many family members, a habit that can unnerve non-Indian teachers who emphasize labeling possessions and taking care of one's *own* belongings. If such teachers do not understand the notion of common ownership, they can easily mislabel certain behaviors as "stealing."

4   Moreover, Native American students may enter school far more advanced than their non-Indian counterparts in such social behaviors as getting along with others, working in groups, taking turns, and sharing. Too often these strengths are not recognized or rewarded in school.

5   Harmony is another core value of Native Americans—harmony with self, with others, and with nature. Paleo-Indians could not have survived had they not used their environment productively. Even today, Native Americans generally take no more than they can use and live in balance with their surroundings.

6   The problem facing educators is to build a warm, supportive learning environment for Native American students without compromising educational goals and without investing a lot of money—which most school districts don't have. The answer to this problem may lie at least partly in an old concept that is receiving renewed emphasis: cooperative learning.

7   To make cooperative learning work, we must rid ourselves of the notion that students who help other students are somehow "cheating." We in American education are so programmed to view learning as an individual—indeed, a competitive—activity that we tend to overlook the value of group methods for reaching individual goals. Certainly, individual effort has its value, and group effort is not always appropriate, but opportunities abound for cooperation that enhances individual achievement.

8   Cooperative learning is based on principles of team sports, and Indian students have a heritage of playing team sports and are avid team competitors. When teachers label Native American students as noncompetitive, they often base their conclusion on pitting one student against another in an academic setting. Such individual competition creates a dilemma for the Native American student whose culture traditionally teaches helping rather than competing with others.

9   The potential benefits of cooperative learning for Native American students are clear. Cooperative learning appears to improve student achievement, and it also matches such traditional Indian values and behaviors as respect for the individual, development of an internal locus of control, cooperation, sharing, and harmony. Cooperative learning can improve the attitudes of students toward themselves, toward others, and toward school, as well as increasing cross-racial sharing, understanding, and acceptance.

EXERCISE 5   # Discussion and Critical Thinking

1. What is Little Soldier's thesis (paragraph 1)?

2. What is the difference between being inner-willed (internal locus of control) and outer-willed (paragraph 2)?

3. Do you feel your reason for behavior comes mainly from inside or outside forces? Or are the reasons complex? Do they vary depending on the situation? Explain.

4. In what way are Native American students advanced (paragraph 4)?

5. According to Little Soldier, is cooperative learning always best?

6. On what principles is cooperative learning based?

7. In what ways are Native American students both competitive and not competitive?

8. In your opinion, which three Native American values and behaviors relate most directly to the intentions of cooperative learning (paragraph 9)?

9. What is your opinion of cooperative, or shared, learning? How does your opinion relate to your own set of values?

EXERCISE 6

Suggestions for Reading-Related Writing

On separate paper, complete one of the following reading-related responses.

1. Write a summary.

2. Write a two-part piece composed of labeled summary and reaction parts.

3. In a reaction response explain how three Native American core values or behaviors such as cooperation, sharing, and harmony relate to cooperative learning.

4. Explain how some of Little Soldier's ideas relate to your experiences with group work, placing you in either agreement or disagreement with her.

5. Explain how your values and behaviors relate to your preferred way(s) of learning.

6. Referring to Little Soldier's essay and to your own experiences, discuss the proper blending of individual and group effort in learning.

Writer's Guidelines

1. Underlining helps you to read with discrimination.

   • Underline the main ideas in paragraphs.
   • Underline the support for those ideas.
   • Underline answers to questions that you bring to the reading assignment.
   • Underline only the key words.

2. Annotating enables you to actively engage the reading material.

   • Number parts if appropriate.
   • Make comments according to your interests and needs.

3. Outlining the passages you read sheds light on the relationship of ideas, including the major divisions of the passage and their relative importance.

4. Summarizing helps you concentrate on main ideas. A summary

   • cites the author and title of the text.
   • is usually shorter than the original by about two-thirds, although the exact reduction will vary depending on the content of the original.
   • concentrates on the main ideas and includes details only infrequently.
   • changes the original wording without changing the idea.
   • does not evaluate the content or give an opinion in any way (even if the original contains an error in logic or fact).

- does not add ideas (even if the writer of the summary has an abundance of related information).
- does not include any personal comments by the writer of the summary (therefore, no use of *I,* referring to self).
- seldom contains quotations (although, if it does, only with quotation marks).
- includes some author tags ("says York," "according to York," or "the author explains") to remind the reader(s) that it is a summary of the material of another writer.

5. Two other types of reading-related writing are

- the reaction, which shows how the reading relates to you, your experiences, and your attitudes; also, often a critique of the worth and logic of the piece.
- the two-part response, which includes a summary and a reaction that are separate.

6. Most ideas in reading-related papers are developed in one or more of these three ways:

- explanation
- direct references
- quotations

7. Documenting is giving credit to borrowed ideas and words.

The Writing Process

Think of writing as swimming. If you were a non-swimmer and you jumped into the water without instructions, at best you would swim awkwardly. At worst you would sink. You may face similar dilemmas in writing. If you choose the sink-or-swim method, hope for hidden talent or good luck. A better choice is the writing process, an approach that all writers use, to some degree, with modifications for different writing situations. Whether you call it the flow of writing or the writing process, it's all here in the next five chapters.

The Writing Process: Stage One
Exploring/Experimenting/Gathering Information

FLOW OF WRITING

The Writing Process Defined   30
The Writing Process Worksheet   30
The Assignment   30
Your Audience   31
Stage One Strategies   31
   Freewriting   31
   Brainstorming   34
   Clustering   36
   Gathering Information   37
Writer's Guidelines   37

"Writing is easy. All you do is stare at a blank sheet of paper until drops of blood form on your forehead."

GENE FOWLER

"My objective is to make the drops of blood smaller."

LEE BRANDON

THE QUIGMANS   by Buddy Hickerson

FRANCINE DISCOVERS THE 5 STAGES of DATING BOB: DENIAL, ANGER, CONFUSION, NAUSEA aND FINALLY, ACCEPTANCE of the CHECK.

SORRY.

B. Hickerson, copyright Los Angeles Times Syndicate. Reprinted by permission.

The Writing Process Defined

The writing process consists of a set of strategies that will help you proceed from idea or purpose to the final statement of a paragraph or an essay. As presented here, the different strategies move from

> **Stage One:** Exploring / Experimenting / Gathering Information
> *to*
> **Stage Two:** Writing the Controlling Idea / Organizing and Developing Support
> *to*
> **Stage Three:** Writing / Revising / Editing.

These stages are described in Chapters 2, 3, and 4, respectively. Collectively they represent what is called the **writing process**.

The process of writing is **recursive**, which means "going back and forth." In this respect, writing is like reading. If you do not understand what you have read, you back up and read it again. After you reread the entire passage, you may still go back and reread selectively. The same can be said of your writing. If, for example, you have reached Stage Two and you are working with an outline only to discover that your subject is too broad, you may want to back up and narrow your topic sentence or thesis and then adjust your outline. You may even return to an early cluster of ideas to see how you can use a smaller grouping of them. Revision, in Stage Three, is usually the most recursive part of all. You will go over your material again and again until you are satisfied that you have expressed yourself the best you can.

The Writing Process Worksheet

The blank Writing Process Worksheet on page 6, with brief directions for the three stages of the writing process, is designed to be duplicated and completed with each major writing assignment. It gives you clear, consistent guidance and provides your instructor with an easy format for finding and checking information. Customarily this worksheet is stapled to the front of your rough and final drafts.

The Assignment

Particulars of the assignment, frequently the most neglected parts of a writing project, are often the most important. If you do not know, or later cannot recall, specifically what you are supposed to do, you cannot do satisfactory work. An otherwise excellent composition on a misunderstood assignment may get you a failing grade, a sad situation for both you and your instructor.

As an aid to recalling just what you should write about, the Writing Process Worksheet provides space and guidance for you to note those details: information about the topic, audience, pattern of writing, length of the paper, whether to include a rough draft or revised drafts, whether your paper must be typed, and the date the assignment is due.

At the time your instructor gives that information, it will probably be clear; a few days later, it may not be. By putting your notes on the assignment portion of the worksheet, you remind yourself of what you should do and also indicate to your instructor what you have done.

Your Audience

More so than most points on the assignment portion of the worksheet, the matter of audience requires special consideration. At the outset of your writing project, you should consider your readers. Their needs, interests, and abilities should determine the focus of your subject, the extent of your explanation, your overall style, and your word choice. We usually make those adjustments automatically when we are speaking; it is easy to forget to do so when we are writing.

Stage One Strategies

Certain strategies commonly grouped under the heading **prewriting** can help you get started and develop your ideas. These strategies—freewriting, brainstorming, clustering, and gathering information—are very much a part of writing. The understandable desire to skip to the finished statement is what causes the most common student-writer grief: that of not filling the blank sheet or of filling it but not significantly improving on the blankness. The prewriting strategies described in this section will help you attack the blank sheet constructively with imaginative thought, analysis, and experimentation. They can lead to clear, effective communication.

Freewriting

Freewriting is an exercise that its originator, Peter Elbow, has called "babbling in print." When you freewrite, you write without stopping, letting your ideas tumble forth. You do not concern yourself unduly with the fundamentals of writing, such as punctuation and spelling. Freewriting is an adventure into your memory and imagination. It is concerned with discovery, invention, and exploration. If you are at a loss for words on your subject, write in a comment such as "I don't know what is coming next" or "blah, blah, blah," and continue when relevant words come. It is important to keep writing. Freewriting immediately eliminates the blank page and thereby helps you break through an emotional barrier, but that is not the only benefit. The words that you sort through in that idea kit will include some you can use. You can then underline or circle those words and even add notes on the side so that the freewriting continues to grow even after its initial spontaneous expression.

The way in which you proceed depends on the type of assignment: working with a topic of your choice, working from a restricted list of topics, or working with a prescribed topic.

The *topic of your choice* affords you the greatest freedom of exploration. You would probably select a subject that interests you and freewrite about it, allowing your mind to wander among its many parts, perhaps mixing fact and fantasy, direct experience, and hearsay. A freewriting about music might uncover areas of special interest and knowledge, such as jazz or folk rock, that you would want to pursue further in freewriting or other prewriting strategies.

Working from a *restricted list* requires a more focused freewriting. With the list, you can, of course, experiment with several topics to discover what is most suitable for you. If, for example, "career choice," "career preparation," "career guidance," and "career prospects" are on the restricted list, you would probably select one and freewrite about it. If it works well for you, you would probably proceed with the next step of your prewriting. If you are not satisfied with what you uncover in freewriting, you would explore another item from the restricted list.

When working with a *prescribed topic,* you focus on a particular topic and try to restrict your freewriting to its boundaries. If your topic specifies a division of a subject area such as "political involvement of your generation," then you would tie those key words to your own information, critical thinking, and imaginative responses. If the topic asks for, let's say, your reactions to a specific poem, then that poem would give you the framework for your free associations with your own experiences, creations, and opinions.

You should learn to use freewriting because it will often serve you well, but you need not use it every time you write. Some very short writing assignments do not call for freewriting. An in-class assignment may not allow time for freewriting.

Nevertheless, freewriting is often a useful strategy in your toolbox of techniques. It can help you get words on paper, break emotional barriers, generate topics, develop new insights, and explore ideas.

Freewriting can lead to other stages of prewriting and writing, and it can also provide content as you develop your topic.

The following example of freewriting, and the writing, revising, and editing examples in Chapters 3 and 4, are from student Betsy Jackson's work titled "If I Were a Traffic Cop." She selected her topic, bad drivers, from a restricted list. If she had been working with a prescribed topic, she might have been told to concentrate on only one aspect of bad drivers, such as the need for driver education, the need for better laws, or the cost of bad driving. Then she would have done some research. However, she had no such limitation and, therefore, thought about bad drivers broadly. After her freewriting, she went back over her work looking for an idea that might be limited enough to use as the basis for a paper. Here is what she wrote:

All kinds

Drunk drivers

If I were a cop

Tailgaters

Lane changers

Left turners on red

Too fast, too slow

Don't yield

Causes

Just driving around on streets and freeways can be a scary experience because of all the bad drivers. Whenever I see them, sometimes I just laugh. Sometimes I get mad. Sometimes I get irritated. Sometimes I get scared. It's not just the young drivers or the old drivers it's <u>all kinds</u>. And all types of people no matter what the nationality or the types of vehicles they drive. Pickup drivers are worse as a group but bad drivers come in all kinds of vehicles. I think someone should do something about them. The worst are the <u>drunk drivers</u>. I don't see them in the morning. But I see them late at night when I'm driving home from work. They should be put away. But a lot of others should be getting serious tickets. Especially the bad ones. <u>Make me a cop</u>—a supercop—a Rambo cop and I'll go after the bad ones. Some of them cause a lot of accidents and get people all mad. Blah. Blah. Blah. Take <u>tailgaters</u> for example. And what about the drivers that go into the emergency lanes on the freeways to pass when there's a jam. And then you've got the <u>lane changers</u> that don't even give signals. And those that just <u>keep going</u> and <u>turn left when</u> the <u>light turns red</u>. Then you've got the ones that drive <u>too fast</u> and <u>too slow</u>. And you've got the ones that <u>don't stop</u> for <u>pedestrians</u>. Blah. Blah. Blah. I guess we all have our pet peeves about bad drivers and everyone would like to be a cop sometimes. I guess if you talked to them some would have reasons. Maybe they're <u>late</u> for work or they are <u>mad</u> about something. Or maybe

Effect   there's an <u>emergency</u>. Whatever it is, I get concerned when they <u>take my life in their hands</u>.

After her freewriting session, Jackson examined what she had written for possible ideas to develop for a writing assignment. As she recognized those ideas, she underlined important words and phrases and made a few notes in the margins. By reading only the underlined words in her freewriting, you can understand what is important to Jackson; it was not necessary for her to underline whole sentences.

In addition to putting some words on that dreaded blank sheet of paper, Jackson discovered that she had quite a lot to say about drivers and that she had selected a favorable topic to develop. The entire process took no more than five minutes. Had she found only a few ideas or no promising ideas at all, she might have freewritten on another topic. Although in going back over her work she saw some errors, especially in wording and sentence structure, she did not correct them because the purpose of freewriting is discovery, not revising or editing. She was confident that she could continue with the process of writing a paper as she followed her flow of thought.

EXERCISE 1

Freewriting

Try freewriting on a broad topic such as one of the following:

an event that was important to you in your youth
a concert, a movie, or a television program
the ways you use your computer
drug use—causes, effects, a friend with a problem
gang membership—causes, effects, an experience
the benefits of using a word processor
ways of disciplining children
why a person is a hero or role model to you
a great or terrible party
a bad or good day at school
why a college education is important

Following the example in Jackson's freewriting, underline and annotate the phrases that may lead to ideas you could explore further.

Brainstorming

Brainstorming features important words and phrases that relate in various ways to the subject area or to the specific topic you are concerned with. Brainstorming includes two basic forms: (1) asking and answering questions and (2) listing.

Big Six Questions

One effective way to get started is to ask the big six questions about your subject: *Who? What? Where? When? Why? How?* Then let your mind run free as you jot down answers in single entries or lists. Some of the big six questions may not fit, and some may be more important than others, depending on the purposes of your writing. For example, if you were writing about the causes of a situation, the *Why?* question could be more important than the others; if you were concerned with how to do something, the *How?* question would predominate. If you were writing in response to a reading selection, you would confine your thinking to questions appropriately related to the content of that reading selection.

Whatever your focus for the questions is, the result is likely to be numerous ideas that will provide information for continued exploration and development of your topic. Thus your pool of information for writing widens and deepens.

Jackson continued with the topic of bad drivers, and her topic tightened to focus on particular areas.

Who?	bad drivers; me as a cop
What?	driving badly, recklessly, unsafely; a cop's job
Where?	on every roadway
When?	all the time
Why?	hurried, disrespectful, self-centered, sick, addiction, hostile, irresponsible
How?	lane-changing, driving illegally in emergency lane, not signaling, passing on the shoulder, tailgating, turning left on red, rolling stop, speeding, driving while intoxicated

Notice that each question is answered in this example, but with some topics some questions may not fit. As Jackson addressed the *Why?* and *How?* questions, her brainstorming produced long lists, suggesting that those areas were strong possibilities for the focus of her paper.

Listing

Simply making a list of words and phrases related to your topic is another effective way to brainstorm, especially if you have a defined topic and a storehouse of information. This strategy is favored by many writers.

Knowing from the outset that she was concerned mainly with the behavior of drivers, Jackson might have gone directly to making a list indicating what drivers do or how they drive. She then might have selected perhaps four ideas from this list for her framework and circled them for future reference.

unsafe lane changers

driving illegally in the emergency lane

not signaling

passing on the shoulder

(tailgating)

(turning left on red)

turning right on red without stop

rolling stop

speeding

driving too slow in fast lane

(driving while intoxicated)

driving while on cell phone

driving while reading road map

truck in car lanes

drivers dumping trash

Even if you do not have a focused topic, you may find a somewhat random listing useful, merely writing phrases as they occur to you. This exploratory activity is similar to freewriting. After you have established such a list, you can sort out and group the phrases as you generate your topic and find its natural divisions. Feel free to accept, reject, or insert phrases.

EXERCISE 2

Brainstorming

Further explore the topic you worked with in Exercise 1 by first answering the big six questions and then making a list.

Big Six Questions

Who? _____

What? _____

Where? _____

When? _____

Why? _____

How? _____

List

_____

_____

_____

_____
_____
_____
_____
_____
_____
_____

Clustering

In **clustering**, double-bubble your topic—that is, write it down in the middle of the page and draw a double circle around it—and then respond to the question "What comes to mind?" Draw a single bubble around other ideas on spokes radiating out from the hub that contains the topic. Any bubble can lead to another bubble or to numerous bubbles in the same way. This strategy is sometimes used instead of, or before, making an outline to organize and develop ideas.

The more restricted the topic inside the double bubble, the fewer the number of spokes that will radiate with single bubbles. For example, a topic such as "high school dropouts" would have more spokes than "reasons for dropping out of high school."

Here is Jackson's cluster on the subject of bad drivers. She has drawn dotted lines around subclusters that seem to relate to a workable, unified topic.

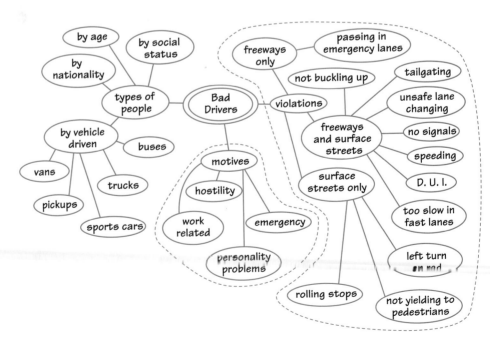

EXERCISE 3   ## Clustering

Continuing with your topic, develop a cluster of related ideas. Draw dotted lines around subclusters that have potential for focus and more development.

Gathering Information

For reading-related writing—especially the kind that requires a close examination of the selection—you will gather information by reading print or electronic sources, such as the Internet, make notes, and perhaps outline or summarize (see Chapter 1) the text. Of course, you may also want to make notes for other topics to write about as they occur to you. This kind of note taking can be combined with other strategies such as brainstorming and clustering. It can even take the place of them. It can also be used in conjunction with strategies such as outlining.

Student Betsy Jackson at this point is writing about personal experience. If she wanted to include statistics or an authoritative statement, she might do some library research or interview a police officer. In either case, she would take notes.

Writer's Guidelines

The writing process consists of strategies that will help you proceed from idea or purpose to the final statement of a paragraph or an essay. Throughout all stages of the writing process, you should consider your audience. Stage One offers four approaches:

1. **Freewriting** consists of writing without stopping, letting ideas tumble forth.

   • Freewriting involves breaking down emotional barriers, generating topics, discovering ideas, and exploring ideas.
   • Your approach to freewriting will depend on whether you work on a topic of your choice (great freedom), a topic from a restricted list (more focused), or an assigned topic (concentration on one idea).

- You need not use freewriting for all writing experiences. You would probably not use it for very short assignments, in-class assignments with limited time, outline and summary assignments, or assignments on topics you know well.

2. **Brainstorming** is used for quickly developing key words and phrases that relate to your topic. It includes two basic forms: the big six questions and listing.

   - You may ask *Who? What? Where? When? Why?* and *How?* questions about your topic, ignoring questions that do not fit.
   - Or you may simply list points on likely divisions of your topic.

3. **Clustering** is a visual way of showing connections and relationships. It is sometimes used with an outline and sometimes in place of one.

   - Start by double-bubbling your topic.
   - Then, in response to the question What comes to mind? single-bubble other ideas on spokes radiating from the hub.

4. **Gathering information** can take the form of reading with underlining, annotating, and note taking.

The Writing Process: Stage Two
Writing the Controlling Idea /
Organizing and Developing Support

FLOW OF WRITING

Defining the Controlling Idea 40

Writing the Controlling Idea as a Topic Sentence
or Thesis 40

Organizing Support 44

    Listing 45

    Clustering 45

    Outlining 45

Writer's Guidelines 50

"If you don't have a controlling idea with related support in mind, your writing will probably be out of control."

LEE BRANDON

© John Callahan, courtesy Levin Represents.

The most important advice this book can offer you is *state your controlling idea and support it*. If you have no controlling idea—no topic sentence for a paragraph or thesis for an essay—your writing will be unfocused, and your readers may be confused or bored. But if you organize your material well, so that it supports and develops your controlling idea, you can present your views to your readers with interest, clarity, and persuasion.

Stating the controlling idea and organizing support can be accomplished effectively and systematically. How? This chapter presents several uncomplicated techniques you can use in Stage Two of the writing process.

Defining the Controlling Idea

If you tell a friend you are about to write a paragraph or an essay, be prepared to hear the question "What are you writing about?" If you answer, "Public schools," your friend will probably be satisfied with the answer but not very interested. The problem is that the phrase *public schools* offers no sense of limitation or direction. It just indicates your subject, not what you are going to do with it. *An effective controlling statement, called the topic sentence for a paragraph and the thesis for an essay, has both a subject **and** a treatment.* The **subject** is what you intend to write about. The **treatment** is what you intend to do with your subject.

Example: <u>Glendora High School</u> <u>offers a well-balanced academic program</u>.
                    subject   treatment

In some instances the subject will follow the treatment:

<u>The time has come for a national law legalizing</u>
                    treatment

<u>physician-assisted suicide for the terminally ill</u>.
                    subject

In other instances the subject will divide the treatment:

<u>Four factors establish</u> <u>Elvis Presley</u> <u>as the greatest</u>
     treatment   subject   treatment

<u>entertainer of the twentieth century: appearance, singing ability, style, and influence</u>.

Writing the Controlling Idea as a Topic Sentence or Thesis

The effective controlling idea presents a treatment that can be developed with supporting information. The ineffective one is vague, too broad, or too narrow.

Vague: <u>Public schools</u> <u>are great</u>.
          subject   treatment

Better: <u>Public schools</u> <u>do as well academically as private schools,</u>
           subject   treatment

<u>according to statistics</u>. [made more specific]

Too Broad: <u>Public schools</u> <u>are too crowded</u>.
           subject   treatment

Better: <u>Bidwell Elementary School</u> <u>is too crowded</u>. [limiting the subject
           subject   treatment

to a particular school]

Too Narrow: <u>American public schools</u> <u>were first established in Philadelphia</u>
           subject   treatment

in 1779. [only a fact]

Better: <u>The first public schools in America</u> <u>were founded to meet certain</u>
           subject   treatment

<u>practical needs</u>. [made more specific by indicating aspects]

In writing a sound controlling idea, be sure that you have included both the subject and the treatment and that the whole statement is not vague, too broad, or too narrow. Instead, it should be phrased so that it invites development. Such phrasing can usually be achieved by limiting time, place, or aspect. The limitation may apply to the subject (instead of schools in general, focus on a particular school), or it may apply to the treatment (you might compare the subject to something else, as in "do as well academically"). You might limit both the subject and the treatment.

EXERCISE 1

Evaluating Topic Sentences

In the following controlling ideas, underline and label the subjects (S) and treatments (T). Also judge each one as effective (E) or ineffective (I). (See Answer Key for answers.)

Example:

   __I__   <u>Basketball</u> <u>is an interesting sport</u>.
                S   T

_____ 1. Students who cheat in school may be trying to relieve certain emotional pressures.

_____ 2. Shakespeare was an Elizabethan writer.

_____ 3. The quarterback in football and the general of an army are alike in significant ways.

_____ 4. Animals use color chiefly for protection.

_____ 5. Portland is a city in Oregon.

_____ 6. Life in the ocean has distinct realms.

_____ 7. Rome has had a glorious and tragic history.

_____ 8. Boston is the capital of Massachusetts.

_____ 9. The word *macho* has a special meaning to the Hispanic community.

_____ 10. The history of plastics is exciting.

Evaluating Topic Sentences

In the following controlling ideas, underline and label the subjects (S) and treatments (T). Also judge each one as effective (E) or ineffective (I).

_____ 1. An experience in the first grade taught me a valuable lesson about honesty.

_____ 2. The Internet has changed the way many people shop.

_____ 3. President Lincoln was assassinated at the Ford Theater.

_____ 4. The dictionary has an interesting history.

_____ 5. The world is a place of many contrasts.

_____ 6. Rap music can be classified on the basis of the intent of its writers / composers.

_____ 7. Bombay is one of the most densely populated cities in the world.

_____ 8. What I've seen while working in a fast-food place has made me lose my appetite.

_____ 9. My physical education teacher is called "Coach."

_____ 10. Count Dracula's reputation is based on his exploits as a nocturnal creature.

Writing Topic Sentences

Complete the following entries to make each one a solid topic sentence. Only a subject and part of the treatment are provided. The missing part may be more than a single word.

Example: Car salespeople behave differently, depending on _the car they are selling and the kind of customer they are serving._

1. A part-time job can offer _____

2. My school's athletic program should be _____

3. It is almost universally accepted that smoking is _____

4. Students caught cheating should be _____

5. Health care should be _____

6. One of the effects of the rising cost of a college education is _____

_____

7. Offering constructive criticism to a friend who didn't ask can _____

_____

8. People who appear on television talk shows are frequently _____

_____

9. The slang of a particular group reveals _____

10. Gestures and facial expressions usually communicate _____

EXERCISE 4

Writing Topic Sentences

Convert each of the following subjects into a topic sentence.

1. Bumper stickers _____

2. Rudeness _____

3. The true character of my neighbor _____

4. Many homeless people _____

5. Being able to use a computer _____

6. Dieting _____

7. The basic forms of jazz and classical music _____

8. Educated citizens _____

9. The required labeling of rock music albums _____

10. Smoking _____

Your topic sentence or thesis can come from any of several places. You may be able to generate it at Stage One, in your initial freewriting, brainstorming, clustering, or gathering information, or you may be given an assigned topic. In any case, your procedure is the same at this point. You need to work on the statement—just that one sentence—until you have developed an interesting subject and a well-focused treatment. The statement may be a bit more mechanical than the one you actually use in your paragraph or essay, but it can easily be reworded once you reach Stage Three of the writing process: writing, revising, and editing.

The controlling idea will probably not pop into your head fully developed. It is more likely to be the result of repeated revisions. Even when you are revising a paper you have written, you may go back and rephrase your topic sentence or thesis. That is part of the back-and-forth (recursive) nature of the writing process.

In the following example, note how Jackson reworks her controlling idea several times before she settles on a statement that is well focused and capable of being developed.

Subject	Treatment
<u>Bad drivers</u>	<u>can be found everywhere.</u> (too broad)
<u>Someone</u>	<u>should do something about bad drivers.</u> (vague)
<u>Bad driving</u>	<u>has existed in the United States for more than a century.</u> (too broad)
<u>If I were a traffic cop</u>	<u>I'd crack down on certain types of bad drivers.</u> (workable)

Jackson has limited the subject by reducing it to the hypothetical situation of being a traffic cop. She has limited the treatment by dealing with only "certain types of bad drivers," not all bad drivers.

EXERCISE 5

Writing Your Topic Sentence

Using a topic you worked with in Chapter 1 or one from the list on page 33, write a topic sentence or thesis. Mark the subject and treatment parts.

Organizing Support

You have now studied the first part of the seven-word sentence "State your controlling idea and support it." In the first stage of the writing process (described in Chapter 2), you explored many ideas, experimented with them, and even developed some approaches to writing about them. You may also have gathered information through reading and note taking. The techniques of that first stage have already given you some initial support. The next step is to organize your ideas and information into a paragraph or an essay that is interesting, understandable, and compelling.

Three tools can help you organize your supporting material: listing (a form of brainstorming), clustering, and outlining. You will probably use only one of these organizing tools, depending on course requirements, the assignment, or individual preference. In the continuing demonstration of Betsy Jackson's work, each tool is shown.

Listing

Lists are the simplest and most flexible of the organizing tools. Listing need be nothing more than a column of items presenting support material in a useful sequence (time, space, or importance). As you work with your support material, you can cross out words or move them around on the list. By leaving vertical space between items, you can easily insert new examples and details. Jackson took phrases from the list she had made in Stage One and wrote them below her topic sentence.

<u>If I were a traffic cop</u>, <u>I'd crack down on certain types of bad drivers</u>.
        subject   treatment

drunk drivers—most dangerous, top priority, off the road

tailgaters—hostile, hurried, cause accidents, irritating

unsafe lane changers—rude, cause accidents

left-turners on red—reckless, accident prone

Clustering

Chains of circles radiating from a central double-bubbled circle form a cluster that shows the relationship of ideas. In the following example, Jackson has developed part of her Stage One cluster (a section noted by a dotted line on page 36).

<u>If I were a traffic cop,</u> <u>I'd crack down on certain types of bad drivers</u>.
        subject   treatment

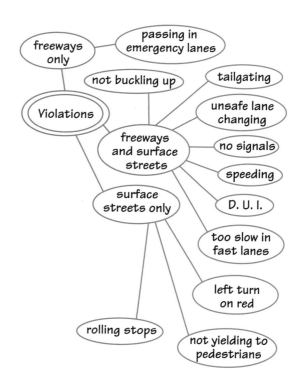

Outlining

Outlining is the tool that most people think of in connection with organizing. Because it is flexible and widely used, it will receive the most emphasis in this stage of the writing process. Outlining does basically the same thing that listing and clustering do. Outlining divides the controlling idea into sections of support material, divides those sections further, and establishes sequence.

An outline is a framework that can be used in two ways: (1) It can indicate the plan for a paragraph or an essay you intend to write, and (2) it can show the organization of a passage you are reading. The outline of a reading passage and the outline as a plan for writing are identical in form. If you intend to write a summary of a reading selection, then a single outline might be used for both purposes.

The two main outline forms are the **sentence outline** (each entry is a complete sentence) and the **topic outline** (each entry is a key word or phrase). The topic outline is more common in writing paragraphs and essays.

In the following topic outline, notice first how the parts are arranged on the page: the indentations, the number and letter sequences, the punctuation, and the placement of words. Then read Jackson's outline and see how the ideas in it relate to one another.

Main Idea (will usually be the topic sentence for a paragraph or the thesis for an essay)

  I. Major support

    A. Minor support

      1. Explanation, detail, example

      2. Explanation, detail, example

    B. Minor support

      1. Explanation, detail, example

      2. Explanation, detail, example

  II. Major support

    A. Minor support

      1. Explanation, detail, example

      2. Explanation, detail, example

    B. Minor support

      1. Explanation, detail, example

      2. Explanation, detail, example

Here is Betsy Jackson's outline:

If I were a traffic cop, I'd crack down on certain types of bad drivers.
      subject   treatment

  I. Drunks

  II. Unsafe lane changers

    A. Attitude

      1. Rude

      2. Bullying

    B. Results

      1. Accidents

      2. People irritated

III. Left-turners on red
  A. Attitude
    1. Self-centered
    2. Putting self above law
  B. Results
    1. Bad collisions
    2. Mass anger
IV. Tailgaters
  A. Motives
    1. Hostility
    2. Rushed
    3. Impatient
  B. Effects
    1. Accidents
    2. Road fights

The foundation of an effective outline, and, hence, of an effective paragraph or essay, is a strong controlling idea. Always begin by writing a sound topic sentence or thesis, one with a specific subject and a well-defined treatment. Then divide the treatment into parts. The nature of the parts will depend on what you are trying to do in the treatment. Just consider the thought process involved. What kinds of material would best support or explain that topic sentence or thesis? How should you organize that material? Should you present a series of examples? A description of a process? A story of human struggle? A combination of methods?

Among the most common forms of dividing and organizing ideas are the following:

- **Narration:** division of time or incident to tell a story
  I. Situation
  II. Conflict
  III. Struggle
  IV. Outcome
  V. Meaning

- **Exemplification:** division into several examples
  I. First example
  II. Second example
  III. Third example

- **Causes and effects:** division into causes or effects
  I. Cause (or effect) one
  II. Cause (or effect) two
  III. Cause (or effect) three

- **Process analysis:** division of a unit into parts (for example, a pencil has an eraser, a wooden barrel, and a lead)
  I. First part
  II. Second part
  III. Third part

- **Analysis by division:** division into steps telling how something is done
  - I. Preparation
  - II. Steps
    - A. Step 1
    - B. Step 2
    - C. Step 3

These patterns and others are the subjects of individual chapters in this book.

EXERCISE 6

Completing Outlines

Fill in the missing parts of the following outlines. It may be helpful to consider, in each case, whether you are dealing with time, examples, causes, effects, parts, or steps. The answers will vary, depending on your individual experiences and views.

1. <u>Borrowing</u> <u>is the mother of trouble.</u>
   subject   treatment

   I. Received five credit cards in mail

   II. Saw numerous commercials on television

      A. One about _____

      B. Another about _____

   III. Made purchases

   IV. Two months later _____

2. <u>A successful job interview</u> <u>depends on several factors.</u>
   subject   treatment

   I. Good appearance

      A. _____

      B. _____

   II. Behaving properly

   III. Being qualified

      A. Education

      B. _____

   IV. Knowing something about the employer

3. <u>Joe's drug addiction</u> <u>had significant effects on his life</u>.
    subject   treatment

    I. Developed mental health problems

        A. _____

        B. _____

    II. Developed _____

    III. Lost his job

    IV. Lost _____

4. <u>A college education</u> <u>is important for several reasons.</u>
    subject   treatment

    I. Offers personal enrichment

    II. Fulfills curiosity

    III. Provides contacts that may be satisfying later

    IV. _____

5. <u>An ordinary person</u> <u>can be an environmentalist every day.</u>
    subject   treatment

    I. Limit use of internal combustion engines

    II. Avoid using and dumping poisonous chemicals

    III. _____

    IV. _____

        A. Save newspapers

        B. Save _____

        C. _____

6. <u>Cooking spaghetti</u> <u>is not difficult.</u>
    subject   treatment

    I. Get pan, water, and pasta

    II. Boil water in pan

    III. _____

    IV. Cook pasta until _____

    V. Remove pasta from pan and rinse in cold water

7. <u>An excellent doctor</u> <u>must have three qualities.</u>
subject   treatment

   I. _____

   II. _____

   III. _____

8. <u>Some drivers</u> <u>break traffic laws selectively.</u>
subject   treatment

   I. Make rolling stops

   II. _____

   III. _____

EXERCISE 7   ## Writing Your Outline

Using the subject you converted into a topic sentence or thesis (Exercise 5), compose a topic outline.

Writer's Guidelines

1. The most important advice this book can offer you is *state your controlling idea and support it*. If you have no controlling idea—no topic sentence for a paragraph or thesis for an essay—your writing will be unfocused and your readers may be confused or bored. But if you organize your material well, so that it supports and develops your controlling idea, you can present your views to your readers with interest, clarity, and persuasion.

2. An effective controlling statement, called the **topic sentence** for a paragraph and the **thesis** for an essay, has both a subject and a treatment. The **subject** is what you intend to write about. The **treatment** is what you intend to do with your subject.

Example: <u>Glendora High School</u> <u>offers a well-balanced academic program</u>.
                         subject   treatment

3. Three tools can help you organize your supporting material: listing, clustering, and outlining.

- Listing presents support material as a column of items in a useful sequence (time, space, or importance).
- Clustering uses chains of circles radiating from a central double-bubbled circle to show the relationship of ideas.
- Outlining can be used in two ways: to plan the structure and content of something you intend to write and to reveal the structure and content of something you read.

A typical outline looks like this:

Main Idea (will usually be the topic sentence for the paragraph or the thesis for the essay)
- I. Major support
  - A. Minor support
    - 1. Explanation, detail, example
    - 2. Explanation, detail, example
  - B. Minor support
    - 1. Explanation, detail, example
    - 2. Explanation, detail, example
- II. Major support
  - A. Minor support
    - 1. Explanation, detail, example
    - 2. Explanation, detail, example
  - B. Minor support
    - 1. Explanation, detail, example
    - 2. Explanation, detail, example

The Writing Process: Stage Three
Writing/Revising/Editing

FLOW OF WRITING

Writing the First Draft   53

Revising   54

 Coherence   54

 Language   56

 Unity   58

 Emphasis   59

 Support   60

 Sentences   61

Editing   63

Student Demonstration of All Stages of the
 Writing Process   64

 Writing Process Worksheet   64

Writer's Guidelines   70

> "I might write four lines or I might write twenty. I subtract and I add until I really hit something I want to do. You don't always whittle down, sometimes you whittle up."
>
> GRACE PALEY

THE QUIGMANS   by Buddy Hickerson

*Repressive Celibate and the Seven Politically Correct Height-Challenged

B. Hickerson, copyright Los Angeles Times Syndicate. Reprinted by permission.

Writing the First Draft

In Stage Three of the writing process, your work begins to assume its final form. Use your outline, or alternative form of organization, as a guide in composing your paragraph or essay. For college work, your controlling idea should almost always be clearly stated early in the paper. The Roman numeral parts of the outline will provide the framework for the main ideas of a paragraph assignment or for the topic sentence ideas in an essay. Supporting information—details, examples, quotations—is likely to be used in approximately the same order as it appears in the outline. Keep in mind that you should not be bound absolutely by the outline. Outlines often need to be redone just as your initial writing needs to be redone.

Most writers do best when they go straight through their first draft without stopping to polish sentences or fix small problems. Try that approach. Using the information in your outline and ideas as they occur to you, go ahead and simply write a paragraph or an essay. Don't be slowed down by possible misspelled words, flawed punctuation, or ungraceful sentences. You can repair those problems later.

Whether you write in longhand or on a computer depends on what works best for you. Some writers prefer to do a first draft by hand, mark it up, and then go to the computer. Computers save you time in all aspects of your writing, especially revision.

The following paragraph is Betsy Jackson's first draft, which includes some errors in spelling, grammar, and punctuation. Notice how it follows the order of topics in her outline; it also includes some new ideas.

Rambo Traffic Cop

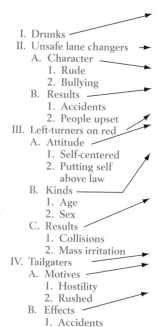

I. Drunks
II. Unsafe lane changers
  A. Character
    1. Rude
    2. Bullying
  B. Results
    1. Accidents
    2. People upset
III. Left-turners on red
  A. Attitude
    1. Self-centered
    2. Putting self
      above law
  B. Kinds
    1. Age
    2. Sex
  C. Results
    1. Collisions
    2. Mass irritation
IV. Tailgaters
  A. Motives
    1. Hostility
    2. Rushed
  B. Effects
    1. Accidents
    2. People upset

Make me a traffic cop, and I'll crack down on certain types of drivers. First off are the drunks. I'd zap them off the highways right off, and any cop would. But what I'm really talking about is the jerks of the highway. Near the top are the uptight lane changers, for example, this morning when I was driving to school, I saw several. I could of carved at least a couple notches in a vilation pad, and I wasn't even cranky. They cut off people and force their way in, and leave behind upset and hurt people. Then there's the left-turn bullies the ones that keep moving out when the yellow turn to red. They come in all ages and sexes, they can be young or old, male or female. Yesterday, I saw this female in a pick-up barrel right out into the teeth of a red light. She had a baby on board. She had lead in her foot. She had evil in her eye. She was hostile and self-centered. Taking advantage of others. She knew that the facing traffic would probably not pull out and risk a head-on crash. The key word there is probably but many times these people with a green light do move out and colide with the left turn bullies. Third, I'd sap the tailgaters. No one goes fast enough for these guys. I'm not alone in this peeve. One bumper sticker reads, "Stay back. I chew tobacky." And James Bond sprayed cars that chased him. Since the first is dirty and the second is against the law, if I had the clout of a Rambo cop I'd just rack up a lot of tailgater tickets. But there's a lot of road demons out there. Maybe it's good I'm not a traffic cop, Rambo or otherwise, cause traffic cops are suppose to inforce hundreds of laws. I don't know if I'd have time cause I have my own pet peeves in mind.

If part of the development of your topic seems out of balance or needs more support, subtract or add material as necessary. Don't be afraid to change the outline. Often going back and forth between the initial draft and the outline will prevent your final work from seeming mechanical. Occasionally, as you discover that you need to expand or diminish a part, it may be useful to review your Stage One for details and opportunities.

EXERCISE 1   ## Writing Your Rough Draft

On a separate sheet of paper, use the topic you developed in Chapters 2 and 3, and write a rough draft of a paragraph or an essay as directed by your instructor.

Revising

The term **first draft** suggests quite accurately that there will be other drafts, or versions, of your writing. Only in the most dire situations, such as an in-class examination when you have time for only one draft, should you be satisfied with a single effort.

What you do beyond the first draft is revision and editing. **Revision** includes checking for organization, content, and language effectiveness. **Editing** (discussed later in this chapter) involves a final correcting of simple mistakes and fundamentals such as spelling, punctuation, and capitalization. In practice, editing and revising are not always separate activities, although writers usually wait until the next-to-the-last draft to edit some minor details and attend to other small points that can be easily overlooked.

Successful revision almost always involves intense, systematic rewriting. You should learn to look for certain aspects of skillful writing as you enrich and repair your first draft. To help you recall these aspects so that you can keep them in mind and examine your material in a comprehensive fashion, this textbook offers a memory device—an acronym in which each letter suggests an important feature of good writing and revision. This device enables you to memorize the features of good writing quickly. Soon you will be able to recall and refer to them automatically. These features need not be attended to individually when you revise your writing, although they may be, and they need not be attended to in the order presented here. The acronym is CLUESS (pronounced "clues"), which provides this guide: Coherence, Language, Unity, Emphasis, Support, and Sentences.

Each of these features of good writing can be approached with a set of techniques you can apply easily to your first draft. They are presented here with some details, examples, and supporting exercises. See the Writer's Guidelines at the end of this chapter for a concise list of these features and a set of questions you can apply to your own writing and to peer editing.

Coherence

Coherence is the orderly relationship of ideas, each leading smoothly and logically to the next. You must weave your ideas together so skillfully that the reader can easily see how one idea connects to another and to the central thought. This central thought, of course, is expressed in the topic sentence for a paragraph and in the thesis for an essay. You can achieve coherence efficiently by using the following:

> Overall pattern
> Transitional terms
> Repetition of key words and important ideas
> Pronouns
> Consistent point of view

Overall Pattern

Several chapters in this book discuss strategies for an overall pattern of organization or order. Three basic patterns prevail: **time** (chronology), **space** (spatial arrangement), and **emphasis** (stress on ideas). Sometimes you will combine patterns. The coherence of each can be strengthened by using transitional words such as the following:

> **For a time pattern:** *first, then, soon, later, following, after, at that point*
> **For a space pattern:** *up, down, right, left, beyond, behind, above, below*
> **For an emphasis pattern:** *first, second, third, most, more*

Transitional Terms

By using transitional terms, you can help your readers move easily from one idea to another. The transitional term in each of the following sentences is italicized.

> *First,* I realized I had to get a job to stay in school.

> *At the same time,* my track coach wanted the team to spend more hours working out.

> We were, *after all,* the defending champions.

> *Finally,* I dropped one of my courses.

Repetition of Key Words and Important Ideas

Repeat key words and phrases to keep the main subject in the reader's mind and to maintain the continuity necessary for a smooth flow of logical thought. (See the section on Emphasis later in this chapter.)

Pronouns

Pronouns, such as *he, her, them,* and *it,* provide natural connecting links in your writing. Why? Every pronoun refers to an earlier noun (called the **antecedent** of the pronoun) and thus carries the reader back to that earlier thought. Here are some examples.

> I tried to buy *tickets* for the concert, but *they* were all sold.

> Assertive *people* tend to make decisions quickly. However, *they* may not make the wisest decisions.

> *Roger* painted a picture of *his* father's pickup truck. *It* was so good that *his* professor asked *him* to enter *it* in an art show.

Consistent Point of View

Point of view shows the writer's relationship to the material, the subject, and it usually does not change within a passage.

If you are conveying personal experience, the point of view will be *first person,* or *I,* which can be either involved (a participant) or detached (an observer).

The *second person, you* and *your,* is usually reserved for how-to writing in college assignments.

If you are presenting something from a distance, geographical or historical (for example, telling a story about George Washington), the point of view will be *third person,* and the participants will be referred to as *he, she,* and *they.*

Along with the consistency of perspective, you should avoid shifts in number (*she* to *they*) and verb tense (*is* to *was*).

Being consistent in these matters will promote coherence.

Language

In the revision process, the word **language** takes on a special meaning, referring to usage, tone, and diction. If you are writing with a computer, consider using the thesaurus feature, but keep in mind that no two words share precisely the same meaning.

Usage

Usage is the kind or general style of language we use. All or almost all of us operate on the principle of appropriateness. If I used *ain't* as part of my explanations in this textbook, you would be surprised and probably disappointed; you would think about my word choice rather than about what I have to say. Why would you be surprised? Because *ain't* is not appropriate for my audience in this situation. If you write an essay containing slang, you will probably be understood, but if the slang is not appropriate, you will draw unfavorable attention to your message. That does not mean that slang does not have its place—it does. It can be imaginative and colorful. Often, though, it is only a weak substitute for a more precise vocabulary.

Usage is an important part of writing and revising. Judge what is appropriate for your audience and your purpose. What kind of language is expected? What kind of language is best suited for accomplishing your purpose?

Most of the material in the Handbook is grammatical explanation of standard, mainly formal, English. Using standard verb tenses and pronoun cases will help you to write effectively. The Handbook offers clear explanations and examples. It also provides exercises supported by answers in the Answer Key. As you practice the principles of standard English in your writing and revising, you will master them.

Tone

Have you ever heard someone say, "Don't talk to me in that tone of voice" or "I accepted what she was saying, but I didn't like the tone she used when she told me"? Tone in these contexts means that the sound of the speaker's voice and maybe the language choices conveyed disrespect to the listener. The tone could have represented any number of feelings about the subject matter and the audience. Tone can have as many variations as you can have feelings: it can, for example, be sarcastic, humorous, serious, cautionary, objective, groveling, angry, bitter, sentimental, enthusiastic, somber, outraged, or loving.

Let's say you are getting a haircut. Looking in those panoramic mirrors bordered with pictures of people with different styles of haircuts, you see that the hair stylist is cutting off too much hair. You could use different tones in giving him or her some timely how-to instructions.

Objective: "If you don't mind, what I meant to say was that I would like a haircut proportioned similar to that one there in the picture of Tom Cruise from *Jerry Maguire.*"

Humorous: "I hesitate to make suggestions to someone who is standing at my back and holding a sharp instrument near my throat, but I'm letting my hair grow out a bit. I don't want you to take off a lot in the back and on the sides."

Angry and sarcastic: "Look man, when I sat down, I said I wanted my hair cut in the design of Tom Cruise in *Jerry Maguire.* The way you're hacking at it, you must've thought I said *Top Gun.*"

Servile: "I really like the way you cut my hair, and I can see that you are proportioning it with great care, but I would like my hair to be a bit longer than the style that I think you're working on. Do you remember how I used to get my hair cut about a year ago, a little longer on the sides and more bushy on top? You came up with a great style that everyone liked. Could you give me one similar to that?"

Overbearing: "Damn it, buddy. Will you watch what you're doing! I asked for a haircut, not a shave. If God had wanted me to have bare skin above my shoulders, he would've put the hair on my feet."

In speech, feelings and attitudes are represented by inflection, loudness, word choice, and language patterns. In writing, tone is conveyed mainly by word choice and order; it is closely related to style—the variations in the way you write, depending on your purpose. Your purpose is simply to present a particular idea in a particular context. The context implies the audience; it is important to use the tone appropriate to your audience.

Usually your tone will be consistent throughout your presentation, although for the informal essay often assigned in college, you may choose to begin in a lighthearted, amusing tone before switching to a more serious, objective mode.

Diction

Diction is word choice. If you use good diction, you are finding the best words for a particular purpose in addressing a certain audience. There is some overlap, therefore, between usage and diction. I may look at an area in the subway and present my reaction in the following way:

Poor Diction:

This part of the subway is really a mess. Everywhere I look I can see things people have thrown away, which have fallen through the grates above. Along with the solid items are liquids. On the walls are a hodgepodge of posters and writing. The whole area is very dirty and very unpleasant.

Note how the scene comes to life with better word choice:

Good Diction:

[Before me I saw] an unspeakable mass of congealed oil, puddles of dubious liquid, and a mishmash of old cigarette packets, mutilated and filthy newspapers, and the debris that filtered down from the street above. [The walls were a display of posters]—here a text from the Bible, there a half-naked girl, here a pair of girl's legs walking up the keys of a cash register—all scribbled over with unknown names and well-known obscenities. . . .

The difference between these two passages is obvious. The first is general. Terms such as "very dirty" and "very unpleasant" carry little meaning. The author has not made us see. The word *very* is an empty modifier. The second passage is specific. You can visualize what the writer is saying through the specific diction, the detail. The first is general and, for content, hardly goes beyond a single phrase—mess in the subway.

The following list shows the difference between general and specific words.

General	Specific	More Specific
food	fruit	juicy, ripe peach
mess	litter	candy wrappers, empty cans
drink	soda	Pepsi Lite
odor	kitchen smell	aroma of coffee brewing

Another aspect of diction is freshness and originality of expression. To achieve those distinctions, you should avoid clichés, which are trite, familiar phrases. Consider this sentence:

> When the Prince married Cinderella, her sisters went green with envy because she was now on easy street, leaving them out in the cold.

Those words were written by a person who doesn't care about communicating in a clear and interesting manner. It would be far better to say:

> When the Prince married Cinderella, her sisters were envious because they had no suitors.

This list shows some clichés to avoid:

young at heart	quick as a flash
rotten to the core	slow but sure
uphill battle	other side of the coin
more than meets the eye	breathless silence
bitter end	acid test
as luck would have it	better late than never
last but not least	six of one, half dozen of the other

Clichés are ready-made expressions. A cliché master manipulates language as if it were a prefabricated building going up, not bothering to use any imagination and leaving little opportunity for his or her audience to use theirs. Good diction, however, reflects the writer as an individual and is fresh, original, and clear.

Unity

A controlling idea, stated or implied, establishes **unity** in every piece of good writing. It is the central point around which the supporting material revolves. For a paragraph, the elements are the topic sentence and the supporting sentences. For an essay, the elements are the thesis and the supporting developmental paragraphs. All the supporting material should be related to the topic sentence or thesis, and it should all be subordinate to the topic sentence or thesis. Unity can be strengthened and made more apparent if you restate the topic sentence or thesis at the end of the unit and if you repeat key words and phrases from time to time. A good check on unity is to ask yourself if everything in your paragraph or essay is subordinate to and derived from the controlling idea.

Don't confuse unity and coherence. Whereas coherence involves the clear movement of thought from sentence to sentence or paragraph to paragraph, unity means staying on the topic. A unified and coherent outline would become incoherent if the parts were scrambled, but the outline technically would still be unified. These qualities of writing go together. You should stay on the topic and make clear connections.

Emphasis

Emphasis, a feature of most good writing, helps the reader focus on the main ideas by stressing what is important. It can be achieved in several ways but mainly through placement of key ideas and through repetition.

Placement of Ideas

The most emphatic part of any passage, whether a sentence or a book, is the last part, because we usually remember most easily what we read last. The second most emphatic part of a passage is the beginning, because our mind is relatively uncluttered when we read it. For these reasons, among others, the topic sentence or thesis is usually at the beginning of a piece, and it is often restated at the end in an echoing statement.

Repetition of Key Words and Important Ideas

Repetition is one of the simplest devices in your writer's toolbox. The words repeated may be single words, phrases, slightly altered sentences, or synonyms. Repetition keeps the dominant subject in the reader's mind and maintains the continuity necessary for a smooth flow of logical thought.

You can use this valuable technique easily. If, as is done in the following example, you are discussing the effects of the school dropout problem, then the word *effect(s)*, along with synonyms such as *result(s)* or *consequence(s)*, and *school dropout(s)*, is likely to be repeated several times. Moreover, phrases giving insight into the issue may be repeated, perhaps with slight variation.

The causes of the school <u>dropout</u> problem have received much attention recently, but the <u>effects</u> are just as important. One obvious <u>result</u> is that of unemployment or low-paying employment. The student who <u>drops out</u> of school is likely to be <u>dropping</u> into poverty, perhaps even into a lifelong condition. Another <u>effect</u> is juvenile crime. The young person who has no prospects for a good job and no hope all too frequently turns to illegal activities. A third <u>result</u> concerns the psychological well-being of the <u>dropout</u>. Although <u>withdrawing</u> from school seems to offer a quick, viable solution to perceived problems, it almost immediately has <u>consequences</u> for the <u>dropout</u>'s self-esteem. Of course, these <u>effects</u> may also be tied to causes, such as drugs, poverty, crime, or psychological problems, but devastating <u>repercussions</u> are there at the far end of the causes-and-effects continuum, and youngsters who are contemplating <u>dropping out</u> should consider them with care.

A word of warning: The effective use of word and phrase repetition should not be confused with an irritating misuse of word repetition. We all at times get stuck on certain words, and the result is a negative response from our audience. Consider this awkward use of repetition:

> She looked at him and frowned. He returned the look and then looked away at a stranger looking for his lost keys.

That's too many *look*'s. Consider this version:

> She looked at him [*or, even better,* She frowned at him]. He glared back and then glanced away at a stranger searching for his lost keys.

The second version preserves the idea of people "looking" by using synonyms. It is more precise and does not grate on the reader's mind as the first does.

Support

How much **support** as evidence or explanation does a piece of writing need? A good developmental paragraph fulfills its function by developing the topic sentence. An essay is complete when it fulfills its function of developing a thesis. Obviously, you will have to judge what is complete. With some subjects, you will need little supporting and explanatory material. With others, you will need much more. Incompleteness, not overdevelopment, is more common among beginning writers. Besides having enough support, be sure that the points of support are presented in the best possible sequence.

Consider the following paragraph. Is it complete? Does the writer make the main idea clear and provide adequate support for it? Are the ideas in the right order?

> A cat's tail is a good barometer of its intentions. By various movements of its tail a cat will signal many of its wants. Other movements indicate its attitudes. An excited or aggressively aroused cat will whip its entire tail back and forth.

At first glance, this paragraph seems complete. It begins with a concise topic sentence telling us that a cat's tail is a good barometer of its intentions. It adds information of a general nature in the following two sentences. Then it presents a supporting example about the aggressively aroused cat. But the paragraph is not explicit; there is insufficient supporting material for the opening generalization. The paragraph leaves the reader with too much information to fill in. What are some other ways that cats communicate their intentions with their tails? How do they communicate specific wishes or desires? Is their communication effective? If the passage is to answer these or other questions that may come into the reader's mind, it must present more material to support the beginning generalization. The original paragraph that follows begins with a concise topic sentence that is then supported with particulars.

> A cat's tail is a good barometer of its intentions. An excited or aggressively aroused cat will whip its entire tail back and forth. When I talk to Sam, he holds up his end of the conversation by occasionally flicking the tip of his tail. Mother cats move their tails back and forth to invite their kittens to play. A kitten raises its tail perpendicularly to beg for attention; older cats may do so to beg for food. When your cat holds its tail aloft while crisscrossing in front of you, it is trying to say, "Follow me"—usually

to the kitchen, or more precisely, to the refrigerator. Unfortunately, many cats have lost their tails in refrigerator doors as a consequence.

We can strengthen our understanding of good support by analyzing the structure of the model paragraph, putting to use the information we have assimilated to this point in the discussion. The paragraph begins with the highest generalization (the main idea in the topic sentence): "A cat's tail is a good barometer of its intentions." It is followed immediately with six supporting statements and ends with a final sentence to add humor to the writing. If we place this material in outline form, we can easily see the recurrent pattern in the flow of thought from general to particular.

Topic sentence (highest generalization)

A cat's tail is a good barometer of its intentions.

Major support
A. An excited or aggressively aroused cat will whip its entire tail back and forth.

Major support
B. When I talk to Sam, he holds up his end of the conversation by occasionally flicking the tip of his tail.

Major support
C. Mother cats move their tails back and forth to invite their kittens to play.

Major support
D. A kitten raises its tail perpendicularly to beg for attention;

Major support
E. older cats may do so to beg for food.

Major support
F. When your cat holds its tail aloft while crisscrossing in front of you, it is trying to say, "Follow me"—usually to the kitchen, or more precisely, to the refrigerator.

Added for humor
Unfortunately, many cats have lost their tails in refrigerator doors as a consequence.

Sentences

In the revision process, the word **sentences** refers to the variety of sentence patterns and the correctness of sentence structure.

Variety of Sentences

A passage that offers a variety of simple and complicated sentences satisfies the reader, just as various simple and complicated foods go together in a good meal. The writer can introduce variety by including both short and long sentences, by using different sentence patterns, and by beginning sentences in different ways (see pp. 432–433).

Length

In revising, examine your writing to make sure that sentences vary in length. A series of short sentences is likely to make the flow seem choppy and the thoughts disconnected. However, single short sentences often work very well. Because they are uncluttered with supporting points and qualifications, they are often direct and forceful. Consider using short sentences to emphasize points and to introduce ideas. Use longer sentences to provide details or show how ideas are related.

Variety of Sentence Patterns

Good writing includes a variety of sentence patterns. Although there is no limit to the number of sentences you can write, you may be pleased to discover that the conventional English sentence appears in only four basic patterns (see pp. 413–414).

Simple: She did the work well.
Compound: She did the work well, and she was well paid.
Complex: Because she did the work well, she was well paid.
Compound-Complex: Because she did the work well, she was well paid, and she was satisfied.

An analysis of these patterns with suggestions and exercises for combining sentences is given in the Handbook.

Each of the four sentence patterns listed has its own purposes and strengths. The simple sentence conveys a single idea. The compound sentence shows, by its structure, that two somewhat equal ideas are connected. The complex sentence shows that one idea is less important than another; that is, it is dependent on, or subordinate to, the idea in the main clause. The compound-complex sentence has the scope of both the compound sentence and the complex sentence.

Variety of Sentence Beginnings

Another way to provide sentence variety is to use different kinds of beginnings. A new beginning may or may not be accompanied by a changed sentence pattern. Among the most common beginnings, other than starting with the subject of the main clause, are those using a prepositional phrase, a dependent clause, or a conjunctive adverb such as *therefore, however,* or *in fact* (see p. 433).

- Prepositional phrase (in italics)

  In your fantasy, you are the star.

  Like casino owners, game show hosts want you to be cheery.

- Dependent clause (in italics)

  When the nighttime "Wheel of Fortune" debuted, the slot was occupied by magazine shows.

  As Pat Sajak noted, viewers often solve the puzzle before the contestants do.

- Conjunctive adverb (in italics)

  Now you know.

  Therefore, you feel happy, excited, and a bit superior.

Problems with Sentences

A complete sentence must generally include an independent clause, which is a group of words that contains a subject and a verb and can stand alone. Some groups of words may sound interesting, but they are not really sentences. Three common problem groupings are the fragment, the comma splice, and the run-on (see p. 434).

- A sentence **fragment** is a word grouping that is structurally incomplete.

  Because he left. [This is a dependent clause, not a complete sentence.]

  Went to the library. [This has no subject.]

  She being the only person there. [This has no verb.]

  Waiting there for help. [This phrase has neither subject nor verb.]

In the back seat under a book. [Here we have two phrases but no subject or verb.]

- A **comma splice** consists of two independent clauses with only a comma between them.

    The weather was bad, we canceled the picnic. [A comma by itself cannot join two independent clauses.]

- A **run-on** differs from the comma splice in only one way: It has no comma between the independent clauses.

    The weather was bad we canceled the picnic.

Fragments, comma splices, and run-ons can easily be fixed (see the Handbook) during the revising and editing stages of your writing. A computerized grammar checker may help you find these problems.

If you frequently have problems with sentence structure and awkwardness of phrasing, be especially suspicious of long sentences. Test each sentence of fifteen or more words for flaws. Try writing shorter, more direct sentences until you gain confidence and competency. Then work with sophisticated patterns.

See the Writer's Guidelines at the end of this chapter for a concise summary of the strategies for effective revision.

Editing

Editing, the final stage of the writing process, involves a careful examination of your work. Look for problems with capitalization, omissions, punctuation, and spelling (COPS). (See capitalization, p. 510; omissions, p. 431; punctuation, p. 496; and spelling, p. 514).

Because you can find spelling errors in writing by others more easily than you can in your own, a computerized spell checker is quite useful. However, it will not detect wrong words that are correctly spelled, so you should always proofread. It is often helpful to leave the piece for a few hours or a day and then reread it as if it were someone else's work.

Before you submit your writing to your instructor, do what almost all professional writers do before sending their material along: Read it aloud, to yourself or to a willing audience. Reading material aloud will help you catch any awkwardness of expression, omission and misplacement of words, and other problems that are easily overlooked by an author.

As you can see, writing is a process and is not a matter of just sitting down and producing a statement. The parts of the process from prewriting to revising to editing are connected, and your movement is ultimately forward, but this process allows you to go back and forth in the recursive manner discussed in Chapters 2 and 3. If your outline is not working, perhaps the flaw is in your topic sentence. You may need to go back and fix it. If one section of your paragraph is skimpy, perhaps you will have to go back and reconsider the pertinent material in your outline or clustering. There you might find more details or alter a statement so that you can move into more fertile areas of thought.

Student Demonstration of All Stages of the Writing Process

Here we see how Betsy Jackson worked through the entire writing process. In Stage One, she freewrote, brainstormed, and developed a cluster of ideas. In Stage Two, she composed a good topic sentence, developed further a part of her cluster from Stage One, and drew up an outline based on the cluster. Then, in Stage Three, we see one of her early drafts, her revision and editing of that draft, and finally the finished version.

Note that Jackson has used a Writing Process Worksheet, which has been lengthened for you to be able to see all parts of her work. You will find a full-size blank worksheet on page 6, which can be photocopied, filled in, and submitted with each assignment if your instructor directs you to do so.

FLOW OF WRITING

Writing Process Worksheet

Title   If I Were a Traffic Cop

Name   Betsy Jackson   **Due Date**   Monday, June 5, 8 a.m.

ASSIGNMENT   In the space below, write whatever you need to know about your assignment, including information about the topic, audience, pattern of writing, length, whether to include a rough draft or revised drafts, and whether your paper must be typed.

Write a paragraph of about 200 to 300 words on a topic from the list—bad drivers. Discuss types for the pattern. Use some examples. Write for readers who have probably shared your experiences. Include this completed worksheet, one or more rough drafts marked for revision, and a typed final paper.

STAGE ONE   **Explore**   Freewrite, brainstorm (list), cluster, or take notes as directed by your instructor. Use the back of this page or separate paper if you need more space.

Freewriting (abbreviated here)

drunks

tailgaters
lane changers
no signals
run lights
too fast/slow
all kinds

Every day when I drive to school I see bad drivers. Sometimes I'm mad. Sometimes I'm irritated. Sometimes I'm scared. I think someone should do something about them. The <u>drunk drivers</u> are the worst. They should be put away. But a lot of the other should be getting tickets too. Some of the drivers are worse than others. Make me a cop, a supercop, a rambo cop, and I'll go after the worst. Maybe I'd just go after the ones that bother me. Some bad drivers cause a lot of accidents and get people all angry. Take the <u>tailgaters</u> for example. And what about the <u>drivers that go into the emergency lanes</u> on the freeways to pass when there's a jam. And then you've got the <u>lane changers</u> and the <u>people that don't signal</u> and <u>those that keep going and turning left when</u> the <u>light turns red</u>. Then you've got the people that <u>drive too fast</u> and <u>too slow</u>. And you've got the ones that <u>don't stop</u> for <u>pedestrians</u>. <u>All kinds</u> of bad drivers are out there—young, old, male, female, insane, drunk, angry, and rushed.

Clustering

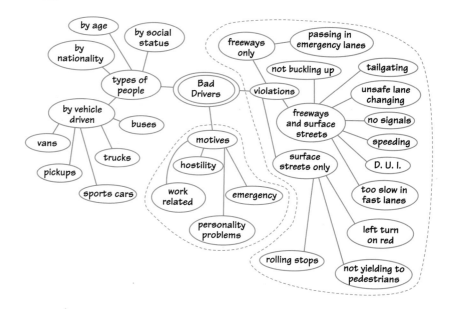

Brainstorming (Big Six Questions)

Who?	bad drivers; me as a cop
What?	driving badly, recklessly, unsafely; a cop's job
Where?	on every roadway
When?	all the time
Why?	hurried, disrespectful, self-centered, sick, addiction, hostile, irresponsible
How?	lane-changing, driving illegally in emergency lane, not signaling, passing on the shoulder, tailgating, turning left on red, rolling stop, speeding, driving while intoxicated

STAGE TWO

Organize   Write a topic sentence or thesis; label the subject and the treatment parts.

<u>If I were a traffic cop,</u> <u>I'd crack down on certain types of drivers</u>.
      subject   treatment

Write an outline or an outline alternative.

I. Drunks
II. Unsafe lane changers
   A. Character
      1. Rude
      2. Bullying
   B. Results
      1. Accidents
      2. People upset
III. Left-turners on red
   A. Attitude
      1. Self-centered
      2. Putting self above law

B. Kinds
1. Age
2. Sex
C. Results
1. Collisions
2. Mass irritation
IV. Tailgaters
A. Motives
1. Hostility
2. Rushed
B. Effects
1. Accidents
2. People upset

STAGE THREE   **Write**   On separate paper, write and then revise your paragraph or essay as many times as necessary for **c**oherence, **l**anguage (usage, tone, and diction), **u**nity, **e**mphasis, **s**upport, and **s**entences (**CLUESS**). Read your work aloud to hear and correct any grammatical errors or awkward-sounding sentences.

Edit any problems in fundamentals, such as **c**apitalization, **o**missions, **p**unctuation, and **s**pelling (**COPS**).

Rough Draft: Writing, Revising, Editing

If I were a Traffic Cop
~~**Rambo Traffic Cop**~~

If I were
~~Make me~~ a traffic cop, and I'll crack down on certain types of drivers. ~~First off~~
My primary
target would be   drivers   arrest   immediately,
~~are the~~ drunks. I'd ~~zap~~ them ~~off the highways right off,~~ and any cop would. But
are   concerned   here.   n   of my hit list
what I'm really ~~talking~~ about is (the jerks of the highway.) Near the top are the
unsafe
~~up-tight~~ lane changers. ~~for example,~~ This morning when I was driving to school, ~~I~~
have   citation
~~saw several.~~ I could ~~of~~ carved at least a couple notches in a ~~vilation~~ pad, and I
other drivers   ing
wasn't even cranky. They cut off ~~people~~ and force their way in, ~~and~~ leave behind
injured   are
upset and ~~hurt~~ people. Then there's the left-turn bullies the ones who keep mov-
s
ing out when the yellow turn to red. They come in all ages and sexes. ~~they can be~~
~~young or old, male or female.~~ Yesterday, I saw this female in a pick-up barrel right
out into the teeth of a red light. She had a baby on board. ~~She had~~ lead in her
and   t
foot. ~~She had~~ evil in her eye. She was hostile and self-centered. Taking advantage
of others. She knew that the facing traffic would probably not pull out and risk a
"   "
head-on crash. The key word there is probably but many times people with a
Fourth   z
green light do move out and collide with the left turn bullies. ~~Third,~~ I'd zap the

tailgaters. No one goes fast enough for ~~these guys~~ them. ~~I'm not alone in this peeve~~ Many of my fellow drivers agree.

One bumper sticker reads, "Stay back. I chew tobacky." And James Bond sprayed oil on cars that chased him. Since the first is ~~dirty~~ unsanitary and the second ~~is against the law~~ illegal, if I had the ~~clout~~ authority of a Rambo-cop I'd just ~~rack up~~ issue a lot of tailgater tickets. ~~But there's a lot of road demons out there.~~ These four types of road demons would feel my wrath. But Maybe it's good I'm not a traffic cop, Rambo or otherwise, cause traffic cops are suppose to ~~inforce~~ enforce hundreds of laws. I don't know if I'd have time cause ~~I have my own pet peeves in mind.~~ I'd be concentrating on this private list of obnoxious drivers.

Final Draft

If I Were a Traffic Cop

Betsy Jackson

Topic sentence	<u>If I were a traffic cop, I'd crack down on certain types of drivers</u>. My primary
Support	target would be <u>drunk drivers</u>. I'd arrest them immediately, and any cop would.
	But the jerks on the highway are what I'm really concerned about here. Near the
Support	top of my hit list are the <u>unsafe lane changers</u>. They cut off other drivers and
	force their way in, leaving behind upset and injured people. This morning when I
	was driving to school, I could have carved at least a couple of notches in a cita-
Support (example)	tion pad, and I wasn't even cranky. Then there are the <u>left-turn bullies</u>, the ones

who keep moving out when the yellow turns to red. They come in all ages and sexes. Yesterday, I saw this female in a pickup barrel right out into the teeth of a red light. She had a baby on board, lead in her foot, and evil in her eye. She was hostile and self-centered, taking advantage of others. She knew that the facing traffic would probably not pull out and risk a head-on crash. The key word there is "probably," but many times people with a green light do move out and collide

Support	with the left-turn bullies. Fourth, I'd zap the <u>tailgaters</u>. No one goes fast enough

for them. Many of my fellow drivers agree. One bumper sticker reads, "Stay back. I chew tobacky." And James Bond sprayed oil on cars that chased him. Since the first is unsanitary and the second illegal, if I had the authority of a Rambo-cop, I'd

Restated topic sentence	just issue a lot of tailgater tickets. <u>These four types of road demons would feel my wrath</u>. But maybe it's good I'm not a traffic cop, Rambo or otherwise, because

traffic cops are supposed to enforce hundreds of laws. I don't know if I'd have time because I'd be concentrating on this private list of obnoxious drivers.

Revising and Editing a First Draft

Revise the following student first draft. Then check for **capitalization, omissions** (oversights or grammar problems), **punctuation,** and **spelling** (COPS). Space is provided for you to add, delete, move, and correct material. (See Answer Key for answers.)

Pain Unforgettable
James Hutchison

One evening in 1968 while I was working the swing shift at the General Tire Recapping Plant. I came up with the greatest pain of my life because of a terible accident. Raw rubber was heated up in a large tank. Pryor to its being fed into an extruder. I was recapping large off-road tires. The lowering platform was in the up position the chain snapped. It sent the heavy platform crashing down into the tank. This caused a huge wave of steaming water to surge out of the tank. Unfortunately, I was in its path the wave hit my back just above my waist. The sudden pain shook me up. I could not move. My clothes were steaming I freaked out. Co-workers ran to my aid and striped the hot clothing from my body, taking skin as they did. I lay face down on the plant floor, naked and shaking for a long time. The paramedics came to pick me up. The painful experience is still scary when I think about it.

Revising and Editing a First Draft

Revise the following student first draft. Then check for **capitalization, omissions** (oversights or grammar problems), **punctuation,** and **spelling** (COPS). Space is provided for you to add, delete, move, and correct material.

Quitting School
Doretta McLain

Quitting school was not a big deal for me until I realize all the effects of quitting would bring to my life. At that time I didn't care. I plan to marry a few months later. I was happy then.

Quitting school was a big mistake because when I went out to look for a job I couldn't qualify for any of the good positions because of my lack of education. Instead, I took a job in a fast-food place where I had no future. Then I went to work in a big company just doing simple office work. When it came time for promotions I couldn't pass the tests they gave. That was not all. As a result of quitting school. I couldn't even help my children with their homework or buy the special things for them.

I started my family when I was not even eighteen years. The first year of my marriage was fine, then things started to fall apart. My husband had quit school too, and he didn't make much money, and as I mentioned, I didn't make much either. We argued a lot mainly over money. We couldn't get a big enough house for our family so that we could have the privacy we needed. I quit work to raise my kids and that when I really got in deep. My car was getting old and money was not enough to make big payments I had to buy another old car, which broke down all the time. I started freaking out. The fighting got worse and we had a divorce.

I was lucky that my parents decided to help me, and now I am dedicated to getting a good education. I will work hard to learn so me and my children can have a better life.

EXERCISE 4

Writing, Revising, and Editing Your Draft

Using the topic you worked with in Stages One and Two (Chapters 2 and 3), on separate paper, write, revise, and edit your paragraph or essay to complete Stage Three. Alternatively, you may delay this stage until after you have worked with paragraphs and essays in the next two chapters.

Writer's Guidelines

1. **Writing**

   Write your first draft, paying close attention to your outline, list, or cluster. Do not concern yourself with perfect spelling, grammar, or punctuation.

2. **Revising**

   Coherence

   - Are the ideas clearly related, each one to the others and to the central idea?
   - Is there a clear pattern of organization (time, space, or emphasis)?
   - Is the pattern supported by words that suggest the basis of that organization (time: *now, then, later*; space: *above, below, up, down*; emphasis: *first, second, last*)?
   - Is coherence enhanced by the use of transitional terms, pronouns, repetition, and a consistent point of view?

   Language

   - Is the general style of language usage appropriate (properly standard and formal or informal) for the purpose of the piece and the intended audience?
   - Is the tone (language use showing attitude toward material and audience) appropriate?
   - Is the word choice (diction) effective? Are the words precise in conveying meaning? Are they fresh and original?

   Unity

   - Are the thesis and every topic sentence clear and well stated? Do they indicate both subject and treatment?
   - Are all points of support clearly related to and subordinate to the topic sentence of each paragraph and to the thesis of the essay?

   Emphasis

   - Are ideas properly placed (especially near the beginning and end) for emphasis?
   - Are important words and phrases repeated for emphasis?

   Support

   - Is there adequate material—such as examples, details, quotations, and explanations—to support each topic sentence and thesis?
   - Are the points of support placed in the best possible order?

   Sentences

   - Are the sentences varied in length and beginnings?
   - Are the sentences varied in pattern (simple, compound, complex, and compound-complex)?
   - Are all problems with sentence structure (fragments, comma splices, and run-ons) corrected?

3. **Editing**

   - Are all problems in such areas as capitalization, omissions, punctuation, and spelling corrected?

Writing the Paragraph

FLOW OF WRITING

The Paragraph Defined   72
Basic Paragraph Patterns   72
The Writing Process and the Paragraph   75
Student Demonstration of All Stages of the
   Writing Process   76
   Writing Process Worksheet   76
Writer's Guidelines   80

"These are the seven most important words about writing a paragraph or an essay: state your controlling idea and support it."

LEE BRANDON

THE QUIGMANS   **by Buddy Hickerson**

hickerson

Writer's strike

B. Hickerson, copyright Los Angeles Times Syndicate. Reprinted by permission.

The Paragraph Defined

Defining the word *paragraph* is no easy task because there are four different kinds of paragraphs, each one having a different purpose:

Introductory: Usually the first paragraph in an essay, it gives the necessary background and indicates the main idea, called the thesis.

Developmental: A unit of several sentences, it expands on an idea. This book features the writing of developmental paragraphs.

Transitional: A very brief paragraph, it merely directs the reader from one point in the essay to another.

Concluding: Usually the last paragraph in an essay, it makes the final comment on the topic.

The following paragraph is both a definition and an example of the developmental paragraph.

Topic sentence

Support

Support

Support

Concluding sentence

The developmental paragraph contains three parts: the subject, the topic sentence, and the support. The **subject** is what you will write about. It is likely to be broad and must be focused or qualified for specific treatment. The **topic sentence** contains both the subject and the treatment—what you will do with the subject. It carries the central idea to which everything else in the paragraph is subordinated. For example, the first sentence of this paragraph is a topic sentence. Even when not stated, the topic sentence as an underlying idea unifies the paragraph. The **support** is the evidence or reasoning by which a topic sentence is developed. It comes in several basic patterns and serves any of the four forms of expression: narration, description, exposition, and argumentation. These forms, which are usually combined in writing, will be presented with both student and professional examples in the following chapters. The **developmental paragraph,** therefore, is a group of sentences, each with the function of supporting a controlling idea called the topic sentence.

Basic Paragraph Patterns

The most important point about a developmental paragraph is that it should state an idea and support it. The support, or development, can take several forms, all of which you already use. It can

- give an account (tell a story).
- describe people, things, or events.
- explain by analyzing, giving examples, comparing, defining, showing how to do something, or showing causes.
- argue that something should be done or resisted, that something is true or untrue, or that something is good or bad.

(All of these forms of expression are discussed with examples in Chapters 7 through 17.) You will not find it difficult to write solid paragraphs once you understand that good writing requires that main ideas have enough support so that your reader can understand how you have arrived at your main conclusions.

Usually the developmental paragraph will be indented only one time. However, you will note in your reading that some writers, especially journalists, break a paragraph into parts and indent more than once in developing a single idea. That arrangement, called a **paragraph unit,** is fairly common in magazine and newspaper articles (frequently with each sentence indented) but less so in college writing.

Two effective patterns of conventional paragraph structure are shown in Figure 5.1. Pattern A merely states the controlling idea, the topic sentence, and develops it; Pattern B adds a concluding sentence following the development.

Figure 5.1
Paragraph Patterns

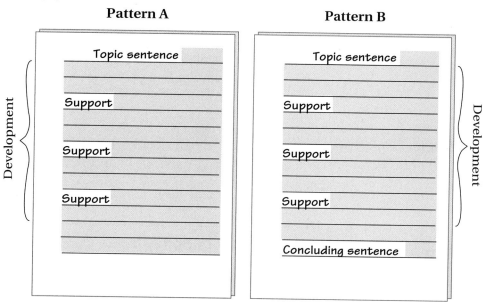

Example of Pattern A:

Pity, Anger, and Achievement Performance

Topic sentence

Support

    It is generally thought that pity and sympathy are "good" emotions and that anger is a "bad" emotion. <u>However, attribution theorists have pointed out that the consequences of these emotional expressions are complex.</u> <u>In one investigation,</u> Graham (1984) gave subjects (twelve-year-old children) false failure feedback during an achievement task. For some children, this was accompanied by the remark: "I feel sorry for you" as well as body postures and facial gestures that accompany sympathy (head down, hands folded, etc.). To other students, the experimenter said: "I am angry with you." Students receiving the pity feedback tended to blame the failure on themselves (low ability) and their performance declined. On the other hand, students receiving anger feedback attributed their failure to lack of

Support

effort and their performance subsequently increased. <u>This is not to advocate that sympathy is always detrimental and anger always facilitative.</u> Rather, the consequences of feedback depend on how that feedback is

Seymour Feshback and Bernard
Weiner, from *Personality*

construed and what it means to the recipient of the communication. Other kinds of feedback, such as praise for success at an easy task and excessive and unsolicited helping, also tend to convey that the student is "unable" and therefore have some negative consequences.

Example of Pattern B:

Primitive Methods of Lie Detection

Topic sentence

Support

<u>Throughout history there have been efforts to distinguish the guilty from the innocent and to tell the liars from the truthful</u>. For example, <u>a method of lie detection practiced in Asia</u> involved giving those suspected of a crime a handful of raw rice to chew. After chewing for some time, the persons were instructed to spit out the rice. The innocent person was anticipated to do this easily, whereas the guilty party was expected to have grains of rice sticking to the roof of the mouth and tongue. This technique relied on the increased sympathetic nervous system activity in the presumably fearful and guilty person. This activity would result in the drying up of saliva that, in turn, would cause grains of rice to stick in the mouth. <u>A similar but more frightening technique</u> involved placing a heated knife blade briefly against the tongue, another method used for criminal detection. An innocent person would not be burned while the guilty party would immediately feel pain, again because of the relative dryness of the mouth. <u>Many of these methods relied (unknowingly) on the basic physiological principles that also guided the creation of the polygraph.</u>

Support

Concluding sentence

Seymour Feshback and Bernard
Weiner, from *Personality*

EXERCISE 1

Analyzing a Paragraph

Read the following paragraph carefully.

1. Is the following paragraph developed in Pattern A (topic sentence/development) or Pattern B (topic sentence/development/restated topic sentence)?

2. Identify the parts of the paragraph pattern by underlining and annotating them. Use the two example paragraphs as models.

Types of Nightclubbers

Jerry Lopez

Dancers aren't the only men who go to nightclubs. Having worked in and attended various clubs, I've come to realize they attract about four different types of guys, who can be grouped by the way they act. First there are the dancers. They are out on the floor most of the night. They aren't concerned with their appearance. They usually wear jeans or shorts and a tee shirt. They're there to dance and sweat. Then there are the posers. They go to model and show off their clothes and hair. They won't dance for fear of messing up their appearance, or even worse, sweating! The third group is the scammers. Scammers go to pick up women. They usually stand around and check out the body parts of other people as they pass by. A person close to them can see the lust in their eyes. There are also the boozers or druggies. They can be seen stumbling around, falling down, or lying in some corner where they have passed out. At times I am a member of a fifth group: the observers.

Analyzing a Paragraph

Read the following paragraph carefully.

1. Is the paragraph developed in Pattern A (topic sentence/development) or Pattern B (topic sentence/development/restated topic sentence)?

2. Identify the parts of the paragraph pattern by underlining and annotating them. Use the two example paragraphs as models.

The Fighting, Founding Mothers
Maxine Johnson

People argue a lot about the prospects of women in the military fighting in combat, but in the War of Independence, several women distinguished themselves in combat situations. In 1775, Paul Revere got the main credit for riding to warn the Patriots that the British were coming on a military move on Concord and Lexington, Massachusetts. The fact is that, although he did warn some Patriots, he was stopped by the British. Who did get through? Several people, including Sybil Ludington, a teenage woman who fearlessly rode her horse like the wind. Another famous woman was known as Molly Pitcher. Her real name was Mary Hayes. She went with her husband to the battlefield, where she brought the men pitchers of water (hence her nickname) and helped load the cannon her husband fired. When her husband was shot at the Battle of Monmouth in 1778, she took over the cannon and fought bravely. At the end of the battle, won by the Patriots, she carried a wounded man for two miles. More than two hundred years ago, these women proved that their gender can be soldiers in every sense.

The Writing Process and the Paragraph

Learning to write a well-designed developmental paragraph will help you write longer assignments, because the developmental paragraph is often an essay in miniature. Therefore, you can approach both the developmental paragraph and the essay in the same manner—namely, by working through the three stages of the writing process described in Chapters 2 through 4. In this chapter, we will go through the basic stages and strategies once again. Here is a summary of them:

- Stage One: Exploring / Experimenting / Gathering Information

  Freewrite, brainstorm (answer questions or make lists), cluster, take notes (if doing research or analyzing a reading selection).

- Stage Two: Writing the Controlling Idea / Organizing and Developing Support

  Compose your topic sentence with a subject and a treatment.
  Complete an outline or an outline alternative.

- Stage Three: Writing / Revising / Editing

  Write a first draft; then revise and edit as many drafts as necessary to reach the final draft.

Student Demonstration of
All Stages of the Writing Process

Here is how one student, Vera Harris, moved from an idea to a topic sentence to an outline to a paragraph. Vera Harris returned to college while she still had a full-time job as a hairdresser. When her instructor asked her to write a paragraph about types of people she had encountered, she naturally considered her customers for the subject of her paragraph—what she would write about. But she also had a special interest in dogs, and cleverly she was able to include that interest. Although she knew her topic rather well, she worked with some prewriting techniques that allowed her to get her ideas flowing onto paper.

She used the Writing Process Worksheet for guidance, thus also providing her instructor with a record of the development of her work. Her worksheet has been lengthened for you to be able to see her work in its entirety. You will find a full-size blank worksheet on page 6, which can be photocopied, filled in, and submitted with each assignment if your instructor directs you to do so.

Writing Process Worksheet

Title Customers Are Like Canines

Name Vera Harris   **Due Date** Monday, Nov. 13, 8 a.m.

ASSIGNMENT   In the space below, write whatever you need to know about your assignment, including information about the topic, audience, pattern of writing, length, whether to include a rough draft or revised drafts, and whether your paper must be typed.

Write a paragraph of classification in which you group people according to their behavior. Keep your audience in mind as you select words and as you develop your ideas in an appropriate way. Submit this completed Writing Process Worksheet, a rough draft marked for revision, and a typed final draft of about 250 words.

STAGE ONE   **Explore**   Freewrite, brainstorm (list), cluster, or take notes as directed by your instructor. Use the back of this page or separate paper if you need more space.

Freewriting (partial)

Types of customers

Both dogs and customers can be grouped

I have worked in beauty shops for a long time, and I've naturally made a lot of observations about my customers. I could write about what they look like and (how they behave) and how they tip and lots of things. When I first started to work, I guess at first I thought of them as pretty much the same but then I started (to see them as types) mainly as to how they acted and I remember way back then I sometimes thought of how they (reminded me of dogs.) I don't mean that in any bad way but just that human beings have their personalities and their appearances and all and so do dogs.

Brainstorming (Big Six Questions)

Who?	my customers
What?	the way they act
Where?	in the beauty salon
When?	for the years I have worked
Why?	their basic nature
How?	behavior sometimes like dogs—hounds, Dobermans, terriers, bulldogs, cockers, poodles, mixed, retrievers, boxers

Brainstorming (Listing)

Kinds of dogs
 hounds
 Dobermans
 terriers
 bulldogs
 cockers
 poodles
 mixed
 retrievers
 pit bulls
 boxers

Clustering

STAGE TWO

Organize Write a topic sentence or thesis; label the subject and the treatment parts.

<u>The customers in the beauty shop where I work</u> <u>remind me of types</u>
                                    subject

<u>of dogs (of which I am fond)</u>.
            treatment

Write an outline or an outline alternative.

I. Poodles (major support)
   A. High-strung (minor support)
   B. Need attention (minor support)
II. Doberman pinschers (major support)
   A. Demanding (minor support)
   B. Need watching (minor support)
III. Bulldogs (major support)
   A. Act mean (minor support)
   B. Will back down (minor support)
IV. Cocker spaniels (major support)
   A. Lovable (minor support)
   B. Faithful (minor support)
   C. Easy to please (minor support)

STAGE THREE

Write On separate paper, write and then revise your paragraph or essay as many times as necessary for **c**oherence, **l**anguage (usage, tone, and diction), **u**nity, **e**mphasis, **s**upport, and **s**entences (**CLUESS**). Read your work aloud to hear and correct any grammatical errors or awkward-sounding sentences.

Edit any problems in fundamentals, such as **c**apitalization, **o**missions, **p**unctuation, and **s**pelling (**COPS**).

Rough Draft: Writing, Revising, Editing

Customers Are Like Canines
Vera Harris

Language
Punctuation

Over the years while working
~~I have worked~~ in a beauty salon ~~for a long time. There,~~ I have come across

Sentences
Punctuation

almost every kind of salon customer, each with her own unique looks and per-

Because
sonality. I am also a dog lover and have observed numerous dogs with care it is

Language

relate them to
easier to classify these people if I ~~compare them with~~ canine types—but in a

playful rather than a mean way. The first group is made up of poodles. Poodles

Language

and high-strung
are very prissy, with a constant need for attention. Their hair is usually over-

Emphasis
Spelling
Omission

last
styled. They think puffballs in soft colors look great. The ~~next group~~ and largest

e   *and*
group—is made up of cocker spanials. The ₵ockers are very lovable the most

Language

groomed and stroked, but they are easy to please.   *to*
faithful. They enjoy being ~~pampered.~~ Cockers like to see me every week and visit

Sentences

with others. Sometimes I can almost see their tails wagging. Then come the

Sentences
Language

s
Doberman pinchers₀this type scares me the most. Dobies are hard to please. If

expose
one hair goes the wrong way/I will see their upper lip rise up to ~~show~~ eyeteeth, as

Punctuation

if they are snarling. I rarely turn my back while working on this type—a Dobie

Language

third   *members,*
might bite. The ~~last~~ group the bulldogs, are not as mean as Dobies. Bulldogs act

Punctuation

one doesn't
mean and tough, but if ~~you don't~~ show fear when they get bossy they will back

I'm
down. This type needs to feel in charge, even if ~~it's me~~ leading them around on a

Language

leash. No matter what, canines and customers are my best friends.

Final Draft

Customers Are Like Canines
Vera Harris

Topic sentence

Over the years while working in a beauty salon, I have come across almost every kind of salon customer, each with her own unique looks and personality. Because I am also a dog lover and have observed numerous dogs with care, it is easier to classify these people if I relate them to canine types—but in a playful

Support

rather than a mean way. The first group is made up of poodles. Poodles are very prissy and high-strung, with a constant need for attention. Their hair is usually

Support

over-styled. They think puffballs in soft colors look great. Then come the Doberman pinschers. This type scares me the most. Dobies are hard to please. If one hair goes the wrong way, I will see their upper lip rise up to expose eyeteeth. I

Support

rarely turn my back while working on this type—a Dobie might bite. The third

Support

group members, the bulldogs, are not as mean as Dobies. Bulldogs act mean and tough, but if one doesn't show fear when they get bossy, they will back down. This type needs to feel in charge, even if I'm leading them around on a leash. The last—and largest—group is made up of cocker spaniels. The cockers are very lovable and the most faithful. They enjoy being groomed and stroked, but they are easy to please. Cockers like to see me every week and to visit with others. Some-

Concluding sentence

times I can almost see their tails wagging. No matter what, canines and customers are my best friends.

EXERCISE 3

Writing a Paragraph

Select one of the following topic sentences and, on separate paper, write a paragraph based on it.

1. I made that argument at the time, but if I had a second chance, I wouldn't repeat it.

2. It was the worst piece of news I ever had to deliver.

3. I confronted authority and learned from the experience.

4. (It) was an act of generosity I will never forget.

5. Sometimes there are good reasons for lying.

6. Alcohol addiction has physical, social, and vocational effects.

7. There are several ways to show affection.

8. The job didn't pay well, but it provided me with a good education in balancing my budget, managing my time, and dealing with the public.

9. Teenagers like music for obvious reasons.

10. Homeless people are in their situation for different reasons.

Writer's Guidelines

1. The **developmental paragraph** is a group of sentences, each with the function of stating or supporting a controlling idea called the topic sentence.

2. The developmental paragraph contains three parts: the subject, the topic sentence, and the support.

3. The two main patterns of the developmental paragraph are (A) topic sentence and support, and (B) topic sentence, support, and concluding sentence.

4. The topic sentence includes what you are writing about—the **subject**—and what you intend to do with that subject—the **treatment.**

<u>Being a good parent</u> <u>is more than providing financial support.</u>
       subject   treatment

Pattern A   **Pattern B**

Topic sentence	Topic sentence
Support	Support
Support	Support
Support	Support
	Concluding sentence

Development (Pattern A) — Development (Pattern B)

5. The **outline** is a pattern for showing the relationship of ideas. It can be used to reveal the structure and content of something you read or to plan the structure and content of something you intend to write. The following topic outline shows how the parts are arranged on the page as well as how the ideas in it relate to one another.

Main Idea (will usually be the topic sentence for the paragraph or the thesis for the essay)
   I. Major support
      A. Minor support
         1. Details (specific information of various kinds)
         2. Details
      B. Minor support
         1. Details
         2. Details
  II. Major support
      A. Minor support
      B. Minor support
         1. Details
         2. Details
         3. Details

Writing the Essay

FLOW OF WRITING

The Essay Defined in Relation to the
Developmental Paragraph   83

Special Paragraphs Within the Essay   85

   Introductions   85

   Conclusions   87

Student Demonstration of All Stages of the
Writing Process   88

   Writing Process Worksheet   89

Writer's Guidelines   96

*"Considered structurally, the essay can
often be an expanded developmental
paragraph."*

LEE BRANDON

THE QUIGMANS　　　　　by **Buddy Hickerson**

TAKE THAT EPITHET BACK, MACK, OR I SHALL IMPACT AGAINST YOUR CRANIUM STRONGLY OR ADVERSELY SO AS TO DISTRESS OR HARM WITHOUT REGARD TO SUCCESS OR FAILURE IN A HAP-HAZARD OR AIMLESS MANNER.

BEER

How the aliens will reveal themselves.

B. Hickerson, copyright Los Angeles Times Syndicate. Reprinted by
permission.

The Essay Defined in Relation to the Developmental Paragraph

The essay is as difficult to define as the paragraph, but the paragraph definition gives us a framework. Consider the definition from Chapter 5: The **developmental paragraph** . . . "is a group of sentences, each with the function of supporting a controlling idea called the topic sentence."

The main parts of the developmental paragraph are the topic sentence (subject and treatment), support (evidence and reasoning), and, often, a concluding sentence. Now let's use that framework to define the essay: The **essay** is a group of paragraphs, each with the function of supporting a controlling idea called the thesis.

These are the main parts of the essay:

Introduction: presents the thesis, which states the controlling idea—much like the topic sentence for a paragraph but on a larger scale.

Development: introduces evidence and reasoning—the support.

Transition: points out divisions of the essay (seldom used in the short essay).

Conclusion: provides an appropriate ending—often a restatement of or reflection on the thesis.

Thus, considered structurally, the essay can be an expanded developmental paragraph. That does not mean that all paragraphs can grow to be essays or that all essays can shrink to become paragraphs. For college writing, however, a good understanding of the parallel between well-organized paragraphs and well-organized essays is useful.

As you learn how to write effective paragraphs—with strong topic sentences and strong support—you also learn how to organize an essay. You just expand the process, as shown in Figure 6.1.

Figure 6.1
Paragraph and Essay Compared

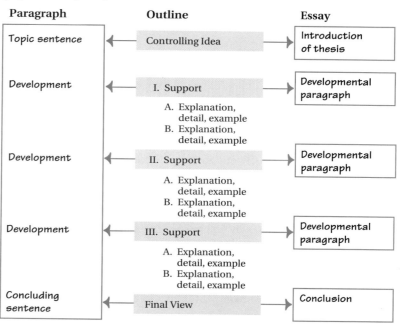

Paragraph:

Short Essay:

Good King Elvis

A messiah, a jester, a reckless jerk—or a soulful singer from the Deep South—Elvis at different times to different people was all these things. <u>His fans mirror every facet of their idol.</u>   Thesis

<u>For some fans the attraction is appearance.</u>   Topic sentence
"I liked him because of his looks," says Sue Scarborough, forty-nine of Lexington, Kentucky, as she waits with her husband to tour Graceland. She grins good-naturedly at her husband and gives him an affectionate nudge in the ribs when he says, "My wife really likes Elvis, but I'm not jealous because he is dead—I think." Her response tells all: "My husband's a good man at drivin' a truck and fishin' for bass, but no one'll ever paint his picture on velvet."   Support

<u>For others, Elvis was a king with a common touch and humanitarian instincts.</u> "He didn't put on airs," says Jeff Graff, twenty, of Cleveland, Ohio. "He went out of his way to help people." His friend nods his head in agreement. "Elvis must've given away a hundred Cadillacs in his day." Others in line break in to tell stories about the generosity of this good man who once walked among them.   Support   Topic sentence

<u>The speakers at Graceland who get the most attention are those who actually met Elvis and have information about his basic goodness.</u>   Topic sentence
"I met him in 1960 when I was twelve years old," says Billie Le Jeune of Memphis, who visits Graceland once or twice a month: "He asked me what my favorite subject was." A few others have stories equally compelling. The crowd listens in awe and envy.   Support

<u>Along with these talkers at Graceland are the writers, who sum up the range of Elvis's qualities.</u> On the pink fieldstone wall outside Graceland, which for years has functioned as an unauthorized bulletin board, the graffiti runs like this: ELVIS IS LOVE; I DID DRUGS WITH ELVIS; and most cryptic of all—ELVIS DIDN'T DESERVE TO BE WHITE.   Conclusion

Introduction

Topic sentence

Good King Elvis

A messiah, a jester, a reckless jerk—or a soulful singer from the Deep South—Elvis at different times to different people was all these things. <u>His fans mirror every facet of their idol.</u> "I liked him because of his looks," says Sue Scarborough, forty-nine, of Lexington, Kentucky, as she waits with her husband to tour Graceland. "He didn't put on airs," says Jeff Graff, twenty, of Cleveland, Ohio. "He went out of his way to help people." "I met him in 1960 when I was twelve years old," says Billie Le Jeune of Memphis, who visits Graceland once or twice a month: "He asked me what my favorite subject was." On the pink fieldstone wall outside Graceland, which for years has functioned as an unauthorized bulletin board, the graffiti runs like this: ELVIS IS LOVE; I DID DRUGS WITH ELVIS; and most cryptic of all—ELVIS DIDN'T DESERVE TO BE WHITE.

Topic sentence

Support

Support

Support

Concluding sentence

I. Appearance

II. Helped people

III. Basic goodness

Jim Miller, "Forever Elvis"

Like the paragraph, the essay may also assume different patterns. It may be principally one form of discourse: narration, description, exposition, or argumentation. It may also be a combination, varying from paragraph to paragraph and even within paragraphs. Regardless of its pattern, the essay will be unified around a central idea, or thesis. The **thesis** is the assertion or controlling purpose. All the other parts of the essay will be subordinate to the thesis and will support it. As with the paragraph, the main point—here, the thesis—will almost certainly be stated, usually in the first paragraph, and again—more often than not—at the end of the essay. The essay on Elvis illustrates this pattern.

The only difference in concept between the topic sentence and the thesis is one of scope: The topic sentence unifies and controls the content of the paragraph, and the thesis does the same for the essay. Because the essay is longer and more complex than the typical paragraph, the thesis may suggest a broader scope and may more explicitly indicate the parts.

Special Paragraphs Within the Essay

Developmental paragraphs were discussed in Chapter 5, and because paragraphs of transition (usually short and having a simple structure) are almost never needed in short essays, we will focus our attention on paragraphs of introduction and conclusion.

Introductions

A good introductory paragraph does many things. It attracts the reader's interest, states or points toward the thesis, and moves the reader smoothly into the body paragraphs, the developmental paragraphs. Here are some introductory methods:

- a direct statement of the thesis
- background
- definition of term(s)
- quotation(s)
- a shocking statement
- question(s)
- a combination of two or more methods on this list

You should not decide that some of the methods are good and some are bad. Indeed, all are valid, and the most common one is the last, the combination. Use the approach that best fits each essay. Resist the temptation to use the same kind of introduction in every essay you write.

Each of the following statements is an introductory paragraph. The thesis is the same in all of them, yet each uses a different introductory method. Notice the great variety here.

Direct Statement of Thesis:

Anyone on the road in any city near midnight on Friday and Saturday is among dangerous people. They're not the product of the witching hour; they're the product of the "happy hour." They're called drunk drivers. Subject / Treatment These threats to our lives and limbs need to be controlled by federal laws with strong provisions.

Background:

In one four-year period in California (1997–2000), 17,354 people were injured and 6,863 were killed by drunk drivers. Each year, the same kinds of figures come in from all our states. The state laws vary. The federal government does virtually nothing. Drunk driving has reached the point of being a national problem of huge proportions. Subject / Treatment This slaughter of innocent citizens should be stopped by following the lead of many other nations and passing federal legislation with strong provisions.

Definition:

Subject
Treatment

Here's a recipe. Take two thousand pounds of plastic, rubber, and steel, pour in ten gallons of gas, and start the engine. Then take one human being of two hundred pounds of flesh, blood, and bones, pour in two glasses of beer in one hour, and put him or her behind the wheel. Mix the two together, and the result may be a drunken driver ready to cause death and destruction. This problem of drunk driving can and should be controlled by federal legislation with strong provisions.

Quotation:

Subject
Treatment

The National Highway Traffic Safety Administration has stated that 50 percent of all fatal accidents involve intoxicated drivers and that "75 percent of those drivers have a Blood Alcohol Content of .10 percent or greater." That kind of information is widely known, yet the carnage on the highways continues. This problem of drunk driving should be addressed by a federal law with strict provisions.

Shocking Statement and Questions:

Subject
Treatment

Almost 60,000 Americans were killed in the Vietnam War. What other war kills more than that number every four years? Give up? It's the war with drunk drivers. The war in Vietnam ended about three decades ago, but our DUI war goes on, and the drunks are winning. This deadly conflict should be controlled by a federal law with strong provisions.

Questions and a Definition:

Subject
Treatment

What is a drunk driver? In California it's a person with a blood alcohol content of .08 percent or more who is operating a motor vehicle. What do those drivers do? Some of them kill. Every year more than 16,000 people nationwide die. Those are easy questions. The difficult one is, What can be done? One answer is clear: Drunk drivers should be controlled by federal laws with strong provisions.

All these introductory methods are effective. Some others, however, are ineffective because they are too vague to carry the thesis or because they carry the thesis in a mechanical way. The mechanical approach may be direct and explicit, but it usually numbs the reader's imagination and interest.

Avoid: The purpose of this essay is to write about the need for strong national laws against drunk driving.

Avoid: I will now write a paper about the need for strong national laws against drunk driving.

The length of an introduction can vary, but the typical length for the introductory paragraph of a student essay is three to five sentences. If your introduction is shorter than three, be certain that it conveys all you want to say. If it is longer than five, be certain that it only introduces and does not try to expand on ideas. That function is reserved for the developmental paragraphs; a long and complicated introduction may make your essay top-heavy.

EXERCISE 1

Writing an Introduction

Select one of the following theses (altering it a bit to suit your own ideas, if you like) and, on separate paper, write at least three introductions for it, using a different method for each one. Underline the thesis in each paragraph, and label the subject and treatment parts.

1. Marriages come in different shapes and sizes.

2. Career choices are greatly influenced by a person's background.

3. *Friendship* is just one word, but friends are of different kinds.

4. The spirit of sports has been corrupted by money.

5. Sexual harassment at work often goes unreported for practical reasons.

Conclusions

Your concluding paragraph should give the reader the feeling that you have said all you want to say about your subject. Like introductory paragraphs, concluding paragraphs are of various types. Here are some effective ways of concluding a paper:

- Conclude with a final paragraph or sentence that is a logical part of the body of the paper; that is, one that functions as part of the support. In the following example, there is no formal conclusion. This form is more common in the published essay than in the student essay.

> One day he hit me. He said he was sorry and even cried, but I could not forgive him. We got a divorce. It took me a while before I could look back and see what the causes really were, but by then it was too late to make any changes.

Maria Campos, "A Divorce with Reasons"

- Conclude with a restatement of the thesis in slightly different words, perhaps pointing out its significance or making applications.

> Don't blame it on the referee. Don't even blame it on the fight managers. Put the blame where it belongs—on the prevailing mores that regard prize fighting as a perfectly proper enterprise and vehicle of entertainment. No one doubts that many people enjoy prize fighting and will miss it if it should be thrown out. And that is precisely the point.

Norman Cousins, "Who Killed Benny Paret?"

- Conclude with a review of the main points of the discussion—a kind of summary. This is appropriate only if the complexity of the essay makes a summary necessary.

> As we have been made all too aware lately in this country, the more energy we conserve now, the more we'll have for the future. The same holds true for skiing. So take the Soft Path of energy conservation as you ski. You'll not only be able to make longer nonstop runs, but you'll have more energy to burn on the dance floor.

Carl Wingus, "Conserving Energy as You Ski"

- Conclude with an anecdote related to the thesis.

> Over the harsh traffic sounds of motors and horns and blaring radios came the faint whang-whang of a would-be musician with a beat-up guitar and a money-drop hat turned up at his feet. It all reminded me of when I

had first experienced the conglomeration of things that now assailed my senses. This jumbled mixture of things both human and nonhuman was, in fact, the reason I had come to live here. Then it was different and exciting. Now it is the reason I am leaving.

- Conclude with a quotation related to the thesis.

Fifty percent of all fatal traffic accidents involve intoxicated drivers, according to the National Highway Traffic Safety Administration. Cavenaugh and Associates, research specialists, say that drunk drivers killed 83,824 people in the five-year period from 1993 through 1999. They go on to say that intoxicated drivers cost us somewhere between $11 and $24 billion each year. It is time to give drunk drivers a message: "Stay off the road. You are costing us pain, injury, and death, and no one has the right to do that."

There are also many ineffective ways of concluding an essay. Do not conclude with the following:

- a summary when a summary is unnecessary
- a complaint about the assignment or an apology about the quality of the work
- an afterthought—that is, something you forgot to discuss in the body of the essay
- a tagged conclusion—that is, a sentence beginning with such phrases as *In conclusion, To conclude, I would like to conclude this discussion,* or *Last but not least*
- a conclusion that raises additional problems that should have been settled during the discussion

The conclusion is an integral part of the essay and is often a reflection of the introduction. If you have trouble with the conclusion, reread your introduction. Then work for a roundness or completeness in the whole paper.

Student Demonstration of All Stages of the Writing Process

Let's see now how one student wrote an essay by working her way through all the stages of the writing process.

Our student writer, Leah, is an inmate at a California prison where, for several years, she was enrolled in a small, low-cost college program. In her English class, her assignment was to write a personal essay of 500 to 800 words. Her instructor suggested she concentrate on a recent development or event at the prison that had changed her life, for better or worse.

Several topics interested her. There was the problem of overcrowding: She lived in an institution built for 900 inmates, and the population was now 2,200. She also considered education. After spending some time in routine prison work and aimless activities, she discovered school and found it highly satisfying. Then there were the accomplishments of her Native-American friends at the prison. After years of arguing their case, they had finally obtained permission from the institution to build a sweat lodge for religious purposes, and it was now in operation. That was a subject she knew well, and it was one for which she held the most enthusiasm. She was ready to proceed, knowing that the writing process would provide her with strategies and give her direction.

Leah used the Writing Process Worksheet for guidance, thus also providing her instructor with a record of the development of her work. Her worksheet has been lengthened for you to be able to see parts of her work in their entirety. You will find a full-size blank worksheet on page 6, which can be photocopied, filled in, and submitted with each assignment if your instructor directs you to do so.

Writing Process Worksheet

Title Prison Sweat Lodge

Name Leah   **Due Date** Tuesday, April 11, at 1 p.m.

ASSIGNMENT In the space below, write whatever you need to know about your assignment, including information about the topic, audience, pattern of writing, length, whether to include a rough draft or revised drafts, and whether your paper must be typed.

Write a personal essay of 500 to 800 words about some aspect of your prison life that has changed recently. This will be mainly about how something is done; therefore, you will probably organize your discussion by time. Write for a general cross section of the population, one that will probably not have shared the experience you write about. Submit this completed worksheet, a rough draft marked for revision, and a typed final draft.

STAGE ONE **Explore** Freewrite, brainstorm (list), cluster, or take notes as directed by your instructor. Use the back of this page or separate paper if you need more space.

Freewriting

• First Leah started freewriting, which enabled her to probe her memory and see which aspects of the subject most interested her. She wrote without stopping, letting her ideas tumble forth in a rich free association on the subject of "sweat lodge." •

For several years I have wanted to worship in the way that I did when I was on the reservation. These people here at prison were discriminating against me, I thought. I knew that the other people here could go to the chaplain and to the chapel and they could do so without people complaining or going to any bother. I didn't know why they did not allow me to follow my own religious preference. Then I talked to the other Indian sisters here at prison and they told me that they had been working for many years to get a sweat lodge. I started working with

Have sweat lodge now them. It took years of work, but it is worth it for now <u>we have a sweat lodge</u> where we can go for our ceremonies. It makes me feel good. I look forward to it. I <u>have used it once a week for most</u> of the <u>last year</u>. When I am nervous and when things are tense on the prison grounds, I think about the sweat lodge and just thinking about it gives me some peace. Then <u>when I go there and sweat</u> for a period of time I seem to feel that I am leaving the prison grounds and I am <u>at peace</u>

Ceremony important with the universe. It is <u>a ceremony</u> that is <u>important</u> to me and also to the prison. We even have women who are not Indians who are interested and we teach them about Indian ways and we all learn from what we do. What else is there to say. I could go on and on. That is what I have to say. I love the sweat lodge which we call the sweats. I think it is the most important thing in my life now. I used to be bitter toward the prison for denying me my rights, but now I am even <u>at peace</u> with them—most of the time. I remember when we were trying to get approval and . . . [partial]

At peace

Brainstorming (Big Six Questions)

• Leah continued with the subject of the prison sweat lodge, and her topic tightened to focus on particular areas. Although she could have listed the annotations and the words she underlined in her freewriting, she began with the big six questions for her framework. •

Who?   American Indian inmates and others
What?   sweat lodge—how it was started—the politics—
          the ceremonies
Where?   California Institution for Women—off the yard
When?   1989, before, after, long time in planning and building
Why?   spiritual, physical, self-esteem, educational
How?   preparation, steps

Brainstorming (Listing)

• Leah then proceeded to write three useful lists based on her answers to the questions. •

Sweat lodge	*Ceremony*	*Result*
Problems in	Preparation	Relaxed
building it	Blankets	Spiritually clean
Reasons	Rocks	Peaceful
Fairness	Fire	
Who helped	Water	
Time to build	Tobacco and	
	sweet grass	
	Sweating	
	Passing pipe	
	Tearing down	

Clustering

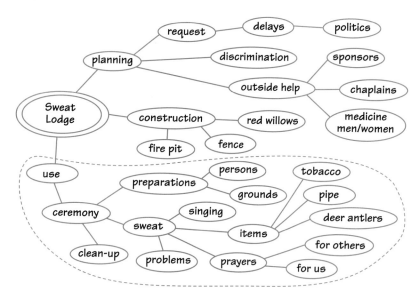

• Notice that after completing her basic cluster, Leah went back and drew a broken boundary around subclusters that offered encouraging areas for focus. Some subclusters, usually with further clustering to provide details, can work as well as an outline for providing structure and content for the development of an essay. •

STAGE TWO

Organize Write a topic sentence or thesis; label the subject and the treatment parts.

• After freewriting, brainstorming, and clustering, Leah was ready to focus. She was ready to concentrate on one aspect of her larger topic that could reasonably be developed in an essay of 500 to 800 words. She also wanted to establish a direction for the essay that would target her audience, who knew little about her topic. It would be necessary to explain her topic in detail so that uninformed readers could easily understand. Moreover, she would avoid any Native-American words that her audience might not know. Although the sweat lodge was developed in an atmosphere of controversy in which she and others often had to be persuasive, she anticipated that readers of this essay would be open-minded and interested. She would simply inform them about her experience with the sweat lodge, giving a personal perspective. She would also have to avoid using prison slang, because this essay was for an assignment in a college writing class.

Leah made three attempts to write a sentence with both a subject (what she would write about) and a treatment (what she would do with her subject). She wanted the treatment to be just right, not vague or too broad or too narrow. •

I want to explain how we use sweats and why.

Using the prison sweat lodge involves specific practices that contribute to my well-being.

I want to discuss the <u>prison sweat lodge, what we do in the prep-</u>
subject
<u>aration period, what we do when we're inside for the ceremony,</u>
treatment
<u>and what we do afterwards.</u>

• Her third attempt satisfied her, and the statement became her thesis. Later she would reword it. •

Write an outline or an outline alternative.

• Leah's next task was to organize her material. Although she might have used the part of her cluster marked by the dotted lines, she chose the outline form.

The outline shows the relationship of ideas, suggests ways to divide the essay according to Leah's thesis, and indicates support. The divisions are Preparation, Ceremony, and Ceremony completion and site restoration. Those items are Leah's Roman numeral headings. •

I. Preparation
   A. Fasting
      1. Duration
      2. Only water
   B. Heat rocks
      1. Thirty to fifty
      2. Build fire
   C. Set up lodge
      1. Permission from sponsor
      2. Cover framework
II. Ceremony
   A. Movement
      1. Going and coming
      2. Passing sacred objects
   B. Establishing attitude
   C. Sweating
   D. Praying and singing
   E. Purification rites
      1. Tobacco ties
      2. Sage
      3. Sweet grass
III. Ceremony completion and site restoration
   A. Personal
      1. Water down
      2. Eat and drink
      3. Change
   B. Site
      1. Remove and store blankets
      2. Move rocks

STAGE THREE   **Write**   On separate paper, write and then revise your paragraph or essay as many times as necessary for **c**oherence, **l**anguage (usage, tone, and diction), **u**nity, **e**mphasis, **s**upport, and **s**entences (**CLUESS**). Read your work aloud to hear and correct any grammatical errors or awkward-sounding sentences.

Edit any problems in fundamentals, such as **c**apitalization, **o**missions, **p**unctuation, and **s**pelling (**COPS**).

• The following is an early draft that shows Leah's revision process. The draft also includes some editing (COPS). •

Razor Wire Sweat Lodge

~~I am a~~ *My tribe is* Pomo ~~Indian~~, one ~~tribe~~ of ~~many here~~ *twenty-one represented* on the prison grounds. I have had *always*

tremendous interest in my ~~Ancestry~~ *ancestors* and *in* their customs, and the cultures of all   ⌉ *Rewrite*

Indian tribes. The sacred sweat ceremonies, I've found to be one of the most

interesting. Many women of ~~all~~ *cultural practices* *other* races here in the facility have also taken   ⌉ *Rewrite*

interest and found ~~peace~~ *other benefits* within themselves from participating in the sweats.

I want to discuss the prison sweat lodge, what we do in the preparation period,

what we do when we're inside for the ceremony, and what we do afterwards.

Rewrite for stronger topic sentence ⌈ The first step to sweating *in our prison facility* is the preparation period. Before anyone can sweat

there are many requirements ~~in~~ *concerning* what we wear/~~how we are instructed (depending~~

~~on how many times we've gone),~~ and how we act. ~~/~~*For* Twenty-four hours before the

sweat we fast. ~~We can only drink~~ *Participants should drink only* water or juices, but if someone has health prob-

lems we will excuse them. The lava rocks have to *heat* in the fire approximately three   ⌉ *Coherence*

hours before we start sweating. The fire has to be built just right in a little house

shape. ~~Putting~~ *We put* all the rocks in the middle with the wood standing like a teepee

Organize Be more concise around them; then the paper *is* stuffed between and around the wood. Once there's

a good fire going then we ~~start~~ tend to the sweat lodge itself. Because we have no

tarp to put on the sweat lodge, the state has provided us with plenty of blankets.

The blankets have to cover the s*w*eat lodge fully. We put at least three layers of

blankets on the sweat lodge. We make sure we leave about eight inches of blan-

ket around the bottom of the sweat lodge. ~~Around~~ *By* this time, some women have

Coherence started making their tobacco ties. These ties are used for ~~putting your~~ *sending* prayer on.

We'~~ve got to~~ *must* make sure the sponsor is somewhere by the sweat lodge at all times.

~~Also about~~ *As for* the rock*s,* we use thirty to fifty of them*;* it depends on their size and

how many women are sweating that day. Then the women are told to change into

only muu muu*s;* the state provides them also. Then we're read*y* to go inside. The

preparation period is very important *but* ~~and~~ everyone looks forward to it being over.

Once everyone is inside the sweat lodge, there are certain things ~~you~~ *we* must do.

~~The way we enter is~~ first we enter counterclockwise and ^{once} inside we ~~maintain~~ ^{conduct all}

~~everything we do~~ ^{parts of the ceremony} counterclockwise. There are four rounds in the sweat which ^{each of}

last about twenty to thirty minutes ~~each~~^s. We stress that no one break our circle ^{should}

inside the sweat lodge, but it ~~is possible.~~ ^{sometimes happens.} Some women can't handle the heat in-

Coherence | side we never make them stay. The praying and singing is in the Sioux language ^{so}

because our outside sponsor is Sioux. Not everyone has to sing or pray. It's up to

Rephrase | ~~them.~~ ^{the individual.} As someone finishes a prayer ~~they say for all their relations~~ ^{she mentions all her relatives} then the next

person prays. Before ~~anyone even~~ enters ^{we} the sweat ~~they~~ ^{we} have to make sure they   *Agreement*

have peace and good feelings with all other members. The tobacco ties hang over   *Be more concise*

our heads in the sweat or around our necks. (Also) we take in sage with us and

smudge ourselves with it. ^{for purification} After each round, new hot rocks are brought in. As

Verb tense | these rocks are place^d in the fire sweet grass is put on them. ~~All~~ ^{What} we do inside the

sweat lodge is not only for ourselves, but ~~for~~ ^{through} our prayers for others. We maintain

ourselves with humility during the whole sweat.

When the sweat is over we enter the final phase. We come out and throw our

tobacco ties in^{to} the fire pit. The ~~first thing~~ we ~~do is~~ hoseⁿ ourselves down with

plenty of cold water. The refreshments are opened and someone goes after food.

Once we've eaten and changed our clothes we start taking down the sweat. The

blankets have to be taken off the same way they were put on and folded up ~~good~~^{carefully.}.

The leftover wood has to be put away and ~~on both~~ the blankets and the wood

~~we put their covers.~~ ^{must be covered.} Any garbage that's been left around is thrown in^{to} the Dump-

ster. Then we lock the gate and bid our farewells until the next weekend. A~~f~~ter

it's all over ~~you really~~ ^{we} feel ~~a sense of~~ ^{physically} refresh~~ness~~^{ed} clean and peaceful.

Move to end | *Rewrite* | ~~T~~he sweat lodge is a custom of most~~ly all~~ Indian tribes. Certain Indian tribes go ^{Using}

about it differently ~~than others~~ ^{from} but once they're all inside everyone feels of one

whole being. All three steps I've gone through are helpful for a successful sweat

ceremony. ~~Many of us members~~ ^{Each week we} look forward to these ceremonies ~~every week~~.

They help us cope better with the prison system.

Final Draft

Razor Wire Sweat Lodge

Leah

My Indian tribe is Pomo, one of twenty-one represented at this prison. I have always had tremendous interest in my ancestors and their customs, and in the cultures of all Indian tribes. The sacred sweat ceremony itself is at the center of my life. Here at prison it has taken on a special meaning. In fact, many women of other races here have also found peace within themselves as a result of partici-

Thesis   pating with me and other Native Americans in the sweats. Each Saturday we have a routine: We make preparations, we sweat, and we conclude with a post-sweat activity.

Topic sentence   Before we sweat, we must prepare ourselves and the facility. For twenty-four hours before the sweat, we fast. We do not eat anything and drink only water or juices, but if someone has a health problem, we will excuse her. As for clothing, we wear simple, loose dresses such as the prison-issued muu muus. We bring tobacco ties, sage leaves, sweet grass, and sometimes a pipe. Preparing the facility is more complicated than preparing ourselves. About thirty-five lava rocks must be heated in a fire approximately three hours before we start sweating. The wood for the fire has to be placed in a tepee shape around the pile of rocks and ignited. Once the fire is hot, we tend to the sweat lodge itself. Because we have no tarp to put on the sweat lodge frame, the state provides us with blankets. We use these to cover the lodge fully, draping it with about three layers and leaving an opening to the east. Finally we are ready to go inside. The preparation period is very important, but everyone looks forward to its being over.

Topic sentence   From this point on through the ceremony, everything must be done according to rules. First we enter counterclockwise, and once inside we conduct all parts of the ceremony counterclockwise. There are four rounds in the sweat, each of which lasts about twenty to thirty minutes. We stress that no one should break our circle inside the sweat lodge, but it sometimes happens. Some women can't handle the steam and the heat, so we never make them stay. Those who do stay are free to participate in the singing and praying or not. The four rounds are similar. For each, six hot rocks are brought in, and six dippers of water are poured onto the rocks. The number six indicates the four directions and the sky and the ground. As someone finishes a prayer (usually in Sioux because our sponsor is a Sioux), she mentions her relatives, for this ceremony is also for others. Then another person follows. As sweet grass burns outside on the fire, we sit in the hot steam and rub sage leaves on our bodies for purification. We maintain ourselves with humility during the whole event.

Topic sentence   When the sweat is over, we enter the final phase. We come out and throw our tobacco ties into the fire pit, and the smoke takes our prayers to the sky. Then we hose ourselves down with plenty of cold water and open the refreshments we brought. Once we've eaten and changed our clothes, we start dismantling the sweat. The blankets have to be taken off the same way they were put up and then folded carefully. The leftover wood has to be put away, and the blankets and wood must be covered. Any garbage that's been left around is thrown into the Dumpster. Then we lock the gate to our facility and bid farewell.

Using a sweat lodge is a custom of most Indian tribes. Certain Indian tribes go about it differently from others, but in here when we are together in the lodge, we feel like one whole being. Each week we look forward to this ceremony. It helps us cope better with the prison system. After it's over, we feel physically re-freshed, clean, and peaceful.

EXERCISE 2

Completing a Writing Process Worksheet

Select one of the following theses (altering it if you like, even by taking the opposite position) and complete a Writing Process Worksheet at least through Stage Two. (Photocopy the blank form on page 6.)

1. The date [marriage, class, game, job] was a disaster [success].

2. I will never forget my first encounter with racial prejudice [cruelty to animals, inhumanity].

3. The kind of music I listen to reflects the kind of person I would like to be.

4. A preoccupation with a single activity or concern throws life out of balance.

5. The importance of student government is often overlooked.

6. A death in the family can teach a person a great deal about life.

7. The way a person drives reveals his or her personality.

8. The way I drive depends on my mood.

9. The way I keep my room [car, house, yard, desk] is a reflection of the way I think [regard life].

10. One of my most embarrassing moments has become, in retrospect, only a hu-morous recollection.

Writer's Guidelines

1. The **essay** is a group of paragraphs, each with the function of stating or support-ing a controlling idea called the thesis.

   • The main parts of an essay are the introduction, development, and conclusion.
   • The essay can be considered an amplification of a developmental paragraph.

2. The **introduction** contains the thesis within a context of comments that give an adequate perspective on the topic. There are many good introductory methods, which include presenting a direct statement of the thesis, background, definition of term(s), quotation(s), a shocking statement, question(s), and a combination of two or more of these methods.

3. The **conclusion** makes a final comment on the development of your thesis. If you do not know how to conclude, reread your introduction for ideas.

4. You can depend on the three stages of the writing process to help you write para-graphs and essays. In the first stage, you are encouraged to explore relevant ideas and perhaps generate a topic sentence or thesis. In the second stage, you move

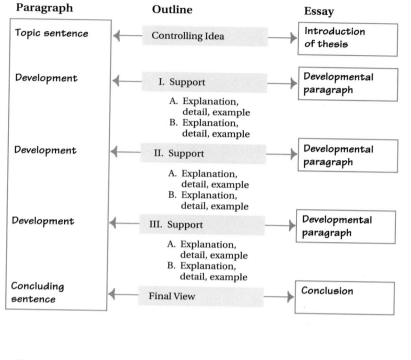

naturally to a precise statement of your topic sentence or thesis and to an organized plan for your support material. Finally, you do the actual writing, revising, and editing of your paragraph or essay. This process also allows for recursive movement: You can go back and forth as you rework your material.

Writing Paragraphs and Essays: Instruction, with Reading Selections

Part III discusses—and also demonstrates through reading selections—how our thoughts often occur in flexible, useful patterns. As you write in classes across the campus, notice how many regular writing assignments—especially papers and essay tests—expect you to describe, narrate, analyze (in many forms such as causes and effects, comparison and contrast, and definition), or argue a point. Following the same principles, you may be asked to use similar forms at the workplace as you write incident reports, proposals, evaluations, and recommendations.

Narration: Moving Through Time

FLOW OF WRITING

Writing Narration   102

   The Narrative Defined   102

   Basic Patterns   102

   Verb Tense   103

   Point of View   103

   Description   104

   Dialogue   104

Practicing Narrative Patterns   105

Connecting Reading and Writing   107

   Professional Writers   107

   "W-A-T-E-R"   107

   "B. B. King Live!"   108

   "No Tears for Frankie"   109

   "Assembly Line Adventure"   111

   Student Writers   115

   "A Moment in the Sun" (demonstration with stages)   117

   "From Survival to Living"   118

Topics for Writing Narration   121

Writer's Guidelines   123

"The art of writing is the art of applying the seat of the pants to the seat of the chair."

M. H. VORSE

THE QUIGMANS   by Buddy Hickerson

Francine's virtue is saved from a reckless advance with the deployment of her first-date air bag.

Writing Narration

The Narrative Defined

A **narrative** is an account of an incident or a series of incidents that make up a complete and significant action. A narrative can be as short as a joke, as long as a novel, or anything between, including a paragraph or an essay. It can function as the major framework for a piece of writing or as a support element. Across the curriculum, students write case studies for psychology classes; observations of other school settings for education classes; and field-trip reports for courses as varied as geology, art history, and music appreciation. Narratives are common at the workplace as investigative, incident, progress, and trip reports, as well as case studies.

Basic Patterns

Each narrative has five properties: situation, conflict, struggle, outcome, and meaning. They are described here as they relate directly to dramatic action. In a broader sense, you might use other terms such as setting, concern, sequence of events, completion, and significance (or recommended action).

Situation

Situation is the background for the action. The situation may be described only briefly, or it may even be implied. ("To celebrate my seventeenth birthday, I went to the Department of Motor Vehicles to take my practical test for my driver's license.")

Conflict

Conflict is friction, such as a problem in the surroundings, with another person, or within the individual. The conflict, which is at the heart of each narrative, produces struggle. ("It was raining and my appointment was the last one of the day. The examiner was a serious, weary-looking man who reminded me of a bad boss I once had, and I was nervous.")

Struggle

Struggle, which need not be physical, is the manner of dealing with conflict. The struggle adds action or engagement and generates the plot. ("After grinding on the ignition because the engine was already on, I had trouble finding the windshield wiper control. Next I forgot to signal until after I had pulled away from the curb. As we crept slowly down the rain-glazed street, the examiner told me to take the emergency brake off. All the while I listened to his pen scratching on his clipboard. 'Pull over and park,' he said solemnly.")

Outcome

Outcome is the result of the struggle. ("After I parked the car, the examiner told me to relax, and then he talked to me about school. When we continued, somehow I didn't make any errors, and I got my license.")

Meaning

Meaning is the significance of the story, which may be deeply philosophical or simple, stated or implied. ("Calmness promotes calmness.")

Verb Tense

Because most narratives relate experience in time order, the verb tense is likely to be the past ("She *walked* into the room") rather than the present ("She *walks* into the room"), although you may use either. An unnecessary change in tense tends to distract or confuse readers.

Two generalizations may be useful as you work with verb tense.

- Most narratives (often summaries) based on literature are written in the present tense.

   Tom Sawyer *pretends* that painting the fence *is* a special pleasure. His friends *watch* him eagerly. He *talks* and *displays* his joy. They *pay* him to do his work.

- Most historical events and personal experiences are written in the past tense.

   The Battle of Gettysburg *was* the decisive encounter in the Civil War. Although General Lee, the Confederate general in charge of the overall strategy, *was* a wise and experienced man, he *made* some tactical blunders that *led* to a devastating victory by the Union forces.

   We *walked* down the path to the well-house, attracted by the fragrance of the honeysuckle with which it *was covered*. Someone *was* drawing water and my teacher *placed* my hand under the spout. As the cool stream *gushed* over one hand she *spelled* into the other the word *water*, first slowly, then rapidly.

Helen Keller, *The Story of My Life*

Although Helen Keller chose the conventional past tense for verbs in the last passage, she might have chosen the present tense for a sense of immediacy.

The two main points about tense are the following:

- The generalizations about verb-tense selection (using past for the historical and the personal and using present for fiction) are useful.
- The verb tense in a passage should change only when the shift is needed for clarity and emphasis.

Point of View

Point of view shows the writer's relationship to the material and the subject, and it usually does not change within a passage.

If you are conveying personal experience, the point of view will be **first person,** which can be either involved (as a participant) or detached (as an observer). The involved perspective uses *I* more prominently than the detached perspective does.

If you are presenting something from a distance—geographical or historical (for example, telling a story about George Washington)—the point of view will usually be **third person,** and the participants will be referred to as "he," "she," and "they."

Description

A good descriptive writer presents material so that the perceptive reader can read and re-experience the writer's ideas. One device important to that writer is imagery. Images can be perceived through the senses (sight, sound, taste, smell, and touch). A good descriptive writer also gives specific details and presents concrete particulars (actual things) in a convincing way. We read, we visualize, we identify, and—*zap*—we connect with a narrative account.

In the following paragraphs, the images are italicized to emphasize how the author has made us hear, smell, touch, and see. Also note the other specific details.

Luis Torres, "Los Chinos Discover el Barrio"

> Before she had quite arisen, she *called* our names and *issued* orders, and *pushed* her large feet into homemade slippers and *across* the *bare lye-washed wooden floor* to *light* the coal-oil lamp.
>
> The *lamplight* in the Store gave a *soft* make-believe feeling to our world which made me want to *whisper* and walk about on tiptoe. The *odors* of onions and oranges and kerosene had been *mixing* all night and wouldn't be disturbed until the wooden slat was removed from the door and the early morning air forced its way in with the bodies of people who had walked miles to reach the pickup place.

Maya Angelou, "Cotton-Picking Time"

Note the use of specific information in the next paragraph.

> On one recent Saturday afternoon a Latino fifth-grader, wearing the same type of hightop tennis shoes I wore as a ten-year-old on that same street corner, strode up to Señor Farrillas' snow-cone pushcart. The kid pulled out a pocketful of dimes and bought two *raspadas*. One for himself, and one for his school chum—a Vietnamese kid. He was wearing hightops, too. They both ordered strawberry, as I recall.

Luis Torres, "Los Chinos Discover el Barrio"

Torres presents the material so you can visualize it. Try to picture this, instead: "The other day I saw a kid buy a refreshment for himself and his friend." Of course, that is what happened, but very little narrative or descriptive communication takes place in this abbreviated version. In Torres's account, you know when and where the action took place. You know what the kids were wearing, and you know that the author (point of view as technique) identifies with the kids. They buy strawberry *raspadas* from Señor Farrillas. The Latino kid pays for the *raspadas* with "a pocketful of dimes." Did you ever, as a kid, put your hand in the pocket of some tight jeans and try to pull out those dimes with a balled fist? We identify, and the imagery registers. We may not have visited that street corner in reality, but vicariously we take a trip with Torres.

Dialogue

Dialogue is used purposefully in narration to characterize, particularize, and support ideas. It shows us how people talk and think, as individuals or as representatives of society. Not every narrative requires dialogue.

Note in the following paragraph that the snatches of dialogue are brief. The language will ring true to Asian immigrants and those who have been around Asian immigrants. It is starkly realistic yet sympathetically engaging in context so that we are convinced of its authenticity and drawn into the story. As narrator, the author was present when the utterances in this paragraph were made.

> My brother was even more fanatical than I about speaking English. He was especially hard on my mother, criticizing her, often cruelly, for her pid-

gin speech—smatterings of Chinese scattered like chop suey in her conversation. "It's not 'What it is,' Mom," he'd say in exasperation. "It's 'What *is* it, what *is* it!'" Sometimes Mom might leave out an occasional "the" or "a," or perhaps a verb of being. He would stop her in mid-sentence: "Say it again, Mom. Say it right." When he tripped over his own tongue, he'd blame it on her: "See, Mom, it's all your fault. You set a bad example."

Elizabeth Wong, "The Struggle to Be an All-American Girl"

Practicing Narrative Patterns

Some narratives are more structured than others, but all have the same basic patterns. The parts, especially conflict and struggle, will vary in extent, depending on the circumstances.

EXERCISE 1

Writing Patterns

Fill in the blanks to complete the pattern for the topic "A Random, Unexpected, and Welcome Act of Kindness" or for another topic of your choice. Add descriptive details as needed.

(Situation) I. _____

(Conflict) II. _____

(Struggle) III. _____

          A. _____

          B. _____

          C. _____

          (Or more) _____

(Outcome) IV. _____

(Meaning) V. _____

EXERCISE 2

Writing Patterns

Fill in the blanks to complete the pattern for the topic "Dealing with an Unpleasant Person at Work" or for another topic of your choice. Add descriptive details as needed.

(Situation) I. _____

(Conflict) II. _____

(Struggle) III. _____

         A. _____

         B. _____

         C. _____

         (Or more) _____

(Outcome) IV. _____

(Meaning) V. _____

EXERCISE 3 | Writing Patterns

Fill in the blanks to complete the pattern for the topic "An Accident in a Retail Store [or Elsewhere]" or for another topic of your choice. Add descriptive details as needed.

(Situation) I. _____

(Conflict) II. _____

(Struggle) III. _____

         A. _____

         B. _____

         C. _____

         (Or more) _____

(Outcome) IV. _____

(Meaning) V. _____

EXERCISE 4 | Completing Narrative Patterns

Fill in the blanks to complete the following pattern of this narrative based on the short story "The Gift of the Magi" by O. Henry.

  I. Situation

    A. A poor man and woman much in love

      1. Man with a watch but no watch chain

      2. Woman with a fine head of hair but no comb

    B. Holiday Time

II. Conflict

    A. Mutual desire to give holiday presents

    B. No money to _____

III. Struggle

    A. Man sells watch to buy woman _____

    B. Woman cuts off hair and sells it to buy man _____

IV. Outcome

    A. Man gives hairless woman _____

    B. Woman gives watchless man _____

V. Meaning

    A. Love in _____

    B. Ends with _____

Before turning to your own writing of narratives, let's look at a range of them, some composed by professional writers and some by students. These examples will show you different forms and different techniques, and they will furnish you with subject material for your own composition in paragraphs and essays.

Connecting Reading and Writing

Professional Writers

W-A-T-E-R

HELEN KELLER

Helen Keller was a remarkable person. With the help of her teacher and companion, Anne Sullivan, she conquered the disabilities of blindness and deafness and became one of the most famous and admired persons of her time. In this paragraph unit, she wrote about what was perhaps the most important, constructive event in her life.

1   One day, while I was playing with my new doll, Miss Sullivan put my big rag doll into my lap also, spelled "d-o-l-l" and tried to make me understand that "d-o-l-l" applied to both. Earlier in the day we had had a tussle over the words "m-u-g" and "w-a-t-e-r." Miss Sullivan had tried to impress it upon me that "m-u-g" is *mug* and that "w-a-t-e-r" is *water,* but I persisted in confounding the two. In despair she had dropped the subject for the time, only to renew it at the first opportunity. I be-

came impatient at her repeated attempts and, seizing the new doll, I dashed it upon the floor. I was keenly delighted when I felt the fragments of the broken doll at my feet. Neither sorrow nor regret followed my passionate outburst. I had not loved the doll. In the still, dark world in which I lived there was no strong sentiment of tenderness. I felt my teacher sweep the fragments to one side of the hearth, and I had a sense of satisfaction that the cause of my discomfort was removed. She brought me my hat, and I knew I was going out into the warm sunshine. This thought, if a wordless sensation may be called a thought, made me hop and skip with pleasure.

2   We walked down the path to the well-house, attracted by the fragrance of the honeysuckle with which it was covered. Someone was drawing water and my teacher placed my hand under the spout. As the cool stream gushed over one hand she spelled into the other the word *water,* first slowly, then rapidly. I stood still, my whole attention fixed upon the motions of her fingers. Suddenly I felt a misty consciousness as of something forgotten—a thrill of returning thought; and somehow the mystery of language was revealed to me. I knew then that "w-a-t-e-r" meant the wonderful cool something that was flowing over my hand. That living word awakened my soul, gave it light, hope, joy, set it free! There were barriers still, it is true, but barriers that could in time be swept away.

EXERCISE 5   ## Discussion and Critical Thinking

1. What is the situation?

2. What is the conflict?

3. What struggle occurs?

4. What is the outcome of the struggle?

5. What is the meaning of this narrative?

B. B. King Live!

ANDREA LEE

As narrated in The Blues Abroad, *the situation here is potentially dramatic. The audience in the concert hall is Russian; the performer is African American. The audience loves music but is not familiar with B. B. King's style. King wants involvement from audience members, but they don't know what to do.*

A slick-haired Russian M.C. announced B. B. King ("A great Negritanski musician"), and then King was on stage with his well-known guitar—Lucille—and a ten-man ensemble. As King and the ensemble swung into "Why I Sing the Blues," one could sense the puzzlement of the Russian audience. "Negro" music to them meant jazz or spirituals, but this was something else. Also, there was the question of response. B. B. King is a great, warm presence when he performs, and he asks his audiences to pour themselves out to him in return. King teases his audiences, urging them to clap along, to whistle, to hoot their appreciation, like the congregations in the Southern churches in which he grew up. But to Russians, such behavior suggests a lack of culture and an almost frightening disorder. Though obviously impressed, the audience at first kept a respectful silence during the numbers, as it might at the symphony. (Only the foreigners shouted and stomped out the beat; we found the Russians around us staring at us open-mouthed.) Then King played an irresistible riff, stopped, and leaned toward the audience with his hand cupped to his ear. The audience caught on and began to clap. King changed the beat, and waited for the audience to catch up. Then he changed it again. Soon the whole place was clapping along to "Get Off My Back, Woman," and there were even a few timid shouts and whistles. King, who has carried the blues to Europe, Africa, and the Far East, had broken the ice one more time.

EXERCISE 6

Discussion and Critical Thinking

1. What is the situation?

2. What is the conflict?

3. What struggle occurs?

4. What is the outcome?

5. What is the meaning?

No Tears for Frankie

GINA GREENLEE

In this essay, freelance writer Gina Greenlee recalls a childhood peer. He died. She attended his funeral. She rejoiced. This article was first published in the "Lives" section of the New York Times Magazine.

1   I was in the fifth grade when Frankie died. It was 1971. My whole class planned to attend the funeral, since we knew him. My father thought going might give me nightmares, but I insisted. I had never seen a dead person before. Most of all, I wanted to be sure that the little creep would never touch me again.

2   Frankie lived in Lower Manhattan where run-down tenements along Avenues A, B and C were on the verge of becoming the crack houses of the '80s. At the time, I lived nearby. Then in 1970 my family moved into an apartment in Coop Village on Grand Street and F.D.R. Drive. It was only three blocks—and a world—away from the projects to a predominantly white middle-class community on the East River. Overnight at school, I became "that black girl who lives in the rich Jew buildings."

Or at least that's what Frankie and my other African-American classmates thought I was. It became a familiar chant of theirs as I made my way through my old neighborhood to get to school.

3   Frankie and I were in the same grade, but I was 10 and he was 12 because he had been left back twice. He tormented all of the girls in our class. But Frankie relished singling me out—the only black girl in a sea of Jewish girls dotted with Latinas—and he had done so since I first arrived from another school in third grade.

4   He never did any schoolwork. Instead, for the first three periods Frankie's curriculum was mayhem; by fourth period he was usually in the principal's office; and by the fifth, he was back in class unremorseful and pumped to do it again. He only got worse in that working-class, urban-blight panacea, the after-school program. It was a nice idea: children whose parents were unavailable at 3 o'clock because they were working stayed after school to study, improve skills and tackle extra-credit projects. I spent those afternoons trying to stay alive.

5   Frankie and his crew would grab my breasts, genitals and buttocks when the teachers weren't looking. Their hands, quick as filthy street rats, darted across my private parts in assembly line, during dance rehearsals and yard processions. They would leave scrawled notes in my book bag that read, "I'm gonna beat you up after school," or "I'll get you in the stairwell."

6   One spring afternoon, I had made it through another harrowing two hours after school, only to be cornered on the stairs by the whole nasty lot. They taunted me to walk down ahead of them. I managed each step as if it were my first, balancing myself on the chalk-blue shellacked handrail as I peered through the landing divider reminiscent of a wire cage, hoping to see another student, teacher, anyone. Frankie shoved me, and I tumbled one full flight, landing on my knees, my favorite brown plaid dress above my ears, easy pickings for the tiny vultures who cackled obscenities while snatching at my body, punching and kicking me. That day, I understood the depth of Frankie's perversity.

7   When I told a friend that our classroom emptied out at 3 P.M., leaving me alone with Frankie's boys, without having to share another detail, she said, "Come to my house after school." I had enjoyed two afternoons of baking cookies and doll playing when I let slip that my parents thought I was in class. My friend's mother welcomed me to play at her home anytime as long as my parents knew. "Why were you at Amy's and not in the after-school program?" my father asked me later that night. I didn't tell him because I didn't think he could help me. His interventions would only inspire retaliations and spiral me deeper into the mess.

8   I did try to tell my teachers, but nobody believed me. They chuckled and said, "Frankie just has a crush on you." That's what I told my father 15 years after the attacks, when he asked me if I had told my teachers. I guess in their world, 12-year-old boys don't sexually attack 10-year-old girls. What world did they come from, anyway? What world was I in, and how could I fix it so Frankie would disappear?

9   One morning when my teachers had stepped away from the classroom, Frankie and his boys shoved me into the coat closet and held the door shut while I was alone with Frankie. It was dark. As he kept touching me, I tried to push him away and screamed to be let out. But Frankie's friends held steadfast until the teachers arrived; then they scrambled to their seats. None of the other kids said a word. But in front of them all, I told Frankie that I hated his guts and hoped he would die.

10   Quite accommodating, he lay in a casket later that year. I didn't shed a tear. My heart was hardened, though. As usual, Frankie was up to no good—tampering with public property with the boys—when he got himself electrocuted. I was 10, and I was glad.

EXERCISE 7

Discussion and Critical Thinking

1. Use phrases or sentences to indicate these parts of this narrative:

   Situation:

   Conflict:

   Struggle:

   Outcome:

   Meaning:

2. Why didn't Gina Greenlee shed a tear?

3. Having read this essay, do you think that this event made Greenlee generally a more compassionate or a less compassionate human being? Explain.

4. Is this an essay that only a person who has been bullied dreadfully can understand or can it be appreciated by anyone? Explain.

5. What would you say to people who would have forgiven Frankie in his casket?

Assembly Line Adventure

LESLEY HAZELTON

A freelance writer who emigrated from England in 1979, Lesley Hazelton has pursued various interests from sports to psychology, but she is best known for her automotive journalism. Seeking firsthand information about the way cars are built and the people who build them, she worked for a day in an auto assembly plant. This essay about that experience comes from her book Driving to Detroit *(1998).*

1   I'd toured many auto plants before, and physically this was not much different. That is, it was an assault on the senses: an enclosed, windowless world of harsh artificial light and hard concrete floors ringing with the discordant cacophony of industrial production. Metal rang on metal. Stamping presses clanked, power tools whined, pulleys groaned, hoists clanged, welding robots whooshed, sparks crackled, lasers beeped, compressed air hissed, bolts banged into place, trolleys rumbled down the aisles, and all the while, conveyor belts carrying cars in one stage or another of production, from bare metal frames to fully painted bodies, clattered and clanketed beside us and behind us and even over our heads.

2   At five in the afternoon, I started work, joining three other workers stationed around a huge rotating machine. Our job was to feed a robot.

3   Officially, we were preparing dashboard molds for foam injection. In fact, we were simply loading and unloading the machine for the robot, which injected the foam and then wiped its own nozzle as though it were wiping its nose—one of those infuriatingly human gestures that make you think, "Cute," and then hate yourself for having thought it.

4   This was one of the simplest tasks on the whole assembly line. Squirt some filler release into a hole. Lift a light plastic mold and place it on a protruding lip of the machine. Bang a board with your knee to drop three locks to hold the mold in place. Check the locks. Push a black button to bring the lip down into the right position for the next guy. Wait for the machine to rotate and present you with a new lip. And that was it. A ten-second job to be repeated *ad infinitum*.

5   Two hours later, I moved from one of the simplest jobs on the line to one of the most complicated: assembling the whole instrument panel. Steering wheel, indicator and wiper wands, gauges, dashboard line, the lot.

6   Audrey, the woman whose task it was to teach me this job, had a tough challenge ahead of her.

7   I guessed she was in her mid-thirties. Despite a mass of long brown curly hair, she had a boyish way to her, maybe because of the leather builder's apron she was wearing, its pockets so full of connectors and screws and bolts that it took me a while to realize she was six months pregnant.

8   "Is this your first?" I asked.

9   She burst out laughing. "Honey, I'm forty-three years old. And a grandmother. I married again not long ago, and"—she spread her arms wide and stared at her belly—"just look what happened. This sure is the last thing I ever expected."

10   "How long will you go on working?"

11   She laughed again. "Do you know how much kids cost? I'm staying right here till the day I pop."

12   She hadn't stopped working for a moment as we talked. She couldn't. The line was rolling, and it was either keep up or bring everything to a halt. We were standing *on* the line, a wide conveyor belt rumbling past an array of shelves piled high with parts, and beneath an overhead rack dangling power tools and bins of screws. On the line with us, every six feet or so, was a workstand holding an empty dashboard shell, placed upside down on the stand so that it was easy to work on. Audrey's job was to make it into a complete instrumental panel.

13   For the first few moments, standing on the moving belt was almost childishly fun. The world was reversed: you stood still and it went past you. Your mind knew it was you moving, not the world, but your senses told you otherwise. And all the time, the belt vibrated gently underfoot; if it weren't for the noise, it might even have been pleasantly sexy.

14   "Watch your head," Audrey said, and I ducked as a power wrench came dangling past my right ear. Followed by another. And yet another. Even though I reminded myself that it was me moving, not them, every time I looked up they seemed to be aiming for my brains with a certain inexorable malevolence.

15   I spent the first half-hour watching Audrey and figuring out how to stay out of the way. So far as I could make out, she had a total of some fifty separate procedures to complete in a logic-defying sequence of about three minutes. Each step had to be performed in perfect timing, so that the right parts and tools were at hand exactly when she needed them. And to add to the pressure, this job was what they called a "show-stopper."

16   Farther on down the line, the completed instrument panel would be lowered into the "smile joint"—a large lazy U going from side to side of the car's frame. If it

didn't fit, the line would stop, and the whole plant would start running behind. "You can't go back and do it again," Audrey said. "You've got to do it perfect the first time."

17   I knew I'd never be able to do this job. Yet Audrey seemed convinced that I was educable. She talked each movement out loud as she worked, with me following her around like a pet dog. Somehow, she convinced me to do a bit here and a bit there, until within an hour, I had the beginning of it down pat:

18   Walk six stands down the line, past the other team members at different stages of the job, and read the manifest hanging on the dashboard shell. Pick up different parts from the shelves alongside the line, depending on whether this is to be a sedan or a wagon, an automatic or a manual shift. Jam a leather sheath over the sharp metal edge to the side of the module. Ease the parts into place. Snap-connect electrical wires: gray to the right, blue to the middle, white to the left.

19   So far so good. I was feeling quite proud of myself. Trouble was, this was only the beginning of the beginning.

20   The rest began to blur: Snap-connect a black fastener, then a yellow one. Don't delay. If you go too slow, the line will take you past the parts you need, and you'll have to start running back and forth for them. Pick up the steering shaft from a shelf and ease its thirty-pound weight down through the center of the module. Arrange the wires to run over the top of the shaft. Slip on and snap a green fastener . . .

21   Or were those last two steps the other way round? "Here," said Audrey, redoing my work.

22   Okay, now pick up two bronze-colored bolts and screws, two black bolts, a circular piece, and two silver bolts from those big bins alongside the line. Insert the silver bolts. Fine. Place the bronze-colored ones in one place, the black ones in another. Great. Pull down a power wrench from the overhead line . . .

23   I grabbed for it and missed. It began to recede from me. I stretched and yanked it down just in time to tighten the bolts. I had no idea of what I was bolting to what, or why. Neither, it turned out, did Audrey.

24   Right, you've got those bolts nice and tight. Now pick different bronze-colored bolts from another bin. No, not alongside the line—right here, hanging overhead. Fine. Insert them and tighten them by hand for now. What about the wrench? Not there yet, that comes soon. First, thread the electrical wires through the back of the module and out through this flap, then loop them over and under the shaft like so, and then . . .

25   Then what? I couldn't remember. And I was only a third of the way through the job.

26   "Don't worry," said Audrey. "It takes most people four days to learn this job. You're doing real good."

27   That was sweet of her, but it didn't feel good to me. My attention strayed for a moment, I lost a beat, and suddenly the power tools and screw bins were bearing down on me way before I was ready for them. I worked as fast as I could, one eye on my hands, the other on the dangling wrench going past. I swore, lunged for it, and yanked at the cord as though if I pulled hard enough I could pull back the whole line and slow things down to my pace. I remembered Charlie Chaplin's desperation in *Modern Times,* and suddenly there was nothing remotely funny about it. I dropped a bolt, reached for the wrong wrench, and watched pathetically as Audrey stepped in and put everything to rights. I hadn't felt quite this incompetent since I was a kid trying to thread a sewing machine at school. I never did master that.

28   Every time I thought I had the hang of it all, another two steps somehow reversed themselves in my mind, or one slipped out of existence altogether. My ears were ringing, my mind was reeling, and my hands had never felt clumsier. I began to fumble the screws, inserting them at an angle so that they wouldn't tighten properly and had to be taken out and inserted anew. Audrey was working as hard as I was by now; we stood shoulder to shoulder, me fouling things up, her fixing them.

29   And suddenly it was ten o'clock, and there was a half-hour break for lunch. Ten at night, that is. By now, I was squinting to stop from seeing double. I was convinced that if I could just work through to the end of the shift, I'd get this job down pat. But as the line came to a halt and everything stopped moving, some remote part of my brain managed to signal a weak but just decipherable message that the pressure was getting to me. It was time to call it quits before I damaged a car, or myself, or worse still, somebody else.

30   "Don't you want some lunch before you go?" said Audrey. But I was too exhausted to even look at food. I needed fresh air. And solitude. And silence. I made my excuses, stuffed my yellow Kevlar gloves into my pocket as a memento, got lost twice trying to find the way out, and finally emerged into the parking lot.

31   Never had a parking lot seemed so beautiful: so quiet, so peaceful, so serene. Even the buzzing yellow of the sodium vapor lights seemed soothing. Behind me, the plant hummed gently, its skylights glowing into the night. Midshift, I was the only person out here, and I had a flash of guilt mixed with giddy freedom, the kind that comes from playing hooky.

32   I found the truck, climbed in, made to start it up. Then stopped, hand in midair, and sat staring at the instrument panel. Something was wrong. I took a moment to figure it out: I'd spent the past few hours working on upside-down instrument panels, and now I was seeing this one the right way up.

33   I reached out and examined it for its component parts, thinking of the man or the woman who'd put it together, and appreciating the way it had been done. This thing I usually took so for granted that I'd never before paid a moment's attention to it, was now an astounding piece of man-made—woman-made—complexity.

34   I started the truck and drove slowly out of the lot, wondering how long I'd keep this awareness that cars are not merely machines, but things put together by human beings, products of real men and real women doing the kind of work that would drive most people crazy. Not long enough, for sure.

| EXERCISE 8 | Vocabulary Highlights |

Write a short definition of each word as it is used in the essay. (Paragraph numbers are given in parentheses.) Be prepared to use the words in your own sentences.

ad infinitum (4)   recede (23)

inexorable (14)   pathetically (27)

malevolence (14)   decipherable (29)

manifest (18)   memento (30)

module (20)   giddy (31)

EXERCISE 9

Discussion and Critical Thinking

1. Indicate the parts of the narrative pattern:

   Situation (What is Hazelton's background and attitude toward the work she is about to attempt?):

   Conflict (How does the sequence of events begin?):

   Struggle (What does she discover about the workers and wrestle with on the assembly line?):

   Outcome (What happens at the end?):

   Meaning (What did she learn?):

2. She quit without finishing her shift. Do you consider her a failure? Why or why not? Did she consider herself a failure?

3. This essay is highly descriptive. Give an example of these images:

   Sight:

   Sound:

   Touch:

4. What is the effect of the dialogue in paragraphs 9 through 11?

5. Have you had the experience of struggling at a new, difficult job? Explain.

Student Writers

Often the difference between star athletes and others is that the star athletes more consistently make the outstanding plays. In this narrative, student Karen Bradley tells of that one moment when she was a star.

Bradley's Writing Process Worksheet, which follows, shows you how her writing evolved from idea to final draft. Because she had her topic clearly in mind, she skipped freewriting and went directly to listing. Her rough draft, marked for revision, has been omitted. The balance of her worksheet has been lengthened for you to be able to see parts of her work in their entirety.

You will find a full-size blank worksheet on page 6, which can be photocopied, filled in, and submitted with each assignment if your instructor directs you to do so.

FLOW OF WRITING

Writing Process Worksheet

Title A Moment in the Sun

Name Karen Bradley   Due Date Friday, April 28, 9 a.m.

ASSIGNMENT

In the space below, write whatever you need to know about your assignment, including information about the topic, audience, pattern of writing, length, whether to include a rough draft or revised drafts, and whether your paper must be typed.

Write a narrative paragraph of two to three hundred words on an occasion when you felt proud of what you had just done. Limit your topic to an incident you can cover in this short assignment. Consider work, school, recreation, and family in your search for subject material. Submit this form, a rough draft marked for revision, and a typed final draft.

STAGE ONE

Explore Freewrite, brainstorm (list), cluster, or take notes as directed by your instructor. Use the back of this page or separate paper if you need more space.

Listing

Situation
Lassie League team: the Ripping Rodents
I'm small, but the catcher
not a championship team
having a good time, not winning most of our games
wanted our team to do better

Conflict
near the end of the season
time to play one of the two best teams in the league
team made fun of us
team had a fast runner who stole bases easily

Struggle
team needed to beat us to win championship
team made rodent jokes
team had a sign saying they were champions
we played well
in the last inning we were ahead by a run
I threw out their fast runner who tried to steal second

Outcome
we won
surprised others, also ourselves
walked away proud

Meaning
like our championship
my moment of glory

STAGE TWO

Organize   Write a topic sentence or thesis; label the subject and the treatment parts.

<u>One event in my childhood</u> <u>stands out clearly in my memory</u>
　　　　subject　　　　　　　　　　　　treatment
<u>and becomes even stronger as I grow older</u>.

Write an outline or an outline alternative.

    I. Situation
      A. Slightly below average team
      B. No All Star game in my future
   II. Conflict
      A. Time to play top team
      B. Little hope for us
      C. Overconfident and arrogant opponents
 III. Struggle
      A. Our team ahead by a run near end of game
      B. Opponent's fastest player tries to steal second
      C. Doesn't expect the best throw of my lifetime
 IV. Outcome
      A. Runner's out
      B. Our team the winner
   V. Meaning
      A. My personal championship
      B. Feeling good

STAGE THREE

Write   On separate paper, write and then revise your paragraph or essay as many times as necessary for **c**oherence, **l**anguage (usage, tone, and diction), **u**nity, **e**mphasis, **s**upport, and **s**entences (**CLUESS**). Read your work aloud to hear and correct any grammatical errors or awkward-sounding sentences.

Edit any problems in fundamentals, such as **c**apitalization, **o**missions, **p**unctuation, and **s**pelling (**COPS**).

A Moment in the Sun

Karen Bradley

Topic sentence   One event in my childhood stands out clearly in my memory and becomes even stronger as I grow older. When I was eleven years old, I wanted to be a great softball player. Unfortunately for me and my ambition, I was only a bit above average in ability and was smaller than my peers. That didn't keep me from becoming catcher on a Lassie League team called the Ripping Rodents. Like me our team was about average in competition. As we approached the last game of the season, I was batting seventh, and we were fourth in a league of seven teams.

Conflict   The team we were playing, the much-dreaded Hotshot Hornets, needed this win to take the league championship. Their players were cocky and boastful before the game. They even made rodent jokes. Then they walked by our dugout after taking infield practice and acted as if we were not there. Finally they posed for some pictures a parent was taking; they even had a sign saying "2A Lassie League Champions." For the first time all year we were angry—at them, at ourselves. And

Struggle

then we went on to surprise ourselves. In the last inning with them at bat, we were leading by one run. After their first two batters made outs, the next one, a speedy, little second baseman named Toni, walked. Everyone knew she would try to steal second. She was the fastest player in the league and had never been thrown out. On the first pitch she took off. The ball was shoulder-high to me. I grabbed it out of my glove and threw it as hard as I could in the direction of second base. To my surprise, and even more so to Toni's, the ball went on a low arc

Outcome

right to our shortstop, knee-high. Toni slid, but she was out by three feet. The game was over, and the Ripping Rodents were all over me. It was as if we had won the

Meaning

championship. It was my only moment of stardom in softball, but it will do.

Discussion and Critical Thinking

1. How does the writer's not being an "All Star player" on an ordinary team make this paragraph more dramatic?

2. Why does the writer remember the incident so well?

3. How important is it for people to have these special moments?

4. How much does the author reveal about herself?

From Survival to Living

JEANNE SEWELL

Jeanne Sewell knows more about survival than participants on reality television shows do. As a fifty-year-old freshman at a community college, she writes, "I had the surgery in 1996, and today, seven years later, I remain cancer free and am doing very well. In my career I am the district administrative secretary for the Gifted and Talented Education Program for Chino Valley Unified School District. Currently I am an organist and choir director at my church, as well as a member of a college Masterworks Chorale. My interests are my family, traveling, classical music, cooking, needlework, attending plays and musical productions, exercising at Curves for Women, and laughing all day long." She wrote this essay for a freshman composition class that grouped students especially interested in medicine as a career.

1   Say the word "cancer" and notice how people will look away. Just hearing the word makes them uncomfortable, afraid, or sad. Many people fear cancer because they see it as a death sentence. My experience taught me that with quick action and a relationship with a trusted surgeon, a person can survive and overcome those negatives associated with cancer.

2   For me, 1996 was a year overflowing with diagnoses of cancer, particularly breast cancer. Working for a school district, calls would come in weekly with news of yet another employee who had been diagnosed with cancer. It seemed to be reaching epidemic proportions. I would react to each report with a nod of concern, but in the back of my mind, I felt relief that it wasn't happening to me. Besides, I reasoned, I had been having regular checkups for years, so I had the "right" to feel safe.

3   In 1965 I had my first breast biopsy; I was 18 years old and newly married when my doctor found a sizable lump in my right breast. Back then, you signed a form stating that if the lump was malignant, your breast would be removed. No discussion. It was not negotiable. Mine was benign, but I went through all the terror and fear from the scary thoughts that still circulate about cancer. My doctor said it was a fibroid cystic condition that is common and almost never becomes cancerous.

4   By 1994 the medical community was changing its opinion about breast lumps. My doctor referred me to a surgeon who was taking a more aggressive approach, and consequently I was having lumps removed every six months. As quickly as they were removed, my body would produce more, but now they were getting larger and deeper into the breast tissue. Because I have chronic asthma, my system could not tolerate being sedated; each biopsy had to be performed solely with local anesthetic. If it wasn't for my surgeon, Dr. Morton, and the caring nurses, I never could have gotten through all those biopsies. I began to dread the thought of painful injections and the stress that accompanied each successive procedure. The time required would get longer and longer as the lumps grew deeper and deeper. It seemed crazy to keep going through this when the reports were always "benign—no evidence of carcinoma."

5   In April 1996 Dr. Morton called me personally at home with the latest lab report. I had been seeing him for more than two years, and we had developed a comfortable doctor-patient relationship. I wasn't particularly surprised to hear his voice. But I was surprised when Dr. Morton said the lab report showed cancer cells. They weren't in the three lumps he removed a few days before. They were located in the surrounding tissues. He asked my husband and me to come to his office the next day to discuss our options.

6   We wasted no time learning and reading and talking to anyone and everyone about cancer. I was a sponge soaking up every drop of information. My husband and I arrived at our meeting looking for a fight, but a medical one.

7   There, we learned how I could go from survival mode to living. Dr. Morton explained that attacking cancer is something akin to a fight-or-flight response from adrenaline coursing through the body. When the cancer is gone, the body can return to normal. We were told that I had ductal carcinoma insitu. Big words that meant I developed cancer of the milk ducts in the right breast. We couldn't be sure about the left side because that tissue hadn't been biopsied for about six months.

8   In Dr. Morton's opinion, this type of cancer almost always afflicts both breasts, and it would be a matter of time. I would require continuous biopsies to monitor

9   any new occurrences. My heart sank as I envisioned removing one breast and then enduring more painful biopsies.

10   I asked about lumpectomy for the right breast, but we ruled it out because of the location of the cancer. I would have been left with a ring of tissue surrounding the breast, but the entire middle needed to be removed down to the chest wall. Reconstruction would be very difficult.

11   My husband and I made eye contact, and he smiled slightly. His gaze shifted to Dr. Morton and he said, "I married Jeanne, not a pair of breasts. She will still be the same person, with or without breasts." What a relief. We chose a bilateral mastectomy, and Dr. Morton assured me that reconstruction after bilateral surgery had a better success rate because the plastic surgeon would have an easier time with size and symmetry.

12   The surgery went very well. I was in the hospital for two days, and recovered comfortably at home with regular doctor visits to monitor my progress. I was given the good news that the type of cancer I had did not migrate to other parts of the body. To be sure, a number of lymph nodes were removed from each underarm, and the lab report came back "clear." I did not have to follow up with radiation or chemotherapy.

13   Prosthetics for cancer patients are continuing to improve. In fact, mine are so comfortable I have decided not to schedule reconstruction for now, but it remains a viable option to consider later.

14   From the beginning, Dr. Morton urged us to work as a team and to talk about our concerns and ask as many questions as we could before and after the surgery. Dr. Morton was actively working to get us out of survival mode and back to living, together.

15   Today I laughingly refer to myself as a "Show and Tell" person for breast cancer. I take advantage of every opportunity to speak to other women to offer the chance for them to learn from my experience, and see what I look like after the surgery and even handle these prosthetics so they have real firsthand information. With the right information and preparation, women with breast cancer can be treated without needless fear and anxiety. I would feel that my experience has been worth it all if I can help even one woman recognize the difference between surviving cancer and getting back to living.

EXERCISE 11

Discussion and Critical Thinking

1. What is the situation?

2. What is the conflict?

3. What is the struggle?

4. What is the outcome?

5. What is the meaning?

Topics for Writing Narration

You will find a blank Writing Process Worksheet on page 6, which can be photocopied, filled in, and submitted with each assignment if your instructor directs you to do so.

Reading-Related Topics

"W-A-T-E-R"

1. This passage is an epiphany—a moment that reveals an important truth (through setup, incident, and understanding). After Helen Keller went through that one experience, her life was transformed. Using the "W-a-t-e-r" passage as a model, write your own epiphany about the first time you knew or understood something about a concept such as love, caring, or family. Or write about the first time you realized you could read or learn another language.

"B. B. King Live!"

2. Using the paragraph on B. B. King as a model for organization, write a narrative account of the first few minutes of a concert you attended, showing how the audience became involved in the event. Or, present the factors that negatively influenced the audience so that it did *not* become involved.

3. Pretend you are a Russian music lover at the B. B. King concert in Moscow. Write a narrative about how you became involved in the audience response.

"No Tears for Frankie"

4. Write a reactive paragraph or essay in which you summarize what occurred and comment on the author's behavior and feeling. Under the circumstances, would you have expected her to feel any sympathy or compassion for her deceased tormentor?

5. Using this essay as a model, write about a time when you were a victim of a bully. How did you feel at the time? How did you feel later, especially if you had the occasion to see the bully again?

"Assembly Line Adventure"

6. Take an imaginary walk with the author through the part of her shift she completed. How do you judge her for character and resourcefulness? Many journalists have posed as workers to get stories. How well did Hazelton do? Was what she did enough?

7. Write about your own experience of working a first shift on a difficult job. Explain what you did and how you felt about the work and yourself.

"A Moment in the Sun"

8. Write about a time when you exceeded expectations in a sport or in another endeavor such as work, family life, school, or a social situation.

9. Discuss the properties of this long paragraph about Bradley's special moment. What factors made this special? Refer directly to the selection as you analyze it.

10. Use your imagination to write about this incident from the point of view of Toni (the speedster who was thrown out).

"From Survival to Living"

11. Using Sewell's account of her ordeal as an example, write about someone you know who has courageously faced a life-threatening illness or other calamity.

General Topics

12. Write a narrative based on a topic sentence such as this: "One experience showed me what _____ [pain, fear, anger, love, sacrifice, dedication, joy, sorrow, shame, pride] was really like."

13. Write a simple narrative about a fire, a riot, an automobile accident, a rescue, shoplifting, or some other unusual happening you witnessed.

14. Write a narrative that supports (or opposes) the idea of a familiar saying such as one of the following:

   a. You never know who a friend is until you need one.

   b. A bird in the hand is worth two in the bush.

   c. A person who is absent is soon forgotten.

   d. Better to be alone than to be in bad company.

   e. A person in a passion rides a mad horse.

   f. Borrowing is the mother of trouble.

   g. A person who marries for money earns it.

   h. The person who lies down with dogs gets up with fleas.

   i. Never give advice to a friend.

   j. If it isn't broken, don't fix it.

   k. Nice people finish last.

   l. It isn't what you know, it's who you know.

   m. Fools and their money are soon parted.

   n. Every person has a price.

   o. You get what you pay for.

   p. Haste makes waste.

   q. The greatest remedy for anger is delay.

   r. A person full of him- or herself is empty.

s. To forget a wrong is the best revenge.

t. Money is honey, my little sonny,
And a rich man's joke is always funny.

Cross-Curricular Topics

15. Write a paragraph or an essay about a visit, an observation, or a field trip to a museum, concert, institution, or workplace.

16. Write about a unit of time in which feverish action occurs. You could select a pivotal moment in history (the assassination of a president, a turning point in a battle, the first encounter between two groups of people), in science (the discovery of a process or product), in music (a composer conducting his or her own musical composition), or in art appreciation (a painter finishing a famous painting). Content from other courses will provide most of the framework; your imagination can provide the details. Be inventive, but base your invention on what you know of individuals and the time period. Consult textbooks. Talk to instructors.

Career-Related Topics

17. Write a narrative account of a work-related encounter between a manager and a worker and briefly explain the significance of the event.

18. Write a narrative account of an encounter between a customer and a salesperson. Explain what went right and what went wrong.

19. Write a narrative account of how a person solved a work-related problem perhaps by using technology.

20. Write a narrative account of a salesperson handling a customer's complaint. Critique the procedure.

21. Using a workplace form you are familiar with, write an incident report about an event such as an accident, a theft, or a disturbance.

Writer's Guidelines: Narration

1. Include these points so you will be sure you have a complete narrative:

   - situation
   - conflict
   - struggle
   - outcome
   - meaning

2. Use these techniques or devices as appropriate:

   - images that appeal to the senses (sight, smell, taste, hearing, touch) and other details to advance action
   - dialogue

- transitional devices (such as *next, soon, after, later, then, finally, when, following*) to indicate chronological order

3. Give details concerning action.

4. Be consistent with point of view and verb tense.

5. Keep in mind that most narratives written as college assignments will have an expository purpose; that is, they explain a specific idea.

6. Consider working with a short time frame for short writing assignments. The scope would usually be no more than one incident of brief duration for one paragraph. For example, writing about an entire graduation ceremony might be too complicated, but concentrating on the moment when you walked forward to receive the diploma or the moment when the relatives and friends come down on the field could work very well.

7. Use the writing process.

- Write and then revise your paragraph or essay as many times as necessary for coherence, language (usage, tone, and diction), unity, emphasis, support, and sentences (**CLUESS**).

- Read your work aloud to hear and correct any grammatical errors or awkward-sounding sentences.

- Edit any problems in fundamentals, such as capitalization, omissions, punctuation, and spelling (**COPS**).

Description: Moving Through Space

FLOW OF WRITING

Writing Description   126

Types of Description   126

Techniques of Descriptive Writing   127

Practicing Descriptive Patterns   130

Connecting Reading and Writing   134

Professional Writers   134

"The Mousetrap"   134

"The Alley"   135

"More"   136

"In the Land of 'Coke-Cola'"   138

Student Writers   141

"The Drag" (demonstration with stages)   143

"My Aircraft Carrier 'Bedroom'"   144

Topics for Writing Description   146

Writer's Guidelines   148

"My task . . . is, by the power of the written word, to make you hear, to make you feel—it is, before all, to make you see. That—and no more—is everything."

JOSEPH CONRAD

THE QUIGMANS   by Buddy Hickerson

B. Hickerson, copyright Los Angeles Times Syndicate. Reprinted by permission.

Writing Description

Description is the use of words to represent the appearance or nature of something. It is not merely the work of an indifferent camera: Instead, often going beyond sight, it includes details that will convey a good representation. Just what details the descriptive writer selects will depend on several factors, especially the type of description and the dominant impression the writer is trying to convey.

Types of Description

Depending on how you wish to treat your subject material, your description is likely to be either objective or subjective.

Effective **objective description** presents the subject clearly and directly as it exists outside the realm of emotions. If you are explaining the function of the heart, the characteristics of a computer chip, or the renovation of a manufacturing facility, your description will probably feature specific, impersonal details. Most technical and scientific writing is objective in this sense. It is likely to be practical and utilitarian, making little use of speculation or poetic technique and featuring mainly what can be seen.

Effective **subjective description** is also concerned with clarity and it may be direct, but it conveys a feeling about the subject and sets a mood while making a point. Because most expression involves personal views, even when it explains by analysis, subjective description (often called **emotional description**) has a broader range of uses than objective description.

Descriptive passages can be a combination of objective and subjective description; only the larger context of the passage will reveal the main intent. The following description of a baseball begins with objective treatment and then moves to subjective.

> It weighs just over five ounces and measures between 2.86 and 2.94 inches in diameter. It is made of a composition-cork nucleus encased in two thin layers of rubber, one black and one red, surrounded by 121 yards of tightly wrapped blue-gray wool yarn, 45 yards of white wool yarn, 53 more yards of blue-gray wool yarn, 150 yards of fine cotton yarn, a coat of rubber cement, and a cowhide (formerly horsehide) exterior, which is held together with 216 slightly raised red cotton stitches. Printed certifications, endorsements, and outdoor advertising spherically attest to its authenticity. . . . Feel the ball, turn it over in your hand; hold it across the seam or the other way, with the seam just to the side of your middle finger. Speculation stirs. You want to get outdoors and throw this spare and sensual object to somebody or, at the very least, watch somebody else throw it. The game has begun.

Objective treatment moving to subjective treatment

Roger Angell, "On the Ball"

The following subjective description, also on the subject of baseball, is designed to move the emotions while informing.

The following details relate to the paradoxes.

> The Babe was a bundle of paradoxes. Somehow one of the most appealing things about him was that he was neither built, nor did he look like, an athlete. He did not even look like a ballplayer. Although he stood six feet two inches and weighed 220 pounds, his body was pear-shaped and even when in tip-top condition he had a bit of a belly. His barrel always seemed too much for his legs, which tapered into a pair of ankles as slender almost

Note the emotional appeals, the subjective approach.

as those of a girl. The great head perched upon a pair of round and unathletic shoulders, presented a moon of a face, the feature of which was the flaring nostrils of a nose that was rather like a snout. His voice was deep and hoarse, his speech crude and earthy, his ever-ready laughter a great, rumbling gurgle that arose from the caverns of his middle. He had an eye that was abnormally quick, nerves and muscular reactions to match, a supple wrist, a murderous swing, and a gorgeously truculent, competitive spirit.

Paul Gallico, "Babe Ruth"

Techniques of Descriptive Writing

As a writer of description, you will need to focus your work to accomplish four specific tasks:

- Emphasize a single point (dominant impression).
- Choose your words with care.
- Establish a perspective from which to describe your subject (point of view).
- Position the details for coherence (order).

Dominant Impression

See if you can find the dominant impression in this description:

> Please help me find my dog. He is a mongrel with the head of a poodle and the body of a wolfhound, and his fur is patchy and dingy-gray. He has only three legs, but despite his arthritis, he uses them pretty well to hobble around and scratch his fleas and mange. His one seeing eye is cloudy, so he runs with his head sideways. His ragged, twisted ears enable him to hear loud sounds, which startle his troubled nervous system and cause him to howl pitifully. If you give him a scrap of food, he will gum it up rapidly and try to wag his broken tail. He answers to the name of Lucky.

Of course, the dominant impression, what is being emphasized, is "misery," or "unlucky," not "lucky." The dominant impression emerges from a pattern of details, often involving repetition of one idea with different particulars. Word choice, which is of paramount importance, depends on your purpose in writing and on your audience.

If you are in a restaurant, and you say to your companion, "This food is good," your companion may understand all he or she needs to understand on the subject. After all, your companion can see you sitting there chewing the food, smacking your lips, and wiping the donut glaze off your chin. But if you write that sentence and send it to someone, your reader may be puzzled. Although the reader may know you fairly well, he or she may not know the meaning of "good" (to eat? to purchase for others? to sell?) or of "this food" (What kind? Where is it? How is it special? How is it prepared? What qualities does it have?).

To convey your main concern effectively to readers, you will want to give some sensory impressions. These sensory impressions, collectively called *imagery,* refer to that which can be experienced by the senses—what we can see, smell, taste, hear, and touch. You may use *figures of speech* to convey these sensory impressions; figures of speech involve comparisons of unlike things that, nevertheless, have something in common.

The imagery in this passage is italicized.

> As I sit here at a little pastry shop called The Donut Man, I am convinced that I am eating the <u>ultimate dessert—the strawberry donut</u>. Jerry

Dominant impression

Walters, the real "donut man," says he invented it. At first glance the strawberry donut looks like a strawberry hamburger. Feeling feathery *light* and *warm* in my hands, the buns are made of donut dough, cooked and glazed. Holding the donut under my nose, I inhale the *blended aroma of fresh pasty and fruit*. I take a no-nonsense bite and taste the *sugary, tart ripeness* of the strawberries. Juice trickles over my napkin and fingers and makes *little red puddles* on the *white vinyl table* below. I *chew noisily* and happily like a puppy at a food bowl, stopping occasionally to flush down the delicacy with a *slurp* from a steaming mug of coffee that clouds my glasses. Back in the kitchen, Jerry Walters has rolled out dough for a fresh batch ready to *plop* into the steaming vat of vegetable oil. I see a cop car roll to a stop outside. A *bunch of students* just out of their evening college class come in from the sidewalk and line up at the counter, calling out orders. They're all saying the same thing, "Strawberry donut. Strawberry donut. Strawberry donut." I should have ordered two. The line is getting long. Jerry's production is not keeping up with consumption.

In reading Clark's enthusiastic endorsement of the strawberry donut, the reader will have no trouble understanding the idea that he liked the food. Through imagery, Clark has involved the reader in what he has seen, smelled, heard, tasted, and touched. He has also used figures of speech, including these examples:

Simile: a comparison using *like* or *as* — "chew noisily and happily like a puppy"

Metaphor: a comparison using word replacement — "feathery [instead of "delicately"] light"

Subjective description is likely to make more use of imagery, figurative language, and words rich in associations than is objective description. But just as a fine line cannot always be drawn between the objective and the subjective, a fine line cannot always be drawn between word choice in one and in the other. However, we can say with certainty that whatever the type of description, careful word choice will always be important. Consider the following points about word choice (diction), point of view, and order.

Word Choice: General and Specific, Abstract and Concrete

To move from the general to the specific is to move from the whole class or group of items to individual ones; for example,

General	Specific	More Specific
food	donut	strawberry donut
mess	juice	little red puddles
drink	coffee	steaming mug
odor	smell from vats	smell of frying donuts

Words are classified as abstract or concrete, depending on what they refer to. **Abstract words** refer to qualities or ideas: *good, ordinary, ultimate, truth, beauty, maturity, love*. **Concrete words** refer to things or a substance; they have reality: *donut, vat, puddle, mug*. Specific concrete words, sometimes called *concrete particulars*, often support generalizations effectively and convince the reader of the accuracy of the description.

Never try to give all the details in a description. Instead, be selective. Pick only those details that you need to project a dominant impression, always taking into account the knowledge and attitudes of your readers. To reintroduce an idea from the beginning of this chapter, description is not photographic. If you wish to describe a person, select the traits that will project your intended dominant impression. If you wish to describe a landscape, do not give all the details that you might find in a picture; on the contrary, pick the details that support your intended dominant impression. That extremely important dominant impression is directly linked to your purpose. It is created by the judicious choice and arrangement of images, figurative language, and revealing details.

Point of View

Point of view shows the writer's relationship to the subject, thereby establishing the perspective from which the subject is described. It rarely changes within a passage. Two terms usually associated with fiction writing, first person and third person, also pertain to descriptive writing.

If you want to convey personal experience, your point of view will be **first person,** which can be either involved (point of view of a participant) or uninvolved (point of view of an observer). The involved perspective uses *I* more prominently than the uninvolved. Ross Clark's paragraph "Strawberry Donut" uses first person, involved.

If you want to present something from a detached position, especially from a geographical or historical distance (see "Babe Ruth" and "On the Ball"), your point of view will be **third person**, and you will refer to your subjects by name or by third-person pronouns such as *he, she, him, her, it, they,* and *them,* without imposing yourself as an *I* person.

Order

The point of view you select may indicate or even dictate the order in which you present descriptive details. If you are describing your immediate surroundings while taking a walk (first person, involved), the descriptive account would naturally develop spatially as well as chronologically—in other words, in both space and time.

- To indicate space, use terms such as *next to, below, under, above, behind, in front of, beyond, in the foreground, in the background, to the left,* and *to the right.*
- To indicate time, use words such as *first, second, then, soon, finally, while, after, next, later, now,* and *before.*

Some descriptive pieces, for example, the one on Babe Ruth, may follow an idea progression for emphasis and not move primarily through space or time. Whatever appropriate techniques you use will guide your reader and thereby aid coherence.

All four elements—dominant impression, word choice, point of view, and order—work together in a well-written description.

The dominant impression of the paragraph "On the Ball" is of an object remarkably well designed for its purpose. The point of view is third person, and the order of the description moves from the core of the baseball outward.

The paragraph "Babe Ruth" emphasizes the idea of paradox (something that appears to be a contradiction). The details are presented from a detached point of view (third person) and appear in order from physique to overall appearance to behavior. The details show a person who wasn't built like an athlete and didn't look like an athlete yet was one of the greatest athletes of all time. Collectively those details convey the dominant impression of "Ruth, the paradox."

Clark's "Strawberry Donut" can also be evaluated for all three elements:

- *Dominant impression:* good food (images, figurative language, other diction). The reader experiences the incident as the writer did because of the diction. The general and abstract have been made clear by use of the specific and the concrete. Of course, not all abstract words need to be tied to the concrete, nor do all general words need to be transformed to the specific. As you describe, use your judgment to decide which words fit your purposes—those needed to enable your audience to understand your ideas and to be persuaded or informed.
- *Word choice:* general or specific; abstract or concrete.
- *Point of view:* first person, involved.
- *Order:* spatial, from seat to kitchen to outside to counter.

Practicing Descriptive Patterns

Description, which is almost always used with other patterns, is very important and often neglected. The following exercises feature descriptive writing that supports a dominant impression of colorful action.

EXERCISE 1

Working with Word Choice

Improve the following sentences by supplying specific and concrete words. Use images when they serve your purposes.

Example: The animal was restless and hungry.
The gaunt lion paced about the cage and chewed hungrily on an old shoe.

1. The fans were happy.
2. She was in love.
3. Confusion surrounded him.
4. The traffic was congested.
5. The dessert impressed the diner.
6. The woman liked her date.
7. The salesman was obnoxious.
8. The room was cluttered.
9. His hair was unkempt.
10. The room smelled bad.

Completing Descriptive Patterns

Fill in the blanks. This is a useful procedure for prewriting a descriptive paragraph or essay. Consider using it for your writing assignment in this chapter. Suggested topic: a location on campus, such as a classroom, the cafeteria, the student aid office, the stadium, a playing field, a lab, or the parking lot at night.

What is your subject? _____

What is the dominant impression? _____

What is the situation? _____

What is the order of details? _____

What details support the dominant impression? (Use listing or clustering.)

Listing

1. _____

2. _____

3. _____

4. _____

5. _____

Clustering

Insert your topic in the double bubble and fill in details in the blank single bubbles.

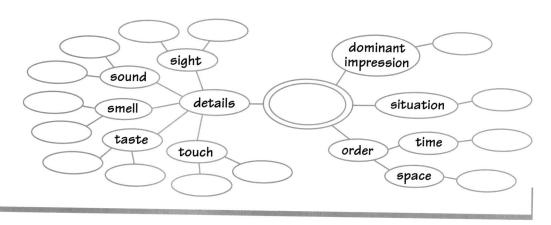

EXERCISE 3

Completing Descriptive Patterns

The colorful action for this topic would probably provide a narrative framework for chronological order. Fill in the blanks to complete the outline.

Walking (a particular location)

I. See

    A. _____

    B. _____

II. Smell

    A. _____

    B. _____

III. Touch

    A. _____

    B. _____

IV. Hear

    A. _____

    B. _____

EXERCISE 4

Completing Descriptive Patterns

Fill in the blanks to complete the outline.

Inside the Movie Theater

I. Getting refreshments

  A. See

    1. _____

    2. _____

  B. Smell

    1. _____

    2. _____

C. Touch

    1. _____

    2. _____

II. Watching the movie

  A. Sights

    1. On the screen

      a. _____

      b. _____

    2. In the audience

      a. _____

      b. _____

  B. Sounds

    1. On the screen

      a. _____

      b. _____

    2. In the audience

      a. _____

      b. _____

  C. Enjoyment

    1. Group experience

    2. Refreshments

      a. _____

      b. _____

Connecting Reading and Writing

Professional Writers

The Mousetrap

CRAIG FINLEY

Freelance writer Craig Finley begins this paragraph with a stark description of the mousetrap and then dispassionately explains its function. In his clear and concise presentation, the paragraph is as practical, effective, and impersonal as the object it depicts.

The mousetrap is a remarkably simple and efficient instrument. The platform is a rectangular piece of soft pine wood, two and a half inches wide, six inches long, and a quarter-inch thick. The plane surface of the piece of wood is evenly divided by a square strike bar, which is attached to the middle by three staples. The staples are evenly spaced, with one in the middle. Between the middle and end staples on each side is a strong metal spring coiled around the bar. Each spring is taut and kept that way by the use of a straight piece of metal thrust out from the coil and tucked up under the kill bar on one side and placed against the board on the other. Also attached to the center kill bar is a bait pad, a little rectangular piece of flat metal with a grooved edge extending up from one side to hold the trigger rod. At the open end of the board, from an eye-screw, dangles the trigger rod, a long piece of metal that can move freely in a half circle from a point behind the screw to the grooved bait pad. To set the trap, place the bait, preferably cheese, on the bait pad, then cock the kill bar by pulling the free end over in a half circle to the other side and tucking it under the trigger rod. Then secure the kill bar by moving the trigger rod into the groove on the side of the bait pad. When the rodent nibbles on the cheese, it will move the bait pad, which will loosen the trigger rod and, in turn, release the kill bar in its fatal arc to pin the rodent against the board.

EXERCISE 5   Discussion and Critical Thinking

1. Underline the topic sentence.

2. Is the description objective or subjective?

3. Write an X to mark the spot where description becomes an explanation of how the mousetrap works.

4. Use the following phrases from the description to label the ten parts (one repeated) of the drawing: eye-screw, trigger rod, staple, kill bar, bait, metal spring, platform, grooved edge, bait pad, spring. If you are artistically inclined, add a rodent.

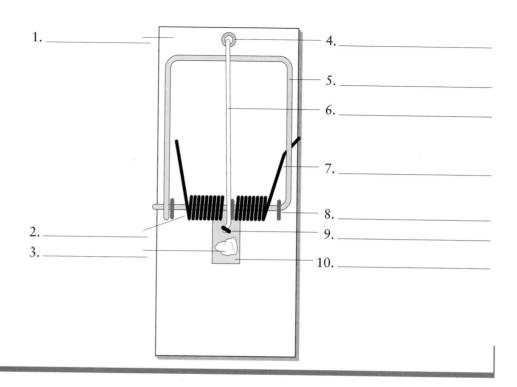

1. _____
2. _____
3. _____
4. _____
5. _____
6. _____
7. _____
8. _____
9. _____
10. _____

The Alley

AMY TAN

These paragraphs are taken from The Joy Luck Club, *a novel composed
of sixteen tales that reflect author Amy Tan's childhood in San Francisco.
Here, in brief narrative and rich descriptive treatment, she reveals her
childhood neighborhood as it lives in her memory.*

1   We lived on Waverly Place, in a warm, clean, two-bedroom flat that sat above a
small Chinese bakery specializing in steamed pastries and dim sum. In the early
morning, when the alley was still quiet, I could smell fragrant red beans as they
were cooked down to a pasty sweetness. By daybreak, our flat was heavy with the
odor of fried sesame balls and sweet curried chicken crescents. From my bed, I
would listen as my father got ready for work, then locked the door behind him,
one-two-three clicks.

2   At the end of our two-block alley was a small sandlot playground with swings
and slides well-shined down the middle with use. The play area was bordered by
wood-slat benches where old-country people sat cracking roasted watermelon
seeds with their golden teeth and scattering the husks to an impatient gathering of
gurgling pigeons. The best playground, however, was the dark alley itself. It was
crammed with daily mysteries and adventures. My brothers and I would peer into
the medicinal herb shop, watching old Li dole out onto a stiff sheet of white paper
the right amount of insect shells, saffron-colored seeds, and pungent leaves for his
ailing customers. It was said that he once cured a woman dying of an ancestral
curse that had eluded the best of American doctors. Next to the pharmacy was a
printer who specialized in gold-embossed wedding invitations and festive red
banners.

| EXERCISE 6 | Discussion and Critical Thinking |

1. Is the dominant impression concerned with a static or a dynamic environment?

2. Which paragraph is based on time, and which is based on space?

3. Give examples of images of touch, smell, sound, sight, and taste.

4. In paragraph 2, what words guide the reader through space?

5. Why do the children prefer the alley to the playground?

More

JUDITH ORTIZ COFER

Born in Puerto Rico in 1952, Judith Ortiz Cofer moved with her parents to New Jersey, where she learned a new language and a new culture while in elementary school. Now an author and a university professor, she writes poignantly about her experiences trying to embrace two cultures with different customs and different languages. This essay comes from Silent Dancing: A Partial Remembrance of a Puerto Rican Childhood *(1990).*

1   My grandmother's house is like a chambered nautilus; it has many rooms, yet it is not a mansion. Its proportions are small and its design simple. It is a house that has grown organically, according to the needs of its inhabitants. To all of us in the family it is known as *la casa de Mamá*. It is the place of our origin; the stage for our memories and dreams of island life.

2   I remember how in my childhood it sat on stilts; this was before it had a downstairs. It rested on its perch like a great blue bird, not a flying sort of bird, more like a nesting hen, but with spread wings. Grandfather had built it soon after their marriage. He was a painter and housebuilder by trade, a poet and meditative man by nature. As each of their eight children were born, new rooms were added. After a few years, the paint did not exactly match, nor the materials, so that there was a chronology to it, like the rings of a tree, and Mamá could tell you the history of each room in her casa, and thus the genealogy of the family along with it.

3   Her room is the heart of the house. Though I have seen it recently, and both woman and room have diminished in size, changed by the new perspective of my eyes, now capable of looking over countertops and tall beds, it is not this picture I

carry in my memory of Mamá's casa. Instead, I see her room as a queen's chamber where a small woman loomed large, a throne-room with a massive four-poster bed in its center which stood taller than a child's head. It was on this bed where her own children had been born that the smallest grandchildren were allowed to take naps in the afternoon; here too was where Mamá secluded herself to dispense private advice to her daughters, sitting on the edge of the bed, looking down at whoever sat on the rocker where generations of babies had been sung to sleep. To me she looked like a wise empress right out of the fairy tales I was addicted to reading.

4   Though the room was dominated by the mahogany four-poster, it also contained all of Mamá's symbols of power. On her dresser instead of cosmetics there were jars filled with herbs: *yerba buena, yerba mala,* the making of purgatives and teas to which we were all subjected during childhood crises. She had a steaming cup for anyone who could not, or would not, get up to face life on any given day. If the acrid aftertaste of her cures for malingering did not get you out of bed, then it was time to call *el doctor.*

5   And there was the monstrous chifforobe she kept locked with a little golden key she did not hide. This was a test of her dominion over us; though my cousins and I wanted a look inside that massive wardrobe more than anything, we never reached for that little key lying on top of her Bible on the dresser. This was also where she placed her earrings and rosary at night. God's word was her security system. This chifforobe was the place where I imagined she kept jewels, satin slippers, and elegant sequined, silk gowns of heart-breaking fineness. I lusted after those imaginary costumes. I had heard that Mamá had been a great beauty in her youth, and the belle of many balls. My cousins had other ideas as to what she kept in that wooden vault: its secret could be money (Mamá did not hand cash to strangers, banks were out of the question, so there were stories that her mattress was stuffed with dollar bills, and that she buried coins in jars in her garden under rosebushes, or kept them in her inviolate chifforobe); there might be that legendary gun salvaged from the Spanish-American conflict over the Island. We went wild over suspected treasures that we made up simply because children have to fill locked trunks with something wonderful.

6   On the wall above the bed hung a heavy silver crucifix. Christ's agonized head hung directly over Mamá's pillow. I avoided looking at this weapon suspended over where her head would lay; and on the rare occasions when I was allowed to sleep on that bed, I scooted down to the safe middle of the mattress, where her body's impression took me in like a mother's lap. Having taken care of the obligatory religious decoration with a crucifix, Mamá covered the other walls with objects sent to her over the years by her children in the States. *Los Nueva Yores* were represented by, among other things, a postcard of Niagara Falls from her son Hernán, postmarked, Buffalo, N.Y. In a conspicuous gold frame hung a large color photograph of her daughter Nena, her husband and their five children at the entrance to Disneyland in California. From us she had gotten a black lace fan. Father had brought it to her from a tour of duty with the Navy in Europe (on Sundays she would remove it from its hook on the wall to fan herself at Sunday mass). Each year more items were added as the family grew and dispersed, and every object in the room had a story attached to it, a *cuento* which Mamá would bestow on anyone who received the privilege of a day alone with her. It was almost worth pretending to be sick, though the bitter herb purgatives of the body were a big price to pay for the spirit revivals of her story-telling.

EXERCISE 7

Vocabulary Highlights

Write a short definition of each word as it is used in the essay. (Paragraph numbers are given in parentheses.) Be prepared to use the words in your own sentences.

perspective (3)	inviolate (5)
massive (3)	suspended (6)
dispense (3)	obligatory (6)
acrid (4)	conspicuous (6)
chifforobe (5)	bestow (6)

EXERCISE 8

Discussion and Critical Thinking

1. Ortiz Cofer says her grandmother's house "is like a chambered nautilus," which is a mollusk with a spiral, pearly lined shellfish with a series of air-filled chambers. In what ways is that figure of speech (simile) a good representation of the house?

2. Name at least two other comparisons she uses in describing the house.

3. Ortiz Cofer helps you imagine what she saw by using details. List five specific, concrete visual images she uses in paragraph 6.

4. What is the benefit of using the Spanish phrases?

5. Reading this essay, do you have the feeling that you are learning more about a particular culture or universal conditions and behavior?

In the Land of "Coke-Cola"

WILLIAM LEAST HEAT-MOON

William Trogdon, of English-Irish-Osage ancestry, writes under the pen name William Least Heat-Moon. Traveling around the country in the old van he called Ghost Dancing, he sought out locales on secondary highways marked in blue on road maps. A collection of his descriptions of these adventures subsequently became the best-selling book Blue Highways. *Here he visits a folksy all-you-can-eat restaurant in rural Georgia.*

1   In the land of "Coke-Cola" it was hot and dry. The artesian water was finished. Along route 72, an hour west of Ninety-Six, I tried not to look for a spring; I knew I wouldn't find one, but I kept looking. The Savannah River, dammed to an unnatural wideness, lay below, wet and cool. I'd come into Georgia. The sun seemed to press on the roadway, and inside the truck, hot light bounced off chrome, flickering like a torch. Then I saw what I was trying not to look for: in a coppice, a long-handled pump.

2   I stopped and took my bottles to the well. A small sign: WATER UNSAFE FOR DRINKING. I drooped like warm tallow. What fungicide, herbicide, nematicide, fumigant, or growth regulant—potions that rebuilt Southern agriculture—had seeped into the ground water? In the old movie Westerns there is commonly a scene where a dehydrated man, crossing the barren waste, at last comes to a water hole; he lies flat to drink the tepid stuff. Just as lips touch water, he sees on the other side a steer skull. I drove off thirsty but feeling a part of mythic history.

3   The thirst subsided when hunger took over. I hadn't eaten since morning. Sunset arrived west of Oglesby, and the air cooled. Then a roadsign:

SWAMP GUINEA'S FISH LODGE
ALL YOU CAN EAT!

An arrow pointed down a county highway. I would gorge myself. A record would be set. They'd ask me to leave. An embarrassment to all.

4   The road through the orange earth of north Georgia passed an old, three-story house with a thin black child hanging out of every window like an illustration for "The Old Woman Who Lived in a Shoe"; on into hills and finally to Swamp Guinea's, a conglomerate of plywood and two-by-fours laid over with the smell of damp pine woods.

5   Inside, wherever an oddity of natural phenomenon could hang, one hung: stuffed rump of a deer, snowshoe, flintlock, hornet's nest. The place looked as if a Boy Scout troop had decorated it. Thirty or so people, black and white, sat around tables almost foundering under piled platters of food. I took a seat by the reproduction of a seventeenth-century woodcut depicting some Rabelaisian banquet at the groaning board.

6   The diners were mostly Oglethorpe County red-dirt farmers. In Georgia tones they talked about their husbandry in terms of rain and nitrogen and hope. An immense woman with a glossy picture of a hooked bass leaping off the front of her shirt said, "I'm gonna be sick from how much I've ate."

7   I was watching everyone else and didn't see the waitress standing quietly by. Her voice was deep and soft like water moving in a cavern. I ordered the $4.50 special. In a few minutes she wheeled up a cart and began offloading dinner: ham and eggs, fried catfish, fried perch fingerlings, fried shrimp, chunks of barbecued beef, fried chicken, French fries, hush puppies, a broad bowl of cole slaw, another of lemon, a quart of ice tea, a quart of ice, and an entire loaf of factory-wrapped white bread. The table was covered.

8   "Call me if y'all want any more." She wasn't joking. I quenched the thirst and then—slowly—went to the eating. I had to stand to reach plates across the table, but I intended to do the supper in. It was all Southern fried and good, except the Southern-style sweetened ice tea; still I took care of a quart of it. As I ate, making up for meals lost, the Old-Woman-in-the-Shoe house flashed before me, lightning in darkness. I had no moral right to eat so much. But I did. Headline: STOMACH PUMP FAILS TO REVIVE TRAVELER.

9   The loaf of bread lay unopened when I finally abandoned the meal. At the register, I paid a man who looked as if he'd been chipped out of Georgia chert. The

Swamp Guinea. I asked about the name. He spoke of himself in the third person like the Wizard of Oz. "The Swamp Guinea only tells regulars."

10   "I'd be one, Mr. Guinea, if I didn't live in Missouri."

11   "Y'all from the North? Here, I got somethin' for you." He went to the office and returned with a 45 rpm record. "It's my daughter singin'. A little promotion we did. Take it along." Later, I heard a husky north Georgia voice let go a down-home lyric rendering of Swamp Guinea's menu:

That's all you can eat
For a dollar fifty,
Hey! The barbecue's nifty!

And so on through the fried chicken and potatoes.

12   As I left, the Swamp Guinea, a former antique dealer whose name was Rudell Burroughs, said, "The nickname don't mean anything. Just made it up. Tried to figure a good one so we can franchise someday."

13   The frogs, high and low, shrilled and bellowed from the trees and ponds. It was cool going into Athens, a city suffering from a nasty case of the sprawls. On the University of Georgia campus, I tried to walk down Swamp Guinea's supper. Everywhere couples entwined like moonflower vines, each waiting for the blossom that opens only once.

EXERCISE 9   **Vocabulary Highlights**

Write a short definition of each word as it is used in the essay. (Paragraph numbers are given in parentheses.) Be prepared to use the words in your own sentences.

artesian (1)   fumigant (2)

coppice (1)   dehydrated (2)

fungicide (2)   conglomerate (4)

herbicide (2)   chert (9)

nematicide (2)   entwined (13)

EXERCISE 10   **Discussion and Critical Thinking**

1. How many of the five senses are represented in the imagery? Give an example of each one you find.

2. Give examples of simile and metaphor.

3. What ideas dominate each section as the writer moves from one phase of his experience to another?

4. You learn a great deal about the location and the residents in this passage. What do you learn about William Least Heat-Moon by the way he describes his experience?

5. What kind of audience does the author anticipate? Why?

Student Writers

When student Mike Kavanagh looked at the assignment to write a descriptive paragraph about something he knew well, he had no trouble in selecting a subject. As a drag racer for sport and prize money, he had built up his car, a 1968 Camaro, to thunder down the track at more than two hundred miles per hour, with all his senses raw to the wind.

His Writing Process Worksheet shows you how his writing evolved from idea to final draft. To conserve space here, the freewriting and the rough draft marked for revision have been omitted. The balance of his worksheet has been lengthened for you to be able to see parts of his work in their entirety.

You will find a full-size blank worksheet on page 6, which can be photocopied, filled in, and submitted with each assignment if your instructor directs you to do so.

Writing Process Worksheet

Title The Drag

Name Mike Kavanagh   **Due Date** Monday, March 27, 9 a.m.

ASSIGNMENT   In the space below, write whatever you need to know about your assignment, including information about the topic, audience, pattern of writing, length, whether to include a rough draft or revised drafts, and whether your paper must be typed.

Write a paragraph of description with a narrative framework about something you have experienced, an event that occurred in a short period of time, maybe a minute or less. Write so that an uninformed audience can understand what you did, how you did it, and how you felt. About 250 to 300 words. Submit this completed worksheet, a rough draft marked for revision, and a typed final draft.

STAGE ONE   **Explore**   Freewrite, brainstorm (list), cluster, or take notes as directed by your instructor. Use the back of this page or separate paper if you need more space.

Clustering

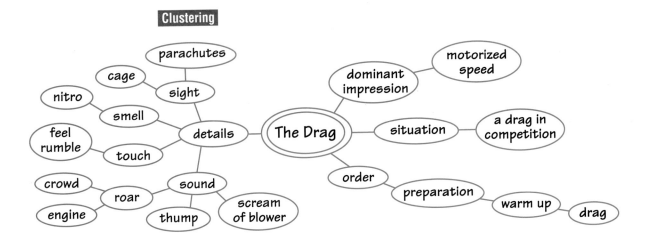

Organize Write a topic sentence or thesis; label the subject and the treatment parts.

I climb into the cockpit for my drag.
subject   treatment

Write an outline or an outline alternative.

I. Preparation
   A. Take position
   B. Strap in
      1. Straps merge
      2. Buckle
II. Warm up
   A. Fire motor
      1. Feel rumble
      2. Hear blower
      3. Smell nitro
   B. Dry hop tires
III. Drag
   A. Green light
   B. Thrust
   C. Braking
      1. Regular brakes
      2. Parachutes
   D. Success
      1. Scoreboard
      2. Feeling

Write On separate paper, write and then review your paragraph or essay as many times as necessary for **c**oherence, **l**anguage (usage, tone, and diction), **u**nity, **e**mphasis, **s**upport, and **s**entences (**CLUESS**). Read your work aloud to hear and correct any grammatical errors or awkward-sounding sentences.

Edit any problems in fundamentals, such as **c**apitalization, **o**missions, **p**unctuation, and **s**pelling (**COPS**).

Final Draft

The Drag

Mike Kavanagh

Topic sentence   As I climb into the cockpit for my drag, I hear the roar of the crowd and the thundering blasts in the background. Engulfed in an iron cage, I strap myself down. First over the shoulders, then from the waist, and finally from between my legs the straps merge and then buckle at my belly button. This is to ensure my stability in the ironclad, two-hundred-and-thirty-miles-per-hour street rocket. My crew then signals me to fire up the three thousand horsepower motor mounted at my back. With the push of a button, I feel the rumble of the motor, hear the scream of the blower, and smell the distinctive odor of nitro in the air. I

Description and narrative frame   then move up to the starting line to dry hop my rear tires for better traction. I quickly thrust the accelerator pedal to the floor. I am shot forward about two hundred feet. Letting off the accelerator pedal and pulling the brake handle allows me to come to a slow stop. A low continuous thump from the motor echoes through my head as I reverse back to the starting line. As I creep forward, I stage the beast and wait for the lights to change to green. This feels like an eternity. The lights flicker yellow, yellow, yellow, GREEN! I stab the pedal to the floor. I am flung thirteen hundred and twenty feet faster than I can say my name. When I pull the brake and parachute handles simultaneously, I lunge back from the force of the billowing chutes. I climb out of the jungle gym and look up at the

Concluding sentence   scoreboard, which reads 5.26 seconds at 230.57. There's nothing else like rocketing down the track at 230 m.p.h.

EXERCISE 11

Discussion and Critical Thinking

1. Is this paragraph mainly descriptive, mainly narrative, or equally balanced?

2. Annotate in the margin and underline at least one image of sound, sight, touch, and smell.

3. Although you probably have not drag raced competitively, you can get a good sense of what it is like to do so by reading this paragraph. What details and what phrasing convince you that the author is writing from experience?

4. What is the dominant impression?

My Aircraft Carrier "Bedroom"

CHANYA WERNER

*After serving in the United States Navy for four years, Chanya Werner
has returned home as a college student, a person who has a greater appreciation of her comforts and opportunities. Here she writes a descriptive
essay about her living quarters on board the aircraft carrier USS Tarawa.*

1   I could never be happier than the day after my enlistment was completed. Four
years in the Navy on board the USS *Tarawa* taught me to truly appreciate what I
was given at home—privacy and comfort. *Tarawa* was tolerable in the sense that I
was guaranteed a mattress to sleep on, two lockers in which to keep my belongings, and a shower after a long day of work.

2   The ships made for combat operations did not have the luxury of cruise ships,
nor did the *Tarawa*. All enlisted females, regardless of rank, were assigned to
sleep in the same area called "berthing." The female berthing was located two
decks, or floors, below the main deck toward the forward end of the ship. When
the ship had to go through high winds and rough seas, the front of the ship
would crash into the waves first, causing terrible rocking and hurling. Many newcomers ended up experiencing seasickness on their first time at sea.

3   There were two sets of narrow ladders leading down to the berthing. The stain-
less steel handrails on the ladders and nonsticks affixed to the steps helped min-
imize the risk of injury. White paint could be found on all of the walls, making the
dirt on the surface obvious. Each female was issued a rack, a military term for bed,
on the day she checked on board. There were about one hundred and ten racks in
the berthing, and twelve racks made up one aisle. Each rack, shaped like a rectangular box, was approximately three feet by three feet by seven feet. Some people
called it a coffin-rack because it appeared as such. There were one rack on top, one
in the middle, and one on the bottom. I was fortunate to be assigned a middle rack.
Because of my height, I found that getting to the top rack was almost as difficult
as climbing a mountain. The blue curtains, with hooks attached to the bar made
for sliding, were the only boundary for my privacy, and a thin sheet of aluminum,
separating my rack and my neighbor's, acted as the partition between my side
and the neighbor's.

4   "Gear adrift" could be a big problem in the berthing. The term referred to anything on a rack or hanging on the hooks. Such a display did not look presentable
and well-organized. Anything left on the rack or on the hooks would be confiscated
and locked up until claimed. As a result, all belongings must be kept tightly and
neatly either in the stand-up locker or inside the rack. Everyone was given one
stand-up locker, which was mainly used to keep the uniforms. However, I used it
to keep anything else that did not fit in the coffin locker. The coffin locker provided
a much larger storage area than the stand-up locker. In order to get inside the
coffin locker, I had to lift up the cover that my mattress lay on and then place a
heavy metal rod in the middle of the locker to provide a support between the
cover and the compartment. There were a total of seven compartments with the

height of about ten inches, four of which served as storage for casual clothing. I learned to fold my clothes in such a way that everything would be compressed and fit snugly inside. I used two compartments to keep my bathroom items and personal belongings. The last compartment was used to keep my shoes; only two pairs would fit.

5   Unlike the males' berthing, where the shower area was built separately from the berthing, female enlisted had the advantage of a shower that was located within, making it somewhat convenient. However, there was a disadvantage to this built-in shower: noise pollution. Whoever slept close or next to the shower area could suffer terribly from the constant noise of running water and, worst of all, people talking in the shower. The shower came in five stalls covered by semitransparent shower curtains on the outside, and each stall served about twenty females. Crowding was not a problem because we managed our time accordingly to avoid having too many people taking a shower at the same time. The aluminum walls reflected on the individuals in the shower. Wearing shower shoes while taking a shower was necessary to enforce the policy on personal hygiene. The mirrors were installed right above the sinks on the opposite side of the shower stalls. A woman could use these unless she needed to take a look at her whole body, then she would have to go near the entrance where a full-length mirror hung.

6   *Tarawa* gave me housing lessons of a lifetime as I experienced the living conditions on board. I do not regret joining the Navy; however, knowing what I had to go through did not encourage me to reenlist either. I learned to value and appreciate the treasure of privacy I had in my possession at home, and I became conscious of the hardship each sailor has to endure on board all naval vessels.

EXERCISE 12

Discussion and Critical Thinking

1. Underline the thesis.

2. How does the thesis prepare the writer for what follows?

3. Is the organization based mainly on direction or emphasis?

4. Is this essay of description mainly objective or subjective? Explain.

5. Is she a complainer? Explain.

6. Of the five kinds of images—sight, sound, taste, smell, and touch—which two did Werner use?

7. Which paragraph has the most images of sound?

8. What is the dominant impression, the one that the descriptive details most directly support?

Topics for Writing Description

You will find a blank Writing Process Worksheet on page 6, which can be photocopied, filled in, and submitted with each assignment if your instructor directs you to do so.

Reading-Related Topics

"The Mousetrap"

1. Describe a simple item and explain how it functions. Consider items such as a yoyo, a Slinky, a flashlight, a pair of scissors, nail clippers, a cigarette lighter, a pocket knife, a baby bottle, a diaper, a music box, a windup toy, a broom, a special wrench, or a can opener.

"The Alley"

2. Describe your neighborhood as it was when you were growing up. Populate it with one or more of the people (not necessarily family members) who influenced you. Limit your description in time and place, and unify it around a dominant impression.

3. Describe an exciting area you visited as a child, perhaps a forbidden place, one that alternately attracted and frightened you.

"More"

4. Pick a house that is or was important to you. Ortiz Cofer compared her grandmother's house to a bird; compare your selected house to some unlike object (Example: It was like a (an) _____.), focus on a single room or work area that reflects/reflected the character of a person, and describe that room or area by using specific details and images. You may want to refer to it as the heart of your subject, or it could be the brains (place for debate or lively discussion), the lungs (for talking or storytelling), or stomach (for cooking or eating).

"In the Land of 'Coke-Cola'"

5. Describe a colorful restaurant, concentrating on food, service, and ambiance. Integrate the parts of your description by presenting a scene involving a customer ordering or eating food, or a waitperson serving food to a customer.

"The Drag"

6. Describe an exciting moment that you experienced; it need not be a sporting event, but it can be. It could be an accident, a rescue, an unexpected pleasure, or any personal triumph. Pick an event you can describe colorfully.

"My Aircraft Carrier 'Bedroom'"

7. Describe a confined area in some institution (camp, school dorm, or the like) where you lived. Give specific information as Werner did. Consider including a drawing to support your description.

General Topics

Objective Description

Give your topic some kind of framework or purpose beyond simply writing a description. As you develop your purpose, consider the knowledge and attitudes of your readers. You might be describing a lung for a biology instructor, a geode for a geology instructor, a painting for an art instructor, or a comet for an astronomy instructor. Or maybe you could pose as the seller of an object, such as a desk, a table, or a bicycle. Describe one of the following topics:

8. A simple object, such as a pencil, cup, sock, dollar bill, coin, ring, or notebook

9. A human organ, such as a heart, liver, lung, or kidney

10. A visible part of your body, such as a toe, finger, ear, nose, or eye

11. A construction, such as a room, desk, chair, commode, or table

12. A mechanism, such as a bicycle, tricycle, wagon, car, motorcycle, can opener, or stapler

Subjective Description

The following topics also should be developed with a purpose other than merely writing a description. Your intent can be as simple as giving a subjective reaction to your topic. However, unless you are dealing with a topic you can present reflectively or a topic as interesting in itself as the one in "On the Ball" (p. 126), you will usually need some kind of situation. The narrative framework (something happening) is especially useful in providing order and vitality to writing. Here are three possibilities for you to consider:

13. Personalize a trip to a supermarket, a stadium, an airport, an unusual house, a mall, the beach, a court, a church, a club, a business, the library, or the police station. Describe a simple conflict in one of those places while emphasizing descriptive details.

14. Pick a high point in any event and describe the most important few seconds. Think how a scene can be captured by a video camera and then give focus by applying the dominant impression principle, using relevant images of sight, sound, taste, touch, and smell. The event might be a ball game, a graduation ceremony, a wedding ceremony, a funeral, a dance, a concert, a family gathering, a class meeting, a rally, a riot, a robbery, a fight, a proposal, or a meal. Focus on subject material that you can cover effectively in the passage you write.

15. Pick a moment when you were angry, sad, happy, confused, lost, rattled, afraid, courageous, meek, depressed, or elated. Describe how the total context of the situation contributed to your feeling.

Cross-Curricular Topics

Use description in the following assignments:

16. Agriculture: Field trip report

17. Art History: Report on a museum or a particular work of art

18. Education: School visit report

19. Ecology: Field trip report

20. Geology: Field trip report

21. Sociology: Field trip to an urban zone, a prison, or another institution

Career-Related Topics

22. Describe a well-furnished, well-functioning office or other work area. Be specific.

23. Describe a computer-related product; give special attention to the dominant trait that gives the product its reputation.

24. Describe a person groomed and attired for a particular job or interview. Be specific in giving details pertaining to the person and in naming the place or situation. Describe yourself from a detached point of view if you like.

Writer's Guidelines: Description

1. In objective description, use direct, practical language appealing mainly to the sense of sight.

2. In subjective description, appeal to the reader's feelings, especially through the use of figurative language and the use of images of sight, sound, smell, taste, and touch.

3. Use concrete, specific words if appropriate.

4. Apply these questions to your writing:

   - What is the subject?

   - What is the dominant impression I am trying to convey?

   - What details support the dominant impression?

   - What is the situation?

   - What is the order of the details?

   - What is the point of view? (First or third person? Involved or objective?)

5. Consider giving the description a narrative framework. Include some action.

6. Use the writing process.

   - Write and then revise your paragraph or essay as many times as necessary for coherence, language (usage, tone, and diction), **unity, emphasis, support,** and **sentences (CLUESS)**.

   - Read your work aloud to hear and correct any grammatical errors or awkward sounding sentences.

   - Edit any problems in fundamentals, such as **capitalization, omissions, punctuation,** and **spelling (COPS)**.

Exemplification: Writing with Examples

FLOW OF WRITING

Surveying Exposition   150

Writing Paragraphs and Essays of
Exemplification   150

   Characteristics of Good Examples   150

   **Techniques for Finding Examples:
   Listing and Clustering   151**

   Number and Order of Examples   152

Practicing Patterns of Exemplification   152

Connecting Reading and Writing   153

   Professional Writers   153

   "Novelty Sells"   153

   "Colorado Springs—Every Which Way"   154

   "Working in a Chicken-Processing Plant"   155

   "Spanglish Creeps into Mainstream'"   157

   Student Writers   159

   "Cheating Is Not Worth the Bother" (demonstration
   with stages)   161

   "Traveling the World at Home"   162

Topics for Writing Exemplification   164

Writer's Guidelines   166

*"Like a picture, a specific vivid example
may be worth a thousand words of explanation."*

KAREN GLEN

THE QUIGMANS   **by Buddy Hickerson**

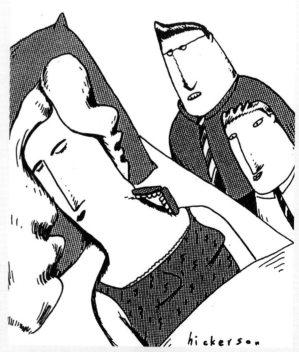

**"Looks like the work of that vampire from the Nursing
Home."**

B. Hickerson, copyright Los Angeles Times Syndicate. Reprinted by
permission.

Surveying Exposition

With this chapter on exemplification, we turn to **exposition,** a form of writing whose main purpose is to explain. This and the following eight chapters will explore these questions:

Examples	Can you give me an example or examples of what you mean?
Analysis by Division	How do the parts work together?
Process Analysis	How do I do it? How is it done?
Cause and Effect	What is the reason for this? What is the outcome?
Classification	What types of things are these?
Comparison and Contrast	How are these things similar and dissimilar?
Definition	What does this term mean?
Literary Analysis	What is a sound interpretation?

In most informative writing, these various methods of organizing and developing thought are used in combination, with one method dominating according to the writer's purpose for explaining. The other forms of discourse can be used in combination with these. You have already learned that narration and description are frequently used for expository purposes. In Chapter 17 you will see how persuasive and expository writing are often blended, becoming interdependent.

Writing Paragraphs and Essays of Exemplification

Exemplification means using examples to explain, convince, or amuse. Lending interest and information to writing, exemplification is one of the most common and effective ways of developing ideas. Examples may be developed in a sentence or more, or they may be only phrases or even single words, as in the following sentence: "Children like packaged breakfast foods, such as *Wheaties, Cheerios,* and *Rice Krispies.*"

Characteristics of Good Examples

As supporting information, the best examples are specific, vivid, and representative. These three qualities are closely linked; collectively, they must support the topic sentence of a paragraph and the thesis of an essay.

You use examples to inform or convince your reader. Of course, an example by itself does not necessarily prove anything. We know that examples can be found on either side of an argument, even at the extreme edges. Therefore, in addition to providing specific examples so that your reader can follow you precisely and vivid ones so that your reader will be interested, you should choose examples that are representative. Representative examples are examples that your reader can consider, accept as appropriate, and, in some instances, even match with examples of his or her own. If you are writing about cheating and you give one specific, vivid, and representative example, your reader should be able to say, "That's exactly what happens. I can imagine just how the incident occurred." The reader might even have in mind examples that are similar.

Techniques for Finding Examples: Listing and Clustering

Writing a good paragraph or essay of exemplification begins, as always, with prewriting. The techniques you use will depend on what you are writing about. If you were writing about cheating at school, you might work effectively with a list, perhaps including a few insights into your topic if you have not already formulated your controlling statement. The following is one such list compiled by student Lara Olivas as she developed her essay in the demonstration on page 160; she has circled items she thinks she can use.

Student Cheating
When I copied homework
Looking at a friend's test answers
A student with hand signals
Jake and his electronic system
Time for planned cheating
Those who got caught
(A person who bought a research paper)
Jess, who copied from me
The Internet "Cheaters" source
The two students who exchanged identities
(More work than it's worth)
(More stress than it's worth)
The teacher's assistant and his friends
(The girl from the biology class)

If you are pretty well settled on your subject and you expect to use several different kinds of examples, clustering may work very well for you. Student Garabed Yegavian, whose paragraph begins on page 162, first used clustering to explore and then transferred much of his information to an outline. Yegavian's cluster is shown here.

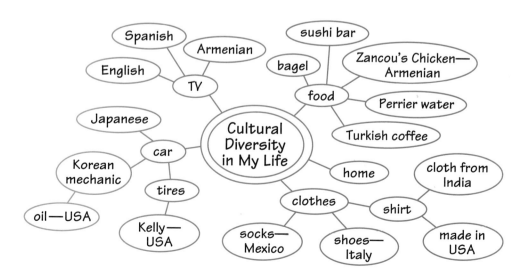

Number and Order of Examples

After you have explored your topic and collected information, you must decide whether to use only one example with a detailed explanation, a few examples with a bit less information, or a cluster of examples. A well-stated topic sentence or thesis will guide you in making this decision. When you are writing about a personal topic, you will probably have far more examples than you can use.

If your example is an incident or a series of incidents, you will probably use time order, reinforcing that arrangement with terms such as *next, then, soon, later, last,* and *finally.* If your examples exist in space (maybe in different parts of a room), then you would use space references (*up, down, left, right, east, west, north,* and *south*). Arranging examples by emphasis means going from the most important example to the least important or from the least to the most important.

Practicing Patterns of Exemplification

The simple patterns in these exercises will help you see the relationship between purpose and example(s).

EXERCISE 1	**Listing**

Make a list of examples that could support the following topic sentence or thesis. Then circle four you might use in writing a paragraph or an essay on that topic. The first item is provided.

Controlling idea: Some people let television watching interfere with their real lives.

Watching television at (examples of specific occasions):

Family gathering on a holiday

_____

_____

_____

_____

_____

_____

_____

EXERCISE 2	**Outlining**

Fill in the blanks based on your list of examples in Exercise 1.

Controlling idea: Some people let television watching interfere with their real lives.

I. Watching a football game at a Thanksgiving Day family party

II. _____

III. _____

IV. _____

Connecting Reading and Writing

Professional Writers

Novelty Sells

WAYNE D. HOYER AND DEBORAH J. MACINNIS

In their college textbook Consumer Behavior, *the authors make extensive use of examples to discuss human behavior in relation to commerce. They are concerned with why we buy and how we buy. Note the specific examples used in explaining the first step in a sales transaction: attracting the prospective customer's attention.*

We are more likely to notice any stimulus that is new or unique—because it stands out relative to other stimuli around us. Products, packages, and brand names that are unusual or novel command attention. A perfume company is attracting attention with novel perfume fragrances—one labeled Dirt smells like potting soil; another labeled Carrot smells like the vegetable. Fragrance marketers are also developing novel packages to attract attention to their brands. For example, Catalyst for Men is packaged in test tubes and laboratory flasks. Because the packaging looks like a chemistry set, the product stands out from other brands on the shelf. The makers of King Tut's Party Mix developed a novel package so the brand would stand out. Unusual looks work even for cars; for example, the Lamborghini Countach is very diffferent in shape from most cars on the road. Marketers sometimes change their products or packages so the otherwise familiar will appear more interesting. Heinz held a major contest a few years ago to get suggestions from consumers about a new trademark to replace its stodgy old one.

Discussion and Critical Thinking

1. Underline the topic sentence.

2. In what ways can items attract attention by being unusual or novel?

3. What are two general items described in the paragraph?

4. Complete this three-tiered listing with examples of unusual or novel stimuli. (Some brand names may be listed more than once.)

Products

_____

_____

Packages

_____

_____

Brand names

_____

_____

Colorado Springs—Every Which Way

ERIC SCHLOSSER

In his best-selling book Fast Food Nation, *Eric Schlosser exposes an ignorant and largely uncaring society dependent on fast food. At the end of unsavory supply lines are rudderless cities thickly populated by fast food chains serving up unhealthful food. One such city is Colorado Springs.*

Colorado Springs now has the feel of a city whose identity is not yet fixed. Many longtime residents strongly oppose the extremism of the newcomers, sporting bumper stickers that say, "Don't Californicate Colorado." The city is now torn between opposing visions of what America should be. Colorado Springs has twenty-eight Charismatic Christian churches and almost twice as many pawnbrokers, a Lord's Vineyard Bookstore and a First Amendment Adult Bookstore, a Christian Medical and Dental Society and a Holey Rollers Tattoo Parlor. It has a Christian summer camp whose founder, David Noebel, outlined the dangers of rock 'n' roll in his pamphlet *Communism, Hypnotism, and the Beatles*. It has a gay entertainment complex called The Hide & Seek, where the Gay Rodeo Association meets. It has a public school principal who recently disciplined a group of sixth-grade girls for reading a book on witchcraft and allegedly casting spells. The loopiness once assoicated with Los Angeles has come full-blown to Colorado Springs—the strange, creative energy that crops up where the future's consciously being made, where people walk the fine line separating a visionary from a total nutcase. At the start of a new century, all sorts of things seem possible there. The cultural and the physical landscapes of Colorado Springs are up for grabs.

EXERCISE 4

Discussion and Critical Thinking

1. Underline the two sentences that focus on the author's main idea.

2. Of the two sentences, which one is directly tied to most of the examples?

3. Circle each example that supports the idea in the third sentence. Notice that they appear in contrasting patterns.

4. How does the last sentence function as part of the paragragh structure.

5. Do you know of other cities that are "torn between visions of what America should be"?

6. If so (for question 5), what are some examples to support your contention?

Working in a Chicken-Processing Plant

GREGORY MOORHEAD AND RICKY W. GRIFFIN

Applied psychologists Gregory Moorhead and Ricky W. Griffin are concerned with the behavior of individuals within an organization: why managers impose conditions and how the workforce reacts. Taken from their textbook Organizational Behavior, *this essay focuses on one example to show what is going on extensively in American industry.*

1   The business press has hit upon what seems to be an interesting trend in work. Business magazines and newspapers are regularly publishing articles about the dynamic nature of work in the Unites States and about how many jobs are being changed. Indeed, because of the publicity given the shift toward service-sector and professional jobs, many people assume that the number of unpleasant and undesirable jobs has declined. In fact, nothing could be further from the truth. It is true that millions of Americans work in gleaming air-conditioned facilities, but many others work in dirty, grimy, and unsafe settings. Consider, for example, the jobs in a chicken-processing facility.

2   Much like a manufacturing assembly line, a chicken-processing facility is organized around a moving conveyor system. Workers call it "the chain." In reality, it's a steel cable with large clips that carries dead chickens down what might be called a "disassembly line." Standing along this line are dozens of workers who do, in fact, take the animals apart as they pass. Even the titles of the jobs are unsavory. Among the first set of jobs along the chain is the "skinner." These people use sharp instruments to cut and pull the skin off the dead chicken. Toward the middle of the line are the "gut pullers." These workers reach inside the chicken carcasses and remove the intestines and other organs. At the end of the line are the "gizzard cutters," who tackle the more difficult organs attached to the inside of the chicken's carcass. These organs have to be individually cut and removed for disposal.

3   The work is obviously distasteful, and the pace of the work is unrelenting: On a good day the chain moves an average of ninety chickens a minute for nine hours. And the workers are essentially held captive by the moving chain. For example, no one can vacate a post to use the bathroom or for other reasons without the permission of the supervisor. And as a supervisor in a chicken-processing plant explained the rules to a new worker, "The rule is, you can't go to the bathroom more than three times a day, unless you've got a doctor's permit." In some plants, taking an unauthorized bathroom break can result in suspension without pay. But the noise in a typical chicken-processing plant is so loud that the supervisor can't hear someone calling for relief unless the person happens to be standing close by.

4   Far from becoming automated and professionalized, jobs such as these are actually becoming increasingly common. Fueled by Americans' growing appetites for lean, easy-to-cook meat, the number of poultry workers has almost doubled since 1980, and today they constitute a work force of around a quarter of a million people. Indeed, the chicken-processing industry has become a major component of the state economies of Georgia, North Carolina, Mississippi, Arkansas, and Alabama.

5   Besides being unpleasant and dirty, many jobs in a chicken-processing plant are dangerous and unhealthy. Some workers, for example, have to fight the live birds when they are first hung on the chains. These workers are routinely scratched and pecked by the chickens. And the air inside a typical chicken-processing plant is difficult to breathe. Workers are usually supplied with paper masks, but most don't use them because they are hot and confining. And the work space itself is so tight that the workers often cut themselves—and sometimes their coworkers—with the knives, scissors, and other instruments they use to perform their jobs. Indeed, poultry processing ranks third among industries in the United States for cumulative trauma injuries such as carpal tunnel syndrome. The inevitable chicken feathers, feces, and blood also contribute to the hazardous and unpleasant work environment.

6   Not all jobs in a chicken-processing plant are as unpleasant as those described above. And certainly many workers in these plants are grateful just to have a job. But the very fact that these jobs are so plentiful underscores a basic problem that confronts many businesses today. That problem is the balancing of organizational pressures for efficiency against individual dignity and work-life quality.

EXERCISE 5

Discussion and Critical Thinking

1. Underline the thesis.

2. Is the essay based mainly on several examples or on one extended example.

3. Does this example represent a particular plant or a typical plant?

4. What has the company done to accommodate workers who need an exception from the rules?

5. Circle the sentence that mentions the four problems with the jobs described in this typical chicken-processing facility.

6. What the authors present is based on their research. Would the example be more compelling if it were based on a specific plant rather than a typical one? Why or why not?

7. Double-underline the sentence in the conclusion that states the main issue— one that is supported by the extended example of the chicken-processing facility.

8. In the conclusion, what two sentences provide partially offsetting factors concerning jobs in the chicken-processing plant?

Spanglish Creeps into Mainstream

DEBORAH KONG

As minority issues writer for the Associated Press, Deborah Kong reports on multicultural clashes, blends, assimiliations, adaptations—all changes to some extent. But change can be controversial, as it is with her topic here: the blending of two languages, Spanish and English, to make Spanglish. This article was first published on the Internet as "AP Breaking News," November 3, 2002.

1   In the wacky cartoon world of the "Mucha Lucha" wrestling school, Buena Girl is trying to help her friend gain weight in preparation for his match with three big "brutos." "And now for the ultimate in buena eats! El Masked Montana's mega torta!" she says, stuffing an enormous sandwich into his mouth. The WB network's new show is peppered with a blend of Spanish and English dialogue often called Spanglish. And TV isn't the only place you'll find it.

2   An Amherst College professor recently completed a Spanglish translation of the first chapter of "Don Quixote," and Hallmark is expanding its line of cards that mix America's most commonly spoken languages. Not everyone is happy to see Spanglish creep into the mainstream. Critics see it as a danger to Hispanic culture and advancement. But Spanglish speakers, who often move nimbly between the two languages and cultures, say it is an expression of ethnic pride. "Spanglish is proof that Latinos have a culture that is made up of two parts. It's not that you are Latino or American," said Ilan Stavans, the professor of Latin American and Latino culture who translated Miguel de Cervantes' masterpiece. "You live on the hyphen, in between. That's what Spanglish is all about, a middle ground."

3   Spanglish speakers span generations, classes and nationalities. Immigrants still learning English may turn to Spanglish out of necessity. Bilingual speakers may dip into one language, then weave in another because it's more convenient. "There are certain words or sayings that are just better in Spanish," said Danny Lopez, 28, who speaks Spanglish with friends and family, though seldom at work. "When I talk to my dad, I'll say, 'Hey Dad, I remember sitting in abuelita's cocina when we were little, and we were drinking a taza of cafe,'" said Lopez, describing memories of his grandmother's kitchen. His family has lived in the United States for four generations. Stavans traces Spanglish's origins back to 1848, when the treaty that ended the U.S.-Mexican War signed over much of the Southwest to the United States, abruptly transforming Spanish-speaking Mexicans into Americans.

4   But the modern phenomenon has plenty of pop culture examples, from Ricky Martin scoring a big hit with "Livin' La Vida Loca" to top-selling Mexican singer Paulina Rubio doing all of her songs in Spanglish as she opens for Enrique Iglesias. At mun2, a cable network that shows music videos, comedies, game shows, extreme sports and other programming targeted at 14- to 34-year-old Hispanics, language has evolved in the last year. When it launched, most of the programs were in Spanish. But the network, a division of NBC-owned Telemundo, will soon be mostly English and Spanglish, in response to viewer preferences, said spokeswoman Claudia Santa Cruz.

5   Stavans translated Cervantes into Spanglish this summer in response to a Spanish-language purist who asserted the linguistic mix would never be taken seriously until it produced a classic like "Don Quixote." "In un placete de La Mancha of which nombre no quiero remembrearme, vivia, not so long ago, uno de esos gentlemen who always tienen una lanza in the rack, una buckler antigua, a skinny caballo y un grayhound para el chase," his translation begins. Stavans' work signals Spanglish's move into academe: He also teaches a class on Spanglish and is working on a Spanglish dictionary, to be published next year.

6   But Antonio Garrido, of the Instituto Cervantes in New York, said a Spanglish "Don Quixote" is "a joke." "The idea is good English and good Spanish. Spanglish has no future," said Garrido, director of the institute created by the Spanish government to promote Spanish and Hispanic-American language and culture. "A person who doesn't speak English well in the United States doesn't have a future."

7   Roberto Gonzalez Echevarria, a professor of Hispanic and comparative literature at Yale University, agreed, saying Hispanics should learn to speak both English and Spanish well. He fears "we're going to end up speaking McSpanish, a sort of anglicized Spanish. I find it offensive the United States' values and cultural mores, all of that, are transmitted through the language filter into Spanish culture." He cited one example of a Spanish pitfall: In a deli in Puerto Rico, he saw a sign that warned parking was for customers only. "Violadores" will be prosecuted, it said. The word was used because it sounds like the English word for violators, but the problem is that "violador" primarily means "rapist" in Spanish, he said.

8   Stavans, who said he speaks Spanglish with his children, doesn't advocate replacing English with Spanglish. But he says it should be recognized as a valid form of communication. "Language is not controlled by a small group of academics that decide what the words are that we should use. Language is created by people and it is the job of academics to record those changes," he said.

9   A recent survey by the Los Angeles-based Cultural Access Group found 74 percent of 250 Hispanic youths surveyed in Los Angeles spoke Spanglish, most often with friends, other young people and at home. The WB network says "Mucha Lucha"—"lucha" means wrestling—reflects that reality. The zippy cartoon doesn't

pause to translate Spanish phrases, but sprinkles them throughout to spice up dialogue. "This is the way that young Latino kids speak," said Donna Friedman, the
10   Kids WB! executive vice president.

Hallmark says its cards also echo how people speak. "Que beautiful it is to do nada, and then descansar despues," reads one, which translates to, "How beautiful it is to do nothing, and then rest afterward." The greeting card company is expanding its line of Spanish-language cards, which includes Spanglish ones. They're aimed at younger recipients rather than mothers, aunts or grandmothers, "who
11   may not approve of mixing languages," according to the company.

In Los Angeles, Lalo Alcaraz and Esteban Zul run a Web site, pocho.com, which offers "satire, news y chat for the Spanglish generation." "We don't live neatly in two worlds. I teach my kids Spanish, yet my wife and I speak English to each other," said Alcaraz, whose new Spanglish comic strip, "La Cucaracha," will appear in newspapers next month. Spanglish is "its own unique point of view. It's more of an empowering thing to us, to say we have a legitimate culture."

EXERCISE 6

Discussion and Critical Thinking

1. Circle the two sentences that make up the thesis.

2. Is the idea supported by an extended example or a number of examples?

3. The specific examples (the actual words) come from different cultural sources. Use paragraph numbers to locate the examples.

   Academic (pertaining to school or college studies): Paragraph(s) _____

   Family: Paragraph(s) _____

   Entertainment: Paragraph(s) _____

4. Do you agree with Antonio Garrido that the wide-ranging use of Spanglish should be viewed with alarm by those who respect the Spanish culture? Why or why not?

5. If Garrido has a valid view, then should native speakers of English be equally concerned about Spanglish? Why or why not?

Student Writers

Lara Olivas was asked to write an essay on unproductive student behavior, developing her ideas mainly with examples. Of numerous topics that came to mind, one stood out: cheating. It was a practice she had observed for years and one that she had very briefly experimented with and rejected. Wanting to do something a bit different, she considered all the reasons that cheating is not a good idea and came up with a practical one: Cheating is hard work, and cheaters sometimes work harder at cheating than others do at their work.

Olivas's Writing Process Worksheet shows how her writing evolved from idea to final draft. To conserve space here, the freewriting and the rough drafts marked for revision have been omitted. The balance of her worksheet has been lengthened for you to be able to see her other work in its entirety.

You will find a full-size blank worksheet on page 6, which can be photocopied, filled in, and submitted with each assignment if your instructor directs you to do so.

Writing Process Worksheet

Title Cheating Is Not Worth the Bother

Name Lara Olivas   **Due Date** Wednesday, May 17, 9:00 a.m.

ASSIGNMENT   In the space below, write whatever you need to know about your assignment, including information about the topic, audience, pattern of writing, length, whether to include a rough draft or revised drafts, and whether your paper must be typed.

Write a 500- to 750-word essay of exemplification on the topic of unproductive student behavior. Fellow students and the instructor will probably be familiar with your subject but not your examples and your view. Submit this completed worksheet, one or more rough drafts marked for revision, and a typed final draft.

STAGE ONE   **Explore**   Freewrite, brainstorm (list), cluster, or take notes as directed by your instructor. Use the back of this page or separate paper if you need more space.

Listing

Student Cheating

When I copied homework
Looking at a friend's test answers
A student with hand signals
Jake and his electronic system
Time for planned cheating
Those who got caught
(A person who bought a research paper)
Jess, who copied from me
The Internet "Cheaters" source
The two students who exchanged identities
(More work than it's worth)
(More stress than it's worth)
The teacher's assistant and his friends
(The girl from the biology class)

STAGE TWO

Organize   Write a topic sentence or thesis; label the subject and the treatment parts.

<u>Cheating students</u> <u>often put themselves under more stress than honest</u>
       subject   treatment
<u>students.</u>

Write an outline or an outline alternative.

  I. Student who bought paper
    A. Had trouble with form
      1. Prewriting
      2. Drafts
    B. Had trouble with quality
    C. Drops class
 II. Student with cheat cards
    A. Had a system
    B. Sometimes under suspicion
    C. Experienced stress

STAGE THREE

Write   On separate paper, write and then revise your paragraph or essay as many times as necessary for **c**oherence, **l**anguage (usage, tone, and diction), **u**nity, **e**mphasis, **s**upport, and **s**entences (**CLUESS**). Read your work aloud to hear and correct any grammatical errors or awkward-sounding sentences.

Edit any problems in fundamentals, such as **c**apitalization, **o**missions, **p**unctuation, and **s**pelling (**COPS**).

Final Draft

Cheating Is Not Worth the Bother

Lara Olivas

I knew many students who took college prep classes all the way through high school and never read a book in an English class. They read Cliff's Notes or Monarch Notes, or they copied work from other people who did. But they weren't cheating just in English classes. They had systems of cheating in every class. Cheating became a way of life. They were always conniving and scheming. I'm not that pure. I've tried cheating, but I soon rejected it. I didn't learn that way, and I lost my self-esteem. I also feared getting caught; and I discovered that most of the time cheating was hard, stressful work. So I never became, like some of my friends, a master cheater, but I did become a master observer of cheaters because students almost always see more than teachers do. <u>What I learned was that</u>

Thesis   <u>cheaters often put themselves under more stress than honest students.</u>

Topic sentence   <u>Even the student who pays for school work can become a victim of stress.</u> I re-

Specific example   member a student in my junior composition class who needed a research paper, so he found a source and bought one for seventy-five dollars. The first trouble was

Order by time   that he had to submit the work in stages: the topic, the working bibliography, the note cards, the outline, the rough draft, and the final. Therefore, he went to the library and started working backwards. Of course, he couldn't turn in only the bib cards actually used in the paper, and next he had to make out note cards for the material he "would be" documenting, and even make out more. After having all kinds of trouble, he realized that the bought paper was of "A" quality, whereas he had been a "C" student. He went back to his source and was told he should change the sentence structure and so on to make the paper weaker. Finally he dropped the class after spending more time on his paper than I did on mine.

Topic sentence

Specific example
Order by time

Then during my senior year, a female student in Biology 4 became another subject for my study in cheating. She was sitting next to me, so I could see every- thing she did. She kept her cheat cards in her bra. This is the way she did it. On the day of the test, she would wear a loose-fitting blouse or dress. Then when the instructor wasn't watching, she would hunch her shoulders like a buzzard sleep- ing and slump so she could look down the front of her own dress. Sometimes she'd have to fiddle around down there to get the cheat card to pop into place. Her writing was tiny. I know about the writing because one day the teacher left the room, and she just took a card out and used it openly. If the instructor stared at her when she was looking down, she would blow inside her dress as if she were trying to cool off her bosom or something. Then she would smile at the in- structor and shake her head and pucker her lips to show how hot it was. Her strategy worked because she did perspire due to the stress. The tests were mainly on muscles and bones and weren't that difficult. She probably worked harder in

Cluster of examples

rigging the cheat cards on her underwear than I did in memorizing information.

There were dozens of other examples—the writing on seats, hands, arms, legs, and cuffs; the hand signs, blinks, and coughs; and the plagiarism of all kinds. There were even the classes where cheating would never be caught because some teach- ers didn't watch carefully during the tests, and others didn't read carefully later. But for the most part, the cheaters were the ones who had the most anxiety and often the ones who did the most work—work that was never directed toward learning.

EXERCISE 7

Discussion and Critical Thinking

1. Why did Olivas give up cheating?

2. What evidence is there that the two students she discusses experienced stress?

3. Does Olivas use a large number of specific examples to support her points or does she develop her examples in detail?

4. As she develops her examples in paragraphs, what other pattern of writing emerges?

Student Writers

Traveling the World at Home
GARABED YEGAVIAN

An Armenian-American student, Garabed Yegavian has traveled to many countries and encountered many cultures. Living in Southern California, he is constantly reminded that he lives in a global community, but this as- signment focused his attention on specific, persuasive examples.

Living in California can be like traveling the world. It is morning! Responding to my alarm clock made in China, I get out of my bed, which was constructed in the United States, and step onto a Persian rug. I'm ready to start my Saturday. I walk to my closet to find my clothes: pants from Indonesia, shirt of fabric from India but made in North Carolina, socks from Mexico, shoes from Italy. For late breakfast I have a bagel and cream cheese. I sit in front of my television to see what's happening in the world today. I flip through the channels—English, Spanish, Chinese—until I get to the local Armenian station for an update. After an hour I'm ready to go. I drive to my Korean friend's garage, where he fills my car with oil refined in a plant down by Long Beach. I pay him with my American dollars, and I'm off for tires. On the way to the tire shop, I stop for some lunch. Zancou's Chicken is the place for me today. I order Armenian-style chicken and a bottle of Perrier water and enjoy my feast. Done with lunch, I motor to the tire shop where an immigrant worker from El Salvador fits American Kelly tires on my car. I drink a small cup of Turkish coffee with the manager and talk about business here in America. After a while, my car is ready, and I leave for a mid-afternoon snack. Where to go? There are just too many choices. I decide to go to a Japanese restaurant near my home. There I eat sushi made with fish caught from the waters off Peru, drink Japanese saki, and reflect on my day's experiences. In miles I hadn't gone far, but who needs to travel the world when one lives in Southern California?

EXERCISE 8

Discussion and Critical Thinking

1. Underline the topic sentence of the paragraph.

2. Circle each specific example.

3. As Yegavian's community becomes more global, does it become less American, more American, or just a different kind of American? Explain.

4. Do you welcome this kind of change and find it rather exciting, as Yegavian apparently does? Why or why not?

5. To what extent is your environment similar to the one presented in this paragraph?

Topics for Writing Exemplification

You will find a blank writing process worksheet on page 6, which can be photocopied, filled in, and submitted with each assignment if your instructor directs you to do so.

Reading-Related Topics

"Novelty Sells"

1. Using the basic idea advanced by Hoyer and MacInnis that novelty sells, write about some specific products you are familiar with that are novel as products, packages, and brand names. Find at least one example for each aspect. Use listing and a simple outline for your search and basic organization.

2. Borrowing the idea about novelty selling, write in detail about either one product that sells because of a particular kind of novelty or about a group of products that sell well because of a particular kind of novelty.

"Colorado Springs—Every Which Way"

3. Using this paragraph as a model of development by examples, write about a similar city, one that exhibits contradictory features of products, services, and individual behavior.

4. Referring to clubs, activities, and course offerings, discuss how a college you are familiar with is torn between opposing visions of what America should be.

"Working in a Chicken-Processing Plant"

5. Using the thesis by Moorhead and Griffin that many people are working at jobs that are unpleasant, describe an unpleasant job that you are familiar with and comment on what the business is doing or could be doing to make the working conditions better.

"Spanglish Creeps into Mainstream"

6. If you know some Spanish and are familiar with Spanglish, write a paragraph or an essay supported with your own examples of language blending. Consider telling a brief story (narrative) in Spanglish.

7. If you know another language, explain how speakers of other languages have come up with their own combinations, such as Chinglish.

"Cheating Is Not Worth the Bother"

8. Using the main idea of this essay as your topic sentence or thesis, develop it with your own example(s) for a paragraph or an essay.

9. Using this essay as a model, write about employee theft or choplifting.

"Traveling the World at Home"

10. Write about a typical day or moment in your community, using examples of products, services, and ideas that make you part of a global village.

11. Write about someone you know who has chosen a simplified life and is only marginally dependent on resources from around the world. Give examples.

General Topics

Choose one of the following statements as a topic sentence for a paragraph or a thesis for an essay. Support the statement with specific examples.

12. Television commercials are often amusing [misleading, irritating, sexist, racist, useless, fascinating].

13. Rap music often carries important messages [makes me sick, brings out the best in people, brings out the worst in people, degrades women, promotes violence, presents reality, appeals to our better instincts, tells funny stories].

14. Rock groups don't have to be sensational in presentation and appearance to be popular.

15. A person can be an environmentalist in everyday life.

16. Many people who consider themselves law-abiding citizens break laws on a selective basis.

17. Television news is full of stories of violence, but we can also find acts of kindness in everyday life.

18. Car salespeople behave differently depending on the kind of car they are selling and the kind of customer they have.

19. The kinds of toys people buy for their children tell us much about their social values.

20. People who do not have a satisfying family life will find a family substitute.

21. One painful experience reminded me of the importance of human rights [student rights, worker rights, gender rights].

22. Drug abuse, including alcohol abuse, may be a problem even with people who seem to be functioning well.

23. Country music appeals to some of our most basic concerns.

Cross-Curricular Topics

Use examples to write paragraphs or essays in these kinds of assignments.

24. Tests or similar written assignments: Supporting information, either specific or extended examples.

25. Reports: Focusing on one or more examples as representation of a much larger group, for example, a focused discussion of one work of art in a museum grouping of pieces by style or a study of a particular typical student in a class visit for an education class. For support in paragraph and essay assignments in any classes.

Career-Related Topics

26. Use specific examples to support one of the following statements as applied to business or work.

    It's not what you know, it's who you know.

    Don't burn your bridges.

    Like Legos, business is a matter of connections.

    Tact is the lubricant that oils the wheels of industry.

    The customer is always right.

    If you take care of the pennies, the dollars will take care of themselves.

    A kind word turns away wrath.

27. Use another common saying or invent one of your own and illustrate it with an example or examples.

28. Discuss how a specific service or product can benefit its users. Use an example or examples.

Writer's Guidelines: Exemplification

1. Use examples to explain, convince, or amuse.

2. Use examples that are vivid, specific, and representative.

   • Vivid examples attract attention.

   • Specific examples are identifiable.

   • Representative examples are typical and therefore the basis for generalization.

3. Tie your examples clearly to your thesis.

4. Draw your examples from what you have read, heard, and experienced.

5. Brainstorm a list or cluster of possible examples before you write.

6. The order and number of your examples will depend on the purpose stated in your topic sentence or thesis.

7. Use the writing process.

   • Write and then revise your paragraph or essay as many times as necessary for coherence, language (usage, tone, and diction), unity, emphasis, support, and sentences (**CLUESS**).

   • Read your work aloud to hear and correct any grammatical errors or awkward-sounding sentences.

   • Edit any problems in fundamentals, such as capitalization, omissions, punctuation, and spelling (**COPS**).

Chapter 10

Analysis by Division:
Examining the Parts

FLOW OF WRITING

Writing Instruction 168
  Procedure 168
  Organization 168
  Sequence of Parts 168
Practicing Patterns of Analysis by Division 169
Connecting Reading and Writing 170
  Professional Writers 170
  "The Family and Its Parts" 170
  "The Zones of the Sea" 171
  "Low Wages, High Skills" 172
  "Growing Up Asian in America" 177
  Student Writers 182
  "Skin" (demonstration with stages) 184
  "Ben Franklin, Renaissance Man" 185
Topics for Writing Analysis by Division 186
Writer's Guidelines 188

"What makes me happy is rewriting. In the first draft you get your ideas and your theme clear. . . . But the next time through it's like cleaning a house, getting rid of all the junk, getting things in the right order, tightening things up. I like the process of making writing neat."

ELLEN GOODMAN

THE QUIGMANS   by Buddy Hickerson

"Woo! Check out the third and seventh segments on THAT babe. YEAH!"

B. Hickerson, copyright Los Angeles Times Syndicate. Reprinted by permission.

Writing Instruction

Procedure

If you need to explain how something works or exists as a unit, you will write an analysis by division. You will break down a unit (your subject) into its parts and explain how each part functions in relation to the operation or existence of the whole. The most important word here is *unit*. You begin with something that can stand alone or can be regarded separately: a poem, a heart, a painting, a car, a bike, a person, a school, a committee. The following procedure will guide you in writing an analysis by division: Move from subject to principle, to division, to relationship.

Step 1. Begin with something that is a unit (subject).

Step 2. State one principle by which the unit can function.

Step 3. Divide the unit into parts according to that principle.

Step 4. Discuss each of the parts in relation to the unit.

You might apply that procedure to writing about a good boss in the following way:

1. Unit	Manager
2. Principle of function	Effective as a leader
3. Parts based on the principle	Fair, intelligent, stable, competent in the field
4. Discussion	Consider each part in relation to the person's effectiveness as a manager.

Organization

In an essay of analysis by division, the main parts are likely to be the main points of your outline or main extensions of your cluster. If they are anything else, reconsider your organization. A basic outline of an analysis by division might look like this:

Thesis: To be effective as a leader, a manager needs specific qualities.
　　I. Fairness
　　II. Intelligence
　　III. Stability
　　IV. Competence in the field

Sequence of Parts

The order in which you discuss the parts will vary according to the nature of the unit and the way in which you view it. Here are some possible sequences for organizing the parts of a unit:

- **Time:** The sequence of the parts in your essay can be mainly chronological, or time-based (if you are dealing with something that functions on its own, such as a heart, with the parts presented in relation to stages of the function).
- **Space:** If your unit is a visual object, especially if, like a pencil, it does nothing by itself, you may discuss the parts in relation to space. In the example of the

pencil, the parts of the pencil begin at the top with the eraser and end at the bottom with the pencil point.

- **Emphasis:** Because the most emphatic location of any piece of writing is the end (the second most emphatic point is the beginning), consider placing the most significant part of the unit at the end.

Practicing Patterns of Analysis by Division

In analysis by division, Roman numeral headings are almost always parts of the unit you are discussing as your subject. Learning to divide the unit into parts will help you move through your assignment quickly and efficiently.

Writing Patterns

Fill in the blanks as if you were organizing material for a paragraph or an essay. Have a specific unit in mind.

1. Unit: friend, relative, hero, or role model

   Principle: that which defines the person

   The name of the person (may be fictitious): _____

   I. _____

   II. _____

   III. _____

   IV. _____

2. Unit: physical object such as a pencil, shoe, baseball, or pair of glasses

   Principle: that which makes the object functional

   Specific name of the unit: _____

   I. _____

   II. _____

   III. _____

   IV. _____

EXERCISE 2

Writing Patterns

Fill in the blanks as if you were organizing material for a paragraph or an essay. Have a specific unit in mind.

1. Unit: movie, television program, or novel

    Principle: that which makes the unit excellent

    Specific name of the unit: _____

    I. _____

    II. _____

    III. _____

    IV. _____

2. Unit: family, relationship, club, or class

    Principle: that which makes the unit excellent

    Specific name of the unit: _____

    I. _____

    II. _____

    III. _____

    IV. _____

Connecting Reading and Writing

Professional Writers

The Family and Its Parts

IAN ROBERTSON

Author and college professor Ian Robertson gives his definition of family with its necessary components.

What characteristics, then, are common to all family forms? First, the family consists of a group of people who are in some way related to one another. Second, its members live together for long periods. Third, the adults in the group assume responsibility for any offspring. And, fourth, the members of the family form an economic unit—often for producing goods and services (as when all members share agricultural tasks) and always for consuming goods and services (such as food or housing). We may say, then, that the "family" is a relatively permanent group of people related by ancestry, marriage, or adoption, who live together, form an economic unit, and take care of their young. If this definition seems a little cumbersome, it is only because it has to include such a great variety of family forms.

EXERCISE 3

Discussion and Critical Thinking

1. According to Robertson, what are the four characteristics of the family?

2. Must this family include children?

3. Does this definition rule out groups of people headed by nonmarried couples or homosexual couples? If not, explain. If so, explain how the definition might be modified to include the two other groups.

4. Do you prefer a broad or narrow definition of *family*? Why?

The Zones of the Sea

LEONARD ENGEL

In this paragraph reprinted from The Sea, *published by Time-Life Books, the author shows that the sea can be divided into four zones.*

The life of the ocean is divided into distinct realms, each with its own group of creatures that feed upon each other and depend on each other in different ways. There is, first of all, the tidal zone, where land and sea meet. Then comes the realm of the shallow seas around the continents, which goes down to about 500 feet. It is in these two zones that the vast majority of marine life occurs. The deep ocean adds two regions, the zone of light and the zone of perpetual darkness. In the clear waters of the western Pacific, light could still be seen at a depth of 1,000 feet through the portholes of the *Trieste* on its seven-mile dive. But for practical purposes the zone of light ends at about 600 feet. Below that level there is too little light to support the growth of the "grass" of the sea—the tiny, single-celled green plants whose ability to form sugar and starch with the aid of sunlight makes them the base of the great food pyramid of the ocean.

EXERCISE 4   Discussion and Critical Thinking

1. What are the four zones of the sea?

2. Is the paragraph organized by space or by time?

3. What characterizes each zone?

4. Draw a cross section of the sea to show the four zones. Make it as elaborate as you like.

Low Wages, High Skills

KATHERINE S. NEWMAN

As an anthropologist Katherine S. Newman specializes in urban life and the working poor. This excerpt is from her well-researched, celebrated book No Shame in My Game *(1999). As the title suggests, the workers have reasons for taking pride in what they do.*

1   Elise has worked the "drive-through" window at Burger Barn for the better part of three years. She is a virtuoso in a role that totally defeated one of my brightest doctoral students, who tried to work alongside her for a week or two. Her job pays only twenty-five cents above the minimum wage (after five years), but it requires that she listen to orders coming in through a speaker, send out a stream of instructions to co-workers who are preparing the food, pick up and check orders for customers already at the window, and receive money and make change, all more or less simultaneously. She has to make sure she keeps the sequence of orders straight so that the Big Burger goes to the man in the blue Mustang and not the woman right behind him in the red Camaro who has now revised her order for the third time. The memory and information-processing skills required to perform this job at a minimally acceptable level are considerable. Elise makes the operation look easy, but it clearly is a skilled job, as demanding as any of the dozen better-paid

positions in the Post Office or the Gap stores where she has tried in vain to find higher-status employment.

2   This is not to suggest that working at Burger Barn is as complex as brain surgery. It is true that the component parts of the ballet, the multiple stations behind the counter, have been broken down into the simplest operations. Yet to make them work together under time pressure while minimizing wastage requires higher-order skills. We can think of these jobs as lowly, repetitive, routinized, and demeaning, or we can recognize that doing them right requires their incumbents to process information, coordinate with others, and track inventory. These valuable competencies are tucked away inside jobs that are popularly characterized as utterly lacking in skill.

3   If coordination were the only task required of these employees, then experience would probably eliminate the difficulty after a while. But there are many unpredictable events in the course of a workday that require some finesse to manage. Chief among them are abrasive encounters with customers, who [. . .] often have nothing better to do than rake a poor working stiff over the coals for a missing catsup packet or a batch of french fries that aren't quite hot enough. One afternoon at a Burger Barn cash register is enough to send most sane people into psychological counseling. It takes patience, forbearance, and an eye for the long-range goal (of holding on to your job, of impressing management with your fortitude) to get through some of these encounters. If ever there was an illustration of "people skills," this would be it.

4   Coping with rude customers and coordinating the many components of the production process are made all the more complex by the fact that in most Harlem Burger Barns, the workers hail from a multitude of countries and speak in a variety of languages. Monolingual Spanish speakers fresh from the Dominican Republic have to figure out orders spoken in Jamaican English. Puerto Ricans, who are generally bilingual, at least in the second generation, have to cope with the English dialects of African Americans. All of these people have to figure out how to serve customers who may be fresh off the boat from Guyana, West Africa, Honduras. The workplace melting pot bubbles along because people from these divergent groups are able to come together and learn bits and snatches of each other's languages— "workplace Spanish" or street English. They can communicate at a very rudimentary level in several dialects, and they know enough about each other's cultural traditions to be able to interpret actions, practices, dress styles, and gender norms in ways that smooth over what can become major conflicts on the street.

5   In a world where residential segregation is sharp and racial antagonism no laughing matter, it is striking how well workers get along with one another. Friendships develop across lines that have hardened in the streets. Romances are born between African Americans and Puerto Ricans, legendary antagonists in the neighborhoods beyond the workplace. This is even more remarkable when one considers the competition that these groups are locked into in a declining labor market. They know very well that employers are using race- and class-based preferences to decide who gets a job, and that their ability to foster the employment chances of friends and family members may well be compromised by a manager's racial biases. One can hear in their conversations behind the counter complaints about how they cannot get their friends jobs because—they believe—the manager wants to pick immigrants first and leave the native-born jobless. In this context, resentment builds against unfair barriers. Even so, workers of different ethnic backgrounds are able to reach across the walls of competition and cultural difference.

6   We are often admonished to remember that the United States is a multicultural society and that the workforce of the future will be increasingly composed of minorities

and foreigners. Consultants make thousands of dollars advising companies in "diversity training" in order to manage the process of amalgamation. Burger Barn is a living laboratory of diversity, the ultimate melting pot for the working poor. They live in segregated spaces, but they work side by side with people whom they would rarely encounter on the block. If we regard the ability to work in a multiethnic, multilingual environment as a skill, as the consulting industry argues we should, then there is much to recommend the cultural capital acquired in the low-wage workplaces of the inner city.

7   Restaurant owners are loath to cut their profits by calling in expensive repair services when their equipment breaks down, the plumbing goes out, or the electrical wiring blows. Indeed, general managers are required to spend time in training centers maintained by Burger Barn's corporate headquarters learning how to disassemble the machinery and rebuild it from scratch. The philosophers in the training centers say this is done to teach managers a "ground-up" appreciation for the equipment they are working with. Any store owner will confess, however, that this knowledge is mainly good for holding labor costs down by making it unnecessary to call a repairman every time a milk shake machine malfunctions. What this means in practice is that managers much teach entry-level workers, especially the men (but the women as well), the art of mechanical repair and press them into service when the need strikes. Indeed, in one Harlem restaurant, workers had learned how to replace floor-to-ceiling windows (needed because of some bullet holes), a task they performed for well below the prevailing rates of a skilled glazier.

8   Then, of course, there is the matter of money. Burger Barn cash registers have been reengineered to make it possible for people with limited math abilities to operate them. Buttons on the face of the machine display the names of the items on the menu, and an internal program belts out the prices, adds them up, and figures out how much change is due a customer, all with no more than the push of a finger on the right "pad." Still, the workers who man the registers have to be careful to account for all the money that is in the till. Anything amiss and they are in deep trouble: they must replace any missing cash out of their wages. If money goes missing more than once, they are routinely fired. And money can disappear for a variety of reasons: someone makes a mistake in making change, an unexpected interloper uses the machine when the main register worker has gone into the back for some extra mustard packets, a customer changes her mind and wants to return an item (a transaction that isn't programmed into the machine). Even though much of the calculation involved in handling funds is done by computer chips, modest management skills are still required to keep everything in order.

9   While this is not computer programming, the demands of the job are nonetheless quite real. This becomes all too clear, even to managers who are of the opinion that these are "no-skill" jobs, when key people are missing. Workers who know the secrets of the trade—how to cut corners with the official procedures mandated by the company on food preparation, how to "trick" the cash register into giving the right amount of change when a mistake has been made, how to keep the orders straight when there are twenty people backed up in the drive-through line, how to teach new employees the real methods of food production (as opposed to the official script), and what to do when a customer throws a screaming fit and disrupts the whole restaurant—keep the complicated ballet of fast food operation moving smoothly. When "experts" disappear from the shift, nothing works the way it should. When they quit, the whole crew is thrown into a state of near-chaos, a situation that can take weeks to remedy as new people come "on line." If these jobs were truly as denuded of skill as they are popularly believed to be, none of this

would matter. In fact, however, they are richer in cognitive complexity and individual responsibility than we acknowledge.

10   This is particularly evident when one watches closely over time how new people are trained. Burger Barn, like most of its competitors, has prepared training tapes designed to show new workers with limited literacy skills how to operate the equipment, assemble the raw materials, and serve customers courteously. Managers are told to use these tapes to instruct all new crew members. In the real world, though, the tapes go missing, the VCR machine doesn't work, and new workers come on board in the middle of the hamburger rush hour when no one has time to sit them down in front of a TV set for a lesson. They have to be taught the old-fashioned way—person to person—with the more experienced and capable workers serving as teachers.

11   One of my graduate students learned this lesson the hard way. A native of Puerto Rico, Ana Ramos-Zayas made her way to a restaurant in the Dominican neighborhood of upper Harlem and put on an apron in the middle of the peak midday demand. Nobody could find the tapes, so she made do by trying to mimic the workers around her. People were screaming at her that she was doing it all wrong, but they were also moving like greased lightning in the kitchen. Ana couldn't figure out how to place the cheese on the hamburger patty so that it fit properly. She tried it one way and then another—nothing came out right. The experienced workers around her, who were all Spanish-speakers, were not initially inclined to help her out, in part because they mistook her for a white girl—something they had not seen behind the counter before. But when they discovered, quite by accident, that Ana was a Latina (she muttered a Spanish curse upon dropping the fifth bun in a row), they embraced her as a fellow migrant and quickly set about making sure she understood the right way to position the cheese.

12   From that day forward, these workers taught Ana all there was to know about the french fry machine, about how to get a milk shake to come out right, about the difference between cooking a fish sandwich and a chicken sandwich, and about how to forecast demand for each so that the bins do not overfill and force wastage. Without their help, provided entirely along informal lines, Ana would have been at sea. Her experience is typical in the way it reveals the hidden knowledge locked up inside what appears to surface observers (and to many employees themselves) as a job that requires no thinking, no planning, and no skill.

13   As entry-level employment, fast food jobs provide the worker with experience and knowledge that ought to be useful as a platform for advancement in the work world. After all, many white-collar positions require similar talents: memory skills, inventory management, the ability to work with a diverse crowd of employees, and versatility in covering for fellow workers when the demand increases. Most jobs require "soft skills" in people management, and those that involve customer contact almost always require the ability to placate angry clients. With experience of this kind, Burger Barn workers ought to be able to parlay their "human capital" into jobs that will boost their incomes and advance them up the status ladder.

14   The fact that this happens so rarely is only partially a function of the diplomas they lack or the mediocre test scores they have to offer employers who use these screening devices. They are equally limited by the popular impression that the jobs they hold now are devoid of value. The fast food industry's reputation for de-skilling its work combines with the low social standing of these inner-city employees to make their skills invisible. Employers with better jobs to offer do recognize that Burger Barn veterans are disciplined: they show up for work on time, they know how to serve the public. Yet if the jobs they are trying to fill require more advanced skills (inventory, the ability to learn new technologies, communication

skills), Burger Barn is just about the last place that comes to mind as an appropriate proving ground. A week behind the counter of the average fast food restaurant might convince them otherwise, but employers are not anthropologists out looking for a fresh view of entry-level employment. They operate on the basis of assumptions that are widely shared and have neither the time nor the inclination to seek out the hidden skills that Burger Barn employees have developed.

15   Perhaps fast food veterans would do better in the search for good jobs if they could reveal that hidden reservoir of human capital. But they are as much the victims of the poor reputation of their jobs as the employers they now seek to impress. When we asked them to explain the skills involved in their work, they invariably looked at us in surprise: "Any fool could do this job. Are you kidding?" They saw themselves as sitting at the bottom of the job chain and the negative valence of their jobs as more or less justified. A lot of energy goes into living with that "truth" and retaining some sense of dignity, but that effort does not involve rethinking the reputation of their work as skillfree. Hence they are the last people to try to overturn a stereotype and sell themselves to other employers as workers who qualify for better jobs.

16   I have suggested here that neither the employers nor the job-seekers have got it right. There are competencies involved in these jobs that should be more widely known and more easily built upon as the basis for advancement in the labor market. Yet even if we could work some magic along these lines, the limitations built into the social networks of most low-wage workers in the inner city could make it hard to parlay that new reputation into success.

EXERCISE 5

Vocabulary Highlights

Write a short definition of each word as it is used in the essay. (Paragraph numbers are given in parentheses.) Be prepared to use the words in your own sentences.

virtuoso (1)	amalgamation (6)
abrasive (3)	interloper (8)
forbearance (3)	amiss (8)
rudimentary (4)	denuded (9)
antagonism (5)	cognitive (9)

EXERCISE 6

Discussion and Critical Thinking

1. Newman maintains that low-wage workers in this ordinary fast food establishment perform tasks that require exceptional skills. To reach her conclusion, she uses analysis by division. Fill in the blanks to indicate how she proceeded.

   Unit (What is she concerned with?):

   Principle of function (What aspect does she focus on?):

Parts based on the principle (What are those potentially transferable skills?)

-
-
-
-
-
-

2. Could the transferable skills discussed in this essay be included effectively on a résumé for a person seeking a higher-paying job?

3. Have you held a low-paying job that requires/required important transferable skills? Discuss.

4. Do you agree with the author's conclusions? Why or why not?

5. How do you interpret the last sentence in the essay: "Yet even if we could work some magic along these lines, the limitations built into the social networks of most low-wage workers in the inner city could make it hard to parlay that new reputation into success"?

Growing Up Asian in America
KESAYA E. NODA

Who are you? Can you classify yourself with a single word? Kesaya E. Noda has grown up Asian in America, but she needs several words to characterize herself because her identity has many facets.

1   Sometimes when I was growing up, my identity seemed to hurtle toward me and paste itself right to my face. I felt that way, encountering the stereotypes of my race perpetuated by non-Japanese people (primarily white) who may or may not have had contact with other Japanese in America. "You don't like cheese, do you?" someone would ask. "I know your people don't like cheese." Sometimes questions came making allusions to history. That was another aspect of the identity. Events that had happened quite apart from the me who stood silent in that moment connected my face with an incomprehensible past. "Your parents were in California? Were they in those camps during the war?" And sometimes there were phrases or nicknames: "Lotus Blossom." I was sometimes addressed or referred to as racially

Japanese, sometimes as Japanese-American, and sometimes as an Asian woman. Confusions and distortions abounded.

2   How is one to know and define oneself? From the inside—within a context that is self-defined from a grounding in community and a connection with culture and history that are comfortably accepted? Or from the outside—in terms of messages received from the media and people who are often ignorant? Even as an adult I can still see two sides of my face and past. I can see from the inside out, in freedom. And I can see from the outside in, driven by the old voices of childhood and lost in anger and fear.

I Am Racially Japanese

3   A voice from my childhood says: "You are other. You are less than. You are unalterably alien." This voice has its own history. We have indeed been seen as other and alien since the early years of our arrival in the United States. The very first immigrants were welcomed and sought as laborers to replace the dwindling numbers of Chinese, whose influx had been cut off by the Chinese Exclusion Act of 1882. The Japanese fell natural heir to the same anti-Asian prejudice that had arisen against the Chinese. As soon as they began striking for better wages, they were no longer welcomed.

4   I can see myself today as a person historically defined by law and custom as being forever alien. Being neither "free white," nor "African," our people in California were deemed "aliens, ineligible for citizenship," no matter how long they intended to stay here. Aliens ineligible for citizenship were prohibited from owning, buying, or leasing land. They did not and could not belong here. The voice in me remembers that I am always a *Japanese*-American in the eyes of many. A third-generation German-American is an American. A third-generation Japanese-American is a Japanese-American. Being Japanese means being a danger to the country during the war and knowing how to use chopsticks. I wear this history on my face.

5   I move to the other side. I see a different light and claim a different context. My race is a line that stretches across ocean and time to link me to the shrine where my grandmother was raised. Two high, white banners lift in the wind at the top of the stone steps leading to the shrine. It is time for the summer festival. Black characters are written against the sky as boldly as the clouds, as lightly as kites, as sharply as the big black crows I used to see above the fields in New Hampshire. At festival time there is liquor and food, ritual, discipline, and abandonment. There is music and drunkenness and invocation. There is hope. Another season has come. Another season has gone.

6   I am racially Japanese. I have a certain claim to this crazy place where the prayers intoned by a neighboring Shinto priest (standing in for my grandmother's nephew who is sick) are drowned out by the rehearsals for the pop singing contest in which most of the villagers will compete later that night. The village elders, the priest, and I stand respectfully upon the immaculate, shining wooden floor of the outer shrine, bowing our heads before the hidden powers. During the patchy intervals when I can hear him, I notice the priest has a stutter. His voice flutters up to my ears only occasionally because two men and a woman are singing gustily into a microphone in the compound, testing the sound system. A prerecorded tape of guitars, samisens, and drums accompanies them. Rock music and Shinto prayers. That night, to loud applause and cheers, a young man is given the award for the most *netsuretsu*—passionate, burning—rendition of a song. We roar our approval of the reward. Never mind that his voice had wandered and slid, now slightly above, now slightly below the given line of the melody. Netsuretsu. Netsuretsu.

7   In the morning, my grandmother's sister kneels at the foot of the stone stairs to offer her morning prayers. She is too crippled to climb the stairs, so each morning she kneels here upon the path. She shuts her eyes for a few seconds, her motions as matter of fact as when she washes rice. I linger longer than she does, so reluctant to leave, savoring the connection I feel with my grandmother in America, the past, and the power that lives and shines in the morning sun.

8   Our family has served this shrine for generations. The family's need to protect this claim to identity and place outweighs any individual claim to any individual hope. I am Japanese.

I Am a Japanese-American

9   "Weak." I hear the voice from my childhood years. "Passive," I hear. Our parents and grandparents were the ones who were put into those camps. They went without resistance, they offered cooperation as proof of loyalty to America. "Victim," I hear. And, "Silent."

10   Our parents are painted as hard workers who were socially uncomfortable and had difficulty expressing even the smallest opinion. Clean, quiet, motivated, and determined to match the American way; that is us, and that is the story of our time here.

11   "Why did you go into those camps?" I raged at my parents, frightened by my own inner silence and timidity. "Why didn't you do anything to resist? Why didn't you name it the injustice it was?" Couldn't our parents even think? Couldn't they? Why were we so passive?

12   I shift my vision and my stance. I am in California. My uncle is in the midst of the sweet potato harvest. He is pressed, trying to get the harvesting crews onto the field as quickly as possible, worried about the flow of equipment and people. His big pickup is pulled off to the side, motor running, door ajar. I see two tractors in the yard in front of an old shed; the flatbed harvesting platform on which the workers will stand has already been brought over from the other field. It's early morning. The workers stand loosely grouped and at ease, but my uncle looks as harried and tense as a police officer trying to unsnarl a New York City traffic jam. Driving toward the shed, I pull my car off the road to make way for an approaching tractor. The front wheels of the car sink luxuriously into the soft, white sand by the roadside and the car slides to a dreamy halt, tail still on the road. I try to move forward. I try to move back. The front bites contentedly into the sand, the back lifts itself at a jaunty angle. My uncle sees me and storms down the road, running. He is shouting before he is even near me.

13   "What's the matter with you?" he screams. "What the hell are you doing?" In his frenzy, he grabs his hat off his head and slashes it through the air across his knee. He is beside himself. "Don't you know how to drive in sand? What's the matter with you? You've blocked the whole roadway. How am I supposed to get my tractors out of here? Can't you use your head? You've cut off the whole roadway, and we've got to get out of here."

14   I stand on the road before him helplessly thinking, "No, I don't know how to drive in sand. I've never driven in sand."

15   "I'm sorry, uncle," I say, burying a smile beneath a look of sincere apology. I notice my deep amusement and my affection for him with great curiosity. I am usually devastated by anger. Not this time.

16   During the several years that follow I learn about the people and the place, and much more about what has happened in this California village where my parents grew up. The *issei,* or grandparents, made this settlement in the desert. Their first crops were eaten by rabbits and ravaged by insects. The land was so barren that men walking from house to house sometimes got lost. Women came here too. They bore children in 114-degree heat, then carried the babies with them into the fields to nurse when they reached the end of each row of grapes or other truck-farm crops.

17   I had no idea what it meant to buy this kind of land and make it grow green. Or how, when the war came, there was no space at all for the subtlety of being who we were—Japanese-Americans. Either/or was the way. I hadn't understood that people were literally afraid for their lives then, that their money had been frozen in banks; that there was a five-mile travel limit; that when the early evening curfew came and they were inside their houses, some of them watched helplessly as people they knew went into their barns to steal their belongings. The police were patrolling the road, interested only in violators of curfew. There was no help for them in the face of thievery. I had not been able to imagine before what it must have felt like to be an American—to know absolutely that one is an American—and yet to have almost everyone else deny it. Not only deny it, but challenge that identity with machine guns and troops of white American soldiers. In those circumstances it was difficult to say, "I'm Japanese-American." "American" had to do.

18   But now I can say that I am a Japanese-American. It means I have a place here in this country, too. I have a place here on the East Coast, where our neighbor is so much a part of our family that my mother never passes her house at night without glancing at the lights to see if she is home and safe; where my parents have hauled hundreds of pounds of rocks from fields and arduously planted Christmas trees and blueberries, lilacs, asparagus, and crab apples, where my father still dreams of angling a stream to a new bed so that he can dig a pond in the field and fill it with water and fish. "The neighbors already came for their Christmas tree?" he asks in December. "Did they like it? Did they like it?"

19   I have a place on the West Coast where my relatives still farm, where I heard the stories of feuds and backbiting, and where I saw that people survived and flourished because fundamentally they trusted and relied upon one another. A death in the family is not just a death in a family; it is a death in the community. I saw people help each other with money, materials, labor, attention, and time. I saw men gather once a year, without fail, to clean the grounds of a ninety-year-old woman who had helped the community before, during, and after the war. I saw her remembering them with birthday cards sent to each of their children.

20   I come from a people with a long memory and a distinctive grace. We live our thanks. And we are Americans. Japanese-Americans.

I Am a Japanese-American Woman

21   Woman. The last piece of my identity. It has been easier by far for me to know myself in Japan and to see my place in America than it has been to accept my line of connection with my own mother. She was my dark self, a figure in whom I thought I saw all that I feared most in myself. Growing into womanhood and looking for some model of strength, I turned away from her. Of course, I could not find what I sought. I was looking for a black feminist or a white feminist. My mother is neither white nor black.

22   My mother is a woman who speaks with her life as much as with her tongue. I think of her with her own mother. Grandmother had Parkinson's disease and it had

frozen her gait and set her fingers, tongue, and feet jerking and trembling in a terrible dance. My aunts and uncles wanted her to be able to live in her own home. They fed her, bathed her, dressed her, awoke at midnight to take her for one last trip to the bathroom. My aunts (her daughters-in-law) did most of the care, but my mother went from New Hampshire to California each summer to spend a month living with Grandmother, because she wanted to and because she wanted to give my aunts at least a small rest. During those hot summer days, mother lay on the couch watching the television or reading, cooking foods that Grandmother liked, and speaking little. Grandmother thrived under her care.

23   The time finally came when it was too dangerous for Grandmother to live alone. My relatives kept finding her on the floor beside her bed when they went to wake her in the mornings. My mother flew to California to help clean the house and make arrangements for Grandmother to enter a local nursing home. On her last day at home, while Grandmother was sitting in her big, overstuffed armchair, hair combed and wearing a green summer dress, my mother went to her and knelt at her feet. "Here, Mamma," she said. "I've polished your shoes." She lifted Grandmother's legs and helped her into the shiny black shoes. My Grandmother looked down and smiled slightly. She left her house walking, supported by her children, carrying her pocketbook, and wearing her polished black shoes. "Look, Mamma," my mom had said, kneeling. "I've polished your shoes."

24   Just the other day, my mother came to Boston to visit. She had recently lost a lot of weight and was pleased with her new shape and her feeling of good health. "Look at me, Kes," she exclaimed, turning toward me, front and back, as naked as the day she was born. I saw her small breasts and the wide, brown scar, belly button to pubic hair, that marked her because my brother and I were both born by Caesarean section. Her hips were small. I was not a large baby, but there was so little room for me in her that when she was carrying me she could not even begin to bend over toward the floor. She hated it, she said.

25   "Don't I look good? Don't you think I look good?"

26   I looked at my mother, smiling and as happy as she, thinking of all the times I have seen her naked. I have seen both my parents naked throughout my life, as they have seen me. From childhood through adulthood we've had our naked moments, sharing baths, idle conversations picked up as we moved between showers and closets, hurried moments at the beginning of days, quiet moments at the end of days.

27   I know this to be Japanese, this ease with the physical, and it makes me think of an old Japanese folk song. A young nursemaid, a fifteen-year-old girl, is singing a lullaby to a baby who is strapped to her back. The nursemaid has been sent as a servant to a place far from her own home. "We're the beggars," she says, "and they are the nice people. Nice people wear fine sashes. Nice clothes."

If I should drop dead,
bury me by the roadside!
I'll give a flower
to everyone who passes.

What kind of flower?
The cam-cam-camellia [tsun-tsun-tsubaki]
watered by Heaven:
alms water.

28   The nursemaid is the intersection of heaven and earth, the intersection of the human, the natural world, the body, and the soul. In this song, with clear eyes, she looks steadily at life, which is sometimes so very terrible and sad. I think of her while looking at my mother, who is standing on the red and purple carpet before me, laughing, without any clothes.

29   I am my mother's daughter. And I am myself.

30   I am a Japanese-American woman.

EXERCISE 7

Discussion and Critical Thinking

1. What is the unit?

2. What is the principle by which the unit is divided?

3. What are the parts of the unit?

4. What does Noda say about the people who stereotyped her?

5. What are some of the characteristics of the stereotyping she encountered?

6. Simply, what does it mean to the author to say she is Japanese-American (paragraph 18)?

7. As a Japanese-American woman, what is her legacy, what values are passed down in her family?

Student Writers

When Selin Simon received her assignment to write a paper of analysis by division on something that was a physical unit, she naturally turned to another class she was taking: biology. From that broad subject she chose *skin* as an organ of the human body.

Her Writing Process Worksheet shows how her writing evolved from idea to final draft. Notice that her clustering as part of Stage One was truly an exploration. She was able to use that information as she slightly reorganized her thoughts in her topic sentence and her well-structured outline. To conserve space here, the freewriting and the rough draft marked for revision have been omitted. The balance of her worksheet has been lengthened for you to be able to see her other work in its entirety.

You will find a full-size blank worksheet on page 6, which can be photocopied, filled in, and submitted with each assignment if your instructor directs you to do so.

Writing Process Worksheet

Title Skin

Name Selin Simon   Due Date Friday, June 2, 8 a.m.

ASSIGNMENT

In the space below, write whatever you need to know about your assignment, including information about the topic, audience, pattern of writing, length, whether to include a rough draft or revised drafts, and whether your paper must be typed.

Write a paragraph of analysis by division about a physical object. Discuss the parts and explain how the object functions. It might be a machine or an organ of the human body. You should assume that your audience knows very little about your subject. Submit this completed worksheet, a rough draft marked for revision, and a typed final draft of about 200 to 250 words.

STAGE ONE

Explore   Freewrite, brainstorm (list), cluster, or take notes as directed by your instructor. Use the back of this page or separate paper if you need more space.

Clustering

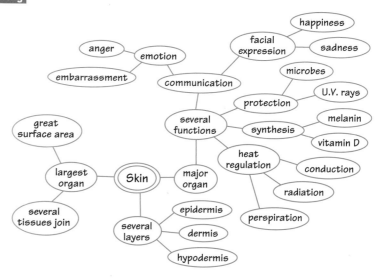

STAGE TWO

Organize   Write a topic sentence or thesis; label the subject and the treatment parts.

The skin is composed of three different layers: epidermis, dermis, and
   subject   treatment

hypodermis.

Write an outline or an outline alternative.

    I. Epidermis
       A. Superficial layer
       B. Protective role
          1. Against organisms

2. Against water
3. Against ultraviolet rays
C. Synthesizes melanin for skin color
D. Synthesizes keratin
1. For bone growth
2. For bone maintenance
II. Dermis
A. Deeper and thicker than epidermis
B. Nourishes tissue
C. Provides for elasticity
D. Cools body with its sweat glands
III. Hypodermis
A. Innermost layer
B. Binds dermis to underlying organs
C. Has fat
1. For insulation
2. For shock absorption
3. For energy

STAGE THREE **Write** On separate paper, write and then revise your paragraph or essay as many times as necessary for **c**oherence, **l**anguage (usage, tone, and diction), **u**nity, **e**mphasis, **s**upport, and **s**entences (**CLUESS**). Read your work aloud to hear and correct any grammatical errors or awkward-sounding sentences.

Edit any problems in fundamentals, such as **c**apitalization, **o**missions, **p**unctuation, and **s**pelling (**COPS**).

[Paragraph structure is indicated with underlining and annotation.]

Final Draft

Skin
Selin Simon

Skin is technically an organ because it is composed of several kinds of tissues that are structurally arranged to function together. In fact, it is the largest organ of the body, occupying approximately 19,344 sq. cm. of surface area. It is composed of three different layers: epidermis, dermis, and hypodermis. Epidermis is the superficial layer of the skin. It plays an important protective role as a physical barrier to organisms, water, and ultraviolet rays. It also helps in the synthesis of melanin, which gives color to the skin, and of keratin, which, as a skin protein with vitamin D, helps in the metabolism of calcium and phosphate in bones. Dermis, deeper and thicker than epidermis, contains blood vessels and nerves to nourish the tissue and elastic fibers that provide skin flexibility. Moreover, it contains glands that produce sweat, thereby helping to regulate the body temperature. Hypodermis, the innermost layer, binds the dermis to the underlying organs. Composed of adipose tissues storing fat, it serves as an insulator, a shock absorber, and a source of energy. These layers work together to perform the major functions of the skin.

EXERCISE 8

Discussion and Critical Thinking

1. What adjustment did Simon make as she moved from her cluster in Stage One to her outline in Stage Two?

2. Circle the words that support the idea of function. You will be looking for words such as *function* and *help*.

Ben Franklin, Renaissance Man

ALLISON UDELL

Benjamin Franklin is one of the most famous and best-loved figures in American history. Those with only a superficial knowledge of him may think of his experiment with electricity by using the kite and the key and of his printing of Poor Richard's Almanac, *but his accomplishments extended well beyond those. According to Allison Udell, Benjamin Franklin was our country's first and greatest Renaissance man.*

1   Anyone who doesn't know the definition of *Renaissance man* would do well to study Benjamin Franklin. When he died in 1790 at the age of eighty-four, he was acknowledged for greatness in numerous areas of endeavor. In short, he was a multigenius, and each area of his accomplishments registered more than almost any other person of his time. Putting the areas together made him probably the greatest Renaissance man that America has ever produced.

2   One side to Benjamin Franklin was his education. Although he went to school for only two years, he was curious, energetic, and determined. He educated himself through reading, and learned six languages. By the age of twenty-four he opened his own print shop, first publishing a newspaper, then *Poor Richard's Almanac*. His *Autobiography* is still read for its brilliance of style.

3   He was also an inventor and a scientist. Almost everyone has heard of his experimentation with electricity, and of his invention of bifocals, the lightning rod, the Franklin stove, and the school chair. Other scholars still read his studies of ocean currents and soil improvement. In his middle years he was elected to the prestigious group of scientists called the Royal Society of London.

4   His work in planning took two directions. In urban life, he planned a hospital, a library, the postal system, the city police, and the city fire department. These institutions were successful and became the models for other cities and even countries. The second direction occurred just before the War of Independence during the French and Indian War. At the request of people in government, he designed strategy that was enormously successful.

5   His involvement as a patriot during the War of Independence was still another area of accomplishment. An acknowledged leader, he signed the Declaration of Independence and later helped write the Constitution, which he also signed. During the war, he served the patriot colonists as the Minister to France. There he arranged for financial and military support from the French, helped negotiate the Treaty of Peace with Great Britain, and now is regarded as probably the most successful diplomat in the history of America.

6   *Renaissance man* means "one who is an expert in several different areas of endeavor." For these more than two hundred years we have found no better example than Benjamin Franklin.

EXERCISE 9   ## Discussion and Critical Thinking

1. What is the unit?

2. What is the principle by which that unit functions? In other words, what does the unit do or represent from this perspective? Write the answer here, and circle the passage that states or suggests the principle.

3. What are the parts that make up the unit according to this principle? Underline them in the text, and write them here.

4. What is the order of the parts (time, space, emphasis, or a combination)?

Topics for Writing Analysis by Division

You will find a blank writing process worksheet on page 6, which can be photocopied, filled in, and submitted with each assignment if your instructor directs you to do so.

Reading-Related Topics

"The Family and Its Parts"

1. Use this definition of a family, with its parts, as a pattern for writing about a family you are familiar with.

2. Use this definition of a family as a model for discussing why a particular family is dysfunctional.

3. Evaluate this definition and discuss how it might be broadened to include parents who are not married or other people with uncommon living arrangements.

"The Zones of the Sea"

4. Using this paragraph as a model, write about something else that has layers, such as a bone, a tree, the atmosphere, the earth, or a snowfield. Consult an encyclopedia or a textbook for specific information on your topic.

5. Use the information and framework of this paragraph to expand on the zones of life, plants, and animals found in different locations.

"Low Wages, High Skills"

6. Write a summary of this essay, stressing the transferable skills Newman uses to judge the nature of the work at Burger Barn. Consider making your writing a two-part response (see Chapter 1).

7. Write a paragraph or an essay about a low-wage job you once held. Explain how you learned and practiced transferable skills that helped you in other jobs or other life situations. The skills will be the parts of your analysis by division. Some of these skills may be the same as or similar to the ones discussed by Newman. Using references to her essay may enrich your own.

"Growing Up Asian in America"

8. Write an analysis by division in which you discuss your own or someone else's origin. *Origin* here may mean ethnic group, class, or region (part of the country, such as South, Midwest, East).

9. Using this essay as a model, write about who you are and why by referring to your parents and grandparents. How are they different from each other and from yourself? More important, what have you learned or inherited from them?

"Skin"

10. Using this paragraph as a model, write about how a particular unit functions. Consider another organ of the human body such as the heart, liver, or lungs. You may also consider other subjects, including a piece of technology such as a computer, a printer, or a scanner.

"Ben Franklin, Renaissance Man"

11. Pick another outstanding figure from history and write about him or her by using analysis by division. Think in terms of special characteristics—roles, abilities, achievements—that can be supported by references to accomplishments. Your subject need not come from a history course; he or she can come from any field. Consult your textbook(s) and library sources.

12. Write about someone else's multiple achievements, such as those mentioned in the previous suggestion.

General Topics

Some of the following topics are too broad for a short writing assignment and should be narrowed. For example, the general "a wedding ceremony" could be narrowed to the particular: "José and María's wedding ceremony." Your focused topic should then be divided into parts and analyzed.

13. A machine such as an automobile, a computer, a camera

14. A city administration, a governmental agency, a school board, a student council

15. A ceremony—wedding, graduation

16. A holiday celebration, a pep rally, a sales convention, a religious revival

17. An offensive team in football (any team in any game)

18. A family, a relationship, a gang, a club, a sorority, a fraternity

19. An album, a performance, a song, a singer, an actor, a musical group, a musical instrument

20. A movie, a television program, a video game

21. Any well-known person—athlete, politician, criminal, writer

Cross-Curricular Topics

22. Consider the units of material in a class you are taking or have taken. Each unit has its parts: a musical composition in a music appreciation class, a short story in an English class, an organ such as a heart in a biology class, a government in a political science class, a management team in a business class, a family in a sociology class, a painting in an art history class, a teacher or student in an education class, and so on. Select one unit, consult your textbook(s), talk to your instructor(s), and follow the procedure for writing an analysis by division. Credit your sources, and use quotation marks around material you borrow.

Career-Related Topics

23. Explain how the parts of a product function as a unit.

24. Explain how each of several qualities of a specific person—such as his or her intelligence, sincerity, knowledgeability, ability to communicate, manner, attitude, and appearance—makes that individual an effective salesperson, manager, or employee.

25. Explain how the demands or requirements for a particular job represent a comprehensive picture of that job.

26. Explain how the aspects of a particular service (such as friendly, competent, punctual, confidential) work together in a satisfactory manner.

Writer's Guidelines: Analysis by Division

Almost anything can be analyzed by division—for example, how the parts of the ear work in hearing, how the parts of the eye work in seeing, or how the parts of the heart work in pumping blood throughout the body. Subjects such as these are all approached with the same systematic procedure.

1. This is the procedure.

   • *Step 1.*   Begin with something that is a unit.

   • *Step 2.*   State the principle by which that unit functions.

- *Step 3.* Divide the unit into parts according to the principle.
- *Step 4.* Discuss each of the parts in relation to the unit.

2. This is the way you might apply that procedure to a good boss.

- Unit   Manager
- Principle of function   Effective as a leader
- Parts based on the principle   Fair, intelligent, stable, competent in the field
- Discussion   Consider each part in relation to the person's effectiveness as a manager.

3. This is how a basic outline of analysis by division might look.

Thesis: To be effective as a leader, a manager needs specific qualities.

   I. Fairness
   II. Intelligence
   III. Stablility
   IV. Competence in the field

4. Use the writing process.

- Write and then revise your paragraph or essay as many times as necessary for coherence, language (usage, tone, and diction), unity, emphasis, support, and sentences (**CLUESS**).

- Read your work aloud to hear and correct any grammatical errors or awkward-sounding sentences.

- Edit any problems in fundamentals, such as capitalization, omissions, punctuation, and spelling (**COPS**).

Chapter

11

Process Analysis:
Writing About Doing

FLOW OF WRITING

"I can't understand how anyone can write without rewriting everything over and over again."

LEO TOLSTOY

Writing Process Analysis   191
  Two Types of Process Analysis: Directive and
    Informative   191
  Working with Stages   191
  Basic Forms   192
  Combined Forms   193
  Useful Prewriting Procedure   193
Practicing Patterns of Process Analysis   193
Connecting Reading and Writing   196
  Professional Writers   196
  "The Birth of an Island"   196
  "Zen and the Art of Pomegranate Eating"   197
  "How Low-Balling Works on Your Mind"   199
  "Fast, Sleek, and Shiny: Using the Internet to Help Buy
    New Cars"   201
  Student Writers   203
  "Sabzi Polo Mahi" (demonstration with stages)   206
  "What's Behind a Brilliant Smile"   207
Topics for Writing Process Analysis   209
Writer's Guidelines   210

THE QUIGMANS   by Buddy Hickerson

The Babysitter Channel.

B. Hickerson, copyright Los Angeles Times Syndicate. Reprinted by permission.

Writing Process Analysis

If you have any doubt about how frequently we use process analysis, just think about how many times you have heard people say, "How do you do it?" or "How is [was] it done?" Even when you are not hearing those questions, you are posing them yourself when you need to make something, cook a meal, assemble an item, take some medicine, repair something, or figure out what happened. In your college classes, you may have to discover how osmosis occurs, how a rock changes form, how a mountain was formed, how a battle was won, or how a bill goes through the legislature.

If you need to explain how to do something or how something was (is) done, you will engage in **process analysis.** You will break down your topic into stages, explaining each so that your reader can duplicate or understand the process.

Two Types of Process Analysis: Directive and Informative

The questions How do I do it? and How is (was) it done? will lead you into two different types of process analysis—directive and informative.

Directive process analysis explains how to do something. As the name suggests, it gives directions for the reader to follow. It says, for example, "Read me, and you can bake a pie (tune up your car, read a book critically, write an essay, take some medicine)." Because it is presented directly to the reader, it usually addresses the reader as "you," or it implies the "you" by saying something such as "First [you] purchase a large pumpkin, and then [you]. . . ." In the same way, this textbook addresses you or implies "you" because it is a long how-to-do-it (directive process analysis) statement.

Informative process analysis explains how something was (is) done by giving data (information). Whereas the directive process analysis tells you what to do in the future, the informative process analysis tells you what has occurred or what is occurring. If it is something in nature, such as the formation of a mountain, you can read and understand the process by which it emerged. In this type of process analysis, you do not tell the reader what to do; therefore, you will seldom use the words *you* or *your*.

Working with Stages

Preparation or Background

In the first stage of directive process analysis, list the materials or equipment needed for the process and discuss the necessary setup arrangements. For some topics, this stage will also provide technical terms and definitions. The degree to which this stage is detailed will depend on both the subject itself and the expected knowledge and experience of the projected audience.

Informative process analysis may begin with background or context rather than with preparation. For example, a statement explaining how mountains form might begin with a description of a flat portion of the earth made up of plates that are arranged like a jigsaw puzzle.

Steps or Sequence

The actual process will be presented here. Each step or sequence must be explained clearly and directly, and phrased to accommodate the audience. The language, especially in directive process analysis, is likely to be simple and concise; however, avoid dropping words such as *and, a, an, the,* and *of,* and thereby lapsing into "recipe language." The steps may be accompanied by explanations about why certain procedures are necessary and how not following directions carefully can lead to trouble.

Order

The order will usually be chronological (time based) in some sense. Certain transitional words are commonly used to promote coherence: *first, second, third, then, soon, now, next, finally, at last, therefore, consequently,* and—especially for informative process analysis—words used to show the passage of time such as hours, days of the week, and so on.

Basic Forms

Consider using this form for the directive process (with topics such as how to cook something or how to fix something).

How to Prepare Spring Rolls

   I. Preparation
      A. Suitable cooking area
      B. Utensils, equipment
      C. Spring roll wrappers
      D. Vegetables, sauce
  II. Steps
      A. Season vegetables
      B. Wrap vegetables
      C. Fold wrappers
      D. Deep-fry rolls
      E. Serve rolls with sauce

Consider using this form for the informative process (with topics such as how a volcano functions or how a battle was won).

How Coal Is Formed

   I. Background or context
      A. Accumulation of land plants
      B. Bacterial action
      C. Muck formation
  II. Sequence
      A. Lignite from pressure
      B. Bituminous from deep burial and heat
      C. Anthracite from metamorphic conditions

Combined Forms

Combination process analysis occurs when directive process analysis and informative process analysis are blended, usually when the writer personalizes the account. For example, if I tell you from a detached view how to write a research paper, my writing is directive process analysis, but if I tell you how I once wrote a research paper and give you the details in an informative account, then you may very well learn enough so that you can duplicate what I did. Thus, you would be both informed and instructed. Often the personalized account is more interesting to the general reader, but if, for example, you need to assemble a toy the night before your child's birthday you just want information.

Many assignments are done as a personalized account. A paper about planting radish seeds may be informative—but uninspiring. However, a paper about the time you helped your grandpa plant his spring garden (giving all the details) may be informative, directive, and entertaining. It is often the cultural framework provided by personal experience that transforms a pedestrian directive account into something memorable. That's why some instructors ask their students to explain how to do something within the context of experience.

Useful Prewriting Procedure

All the strategies of freewriting, brainstorming, and clustering can be useful in writing a process analysis. However, if you already know your subject well, you can simply make two lists, one headed *Preparation* or *Background* and the other *Steps* or *Sequence*. Then jot down ideas for each. After you have finished with your listing, you can delete parts, combine parts, and rearrange parts for better order. That editing of your lists will lead directly to a formal outline you can use in Stage Two of the writing process. Following is an example of listing for the topic of how to prepare spring rolls.

Preparation	*Steps*
stainless steel bowl	slice and mix vegetables
deep-fry pan	add sauce to vegetables
spoon	beat eggs
damp cloth	place wrappers on damp cloth
spring roll wrappers	add 2 to 3 tablespoons of vegetables per wrapper
eggs	fold and seal wrapper with egg
sauce	freeze for later or deep-fry immediately
cabbage	serve with sweet-and-sour sauce
celery	
carrots	
bean sprouts	

Practicing Patterns of Process Analysis

A definite pattern underlies a process analysis. In some presentations, such as with merchandise to be assembled, the content reads as mechanically as an outline, and no reader objects. In other presentations, such as your typical college assignments, the writing should be well-developed and interesting. Regardless of the form you use or the audience you anticipate, keep in mind that in process analysis the pattern will provide a foundation for the content.

EXERCISE 1

Completing Patterns of Directive Process Analysis

Using directive process analysis, fill in the blanks to complete this pattern for "writing an essay."

    I. Preparation (Prewriting)

       A. Understand assignment

       B. _____

       C. Write the controlling idea

       D. _____

    II. Steps (Writing)

       A. Draft

       B. _____

       C. _____

EXERCISE 2

Completing Patterns of Directive Process Analysis

Using directive process analysis, fill in the blanks to complete this pattern for "planting a lawn."

    I. Preparation

       A. Obtain tools

       B. Obtain _____

       C. Obtain _____

       D. Obtain _____

    II. Steps

       A. _____

       B. _____

       C. Cultivate soil

       D. _____

222222222222222

E. Cover seed with mulch and fertilizer

F. _____

EXERCISE 3

Completing Patterns of Informative Process Analysis

Using informative process analysis, fill in the blanks to complete this pattern. Use a topic from a subject you are studying or have studied and explain some phenomenon such as how a volcano, a hurricane, a tidal wave, cell division, tree growth, a common cold, a sunburn, a blister, a headache, chapped lips, land erosion, quicksand, a bill going through legislature, jury trial, baseball curving, or the like occurs.

I. Background

A. _____

B. _____

C. _____

II. Sequence

A. _____

B. _____

C. _____

D. _____

EXERCISE 4

Completing Patterns of Informative Process Analysis

Using informative process analysis, fill in the blanks to complete this pattern. Use a topic from a subject you are studying or have studied and explain some phenomenon such as how a volcano, a hurricane, a tidal wave, cell division, tree growth, a common cold, a sunburn, a blister, a headache, chapped lips, land erosion, quicksand, a bill going through legislature, jury trial, baseball curving, or the like occurs.

I. Background

A. _____

B. _____

C. _____

II. Sequence

A. _____

B. _____

C. _____

D. _____

Connecting Reading and Writing

Professional Writers

The Birth of an Island
RACHEL CARSON

We usually think of birth in a biological sense, but Rachel Carson describes a different kind—a geological birth. It requires no coach, no midwife, no obstetrician. But unless you can live for thousands or even millions of years, you cannot witness the whole process. Nevertheless, it is a process, and it can be described in steps.

The birth of a volcanic island is an event marked by prolonged and violent travail: the forces of the earth striving to create, and all the forces of the sea opposing. The sea floor, where an island begins, is probably nowhere more than about fifty miles thick—a thin covering over the vast bulk of the earth. In it are deep cracks and fissures, the results of unequal cooling and shrinkage in past ages. Along such lines of weakness the molten lava from the earth's interior presses up and finally bursts forth into the sea. But a submarine volcano is different from a terrestrial eruption, where lava, molten rocks, gases, and other ejecta are hurled into the air through an open crater. Here on the bottom of the ocean the volcano has resisting it all the weight of the ocean water above it. Despite the immense pressure of, it may be, two or three miles of sea water, the new volcanic cone builds upward toward the surface in flow after flow of lava. Once within reach of the waves, its soft ash and tuff are violently attacked, and for a long period the potential island may remain a shoal, unable to emerge. But, eventually, in new eruptions, the cone is pushed up into the air and a rampart against the attacks of the waves is built of hardened lava.

EXERCISE 5 | **Discussion and Critical Thinking**

1. What type of process analysis (informative or directive) is used here?

2. To what type of audience (well informed, moderately informed, or poorly informed on the topic) does Carson direct this selection?

3. What is the prevailing tone of this material (objective, humorous, reverent, argumentative, cautionary, playful, ironic, ridiculing)?

4. Underline the sentence that shows at which point the setup material ends and the informative process begins.

5. How many stages are there? Number them in the margin of the text.

6. Underline the five transitional terms that are used.

Zen and the Art of Pomegranate Eating

WILL BROCK

In a Zen experience, one loses oneself in the object of attention, and the person becomes one with that object. Freelance writer Will Brock suggests that eating a pomegranate, done properly, can be such an engaging experience. The procedure and the eating are one with the person, combining therapy, nutrition, and human senses. But he admits it doesn't have to be that way. You can just eat a pomegranate—if you dare.

1   The pomegranate is to me the most beautiful and remarkable of fruits, but it is not eaten by many people, perhaps because they do not know how to do so.

2   First I have a word of caution. Properly done, eating a pomegranate will take more time than, say, eating a banana. You don't have to be a Zen master, but you should have patience, and you should enjoy the doing of something well, for which you will be richly rewarded.

3   For this endeavor, you need only a pomegranate, a sharp knife, and a receptive mind. Selecting a ripe pomegranate is not an easy task. Here we deal only with likelihood. There are no absolutes in pomegranate selection. The big ones tend to have larger grains and to be juicier. The color, which varies from deep red to a pale greenish-yellow, may not be a good indicator, though the deep red usually indicates ripeness and, of course, looks better in the fruit bowl. Another factor is the skin. Only about an eighth of an inch thick, it sometimes splits in the late warm days of autumn as the grains swell with succulence. Through those splits, you can determine both the color and size of the grains. You will want the deep red and large ones.

4   Now you are ready to open the fruit. First, use your sharp knife to slice off the stem nub and blossom tube. Then make a polar incision through the skin, tracing the circumference of the fruit. Next, ever so carefully, place the knife in the cut marks and work it back and forth to split the pomegranate initially into two lumpy parts and then, by making two lateral slashes, into

four or more. Each part of the pomegranate will have its own sections in-side, each draped by white membranes like curtains. Finally, pull these membranes off as you would remove wrappers from candies. Inside you will find clusters of translucent grains as red as precious rubies from Man-dalay, each with a seed in the middle. Each grain will be lightly attached to a rind which winds around, skeletonlike, throughout the fruit.

5   Gently remove the grains from the rind and eat them according to your inclinations, perhaps according to the degree of your hunger. Pomegranate connoisseurs crunch the seeds as part of the feast. At your best, in your most reflective, patient mood, you will likely eat the fruit one grain at a time, savoring the experience by prolonging it. Yet, at your worst, succumb-ing to ravenous appetite, you may dislodge a fistful of grains and cram them into your mouth. To heighten the joy of the palate, some eaters will remove the grains and place them in a container for chilling in the refrigerator be-fore the eating. Keep in mind that along with the rich color of the grains and the sweet, tangy flavor comes a juice that can stain clothing, carpets, and furniture.

6   You will find the intricacies of preparing the pomegranate and the risk of collateral damage more than compensated by the pleasure afforded by the eating. Whether you regard the whole ritual as Zen or secular makes no dif-ference. The result is the same. Eating a pomegranate properly can satisfy both stomach and spirit. Moreover, with advances in the healing arts, don't be surprised if someday when you call your doctor for a sedative to ease the stress from this troubled world, the prescriptive advice is to "eat a pome-granate and call me in the morning."

EXERCISE 6   ## Discussion and Critical Thinking

1. What preparation is necessary?

2. What other form of writing is well represented in this essay?

3. How many steps are included?

4. Draw a vertical line in the margin to identify the preparation.

5. Underline the words that provide coherence in paragraph 4.

6. What in the food industry is the opposite of eating pomegranates ritualistically?

7. What other foods are sometimes consumed in a manner as ritualistic as the one discussed here?

How Low-Balling Works on Your Mind

SHARON S. BREHM, SAUL M. KASSIN, AND STEVEN FEIN

You may not have heard the term low-balling, *but if you have spent much time shopping for cars on site, you're probably familiar with the technique. In their textbook* Social Psychology, *Sharon S. Brehm, Saul M. Kassin, and Steven Fein analyze why people are taken in by this simple technique.*

1   Perhaps the most unscrupulous of all compliance techniques is *low-balling,* which is based on the "start small" idea.

2   Imagine yourself in the following situation. You're at a local automobile dealership. After some negotiation, the salesperson offers a great price on the car of your choice. You cast aside other considerations and shake hands on the deal; and as the salesperson goes off to "write it up," you begin to feel the thrill of owning the car of your dreams. Absorbed in fantasy, you are interrupted by the sudden return of the salesperson. "I'm sorry," he says. "The manager would not approve the sale. We have to raise the price by another $450. I'm afraid that's the best we can do." As the victim of an all-too-common trick known as low-balling, you are now faced with a tough decision. On the one hand, you're wild about the car. You've already enjoyed the pleasure of thinking it's yours; and the more you think about it, the better it looks. On the other hand, you don't want to pay more than you bargained for, and you have an uneasy feeling in the pit of your stomach that you're being duped. What do you do?

3   Salespeople who use this tactic are betting that you'll go ahead with the purchase despite the added cost. If the way research participants behave is any indication, they are often right. In one study, experimenters phoned introductory psychology students and asked if they would be willing to participate in a study for extra credit. Some were told up front that the session would begin at the uncivilized hour of 7 A.M. Knowing that, only 31 percent volunteered. But other participants were low-balled. Only *after* they agreed to participate did the experimenter inform them of the 7 A.M. starting time. Would that be okay? Whether or not it was, the procedure achieved its objective—the sign-up rate rose to 56 percent.

4   Low-balling is an interesting technique. Surely, once the low ball has been thrown, many recipients suspect that they were misled. Yet they go along. Why? The reason appears to be based on the psychology of commitment. Once people make a particular decision, they justify it to themselves by thinking of all its positive aspects. As they get increasingly committed to a course of action, they grow more resistant to changing their mind, even if the initial reasons for the action have been changed or withdrawn entirely. In the automobile dealership scenario, you might very well have decided to purchase the car because of the price. But then you would have thought about its sleek appearance, the leather interior, the sun roof, and the CD player. By the time you learned that the price would be more than you'd bargained for, it was too late—you were already hooked.

5   Low-balling also produced another form of commitment. When people do not suspect duplicity, they feel a nagging sense of unfulfilled obligation to the person with whom they negotiated. Thus, even though the salesperson was unable to complete the original deal, you might feel obligated to buy anyway, having already agreed to make the purchase. This commitment to the other person may account

for why low-balling works better when the second request is made by the same person than by someone else.

6   Being able to resist the pressure of compliance rests, first and foremost, on being vigilant. If a stranger hands you a gift and then launches into a sales pitch, you should recognize the tactic for what it is and not feel indebted by the norm of reciprocity. And if you strike a deal with a salesperson who later reneges on the terms, you should be aware that you're being thrown a low ball. Indeed, that is exactly what happened to one of the authors of this book. After a full Saturday afternoon of careful negotiation at a local car dealer, he and his wife finally came to terms on a price. Minutes later, however, the salesman returned with the news that the manager would not approve the deal. The cost of an air conditioner, which was to be included, would have to be added on. Familiar with the research, the author turned to his wife and exclaimed, "It's a trick; they're low-balling us!" Realizing what was happening, she became furious, went straight to the manager, and made such a scene in front of other customers that he backed down and honored the original deal.

7   What happened in this instance? Why did recognizing the attempted manipulation produce such anger and resistance? As this story illustrates, compliance techniques work smoothly only if they are hidden from view. The problem is not only that they are attempts to influence us but that they are deceptive.

EXERCISE 7   ## Discussion and Critical Thinking

1. Is this essay informative or directive?

2. What is the purpose of informing readers about low-balling?

3. What are the basic steps to low-balling?

    1. _____

    2. _____

4. What two forms of writing are used in paragraphs 2 and 5?

5. If paragraph 2 is concerned with how low-balling works, and paragraphs 4 and 5 are concerned with why it works so well, what is paragraph 6 concerned with?

6. How do salespersons for health clubs and gyms often use low-balling?

Fast, Sleek, and Shiny: Using the Internet to Help Buy New Cars

PRESTON GRALLA

In this essay adapted from The Complete Idiot's Guide to Online Shopping, *Preston Gralla presents down-to-earth advice on how to shop for a car on the Internet and how to avoid getting taken. Cars are only one of the many products featured in this book. This essay includes a discussion on how to buy a car and finance it, all through using your computer.*

1   Whether or not you plan to buy your new car over the Internet, make sure to do your prepurchase research online. Use the Internet to help decide which car to buy and to get the best deal possible from the dealer—or even to buy online. You'll get pleasure not only out of saving money, but also out of seeing car dealers gnash their teeth over the thought of how you were able to bargain them down to very little profit. There goes their trip to Cancun this year!

Step 1: Go Online to Research and Find Your Dream Machine

2   Your clunker has finally spit the last bit of black exhaust out of its tail pipe, and it's time to get a new dream machine. But what should you get? Should it be a super-macho, ego-enhancing sports utility vehicle? A trusty family station wagon? A hell-bent-for-leather sports car? Or just a plain old sedan? And which is the best model for your needs and pocketbook?

3   You'll find many sites to help you narrow down what you should buy. If you're not quite sure what you want, immediately head to the GTE Superpages Consumer Guide at www.consumerguide.com. Use the Interactive Car Finder—think of it as the "Complete Idiot's Guide to Choosing a Car." You select the kind of car (compact, sports utility vehicle, and so on), the price range, fuel economy, and features such as air-conditioning, and voilà—you'll get a list of cars that match your pocketbook and the features you want.

4   Car aficionados who want to know what the insiders think about cars should head to the online site of *Car and Driver* magazine at www.caranddriver.com. As you might guess, many, many more car sites online can help you decide which car to buy, and many also offer car reviews. I'd suggest that after you use the Consumer Guide and the *Car and Driver* site to narrow down your choices, you check in with as many sites as possible to get their takes on the cars of your dreams. One excellent site is Edmund's at www.edmunds.com.

Step 2: Get Ready to Bargain—Find Out the True Dealer Invoice Price

5   Sure, the last time you bought a car, you probably thought you got a pretty good deal. The dealer may even have said something like, "You got the best of me that time, Buddy." Guess what? The dealer was lying. (What a shock!) You got taken for a ride. The dealer got the best of you. And it's not because you're not smart enough to drive a good bargain. It's because the dealer knows exactly how much the car cost, and you don't have a clue. Sticker price, retail price, rebates, MSRP (what in the world does that stand for, anyway?—oh, yeah, Manufacturer's Suggested Retail Price), the costs of all the "extras" (such as doors and an engine, it seems)—trying to put it all together makes your head start to spin. The whole pricing scheme for new cars is designed to confuse you. So what's a poor car buyer to do?

6   It's simple. Head to the Internet and find out exactly how much the dealer paid for the car (the dealer cost) to the dollar—including all the extras. When you're armed with that information, you can force the dealer to meet your price—or you can walk out the door and find a dealer who *will* meet it.

7   You can find the dealer invoice price at a number of sites on the Internet. But head to www.edmunds.com to get the best lowdown. It not only provides the most comprehensive information but also explains the ins and outs of car pricing, which is arcane enough to have confused a medieval philosopher. This site offers excellent how-to-buy articles as well.

8   The MSRP is the car's base price that the dealer will quote to you. Never, ever, ever pay that price for a car. If you do, the dealer and salesperson will be breaking out the champagne after you leave.

9   Find the invoice price. That's the most important number on the page. It's the price that the dealer pays the manufacturer for the base model of the car, without any extras. That's the number you're going to use when you start to bargain. Do you notice something interesting about the MSRP price and the invoice price? I thought you did; you have sharp eyes. The MSRP (sticker) price is several thousand dollars higher than the invoice price. So if a dealer knocks off $1,000 from the sticker price, you might think you're getting a good deal, but you're not—the dealer is still making out like a bandit.

10   Next, check out the invoice prices of the options you want—things like automatic transmission, a luggage rack, and a stereo. As you can see, each item has an MSRP as well as an invoice price, which means that the dealer is making money by marking up all your extras as well. The dealer also has to pay a destination charge, which can be $500 or more. Edmund's reports that charge as well.

11   To figure out the true cost to the dealer of the car you're interested in buying, do this math:

Invoice Price + Invoice Price of Extras + Destination Charge = Dealer's Costs

Now here's a strange fact: Even if you pay only the dealer's invoice costs for a car, in most instances the dealer *still* makes a profit. That's because of a little-known program called the "Dealer Hold Back." The dealer hold back is a percentage of the MSRP of the vehicle, including all extras. When a dealer sells a vehicle, the manufacturer sends the dealer a check based on the hold back percentage and the MSRP of the vehicle. Domestic carmakers typically pay a 3 percent dealer hold back, and foreign makers often pay 2 percent. But the amount varies from manufacturer to manufacturer. Edmund's tells you the dealer hold back for the car you're buying.

12   Let's take an example. Say the MSRP of the car and extras you've bought is $25,000, and the dealer hold back is 3 percent. According to this formula, after you buy the car, the manufacturer sends the dealer a check for $750. Therefore, even if the dealer sells the car at invoice price, he or she is still making money. Note, though, that the money doesn't go to your salesperson—it goes straight to the dealer. So, no salesperson is going to agree to give you a car at invoice price.

13   Another way to save hundreds or even thousands of dollars when buying your next car is to find out what kinds of rebates and dealer incentives are available, on the www.edmunds.com site, just click on Incentives and Rebates.

Step 3: Psyching Out Your Dealer with Information You Got Online

14   So now you know the invoice cost of the car you want to buy, the destination charge, the dealer hold back, and any kinds of rebates and incentives available on the car you're interested in buying. What next? Let's say you want to buy a car from a dealer, not through the Web.

15   First, print everything out directly from the Web so that you have a sheaf of papers you can refer to. When you walk in with the printouts, the dealer will realize you know your business and won't try to pull a fast one on you. (Well, the dealer may *try* to pull a fast one, but won't be able to succeed.)

16   Also, figure out on a sheet of paper how much you're willing to pay for the car. Base it on the invoice price of the car. You should hold the line at 3 percent over invoice cost if you can—and if the car isn't very popular or new models are about to come out, try to get it at 2 percent or less over invoice cost. If you're looking to buy a hot-selling car, you might not be able to drive such a hard bargain, but it's worth a try. For cars that aren't moving fast, you should be able to bargain down to your 2 percent or 3 percent figure. Also, when figuring the price you should pay for a car, be sure to consider any rebates or incentives.

EXERCISE 8

Discussion and Critical Thinking

1. Is this essay informative or directive?

2. Sometimes the preparation stage is implied or assumed. To shop on the Internet, of course, a person needs a computer with Internet access. Does Gralla specify the preparation stage, or does he simply make an assumption about the computer and Internet access?

3. Gralla gives much information, but he also is writing with a particular audience in mind. Just what does he expect the reader to know about computers?

4. How many steps does Gralla use?

5. In tone (the way the author regards the subject and the reader), what distinguishes this essay from many directive process analysis statements?

Student Writers

Many of us reclaim our ethnic origin at our New Year as we celebrate by eating a meal that is intended to bring us happiness, peace, and prosperity for the next twelve months. For Maysim Mondegaran, the meal is Sabzi Polo Mahi, and each phase of the preparation and cooking is done with care and feeling. Reading her paragraph will make you hungry. Notice how she includes both directive and informative elements.

Mondegaran's Writing Process Worksheet shows you how her writing evolved from idea to final draft. To conserve space here, the free writing and the rough drafts marked for revision have been omitted. The balance of her worksheet has been lengthened for you to be able to see her other work in its entirety.

You will find a full-size blank worksheet on page 6, which can be photocopied, filled in, and submitted with each assignment if your instructor directs you to do so.

Writing Process Worksheet

Title Sabzi Polo Mahi

Name Maysim Mondegaran   Due Date Thursday, March 9, 11 a.m.

ASSIGNMENT   In the space below, write whatever you need to know about your assignment, including information about the topic, audience, pattern of writing, length, whether to include a rough draft or revised drafts, and whether your paper must be typed.

Write a long paragraph (about 300 words) about a holiday meal, dish, or ritual. Explain how something is done, and place your subject within a cultural framework. Submit your completed Writing Process Worksheet, a rough draft marked for revision, and a typed final draft.

STAGE ONE   Explore   Freewrite, brainstorm (list), cluster, or take notes as directed by your instructor. Use the back of this page or separate paper if you need more space.

Clustering

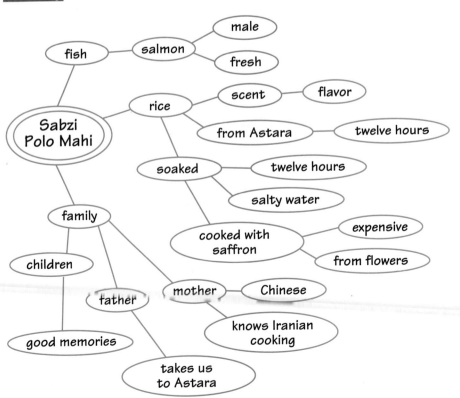

Listing

Preparation	Steps
Get fish	Cook fish
Find good rice	Cook rice
Get vegetables	Cook vegetables
Butter	Season
Saffron	

STAGE TWO

Organize   Write a topic sentence or thesis; label the subject and the treatment parts.

In order to make Sabzi Polo Mahi properly, you need to know how to pick
                    subject   treatment
the right ingredients and how to cook them.

Write an outline or an outline alternative.

I. Preparation
  A. Picking the fish
    1. Fresh
    2. Salmon
    3. Male
  B. Picking the rice
    1. Appearance
    2. Scent
    3. Where found
  C. Vegetables
    1. Leafy
    2. Garlic
  D. Picking the seasoning
    1. Butter
    2. Saffron
II. Cooking
  A. Fish
    1. Baked
    2. Flaky, white, juicy
  B. Rice
    1. Soaked for twelve hours
    2. Boiled
    3. Drained
  C. Vegetables
    1. Stir-fried
    2. Steamed with rice
  D. Seasoning
    1. Butter
    2. Saffron

STAGE THREE

Write   On separate paper, write and then revise your paragraph or essay as many times as necessary for **c**oherence, **l**anguage (usage, tone, and diction), **u**nity, **e**mphasis, **s**upport, and **s**entences (**CLUESS**). Read your work aloud to hear and correct any grammatical errors or awkward-sounding sentences.

Edit any problems in fundamentals, such as **c**apitalization, **o**missions, **p**unctuation, and **s**pelling (**COPS**).

Final Draft

Sabzi Polo Mahi

Maysim Mondegaran

Transitional words are circled

Preparation

Steps

1

2

3

4

5

6

In Iran, families like to celebrate the beginning of the New Year each spring with a meal called Sabzi Polo Mahi, which means fish with vegetables and rice. The preparation is as important as the cooking. In order to make this special dish, one must (first) know how to pick the right fish, rice, vegetables, and seasoning. A fresh fish is required for the main part of the meal. It should have shiny bright eyes, nonsticky light grey skin, and pale pink meat. Salmon is recommended. In my family we usually buy one that weighs about eight kilograms. It is best to pick a male fish because the meat is more tender and tastier than that of the female. The males always have several black round dots that look like moles on top of their heads. (Second) the rice must be excellent, and the best is grown in Astara, in Northern Iran. Although my mother is Chinese, she likes to follow the Iranian custom, so every now and then we drive six hours to Astara and buy several big bags of Astarian rice with long grains and a good scent. To get the best results, the rice must be soaked in salty water for twelve hours before it is cooked. When the rice is almost through soaking, the fish is placed in the oven preheated to about 350 degrees and baked. (From time to time) it should be basted. The baking time will vary, depending on the size of the fish. It is done when the flesh is white and flaky but still moist. (While) the fish is cooking, the rice should be boiled and drained. (While) the rice is draining, the vegetables should be prepared. The vegetables (in my family, mainly leafy green ones like spinach or parsley) are chopped fine and stir-fried with garlic. (After) the vegetables are done, they should be combined with the rice and steamed so that the flavors mix. (After) they are steamed, melted butter and ground saffron mixed with a few drops of water are poured over them. Saffron has a bright yellow color and a rich flavor. My mother buys it raw and grinds it specially for this meal. (At last) the Sabzi Polo Mahi is ready—the succulent baked fish and the mixture of spicy green vegetables and rice, (now) made vibrant yellow and flavorful by the saffron and butter. This is one of my favorite dishes, and I look forward to the next time when I can have it with my family.

EXERCISE 9

Discussion and Critical Thinking

1. What type of process analysis (informative, directive, or both) is used?

2. To what kind of audience (well informed, moderately informed, or poorly informed on the topic) does the writer direct this selection?

3. What is the prevailing tone (objective, humorous, reverent, argumentative, cautionary, playful, ironic, ridiculing) of this material?

What's Behind a Brilliant Smile

CHANYA WERNER

Student Chanya Werner is not an orthodontist yet, but her workplace experience and college studies inform her about the procedure for performing orthodontic treatment.

1   Some genetically blessed people are born with the complete potential for a brilliant smile. They have the right genes, which means teeth all aligned and proportioned on precision jaws. Others have noticeable irregularities. Those are the ones who may need help from an orthodontist. The treatment obtained there may take up to four years—two years with braces and two more years with retainers to keep the teeth in place. For one to acquire that brilliant smile, many procedures are involved, and the patient's cooperation is essential.

2   A doctor visit is the initial movement toward the goal. Usually the consultation requires an examination of the teeth and a discussion of treatment fee. After the patient fully acknowledges the entire course of treatment, the doctor will take some x-rays of the teeth, which she will use to determine the problems and steps required to correct them. Some pictures of the teeth and the patient's face will also be taken as a record prior to starting treatment. The next part of the preparation involves making a model of the teeth. This can be done by mixing the Algenate with water. The Algenate is a powder-like material that will harden after coming in contact with the heat inside the mouth. The Algenate paste will be applied on the upper and lower trays that are used to impress the teeth. After this phase, the patient will be scheduled to come back in two to three weeks.

3   By the time the patient comes back for the second appointment, the doctor will already have in mind what to do with the teeth. She will explain the problems to the patient and make some suggestions as she sees appropriate. For example, if extracting some teeth will yield the optimum result of treatment, she will explain so at this time. At the end of the discussion, the doctor will begin to place the appliances on the teeth, starting with brackets. These tiny individual brackets serve as a means of fastening the arch wire that is used to move the teeth. The brackets are bonded on the teeth by cement called Fuji. This next step can sometimes be taken care of on the third visit; however, it can also be done on the second visit. The doctor will put a band, a metal ring that is used to hold on parts of the braces, on each of the molar teeth. The same idea applies here; the bands will be chemically glued onto the molar teeth. When everything is dried up, an arch wire will be placed on the brackets, inserted into the bands, and held in place by pieces of elastics. From now until the end of the treatment, the patient will be asked to come back once a month for adjustment. If the patient comes regularly as scheduled, the treatment will be completed within two years. On the other hand, if the patient misses the appointment frequently, then the course of treatment will take longer than expected.

4   Toward the end of the course of treatment, after both the doctor and her patient are absolutely satisfied with the position of the teeth, the doctor will begin the process called debanding, removing braces and cleaning off the excess glue on the surface of the teeth. At the end of debanding, the doctor will take a final set of x-rays and photos of the teeth for the record. Another impression of the teeth will be taken in order to make a set of retainers. The patient is given two choices of retainers—a clear retainer and a wire retainer. As the name implies, the material used for the clear retainer is clear plastic, constructed from the impression and, therefore, shaped like teeth. With a wire retainer, usually done by the dental art lab, the doctor has the choice to make any further adjustment. It has a wire stretched from one end of the arch to the other end, and the wire is attached to a piece of hard plastic-like material. Most patients will preferably choose to wear the clear retainers. A three-month check-up will be scheduled for the next year and six months thereafter. Occasionally, the patient may be asked to come back in a year for a check-up. When the doctor feels certain that the teeth would not move back to their original positions, she will ask the patient to stop wearing retainers, placing an end to the orthodontic treatment.

5   The cost to have an orthodontic treatment is fairly expensive, considering that it is a cosmetic treatment. The price can range from three to five thousand dollars. However, under certain circumstances, such as open-bite or under-bite cases, the treatment becomes necessary. The goal of a successful treatment is reached by making a patient content with his or her smile.

EXERCISE 10   ## Discussion and Critical Thinking

1. Is this essay mainly directive or informative?

2. Circle the thesis.

3. Underline and annotate the preparation and steps.

Topics for Writing Process Analysis

You will find a blank Writing Process Worksheet on page 6, which can be photocopied, filled in, and submitted if your instructor directs you to do so.

Reading-Related Topics

"The Birth of an Island"

1. Using this reading selection as a model, write about the formation of some other geological feature: an alluvial plain, a beach, a mountain lake, a mountain, a desert, or a delta. Consult a science textbook or encyclopedia for basic information.

"Zen and the Art of Pomegranate Eating"

2. Using this essay as a model, write a paragraph or an essay on preparing and/or eating a food. Consider these: watermelon, coconut, pineapple, sushi.

"How Low-Balling Works on Your Mind"

3. Using information from this excerpt, describe how and why you or someone you know was tricked by the low-balling technique.

4. Using this article as a model, write about another technique, such as "bait and switch," for selling products.

"Fast, Sleek, and Shiny: Using the Internet to Help Buy New Cars"

5. Using this essay as a model, explain how to purchase another item on the Internet.

6. Using the steps presented in this essay, write an informative process analysis in which you explain how you shopped for a car or a similar product on the Internet.

"Sabzi Polo Mahi"

7. Write about a special holiday dish prepared in your home. Follow Mondegaran's lead in discussing the source and quality of the foods, and try to capture her warmth of tone. Try to blend the directive and informative approaches.

"What's Behind a Brilliant Smile"

8. Using this essay as a model, write a paragraph or an essay about a workplace procedure you are familiar with.

General Topics

Write a paragraph or an essay on one of the following topics. Although they are phrased as directive topics, each can be transformed into a how-it-was-done informative topic by personalizing it and explaining stage by stage how you, someone else, or a group did something. For example, you could write either a directive process analysis about how to deal with an obnoxious person or an informative process analysis about how you or someone else dealt with an obnoxious person. Keep in mind that the two types of process analysis are often blended, especially in the personal approach. Many of these topics will be more interesting to you and your readers if they are personalized.

Most of the topics require some narrowing to be treated in a paragraph. For example, writing about playing baseball is too broad; writing about how to throw a curve ball may be manageable.

9. How to end a relationship without hurting someone's feelings

10. How to pass a test for a driver's license

11. How to get a job at _____

12. How to eat _____

13. How to perform a magic trick

14. How to repair _____

15. How to assemble _____

16. How to learn about another culture

17. How to approach someone you would like to know better

Cross-Curricular Topics

18. Write a paragraph or an essay about a procedure you follow in your college work in a science (chemistry, biology, geology) lab. You may explain how to analyze a rock, how to dissect something, how to operate something, how to perform an experiment.

19. Write a paragraph or an essay about how to do something in an activity or performance class, such as drama, physical education, art, or music.

Career-Related Topics

20. Explain how to display, package, sell, or demonstrate a product.

21. Explain how to perform a service or to repair or install a product.

22. Explain the procedure for operating a machine, a computer, a piece of equipment, or another device.

23. Explain how to manufacture, construct, or cook something.

Writer's Guidelines: Process Analysis

1. Decide whether your process analysis is mainly directive or informative, and be appropriately consistent in using pronouns and other designations.

   • For directive process analysis, use the second person, addressing the reader as *you*. The *you* may be understood, even if it is not written.

   • For informative process analysis, use the first person, speaking as *I* or *we*, or the third person, speaking about the subject as *he, she, it,* or *they,* or by name.

2. Consider using these basic forms.

Directive	Informative
I. Preparation	I. Background
A.	A.
B.	B.
II. Steps	II. Sequence
A.	A.
B.	B.
C.	C.

3. Listing is a useful prewriting activity for process analysis. Begin with the Roman-numeral headings indicated in number 2.

4. The order of a process analysis will usually be chronological (time based) in some sense. Certain transitional words are commonly used to promote coherence: *first, second, third, then, soon, now, next, finally, at last, therefore,* and *consequently.*

5. Use the writing process.

- Write and then revise your paragraph or essay as many times as necessary for coherence, language (usage, tone, and diction), unity, emphasis, support, and sentences (**CLUESS**).

- Read your work aloud to hear and correct any grammatical errors or awkward-sounding sentences.

- Edit any problems in fundamentals, such as capitalization, omissions, punctuation, and spelling (**COPS**).

Cause and Effect: Determining Reasons and Outcomes

FLOW OF WRITING

Writing Cause and Effect   213
   Exploring and Organizing   213
   Composing a Topic Sentence or a Thesis   213
   Writing an Outline   214
   Considering Kinds of Causes and Effects   214
   Evaluating the Importance of Sequence   215
   **Introducing Ideas and Working with
    Patterns   215**
Practicing Patterns of Cause and Effect   216
Connecting Reading and Writing   218
   Professional Writers   218
   "What Happens to Steroid Studs?"   218
   "Family Heroes and Role Models"   219
   "The Purposes of Shopping"   220
   "Living in Sin"   221
   "The Seven Sustainable Wonders of the World"   226
   Student Writers   228
   "More Than the Classroom" (demonstration with
    stages)   230
   "Getting High and Living Low"   230
Topics for Writing Cause and Effect   232
Writer's Guidelines   234

*"Originality doesn't mean saying what no
one has ever said before; it means saying
exactly what you think yourself."*

JAMES STEPHEN

THE QUIGMANS   by **Buddy Hickerson**

"Francine! Have you seen my flare gun?"

B. Hickerson, copyright Los Angeles Times Syndicate. Reprinted by
permission.

Writing Cause and Effect

Causes and effects deal with reasons and results; they are sometimes discussed together and sometimes separately. Like other forms of writing to explain, writing about causes and effects is based on natural thought processes. The shortest, and arguably the most provocative, poem in the English language—"I/Why?"—is posed by an anonymous author about cause. Children are preoccupied with delightful and often exasperating "why" questions. Daily we encounter all kinds of causes and effects. The same subject may raise questions of both kinds.

> The car won't start. Why? *(cause)*
> The car won't start. What now? *(effect)*

At school, from the biology lab to the political science classroom, and at work, from maintaining relationships to changing procedures, causes and effects are found everywhere.

Exploring and Organizing

One useful approach to developing a cause-and-effect analysis is listing. Write down the event, situation, or trend you are concerned about. Then on the left side, list the causes, and on the right side, list the effects. From them you will select the main causes or effects for your paragraph or essay. Here is an example.

Causes	Event, Situation, or Trend	Effects
Low self-esteem	Joining a gang	Life of crime
Drugs		Drug addiction
Tradition		Surrogate family relationship
Fear		Protection
Surrogate family		Ostracism
Protection		Restricted vocational opportunities
Neighborhood status		

As you use prewriting techniques to explore your ideas, you need to decide whether your topic should mainly inform or mainly persuade. If you intend to inform, your tone should be coolly objective. If you intend to persuade, your tone should be subjective. In either case, you should take into account the views of your audience as you phrase your ideas. You should also take into account how much your audience understands about your topic and develop your ideas accordingly.

Composing a Topic Sentence or a Thesis

Now that you have listed your ideas under causes and effects, you are ready to focus on the causes, on the effects, or, occasionally, on both.

Your controlling idea, the topic sentence or the thesis, might be one of the causes: "It is not just chance; people have reasons for joining gangs." Later, as you use the idea, you would rephrase it to make it less mechanical, allowing it to become part of the flow of your discussion. If you wanted to personalize the work—thereby probably making it more interesting—you could write about someone you know who joined a gang. You could use the same basic framework, the main causes, to indicate why this particular person joined a gang.

Writing an Outline

Your selection of a controlling idea takes you to the next writing phase: completing an outline or outline alternative. There you need to

- consider kinds of causes and effects.
- evaluate the importance of sequence.
- introduce ideas and work with patterns.

In its most basic form, your outline, derived mainly from points in your listing, might look like one of the following:

Paragraph of causes
Topic sentence: It is not just chance; people have reasons for joining gangs.
   I. Low self-esteem (cause 1)
   II. Surrogate family (cause 2)
   III. Protection (cause 3)

Essay of effects
Thesis: One is not a gang member without consequences.
   I. Restricted vocational opportunities (effect 1)
   II. Life of crime (effect 2)
   III. Drug addiction (effect 3)
   IV. Ostracism from mainstream society (effect 4)

Considering Kinds of Causes and Effects

Causes and effects can be primary or secondary, immediate or remote.

Primary or Secondary

Primary means "major," and **secondary** means "minor." A primary cause may be sufficient to bring about the situation (subject). For example, infidelity may be a primary (and possibly sufficient by itself) cause of divorce for some people but not for others, who regard it as secondary. Or if country X is attacked by country Y, the attack itself, as a primary cause, may be sufficient to bring on a declaration of war. But a diplomatic blunder regarding visas for workers may be of secondary importance, and though significant, it is certainly not enough to start a war over.

Immediate or Remote

Causes and effects often occur at a distance in time or place from the situation. The immediate effect of sulfur in the atmosphere may be atmospheric pollution, but the long-range, or remote, effect may be acid rain and the loss of species. The immediate cause of the greenhouse effect may be the depletion of the ozone layer, whereas the long-range, or remote, cause is the use of CFCs (commonly called Freon, which is found in such items as Styrofoam cups). Even more remote, the ultimate cause may be the people who use the products containing Freon. Your purpose will determine the causes and effects appropriate for your essay.

Evaluating the Importance of Sequence

The sequence in which events occur(red) may or may not be significant. When you are dealing with several sequential events, determine whether the sequence of events has causal connections; that is, does one event bring about another?

Consider this sequence of events: Joe's parents get divorced, and Joe joins a gang. We know that one reason for joining a gang is to gain family companionship. Therefore, we may conclude that Joe joined the gang to satisfy his need for family companionship, which he lost when his parents divorced. But if we do so, we may have reached a wrong conclusion, because Joe's joining the gang after the family breakup does not necessarily mean that the two events are related. Maybe Joe joined the gang because of drug dependency, low self-esteem, or a need for protection.

In each case, examine the connections. To assume that one event is *caused* by another just because it *follows* the other is a logical error called a ***post hoc*** (**"after this"**) **fallacy.** An economic depression may occur after a president takes office, but that does not necessarily mean the depression was caused by the new administration. It might have occurred anyway, perhaps in an even more severe form.

Order

The order of the causes and effects you discuss in your paper may be based on time, space, emphasis, or a combination.

- *Time:* If one stage leads to another, as in a discussion of the causes and effects of upper atmospheric pollution, your paper would be organized best by time.
- *Space:* In some instances, causes and effects are best organized by their relation in space. For example, the causes of an economic recession could be discussed in terms of local factors, regional factors, national factors, and international factors.
- *Emphasis:* Some causes and effects may be more important than others. For instance, if some causes of divorce are primary (perhaps infidelity and physical abuse) and others are secondary (such as annoying habits and laziness), a paper about divorce could present the secondary causes first, and then move on to primary causes to emphasize the latter as more important.

In some situations, two or more factors (such as time and emphasis) may be linked; in that case, select the order that best fits what you are trying to say, or combine orders.

Introducing Ideas and Working with Patterns

In presenting your controlling idea—probably near the beginning for a paragraph or in an introductory paragraph for an essay—you will almost certainly want to perform two functions:

1. *Discuss your subject.* For example, if you are writing about the causes or effects of divorce, begin with a statement about divorce as a subject.

2. *Indicate whether you will concentrate on causes or effects or combine them.* That indication should be made clear early in the paper. Concentrating on one—causes or effects—does not mean you will not mention the other; it only means you will

emphasize one of them. You can bring attention to your main concern(s)—causes, effects, or a combination—by repeating key words such as *cause, reason, effect, result, consequence,* and *outcome.*

The most likely pattern for your work is one of those shown in Figure 12.1. These patterns may look familiar to you. We discussed similar patterns in Chapters 4 and 5.

Figure 12.1
Patterns for Paragraph and Essay

For Paragraph

| Subject and Topic Sentence |
| Cause or Effect 1 |
| Cause or Effect 2 |
| Cause or Effect 3 |
| Reflection on Topic Sentence |

For Essay

| Subject and Thesis |
| Topic Sentence |
| Cause or Effect 1 |
| Topic Sentence |
| Cause or Effect 2 |
| Topic Sentence |
| Cause or Effect 3 |
| Conclusion |

Practicing Patterns of Cause and Effect

A detailed outline and your subsequent writing may include a combination of causes and effects, but almost always either causes *or* effects will be emphasized and will provide the main structure of your paper. Whether you are writing a basic outline for an assignment outside of class without a significant time constraint or you are writing in class under the pressure of time, you will always have a chance to jot down prewriting lists and a simple outline.

EXERCISE 1   ## Completing Patterns of Cause and Effect

Complete the following cluster on teenage parenthood. Then select three primary causes or three primary effects that could be used in writing a paragraph or an essay on this topic.

Causes   Effects

Primary causes   Primary effects

1. _____   1. _____

2. _____   2. _____

3. _____   3. _____

EXERCISE 2

Completing Patterns of Cause and Effect

Complete the following cluster on a bad diet. Then select three primary causes or three primary effects that could be used in writing a paragraph or an essay on this topic.

Causes   Effects

Primary causes   Primary effects

1. _____   1. _____

2. _____   2. _____

3. _____   3. _____

EXERCISE 3

Completing a Pattern of Cause

Fill in the blanks to complete this outline of cause.

Causes for dropping out of high school

  I. Family tradition

 II. _____

III. _____

IV. _____

| EXERCISE 4 | Completing a Pattern of Effect |

Fill in the blanks to complete this outline of effect.

Effects of becoming a parent

    I. Pride

   II. _____

  III. _____

  IV. _____

Connecting Reading and Writing

Professional Writers

What Happens to Steroid Studs?

ANASTASIA TOUFEXIS

Young men take steroids because they want the Rambo look. But they get much more than muscles in their steroids effects package—and what they get, no one wants.

But the drug-enhanced physiques are a hazardous bargain. Steroids can cause temporary acne and balding, upset hormonal production, and damage the heart and kidneys. Doctors suspect they may contribute to liver cancer and atherosclerosis. Teens, who are already undergoing physical and psychological stresses, may run some enhanced risks. The drugs can stunt growth by accelerating bone maturation. Physicians also speculate that the chemicals may compromise youngsters' still developing reproductive systems. Steroid users have experienced a shrinking of the testicles and impotence. Dr. Richard Dominguez, a sports specialist in suburban Chicago, starts his lectures to youths with a surefire attention grabber: "You want to shrink your balls? Take steroids." Just as worrisome is the threat to mental health. Drug users are prone to moodiness, depression, irritability and what are known as "roid rages." Ex-user Darren Allen Chamberlain, 26, of Pasadena, California, describes himself as an "easy-going guy" before picking up steroids at age 16. Then he turned into a teen Terminator.

EXERCISE 5

Discussion and Critical Thinking

1. What is the subject (a situation, circumstances, or trend) at the center of this discussion?

2. Which sentence most clearly indicates the author's intention of writing about cause, effect, or a combination?

3. Is this passage concerned most with causes, effects, or a combination of both?

4. Underline the sentences that indicate the specific effects.

5. In what order (time, space, emphasis, or a combination) are the parts presented?

6. Is the author's purpose mainly to inform or to persuade?

Family Heroes and Role Models

MARIAN WRIGHT EDELMAN

We are not born with values. We do not survive and prosper by ourselves. Any person who has succeeded should be able to look back and recognize those who provided a heritage through example and instruction. Marian Wright Edelman pays homage to her family and community for what her generation of black children received. This paragraph comes from her book The Measure of Our Success: A Letter to My Children and Yours *(1992).*

The legacies that parents and church and teachers left to my generation of Black children were priceless but not material: a living faith reflected in daily service, the discipline of hard work and stick-to-it-ness, and a capacity to struggle in the face of adversity. Giving up and "burnout" were not part of the language of my elders—you got up every morning and you did what you had to do and you got up every time you fell down and tried as many times as you had to to get it done right. They had grit. They valued family life, family rituals, and tried to be and to expose us to good role models. Role models were of two kinds: those who achieved in the outside world (like Marian Anderson, my namesake) and those who didn't have a whole lot of education or fancy clothes but who taught us by the special grace of their lives the message of Christ and Tolstoy and Gandhi and Heschel and Dorothy Day and Romero and King that the Kingdom of God was within—in what you are, not what you have. I still hope I can be half as good as Black church and community elders like Miz Lucy McQueen, Miz Tee Kelly, and Miz Kate Winston, extraordinary women who were kind and patient and loving with children and others and who, when I went to Spelman College, sent me shoeboxes with chicken and biscuits and greasy dollar bills.

EXERCISE 6

Discussion and Critical Thinking

1. What is the subject at the center of this discussion?

2. Which sentence most clearly indicates why black children of Edelman's generation developed a good set of values?

3. What were the three main legacies, or causes, of the value system of Edelman's generation?

4. What kinds of role models were causal factors?

5. Give two examples of role models (one of each kind) offered by Edelman.

The Purposes of Shopping

PHYLLIS ROSE

Author of scholarly books, university professor, book reviewer, and free-lance writer—Phyllis Rose is also a student of shopping. To her, shopping is not just something we do to acquire the necessities or a few frills. This brief paragraph comes from her essay "Shopping and Other Spiritual Adventures."

It is a misunderstanding of the American retail store to think we go there necessarily to buy. Some of us shop. There's a difference. Shopping has many purposes, the least interesting of which is to acquire new articles. We shop to cheer ourselves up. We shop to practice decision-making. We shop to be useful and productive members of our class and society. We shop to remind ourselves how much is available to us. We shop to remind ourselves how much is to be striven for. We shop to assert our superiority to the material objects that spread themselves before us.

EXERCISE 7

Discussion and Critical Thinking

1. Is the emphasis mainly causes or effects?

2. Underline the topic sentence.

3. Place numbers in the text to indicate the reasons (causes) for shopping.

4. According to Phyllis Rose, what is the difference between buying and shopping?

5. Which of these reasons for shopping apply to you? What place does shopping occupy in your life? What are the items you buy and what are the items you shop for?

6. Does the paragraph convey an implied philosophy or value system?

Living in Sin

DAYANA YOCHIM

A specialist in business writing, Dayana Yochim works for The Motley Fool, a highly successful, unconventional investment company. You can find her musings on Fool.com, in The Motley Fool's syndicated newspaper column, as well as on television, on radio, and in various magazines. She is the author of The Motley Fool's Guide to Couples & Cash *and the co-author of* The Motley Fool Personal Finance Workbook.

1   Living in sin and loving it? Why not? The legal rights and financial rewards available to unmarried couples have come a long way. In fact, more than ever, these unions resemble those of the officially hitched. But even if your goldfish get along and your mother is cool with your cohabitation, affairs of the heart are riddled with financial issues. Here's what you need to know about shacking up.

2   It's not just about splitting your rent or doubling the size of your CD collection. Shacking up outside of the official bonds of matrimony is becoming more like marriage in a lot of ways.

3   The rights and privileges for those who lack the license from their county courthouse have come a long way. Everyone from employers to warehouse clubs are catching up to the times, recognizing the modern reality of unmarried love and offering couples the same perks afforded to the wedded set. These days, you and your sweetheart can get health insurance, discounted dental care, and even the family rate at the local gym—saving thousands of dollars, even while your nagging relatives *tsk tsk* your unofficial union.

4   But before you uncork the champagne, consider the following: 55 percent of different-sex cohabitants marry within five years of moving in together; but a whopping 40 percent break up within that same time period. About 10 percent remain in an unmarried relationship five years or longer, according to "Cohabitation in the United States," a study published in the *Annual Review of Sociology.*

5   We know that impersonal, black-and-white statistics don't capture the depth of your commitment to one another. Unmarried couples who live together face almost all of the same—and sometimes more—administrative money issues as their matrimonially bound counterparts.

6   Forgive us for interrupting your giddy state of unwedded bliss with a dose of relationship reality. However, there are some things to consider if you and your love muffin share a roof.

But Mom, *Everybody's* Doing It

7   It's true. More and more people are shacking up outside of the official bonds of marriage. There are 5.5 million unmarried partner households in the U.S., including gay and straight couples, according to year 2000 U.S. Census statistics. That's up 72 percent from 1990. And it's not just twosomes in those households. Census data released last week reveals that unmarried couples who live together are just as likely as their married counterparts to raise children in the household.

8   Living in sin is not so thoroughly modern a trend as you might think. Look no further than your multiplex or library for examples. Goldie Hawn and Kurt Russell have been together since 1984, with no marriage plans. Author Simone de Beauvoir and philosopher Jean-Paul Sartre shacked up for nearly 50 years, until Sartre's death.

9   Even grams and gramps are getting in on the action. (Think Spencer Tracy and Katharine Hepburn.) Census data shows that the number of households containing an unmarried man and woman, at least one of whom is over age 65, grew 60 percent to 203,000 households between 1990 and 2000.

Why Not Tie the Knot?

10   In the case of Hepburn and Tracy, his faith prevented him from divorcing his wife. Others who choose the unmarried life don't believe in the institution, don't feel it's necessary in their relationship, or, in the case of same-sex partners, don't have the option of official marriage.

11   But for many, the marriage workaround is a financial necessity. Widowed senior citizens, in particular, risk losing pension benefits if they tie the knot a second, third, or Liz Taylor-like seventh time.

12   For many, living together is simply a prelude to taking that next step down the aisle. About 75 percent of cohabitants (about 6.2 million people) say they plan to marry their partners, according to the "Cohabitation in the United States" study. In fact, the majority of couples marrying today have lived together first (53 percent of women's first marriages are preceded by cohabitation).

Shack Up and Save Money!

13   What perks—including financial plusses—can unmarried partners expect? These days, live-ins are eligible for:

- "Family" memberships at Costco, AAA, and the local YMCA.
- Continued access to pension and health insurance for senior citizens.
- Perks that were previously off limits to domestic partners—health, disability and life insurance, pension benefits, family leave, and mental-health counseling.
- A live, live-in dishwasher with an already established personal CD collection!
- A break on homeowners and car insurance from some insurance companies, such as State Farm and Allstate.
- Official recognition of your relationship. According to a recent article in *The Wall Street Journal*, unmarried couples can make their bond official through a domestic-partner registry in about 60 municipalities or states.
- Price breaks at rental car businesses.

Then there's the downside:

- Less access to insurance price breaks. Though it is improving, depending on which you believe, anywhere from 25 percent to 90 percent of employers offer domestic partner benefits.
- More complicated legal rights. Inheritance and retirement benefits, and medical decisions are not automatically granted to life partners, as they are to married life partners.
- No ring? No acknowledgment—at least as a bona fide member of the family by his great-grandmother.
- No right to alimony if you split. Recently, however, the American Law Institute suggested that this standard should be changed.
- Difficulty choosing an appropriate term of endearment when introducing your partner. According to "Unmarried to Each Other: The Essential Guide to Living Together as an Unmarried Partner," the top three introductions are "partner," "boyfriend/girlfriend," and "significant other." The overly descriptive term "lover" is No. 8 on the list.
- Uncle Sam considers you single in terms of income taxes. So, you'll be paying the piper on your own salary, in addition to paying taxes on the value of perks afforded to you by an employer.

Making It Official

14   Though many of the same estate planning and medical directive rights are available to unmarried couples, the difference is they don't happen automatically. You've got to fill out the paperwork to make your wishes recognized in the eyes of the law.

15   Trust us; it can get ugly without the necessary legal documents. Thankfully, it doesn't take much to put a few safeguards in place, and you can go on, skipping through life, with that smile your sweetie loves so much.

16   First, complete these important documents:

- **Your will (last will and testament).** You can get this from an attorney, or opt for preprinted, fill-in-the-blank forms—though make sure they are up to date and conform to the laws of your state.
- **A living will (advance medical directive).** Available free at virtually every hospital in the nation.
- **Durable and medical power of attorney (health-care proxy).** See a lawyer for this.

17   As you're filling out the paperwork, make your heirs apparent. Update all of your beneficiary information—everything from your 401(k), 403(b), pension, profit-sharing, IRAs, and insurance policies to your coveted bicentennial quarter collection. If children are part of the union (as they are in one in three unmarried households), these protections are that much more important. Lawyers recommend that unmarried couples sign an "acknowledgment of parenthood" or a paternity for additional legal protection, in the case of one parent's death or a breakup.

18   Other ownership issues arise when you make big purchases together—such as homes and cars. Discuss whether they will be jointly or individually owned/titled. And don't forget to let important people know where you keep your documents. There's only one thing worse than filling out a guy's tax forms, and that's doing it without access to his financial records.

19   Grim? Yes. Necessary? Afraid so.

Happily Ever After, Financially Speaking

20   Another thing that unwed unions have in common with official married ones is what makes them last. Communication and contingency planning—though far from romantic—are the keys to a happy financial coupling. When the money communication is good, the satisfaction rubs off in other areas of the relationship. (We're trying to keep this article G-rated, so you'll just have to take our word for it.)

21   Assuming your love will last forever can leave you in a world of financial hurt, should things not work out. Why not set yourselves up for success? The couples who shared their dirty little financial secrets with us in *Couples & Cash: How to Handle Money with Your Honey* all agreed: Communication is the key.

22   Yeah, we know. No surprise there. But just think about this: With money as one of the leading causes of breakups, make this one thing work, and your relationship has that much better a chance of succeeding.

23   If you're considering shacking up, or already do so on an informal basis, there are a lot of joint decisions to be made outside of whose couch you're going to keep. Consider some key money questions and get talking—together. WIFE.org (that stands for Women's Institute for Financial Education, though their advice is good for both genders) advises domestic partners to put things in writing in a "Living Together Agreement." Yeah, it may feel weird to do so, which is why you should write your drafts over a decent bottle of merlot!

24   With more and more perks available to the unwed, now's a great time to have a heart-to-heart about money in your relationship.

25   Oh, and one more piece of advice: Remember to screw the cap back on the toothpaste when you're done. Always.

States with Highest Percentages of Unmarried Cohabiting Partners (including same-sex and different-sex):

1. Vermont—highest percentage of unmarried couples living together

2. Alaska

3. Maine

4. Nevada

5. New Hampshire

6. New Mexico

7. Oregon

8. Arizona

9. Washington

10. Delaware

States with Lowest Percentages of Unmarried Cohabiting Partners (including same-sex and different-sex):

1. Alabama—lowest percentage in unmarrieds

2. Utah

3. Arkansas

4. Oklahoma

5. Kansas

6. Tennessee

7. North Dakota

8. Texas

9. Nebraska

10. Mississippi

Discussion and Critical Thinking

1. Is this essay more about causes or effects?

2. This essay also uses the form of comparison and contrast. Within that form, are causes or are effects more relevant?

3. What heading carries a list of effects?

4. How are effects related to suggestions of what to do?

5. Does Yochim take a position on the issue of living together?

6. Does your knowledge of experiences in living together match what Yochim says?

7. If you were writing this essay, would you add or subtract anything? If so, what?

8. This article was published on the Internet by The Motley Fool, a business group that sells advice and services in managing money. How is that circumstance reflected in the subject material?

The Seven Sustainable Wonders of the World

ALAN THEIN DURNING

Alan Thein Durning is the director of Northwest Environment Watch *in Seattle and author of* This Place on Earth *(1996). This essay first appeared in the* Utne Reader.

1   I've never seen any of the Seven Wonders of the World, and to tell you the truth I wouldn't really want to. To me, the real wonders are all the little things—little things that work, especially when they do it without hurting the earth. Here's my list of simple things that, though we take them for granted, are absolute wonders. These implements solve every-day problems so elegantly that everyone in the world today—and everyone who is likely to live in it the next century—could make use of them without Mother Nature's being any the worse for wear.

1. The Bicycle

2   The most thermodynamically efficient transportation device ever created and the most widely used private vehicle in the world, the bicycle lets you travel three times as far on a plateful of calories as you could walking. And they're 53 times more energy efficient—comparing food calories with gasoline calories—than the typical car. Not to mention the fact that they don't pollute the air, lead to oil spills (and oil wars), change the climate, send cities sprawling over the countryside, lock up half of urban space in roads and parking lots, or kill a quarter million people in traffic accidents each year.

3   The world doesn't yet have enough bikes for everybody to ride, but it's getting there quickly: Best estimates put the world's expanding fleet of two-wheelers at 850 million—double the number of autos. We Americans have no excuses on this count: We have more bikes per person than China, where they are the principal vehicle. We just don't ride them much.

2. The Ceiling Fan

4   Appropriate technology's answer to air conditioning, ceiling fans cool tens of millions of people in Asia and Africa. A fan over your bed brings relief in sweltering climes, as I've had plenty of time to reflect on during episodes of digestive turmoil in cheap tropical hotels.

5   Air conditioning, found in two-thirds of U.S. homes, is a juice hog and the bane of the stratospheric ozone layer because of its CFC coolants. Ceiling fans, on the other hand, are simple, durable, and repairable and take little energy to run.

3. The Clothesline

6   A few years ago, I read about an engineering laboratory that claimed it had all but perfected a microwave clothes dryer. The dryer, the story went, would get the moisture out of the wash with one-third the energy of a conventional unit and cause less wear and tear on the fabric.

7   I don't know if they ever got it on the market, but it struck me at the time that if simple wonders had a PR agent, there might have been a news story instead about the perfection of a solar clothes dryer. It takes few materials to manufacture, is safe

for kids, requires absolutely no electricity or fuel, and even gets people outdoors where they can talk to their neighbors.

4. The Telephone

8   The greatest innovation in human communications since Gutenberg's printing press, telephone systems are the only entry on my wonders list invented in this century, and—hype of the information age notwithstanding—I'll wager that they never lose ground to other communications technologies. Unlike fax machines, personal computers and computer networks, televisions, VCRs and camcorders, CD-ROMs, and all the other flotsam and jetsam of the information age, telephones are a simple extension of the most time-tested means of human communication: speech.

5. The Public Library

9   Public libraries are the most democratic institutions yet invented. Think of it! Equal access to information for any citizen who comes inside. A lifetime of learning, all free. Libraries foster community, too, by bringing people of different classes, races, and ages together in that endangered form of human habitat: non-commercial public space.

10 Although conceived without any ecological intention whatsoever, libraries are waste reduction at its best. Each library saves a forestful of trees by making thousands of personal copies of books and periodicals unnecessary. All that paper savings means huge reductions in energy use and water and air pollution, too. In principle, the library concept could be applied to other things—cameras and camcorders, tapes and CDs, cleaning equipment and extra dining chairs—further reducing the number of things our society needs without reducing people's access to them. The town of Takoma Park, Maryland, for example, has a tool library where people can check out a lawn mower, a ratchet set, or a sledgehammer.

6. The Interdepartmental Envelope

11 I don't know what they're really called: those old-fashioned slotted manila envelopes bound with a string and covered with lines for routing papers to one person after another. Whatever they're called, they put modern recycling to shame.

7. The Condom

12 It's a remarkable little device: highly effective, inexpensive, and portable. A few purist Greens might complain about disposability and excess packaging, but these objections are trivial considering the work the condom has to do—battling the scourge of AIDS and stabilizing the human population at a level the earth can comfortably support.

EXERCISE 9

Discussion and Critical Thinking

1. Are these wonders discussed mainly as causes or effects?

2. Briefly indicate the effects of each of Durning's seven wonders:

- the bicycle

- the ceiling fan

- the clothesline

- the telephone

- the public library

- the interdepartmental envelope

- the condom

3. What statements reveal the author's concern for the environment?

Student Writers

Responding to an assignment on a topic organized mainly around causes and effects, Richard Blaylock chose to write about the consequences of his becoming a college student. With much trepidation, at thirty-three he had enrolled in the evening program at a local community college. The reasons for his being there were multiple, and so, surprising to him, were the results.

Blaylock's Writing Process Worksheet shows how his writing evolved from idea to final draft. To conserve space here, the freewriting and the rough drafts marked for revision have been omitted. The balance of his worksheet has been lengthened for you to be able to see his other work in its entirety.

You will find a full-size blank worksheet on page 6, which can be photocopied, filled in, and submitted with each assignment if your instructor directs you to do so.

FLOW OF WRITING

Writing Process Worksheet

Title More Than the Classroom

Name Richard Blaylock   Due Date Tuesday, May 9, noon

ASSIGNMENT In the space below, write whatever you need to know about your assignment, including information about the topic, audience, pattern of writing, length, whether to include a rough draft or revised drafts, and whether your paper must be typed.

In a paragraph of 200 to 300 words, discuss the causes or effects of any new element in your life at any point. The element could be a relationship, death, health problem, marriage, college program, new job, or winning ticket in the lottery. Submit this completed worksheet, a rough draft marked for revision, and a typed final draft.

STAGE ONE

Explore   Freewrite, brainstorm (list), cluster, or take notes as directed by your instructor. Use the back of this page or separate paper if you need more space.

Listing

Causes	Event, Situation, or Trend	Effects
Boss's suggestion	My going to college	Family pride
Company pays		Wife inspired
My desire		Personal growth
Family support		More competitive at work
		Better pay
		Work scholarship
		Tired
		School friendships

STAGE TWO

Organize   Write a topic sentence or thesis; label the subject and the treatment parts.

<u>My decision to enroll in college night school</u> <u>would offer more benefits than I</u>
                subject   treatment
<u>could have imagined.</u>

Write an outline or an outline alternative.

  I. Effects on family
    A. Wife inspired
    B. Family proud
 II. Effects on me
    A. Learn usable skills
    B. More confident
    C. More curious
III. Effects at work
    A. In line for better pay
    B. Soon given new responsibilities
    C. Given new respect

STAGE THREE

Write   On separate paper, write and then revise your paragraph or essay as many times as necessary for **c**oherence, **l**anguage (usage, tone, and diction), **u**nity, **e**mphasis, **s**upport, and **s**entences (**CLUESS**). Read your work aloud to hear and correct any grammatical errors or awkward-sounding sentences.

Edit any problems in fundamentals, such as **c**apitalization, **o**missions, **p**unctuation, and **s**pelling (**COPS**).

More Than the Classroom
Richard Blaylock

"We think you would benefit from our work-study program," he said to me. He wasn't my high school counselor, and I wasn't 18. He was the division manager, and he had just offered to pay my expenses for attending a local community college. At 33, I was working for a large company in a dead-end job, dead-end because I wasn't qualified for any management positions. Naturally, I enrolled in college. More benefits than I expected were to follow. I had hardly started when the first response greeted me: my family was clearly proud. I heard my two kids in elementary school bragging about me to kids in the neighborhood. They even brought me some of their tough homework questions. My wife had lots of questions about college. We talked about taking a class together. Unlike me, she had been a good student in high school. Then I had had no interest in going on to college. Now I did, and one thing led to another. A geography class connected me with a geology class. A political science class moved me to subscribe to the Los Angeles Times. I became more curious about a variety of subjects, and I felt more confident in dealing with ideas. At work my supervisors started asking me to become more involved in ongoing projects and planning. By the time I had taken my second English class, I was writing reports with much more confidence and skill. Now, after receiving a good job review and being interviewed by my plant manager, I am in line for a promotion that I once though was beyond my reach. I had expected mainly a classroom. I found much more.

EXERCISE 10

Discussion and Critical Thinking

1. Is this an essay mainly of causes or effects?

2. Circle the topic sentence.

3. Underline each effect.

Getting High and Living Low

SERGIO RAMOS

Student Sergio Ramos writes about growing up in a school rife with illegal drugs. Ramos escaped drug free. Two of his friends were less fortunate.

1   The use of drugs and alcohol from grade school through high school has been a major concern in recent years. Myriads of young kids turn to stealing for the means of satisfying their addictions. The high school drop-out rate is at an all-time high across the nation, and one of the main causes is alcohol and drug

abuse. Most of the convicts in prison were locked up because of drug-related crimes. The repeated use of drugs and alcohol at an early age sets a pattern and leads to failure during adulthood; that's what happened to some of my close friends.

2   I had a friend named Gerardo who drank beer and smoked marijuana when he was in the fifth grade. He was influenced by his older brother Luis. The only thing that Gerardo talked about at school all day was that he could not wait to get home to smoke marijuana with his brother in their clubhouse. I lived next door, and I would usually go over to watch them get high. They constantly attempted to convince me to try it, but to their dismay, they always failed. Once it was time for Gerardo to do his homework, he would eagerly ask me for help. When Gerardo was sent to the store to buy items for his mother, he would usually steal the items and keep the money to buy beer or marijuana.

3   When I got to junior high school, I really began to notice the heavy use of drugs and alcohol. I saw students "snort" cocaine behind their open books in class while the teachers wrote notes on the board. I also saw students smoking angel dust on the physical education field during lunchtime. They brought alcoholic beverages on campus and many students smoked a joint before their classes began. Most of these youngsters eventually were caught and expelled from school. Luis was a football player in high school while Gerardo and I were in junior high. Luis "snorted" half a gram of cocaine before every game he played. Gerardo had begun to sniff typewriter correction fluid just for fun.

4   Once when we were in the eighth grade, we decided that we were going to smoke a marijuana cigarette with two girls from school. After school, at the clubhouse, we could not find the joint we had promised the girls. I felt extremely happy that I was not going to go through with it. Then the two girls began to get upset, and said that we had lied to them. Gerardo immediately handed each of them a sandwich bag with typewriter correction fluid inside. After the three of them began inhaling the substance, they began behaving erratically. Then one of the girls, whom I had an extremely strong crush on, handed me her bag and asked me to try it. I had never felt peer pressure as strong as I did that day. I hesitated at first, but after she moved close and kissed me, I felt obligated to try. It was the worst hallucinating effect I have ever experienced. Gerardo began crawling on the ground because he could not walk, and we all laughed at him.

5   Luis and Gerardo both dropped out of high school because of their addiction to drugs. They both became crack addicts, and Luis was also an alcoholic. Gerardo ended up in prison for robbery, which he did often in order to support his expensive drug habit. After his release, he went through counseling and treatment, and he was able to stop smoking crack, but he still drinks beer and smokes marijuana. Luis remains a crack addict and an alcoholic. He continues to live at home, and he refuses to get treatment for his disease. Working as a security guard, he spends his entire paycheck on drugs and alcohol. These are only two examples of the tragedies that exist all across this nation.

Discussion and Critical Thinking

1. Is this mainly an essay of causes, effects, or equal combination?

2. Underline the thesis.

3. Use annotation in the left-hand margin to indiciate the multiple effects and at least one cause.

4. How does the last paragraph relate to the thesis?

Topics for Writing Cause and Effect

You will find a blank Writing Process Worksheet on page 6, which can be photocopied, filled in, and submitted with each assignment if your instructor directs you to do so.

Reading-Related Topics

"What Happens to Steroid Studs?"

1. Write about the causes or effects of steroid use on someone you know.

2. Write about the effects of other drugs such as tobacco, heroin, cocaine, marijuana, LSD, or alcohol on someone you know. Consider doing a detailed study based on information from the counseling office, health office, library, American Heart Association, American Lung Association, or a police station. Pamphlets are readily available.

"Family Heroes and Role Models"

3. Write about people who have influenced you in important ways. How have they caused you to be who you are? Consider family members, friends, and people you know at church, at school, or in the community. Or write about the ways a public figure has influenced you.

4. Write about one role model who has influenced you in three or more important ways, or about three or more role models, each of whom has influenced you in an important way.

"The Purposes of Shopping"

5. Discuss buying and shopping in terms of the causes and effects of each activity.

6. Use Rose's ideas to discuss online shopping. Explain whether the causes and effects are the same.

7. As a buyer, explain why you go to a particular store.

8. As a shopper, explain why you go to a particular store.

9. Rose does not discuss big sales days. Explain how the whole sales atmosphere in a store contributes to the shopping experience and suggests the reasons for and the results of the activity.

"Living in Sin"

10. Using some of the observations (with credit) from this essay, write about the experiences of a "living-in" couple you are familiar with.

11. Write an evaluation of this article in which you generally agree or disagree with the author. Base your statement on your own value system, as well as your experience and/or observations.

"Seven Sustainable Wonders of the World"

12. Using Durning's essay as a model, write about your own three or more "wonders . . . the little things that work . . . especially when they do it without hurting the earth."

"More Than the Classroom"

13. Using this selection as a model, write a paragraph or an essay about the causes and effects of any new element in your life at any point. The element could be a relationship, death, health problem, marriage, college program, new job, or winning ticket in the lottery.

"Getting High and Living Low"

14. Using this essay as a model, write about someone you know who has gone through a similar experience.

15. Write about a problem in a larger sense, generalizing about mainly the causes or mainly the effects of drug addiction, among young people.

General Topics

Select one of the following topics as a subject (situation, circumstance, or trend) for your paragraph or essay and then determine whether you will concentrate on causes, effects, or a combination. You can probably write a more interesting, well-developed, and therefore successful paragraph or essay on a topic you can personalize. For example, a discussion about a specific young person who contemplated, attempted, or committed suicide is probably a better topic idea than a general discussion of suicide. If you do not personalize the topic, you will probably have to do some basic research to supply details for development.

16. Attending or completing college

17. Having or getting a job

18. Change in policy or administration

19. Change in coaches, teachers, officeholder(s)

20. Alcoholism

21. Gambling

22. Moving to another country, state, or home

23. Exercise

24. Passing or failing a test or a course

25. Popularity of a certain TV program or song

26. Early marriage

Cross-Curricular Topics

27. From a class that you are taking or have taken, select a subject that is especially concerned with causes and effects and develop a topic. Begin by selecting an event, situation, or trend in the class content and make a list of the causes and effects; that procedure will almost immediately show you whether you have a topic you can discuss effectively. Class notes and textbooks can provide you with more specific information. If you use textbooks or other materials, give credit or make copies of the sources. Instructors across the campus may have suggestions for studies of cause and effect. Some areas for your search include history, political science, geology, astronomy, psychology, philosophy, sociology, business, real estate, child development, education, fashion merchandising and design, psychiatric technician program, nursing, police science, fire science, nutrition and food, physical education, and restaurant and food-service management.

Career-Related Topics

28. Discuss the effects (benefits) of a particular product or service on the business community, family life, society generally, a specific group (age, income, interest), or an individual.

29. Discuss the needs (thus the cause of development) by individuals, families, or institutions for a particular product or type of product.

30. Discuss the effects of using a certain approach or philosophy in sales, human resources management, or customer service.

Writer's Guidelines: Cause and Effect

FLOW OF WRITING

1. Determine whether your topic should mainly inform or mainly persuade, and use the right tone for your purpose and audience.

2. Use listing to brainstorm cause-and-effect ideas. This is a useful form:

Causes	Event, Situation, or Trend	Effects
1.		1.
2.		2.
3.		3.
4.		4.

3. Decide whether to concentrate on causes, effects, or a combination of causes and effects. Most paragraphs will focus only on causes or only on effects. Many short

essays will discuss causes and effects but will use one as the framework for the piece. A typical basic outline might look like this:

Topic sentence of paragraph or thesis of essay
   I. Cause or Effect 1
  II. Cause or Effect 2
 III. Cause or Effect 3

4. Do not conclude that something is an effect merely because it follows something else.

5. Lend emphasis to your main concern(s)—causes, effects, or a combination—by repeating key words such as *cause, reason, effect, result, consequence,* and *outcome.*

6. Causes and effects can be primary or secondary, immediate or remote.

7. The order of causes and effects in your paper may be based on time, space, emphasis, or a combination.

8. Use the writing process.

- Write and then revise your paragraph or essay as many times as necessary for coherence, language (usage, tone, and diction), unity, emphasis, support, and sentences (**CLUESS**).

- Read your work aloud to hear and correct any grammatical errors or awkward-sounding sentences.

- Edit any problems in fundamentals, such as capitalization, omissions, punctuation, and spelling (**COPS**).

Chapter 13

Classification: Establishing Groups

FLOW OF WRITING

Writing Classification   237

   Selecting a Subject   237

   Using a Principle to Avoid Overlapping   237

   Establishing Classes   237

   Using Simple and Complex Forms   238

Practicing Patterns of Classification   241

Connecting Reading and Writing   242

   Professional Writers   242

   "Styles of Leadership"   242

   "Nobles, Peasants, and Clergy"   244

   "Which Stooge Are You?"   245

   "The Different Ways of Being Smart"   249

   "How to Deal with a Difficult Boss"   253

   Student Writers   257

   "Doctors Have Their Symptoms, Too" (demonstration
    with stages)   259

   "Types of Hepatitis"   260

Topics for Writing Classification   261

Writer's Guidelines   264

"Writers can grow into originality . . . after they master the fundamentals. Being your own diagnostician, your own toughest editor—and your staunchest supporter—will take you far."

LAUREN KESSLER

THE QUIGMANS   by **Buddy Hickerson**

B. Hickerson, copyright Los Angeles Times Syndicate. Reprinted by permission.

Writing Classification

To explain by classification, you put persons, places, things, or ideas into groups or classes based on their characteristics. Whereas analysis by division deals with the characteristics of just one unit, classification deals with more than one unit, so the subject is plural.

To classify efficiently, try following this procedure:

1. Select a plural subject.

2. Decide on a principle for grouping the units of your subject.

3. Establish the groups, or classes.

4. Write about the classes.

Selecting a Subject

When you say you have different kinds of neighbors, friends, teachers, bosses, or interests, you are classifying; that is, you are forming groups.

In naming the different kinds of people in your neighborhood, you might think of different groupings of your neighbors, the units. For example, some neighbors are friendly, some are meddlesome, and some are private. Some neighbors have yards like Japanese gardens, some have yards like neat-but-cozy parks, and some have yards like abandoned lots. Some neighbors are affluent, some are comfortable, and some are struggling. Each of these sets is a classification system and could be the focus of one paragraph in your essay.

Using a Principle to Avoid Overlapping

All the sets in the preceding section are sound because each group is based on a single concern: neighborly involvement, appearance of the yard, or wealth. This one concern, or controlling idea, is called the **principle.** For example, the principle of neighborly involvement controls the grouping of neighbors into three classes: friendly, meddlesome, and private.

All the classes in any one group must adhere to the controlling principle for that group. You would not say, for example, that your neighbors can be classified as friendly, meddlesome, private, and affluent, because the first three classes relate to neighborly involvement, but the fourth, relating to wealth, refers to another principle. Any one of the first three—the friendly, meddlesome, and private—might also be affluent. The classes should not overlap in this way. Also, every member should fit into one of the available classes.

Establishing Classes

As you name your classes, rule out easy, unimaginative phrasing such as *fast/medium/slow, good/average/bad,* and *beautiful/ordinary/ugly.* Look for creative, original phrases and unusual perspectives.

Subject:	neighbors
Principle:	neighborhood involvement
Classes:	friendly, meddlesome, private

Subject: neighbors
Principle: yard upkeep
Classes: immaculate, neat, messy

Subject: neighbors
Principle: wealth
Classes: affluent, comfortable, struggling

Using Simple and Complex Forms

Classification can take two forms: simple and complex. The simple form does not go beyond main divisions in its groupings.

Subject: Neighbors
Principle: Involvement
Classes: I. Friendly
               II. Meddlesome
               III. Private

Complex classifications are based on one principle and then subgrouped by another related principle. The following example classifies neighbors by their neighborly involvement. It then subgroups the classes on the basis of motive.

I. Friendly
  A. Civic-minded
  B. Want to be accepted
  C. Gregarious
II. Meddlesome
  A. Controlling
  B. Emotionally needy
  C. Suspicious of others
III. Private
  A. Shy
  B. Snobbish
  C. Secretive

Here are two examples by professional writers on other topics, one organized as a simple form and the other organized as a complex form.

Simple:

Subject
Development of classes
I. Some do not listen.
II. Some only half-listen.
III. Some listen with passive acceptance.
IV. Some listen with discrimination.

Glenn R. Capp, *Listen Up!*

Listeners can be classified into four groups: (1) Some do not listen; they "tune the speaker out" and think of matters foreign to the speaker's subject. They get little from a speech. (2) Some only half-listen; their spasmodic listening fluctuates all the way from careful attention to no attention. They understand fragments of the speech, but they do not see the idea as a whole. (3) Some listen with passive acceptance; they accept all the speaker says without question. Because of their lack of discrimination, they add little to what the speaker says from their own experiences. (4) Some listen with discrimination; this critical type of listener gets the most from a speech.

Complex:

Subject main class
Main class I
Principle

    There are two principal types of <u>glaciers</u>: the <u>continental</u> and the <u>valley</u>. The <u>continental glaciers</u> are great sheets of ice, called ice caps, that cover parts of continents. The earth has two continental glaciers at present: one spreads over most of Greenland and one over all of Antarctica save for a small window of rock and the peaks of several ranges. The Greenland ice sheet is over 10,000 ft. thick in the central part and covers an area of about 650,000 sq. miles. The Antarctic sheet has been sounded, in one place at least, to a depth of 14,000 ft., and it spreads over an area of 5,500,000 sq. miles. This is larger than the conterminous United States in the proportion of $5\frac{1}{2}:3$. It is calculated to store 7 million cu. miles of ice, which if melted would raise the ocean level 250 ft.

Main class II

Subclass A
(conventional)

Subclass B

Subclass C

    <u>Valley glaciers</u> are ice streams that originate in the high snow fields of mountain ranges and flow down valleys to warmer climates, where they melt. <u>Some break up</u> into icebergs and eventually melt in the ocean. In certain places the valley glaciers flow down the mountain valleys to adjacent plains and there spread out as lobate feet. These are called <u>expanded-foot glaciers</u>. Generally the sprawling feet of several valley glaciers coalesce to form one major sheet, and this is called a <u>piedmont glacier</u>.

    Notice that the valley glacier is subdivided:

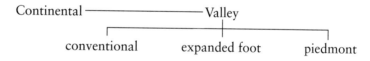

A. J. Eardley, "Glaciers: Types and Subtypes"

    As you can see, glaciers are of two types based on their location (with implications for size:): (1) the continental glacier, such as the huge one in the Antarctic, and (2) the valley glacier. The valley glacier can be subdivided into the conventional valley glacier, flowing straight; the expanded-foot glacier, which spreads out; and the piedmont glacier, which is made up of several expanded-foot glaciers. This information could be organized in a complex outline as follows:

    I. Continental glacier
   II. Valley glacier
      A. Conventional
      B. Expanded foot
      C. Piedmont

    This outline on glaciers could be cut down to just the "valley glacier" part and developed into a paragraph or an essay. Moving in the other direction, we can say that almost all classifications can be part of a higher level of classification. For example, glaciers are one type of earth-altering process. (Others include earthquakes, volcanoes, and wind erosion.)

    Most papers of classification will be simple (based on one principle) in concept, informative in purpose, and organized class by class.

EXERCISE 1	Avoiding Overlapped Classes

Mark each set of classes as OK or OL (overlapping); circle the classes that overlap.

	Subject	Principle	Classes
	Example:		
OL	community college students	intentions	vocational
			academic transfer
			specialty needs
			(hardworking)
OK	1. airline flights	passenger seating	first class
			business
			coach
OL	2. country singers	clothing trademark	hat
			overalls
			decorative costume
			expensive
OL	3. schools	ownership	private
			religious
			public
OL	4. faces	shape	round
			square
			oval
			beautiful
			broad
			long

_____OL_____ 5. dates

behavior resembling
aquatic animals

sharks

clams

jellyfish

cute

octopuses

Practicing Patterns of Classification

Because the basic pattern of classification consists of classes, the initial outline is predictable: It uses Roman-numeral headings for the classes, although some classes may be longer and more complex than others.

EXERCISE 2 　Completing Patterns of Classification

Fill in the blanks to identify classes that could be discussed for each subject.

1. *Subject:* Professional athletes

   Principle: Why they participate in sports

   Classes:

   I. Glory

   II. _____

   III. _____

2. *Subject:* Pet owners

   Principle: Why they own (need) pets

   Classes:

   I. Companionship

   II. _____

   III. _____

3. *Subject:* Dates or prospective spouses

Principle: The way they can be compared to vehicles

Classes:

I. Economy (Taurus, Corolla, Civic)

   A. Low cost

   B. Low maintenance

   C. _____

II. Minivans (Caravan, Quest, Odyssey)

   A. Practical

   B. _____

   C. _____

III. Luxury (Porsche, BMW, Mercedes, Lexus)

   A. High cost

      1. Initial

      2. _____

   B. _____

   C. Impressive features

      1. _____

      2. Unnecessary

Connecting Reading and Writing

Professional Writers

Styles of Leadership

WILLIAM M, PRIDE, ROBERT J. HUGHES, AND JACK R. KAPOOR

Written by three business professors, this paragraph is excerpted from a college textbook. It refers mainly to business institutions and the work-place, but it also covers all social units that depend on leadership, from the family to nations.

For many years, leadership was viewed as a combination of personality traits, such as self-confidence, concern for people, intelligence, and dependability. Achieving a consensus on which traits were most important was difficult, however, and attention turned to styles of leadership behavior. In the last few decades, several styles of leadership have been identified: authoritarian, laissez-faire, and democratic. The **authoritarian leader** holds all authority and responsibility, with communication usually moving from top to bottom. This leader assigns workers to specific tasks and expects orderly, precise results. The leaders at United Parcel Service employ authoritarian leadership. At the other extreme is the **laissez-faire leader,** who gives authority to employees. With the laissez-faire style, subordinates are allowed to work as they choose with a minimum of interference. Communication flows horizontally among group members. Leaders at Apple Computer are known to employ a laissez-faire leadership style in order to give employees as much freedom as possible to develop new products. The **democratic leader** holds final responsibility but also delegates authority to others, who participate in determining work assignments. In this leadership style, communication is active both upward and downward. Employee commitment is high because of participation in the decision-making process. Managers for both Wal-Mart and Saturn have used the democratic leadership style to encourage employees to become more than just rank-and-file workers.

EXERCISE 3

Discussion and Critical Thinking

1. Underline the topic sentence.

2. What is the subject of this paragraph?

3. What is the principle that divides the subject into classes?

4. This paragraph is obviously concerned with explaining the different styles of leadership, without showing favor. Do you have a preference? If so, what is your preference and why?

5. In the textbook *Business,* Seventh Edition, this paragraph is followed by another with this first sentence: "Today most management experts agree that no one 'best' managerial leadership style exists." How do you think the authors explain such a statement?

Nobles, Peasants, and Clergy

T. WALTER WALLBANK

In this passage taken from The Story of Civilization, *historian T. Walter Wallbank classifies medieval society (456–1453 C.E.) into three groups.*

    Though at times there was considerable social mobility, medieval society conventionally consisted of three classes: the nobles, the peasants, and the clergy. Each of these groups had its own task to perform. Since the vassals [land owners] usually gave military service to their lord in return for their fiefs [estates], the nobles were primarily fighters, belonging to an honored society distinct from the peasant people—freemen, villeins, and serfs. In an age of physical violence, society obviously would accord first place to the man with the sword rather than to the man with the hoe. The peasants were the workers; attached to the manors, they produced the crops and did all the menial labor. The Church drew on both the noble and the peasant classes for the clergy. Although the higher churchmen held land as vassals under the feudal system, the clergy formed a class which was considered separate from the nobility and peasantry.

EXERCISE 4

Discussion and Critical Thinking

1. What sentence carries the topic idea?

2. Into what classes does Wallbank divide his subject?

3. What principle does Wallbank use as a basis for classifying members of society?

4. Why was it necessary to discuss the clergy class more fully than the other two classes?

5. Were the classes set inflexibly?

Which Stooge Are You?

RON GERACI

*Who would expect to find an article about the Three Stooges in a maga-
zine named* Men's Health? *Pratfalling, eye-gouging, ear-pulling, nose-
twisting, and head-butting their way through life, Moe, Larry, and Curly
are not the stuff we hold in the same thought as* health—*mental or physical. Perhaps because no freelance writer would have dared submit an
article on this topic for publication, the feature editor, Ron Geraci, wrote
one himself. He not only wrote about the Stooges as a team of nitwits;
he wrote about them as individual casebook studies of mental health and
invited us to identify with one or more. Prepare to laught and learn. Hey,
before you start, what's that on your shirt? Gotcha!*

1   Men spend millions of dollars on psychotherapy trying to figure out why they're
unhappy, why their kids don't respect them, why women treat them like idiots. Perhaps shrinks help some men, but for many others, it's money that would have been
better spent on popcorn and videotapes. To solve many of life's problems, all you
really need to do is watch the *Three Stooges.*

2   We're all variations of Moe, Larry, or Curly, and our lives are often short subjects filled with cosmic slapstick. When Moe (your boss) hits Curly (your buddy)
with a corporate board and then blindsides you when you try to make it all nice,
you're living a Stooge moment. Here you'll find the personality type each Stooge
represents. Once you determine which Stooge you are, you'll better understand the
problems you bring on yourself—and how you can be a generally happier, more
successful knucklehead.

3   Everyone knows more than one Moe. These men are the insufferable know-it-
alls who become driving instructors, gym teachers, and divorce attorneys. The
coach who had you do pushups in front of the team? He was a Moe. So was that
boss who made you carry his golf bag.

4   In short, Moes are hot-tempered men who intimidate people with verbal slaps
and managerial eye pokes, according to Stuart Fischoff, Ph.D., a psychologist at
California State University. "Moe has a paternalistic personality, which is pretty
common among men," Fischoff says. "He treats everyone like a child and bullies
people to keep them off balance." Being a temperamental loudmouth also helps
Moe scare off critics who might expose his little secret: He's no smarter than the
saps he terrorizes. Moe himself proved that point. Although he served up most of
the nose gnashings and belly bonks in 190 shorts, he always ended up back in the
mud with Larry and Curly.

5   Even if you've never actually threatened to tear somebody's tonsils out, there are
a few other clues that can tag you as a Moe. First, naturally, Moes are explosive
hot-heads who storm through life constantly infuriated by other people. "These
men suffer from classic low frustration tolerance," says Allen Elkin, Ph.D., a psychologist in New York. "This not only makes them difficult to work with, but it
also gives them high blood pressure, high cholesterol, and a much greater risk of
heart attack." In fact, Moes often end up seeking counseling to control their anger,
usually after it costs them a job, a marriage, or a couple of good pals. "I tell them
to just get away from infuriating situations quickly," says Elkin. "Remember, you
don't *have* to poke Curly in the eye because he destroyed the plumbing."

6   Second, in the likely event that a Moe manages to foul things up himself, he'll
find a way to blame his mistakes on other people, says Fischoff. In *Healthy,*

Wealthy, and Dumb (1938), for example, Moe breaks a $5,000 vase with a 2-by-4 and screams at Larry, "Why didn't you bring me a softer board?!"

7   Your habits on the job are the most telling signs. If you're a Moe, you're probably the hardest-driving wise guy at work. "High-strung, bossy men with Moe personalities tend to live at their jobs," says Elkin. To help stop overloading themselves with work they can't possibly finish (a common Moe peccadillo), workaholic Moes should make a list of projects they *won't* do each day—and then make sure they keep their hands off those folders.

8   Moe Howard (1897–1975) had a classic Moe personality. Even offscreen, he was the fiery, short-fused leader of the trio who made all the decisions. Of course, this put a lot of worries on Moe's shoulders. "My father was an anxiety-ridden, nervous man," says Paul Howard, Moe's son. "He didn't have much patience. He always worried about his kid brother Curly, and if Larry flubbed a line, my father could become upset and criticize him almost like a director." Larry probably shaped up fast; Moe could always put some English into the next eye gouge.

9   Now, in fairness to all men with bowl cuts and bad attitudes, there are some big advantages to having a Moe personality. "If I could choose my Stooge, I'd sure as hell be a Moe," says Fischoff. Because they're usually so domineering and assertive, Moes are often able to bark their way into leadership positions quickly. (Kennedy and Nixon were Moes; Carter was a Larry.) If you crammed all the *Fortune*-100 CEOs into one Bennigan's, you'd have Moe Central with a wet bar.

10   Another Moe perk: Women flock to you like geeks to a *Star Trek* premier. Moe is an aggressive, tenacious SOB, and women are genetically programmed to find those traits sexually attractive, says Barbara Keesling, Ph.D., a Southern California sex therapist. That's because prehistoric Moes used their superior eye-poking abilities to scare off those wise-guy tigers. It's why that Moe who gave you noogies in high school went through skirts faster than J. Edgar Hoover—and why he's probably divorced now.

11   "Moes are control freaks," says Keesling. "That can be sexually exciting at first, but women get tired of it very quickly. I know—I've dated examples of all three Stooges. I'm thankful they didn't all try to sleep in my bed at once."

12   Larry is the passive, agreeable fellow who scrapes through life by taking his licks and collecting his paycheck. "Generally, things happen *to* a Larry; he doesn't make them happen," says Alan Entin, Ph.D., a psychologist with the American Psychological Association. Larry is the ubiquitous "nice guy" who commutes to his mediocre job, congenially tries to cover Curly's ass, and spends his day trying to avoid getting whacked in the nose by Moe.

13   That's right: John Q. Taxpayer is a Larry.

14   A subtle testosterone shift, though, can make all the difference in what kind of life this lovable sap leads. Give the classic Larry a little more testicularity, and you have a good-natured man who isn't a biological doormat. He'll kick a wino off your lawn but won't fink on your free cable. That makes him a perfect coworker, neighbor, and pal.

15   But subtract a little gonad power, and a Larry can be an indecisive wimp whose greatest ambition in life is to watch *Everybody Loves Raymond*. These pitiful, wishy-washy slobs constantly get clobbered for being—as Larry put it—"a victim of soicumstance," and that typically makes them passive-aggressive, says Fischoff.

16   "A Larry doesn't have the nerve to be assertive, so he protests by not doing something," Fischoff says: not securing the ladder on the triple-bunk bed, or not mentioning that the coffee is actually rat poison. Consequently, Larrys are rarely promoted. If a Larry usually does work up the courage to ask for a raise, the Moe

he works for will usually give a meaningless title upgrade—or say, "Get outta here before I murder ya."

17   To determine if you're an overly passive Larry, answer these three questions.

18   *What's new?* If you're a classic Larry, nothing is new. Your answer will be the latest yarn about the office Curly who once photocopied his own butt. "Larrys live vicariously through Moes and Curlys," says Fischoff. "They don't really have a strong identity of their own."

19   *Still dream about writing a screenplay?* "Larrys don't have a life plan," says Fischoff. They bumble from one opportunity to the next while awaiting their "break"; a Moe plots his life like a war and a Curly flatly avoids challenges.

20   *Do you weasel out of big projects?* Larrys become good at deflecting responsibility. This lets them avoid the risk of failure (and success) without looking like a bum. In *Idiots Deluxe* (1945), as Curly is being attacked by a giant bear, Moe screams, "Go out there and help him!" "The bear don't need no help!" Larry yells back.

21   The chief bonus in being a Larry of course, is that almost everyone thinks you're a swell chum. The dames eventually warm up to you, too, although it might take a few decades. Women reeling from years of turbulent relationships with Moes and Curlys often settle down with a Larry, says Keesling, because he's a stable, predictable, okeydokey guy who won't mind heading to the 7-Eleven for tampons. That makes him husband material. "I'd date Moe and Curly, but I'd marry Larry," confided several women we asked.

22   Like most Larrys, Larry Fine (1902–1975) spent his career following Moe and his free time ducking him. "Larry and Moe weren't friends," says Lyla Budnick, Larry's sister. "Their dealings were all business." Like any good Larry, he found passive-aggressive ways to make Moe fume. "My father would be at an airport hours early," says Joan Maurer, Moe's daughter, "but Larry would show up 5 minutes before the plane took off. This made my dad very upset." For Larry, making Moe sweat in a crowded airport terminal was probably a tiny payback for the daily humiliations.

23   In *The Sweet Pie and Pie* (1941), Curly tries to throw a pie at the usual gang of rich idiots but gets nailed with a pastry each time he cocks his arm. Finally he bashes himself with the pie to deprive others of the satisfaction. This illustrates Curly's strategy for life. "These men laugh at themselves so other people can't ridicule them first," says Elkin. "It comes across as funny, but this kind of defense mechanism really stems from a large reservoir of anger and resentment."

24   Curly had what's called an oral personality, and a particularly self-destructive one. Boisterous, attention-seeking men, especially those who are secretly ashamed of something, like a beer gut or a bald head, often feel that they must perform in order to be liked, says Keesling. "These guys always come in for counseling, because they experience mood swings and addiction problems. It's what killed Curly and his modern-day version, Chris Farley."

25   Men with Curly personalities are almost always fat, says Fischoff, because they live to binge. They overdose on food, booze, gambling, drugs, or sex—and sometimes on all five in one badly soiled hotel bed. Curly, a consummate binger, even outlined his plans for a utopian life in *Healthy, Wealthy, and Dumb*: "Oh boy! Pie à la mode with beer chasers three times a day!"

26   On the job, Curlys pride themselves on providing comedic relief. "A Curly senses he's no leader, so he garners attention by being a fool," says Fischoff. This nets him no respect, but it does defuse criticism. Who can fire a guy when he's down on the carpet running in circles?

27   Just like his two nitwit cohorts, Curly Howard's offscreen personality was pretty similar to that of the Stooge he portrayed. He drank heavily, overate, and smoked several cigars a day. "He would always be out carousing and drinking, and playing the spoons in nightclubs," remembers Paul Howard, his nephew.

28   "I've heard stories that my father sometimes had to pay for the damage Curly caused while drinking," says Joan Maurer, Moe's daughter. If woo-wooing was enough to get Curly belted onscreen, can you imagine what Moe dished out over a real-life antic like this?

29   Curly's lifestyle apparently made him foggy at work, too. When he barked at women or said "nyuk-nyuk-nyuk!" it was often because he had forgotten his lines. After having a series of obvious mini-strokes (he could barely grumble out his woos in 1945's *If a Body Meets a Body),* Curly had a career-ending stroke in 1946 and died in 1952 at age 48.

30   He had a hoot along the way, of course. Everybody loves a clown, so Curlys get plenty of party invites—and nightcaps with attractive women. "If each of the Stooges were to flirt with a woman, Curly would probably take her home, because his humor radiates confidence," Keesling says. (And what woman could resist an opener like "Hiya, Toots"?) But a Curly's neuroses usually shine through within a few dates, which explains why Curlys tend to have few long-term sex partners, says Keesling.

31   Curly Howard was married four times. "With the exception of his fourth marriage, his best relationship was with his dogs," says Paul Howard. Curly expressed his marital outlook pretty clearly in 1941's *An Ache in Every Stake,* as he shaved a lathered block of ice with a razor: "Are you married or happy?"

EXERCISE 5   Vocabulary Highlights

Write a short definition of each word as it is used in the essay. (Paragraph numbers are given in parentheses.) Be prepared to use the words in your own sentences.

peccadillo (7)	passive-aggressive (15)
ubiquitous (12)	vicariously (18)
mediocre (12)	boisterous (24)
congenially (12)	consummate (25)
testosterone (14)	utopian (25)

EXERCISE 6   Discussion and Critical Thinking

1. Why is Stooge-watching good therapy?

2. Complete the following outline for a study in classification:

    Subject: The Three Stooges

Principle: What they represent as psychological types

Classes (types): Moes, Larrys, and Curlys

What each type represents:

Personality or character traits

I. Moes as control freaks

   A. _____

   B. _____

   C. _____

Personality or character traits

II. Larrys as passive or passive-aggressive

   A. _____

   B. _____

   C. _____

Personality or character traits

III. Curlys as oral personality

   A. _____

   B. _____

   C. _____

3. To what extent are you or someone you know somewhat similar to Moe, Larry, or Curly?

4. Who is your favorite Stooge and why?

The Different Ways of Being Smart

SARA GILBERT

We are likely to think of being smart as being educated, but Sara Gilbert explains that being smart has many applications. Some people are smart in more than one way. This excerpt comes from Gilbert's book Using Your Head: The Many Ways of Being Smart.

1   Book smarts, art smarts, body smarts, street smarts, and people smarts: These . . . labels . . . describe the various forms of intelligence and their use. As you might imagine, psychologists and other researchers into the nature of intelligence have come up with more formal terms for the types that they have isolated. One set of labels in common use is: convergent, divergent, assimilating, and accommodating.

The converger and assimilator are like our book-smart person; the diverger, like our art-smart; and the accommodator, like our street-smart and people-smart. . . .

2   Whatever categorization we use, we will find some overlap within any individual. In fact, there are probably as many answers to the question "What are the different ways of being smart?" as there are people in the universe, because each of us is unique. We can't be typecast; we each have a wide spectrum of special talents.

3   Still, you probably know well at least one person whose talents generally fall into each of our categories. Keep those people in mind as you read through the detailed descriptions of them. . . .

4   At first it might seem that each of those types must call on very different sorts of abilities to be smart in his or her own ways. But in fact, each of the categories of intelligence on our list must use the same ingredients . . . learning ability, memory, speed, judgment, problem-solving skill, good use of language and other symbols, and creativity. Also, the thought processes that go on inside the heads of people with those varying kinds of smarts include the same steps: planning, perceiving, imaging, remembering, feeling, and acting.

5   Intelligence expresses itself in different forms, in part because of the differing physical qualities born and built into each person's body and brain, and in part because of the values and motivations that each person has learned.

6   However, the fact that each kind of smarts makes use of the same steps means that anyone can learn or develop skills in any or all of the categories. . . . Let's take a closer look at the many ways of being smart.

7   A *book-smart* person is one who tends to do well in school, to score high on tests, including intelligence tests. He or she is likely to be well-organized, to go about solving problems in a logical, step-by-step fashion, and to have a highly developed language ability. Another label for a book-smart person is "intellectual," meaning someone who uses the mind more to *know* than to feel or to control, and a book-smart person is especially proud of having knowledge. That knowledge may range from literature through science to math, but it is probable that it is concentrated in one area. Research shows that different knowledge areas occupy different clusters in the brain, so that someone whose connections for complicated calculations are highly developed may have less development in the areas controlling speech and writing.

8   Although as we've said, current research indicates that learning centers may be scattered throughout both hemispheres of the brain, the activities of the "logical" left side are probably most important in the lives of book-smart people. Book-smart people may also be creative: many mathematical or scientific problems could not be solved, for instance, without creative insights, but the primary focus of a book-smart person is the increase of knowledge.

9   *Art-smart* people, on the other hand, rely primarily on creativity. They create music, paintings, sculpture, plays, photographs, or other forms of art often without being able to explain why or how they chose a particular form or design. They are said to be "right-brained" people, because it appears that the control centers for such skills as touch perception and intuition—the formation of ideas without the use of words—lie in the right hemisphere. Artistic people tend to take in knowledge more often by seeing, hearing, and feeling than by conscientious reading and memorizing.

10   An art-smart person may not do too well in school, not because he or she is not bright, but because of an approach to problem solving that does not fit in well with the formats usually used by teachers and tests. A book-smart person might approach a problem on a math test logically, working step-by-step toward the right answer, while an art-smart person may simply "know" the answer without being

able to demonstrate the calculations involved. On a social studies exam, the book-smart person will carefully recount all the facts, while the more artistic one may weave stories and fantasies using the facts only as a base. In both cases, it's a good bet that the book-smart student will get the higher grade.

11   People who are serious about becoming artists, of course, may need to absorb a great deal of "book knowledge" in order to develop a solid background for their skills. There are other overlaps, as well: People with great musical ability, for instance, also tend to be skilled at mathematics, perhaps because of brain-cell interactions that are common to both processes. And in order to make use of any talent, art-smart people must have good body control as well.

12   The people we're calling *body smart* have a lot of that kind of body control. Most of them start out with bodies that are well put together for some kind of athletics—they may have inherited good muscular development for a sport like football, or loose and limber joints for gymnastic-style athletics. Or they may be people whose hands are naturally well coordinated for performing intricate tasks.

13   But although the physical basis for their talent may come from their genes and from especially sensitive brain centers for motor control, to make use of their "natural" skills they must be able to observe accurately—to figure out how a move is made or an object is constructed—and they must think about how to do it themselves. This thinking involves a complex use of symbols that enables the brain to "tell" another part of itself what to do. In other situations, such as school, a body-smart person is probably best able to learn through some physical technique: In studying for an exam, for instance, he or she will retain information by saying it out loud, acting out the facts, or counting them off with finger taps. Although athletes or the manually talented are often teased as being "dumb" in schoolwork, that is not necessarily an accurate picture. To be good in using physical talents, a person must put in a lot of practice, be able to concentrate intently, and be stubbornly persistent in achieving a goal. And those qualities of will and self-control can also be put to good use in more "intellectual" achievements.

14   Persistence is also an important quality of *street-smart* people. They are the ones who are able to see difficulties as challenges, to turn almost any situation to advantage for themselves. As young people, they are the ones who are able to make the most money doing odd jobs, or who can get free tickets to a concert that others believe is completely sold out. As adults, they are the business tycoons, for instance, or the personalities who shoot to stardom no matter how much or little talent they have. A street-smart student may do well in the school subjects that he or she knows count for the most and will all but ignore the rest. When taking exams, street-smart people are likely to get better grades than their knowledge merits because they can "psych out" the test, and because, when facing a problem or question they can't answer, they are skilled at putting on the paper something that looks good.

15   To be street smart in these ways—to be able to achieve highly individualistic goals and to be able to get around obstacles that totally stump others—a person must draw upon a wide scope of mental powers. It takes excellent problem-solving ability, creative thought, good planning and goal setting, accurate perception, persistent effort, skill with language, quick thinking, and strong sense of intuition.

16   Intuition plays a major role in *people smarts* as well. This kind of intelligence allows a person to sense what others are thinking, feeling, wanting, and planning. Although we might tend to put this sort of skill down as basic "instinct," it actually relies on higher activities of the brain. People smarts rely on very accurate and quick perceptions of clues and relationships that escape the notice of many, and they include the ability to analyze the information taken in. A people-smart student

can do well in school simply by dealing with individual teachers in the most productive way: Some can be charmed, some respond well to special requests for help, some reward hard work no matter what the results, and so forth. The people-smart student figures out easily what is the best approach to take. People with these talents also achieve well in other activities, of course—they become the leaders in clubs, and organizations, and they are able to win important individuals, like potential employers, over to their side. They would probably be typed as right-brained people, like artists, but their skill with language, both spoken and unspoken, is one that draws heavily on the left side.

17   Have you been able to compare these types with people you know in your class, family, or neighborhood? Of course, no individual is actually a type: People with any one of the kind of smarts that we've described also have some of the others. . . .

EXERCISE 7   Vocabulary Highlights

Write a short definition of each word as it is used in the essay. (Paragraph numbers are given in parentheses.) Be prepared to use the words in your own sentences.

unique (2)   coordinated (12)

spectrum (2)   intently (13)

hemispheres (8)   persistent (13)

conscientious (9)   tycoons (14)

symbols (4, 13)   merits (14)

EXERCISE 8   Discussion and Critical Thinking

1. Complete the following brief outline:

   Subject: People

   Principle: How people are smart

   I. Book smarts

   II. _____

   III. _____

   IV. _____

   V. _____

2. In paragraph 2, what qualification (limitation) does Gilbert place on her system of classification?

3. Circle words (such as repeated words, pronouns, or transitional connectives—*however, still, on the other hand*) that help connect thoughts between sentences.

4. How do these ideas relate to the way most people define intelligence?

5. Drawing on your experience, give an example of each class of "smarts."

How to Deal with a Difficult Boss

DONNA BROWN HOGARTY

Journalist Donna Brown Hogarty makes it clear that if you've ever had a boss, you've had a bad boss in certain respects. Bosses who are particularly bad, she says, can be grouped in five categories, and being able to recognize the kind of bad boss you have is the first step in dealing with discomfort and frustration at work. This article was published in Reader's Digest *in 1993.*

1   Harvey Gittler knew his new boss was high-strung—the two had worked together on the factory floor. But Gittler was not prepared for his co-worker's personality change when the man was promoted to plant manager.

2   Just two days later, the boss angrily ordered a standing desk removed because he'd seen a worker leaning on it to look up an order. He routinely dressed down employees at the top of his lungs. At one time or another he threatened to fire almost everyone in the plant. And after employees went home, he searched through trash cans for evidence of treason.

3   For many workers, Gittler's experience is frighteningly familiar. Millions of Americans have temperamental bosses. In a 1984 Center for Creative Leadership study of corporate executives, nearly 75 percent of the subjects reported having had at least one intolerable boss.

4   "Virtually all bosses are problem bosses, in one way or another," says psychologist Mardy Grothe, co-author with Peter Wylie of *Problem Bosses: Who They Are and How to Deal with Them.* The reason, he said, lies in lack of training. Most bosses were promoted to management because they excelled at earlier jobs—not because they have experience motivating others.

5   Uncertain economic times worsen the bad-boss syndrome. "There is an acceptance of getting results at any price," says Stanley Bing, a business executive and author of *Crazy Bosses.* "As a result, the people corporations select to be bosses are the most rigid and demanding, and the least able to roll with the punches."

6   Bad bosses often have a recognizable *modus operandi.* Harry Levinson, a management psychologist in Waltham, Massachusetts, has catalogued problem bosses, from the bully to the jellyfish to the disapproving perfectionist. If you're suffering from a bad boss, chances are he or she combines several of these traits and can be dealt with effectively if you use the right strategy.

The Bully

7   During his first week on the job, a new account manager at a small Pennsylvania advertising agency agreed to return some materials to a client. When he mentioned

this at a staff meeting, the boss turned beet red, his lips began to quiver and he shouted that the new employee should call his client and confess he didn't know anything about the advertising business, and would *not* be returning the materials.

8   Over the next few months, as the account manager watched co-workers cower under the boss's browbeating, he realized that the tyrant fed on fear. Employees who tried hardest to avoid his ire were most likely to catch it. "He was like a schoolyard bully," the manager recalls, "and I've known since childhood that, when confronted, most bullies back down."

9   Armed with new-found confidence and growing knowledge of the ad business, he matched his boss's behavior. "If he raised his voice, I'd raise mine," the manager recalls. True to type, the boss started to treat him with grudging respect. Eventually, the young man moved up the ranks and was rarely subjected to his boss's outbursts.

10   Although standing up to the bully often works, it *could* make matters worse. Mardy Grothe recommends a different strategy: reasoning with him after he's calmed down. "Some bosses have had a problem with temper control all their lives, and are not pleased with this aspect of their personality," he explains. Want a litmus test? If the boss attempts to compensate for his outburst by overreacting and trying to "make nice" the next day, says Grothe, he or she feels guilty about yesterday's bad behavior.

11   Grothe suggests explaining to your boss how his temper affects you. For instance, you might say, "I know you're trying to improve my performance, but yelling makes me less productive because it upsets me."

12   Whatever strategy you choose, deal with the bully as soon as possible, because "once a dominant/subservient relationship is established, it becomes difficult to loosen," warns industrial psychologist James Fisher. Fisher also suggests confronting your boss behind closed doors whenever possible, to avoid being disrespectful. If your boss continues to be overbearing, try these strategies from psychologist Leonard Felder, author of *Does Someone at Work Treat You Badly?*

13   • To keep your composure while the boss is screaming, repeat a calming phrase to yourself, such as "Ignore the anger. It isn't yours."

14   • Focus on a humorous aspect of your boss's appearance. If she's got a double chin, watch her flesh shake while she's yammering. "By realizing that even the most intimidating people are vulnerable, you can more easily relax," explains Felder.

15   • Wait for your boss to take a breath, then try this comeback line: "I want to hear what you're saying. You've got to slow down."

16   Finally, never relax with an abusive boss, no matter how charming he or she can be, says Stanley Bing. "The bully will worm his or her way into your heart as a way of positioning your face under his foot."

The Workaholic

17   "Some bosses don't know the difference between work and play," says Nancy Ahlrichs, vice president of client services at the Indianapolis office of Right Associates, an international outplacement firm. "If you want to reach them at night or on a Saturday, just call the office." Worse, such a boss invades your every waking hour, making it all but impossible to separate your own home life from the office.

18   Ahlrichs advises setting limits on your availability. Make sure the boss knows you can be reached in crisis, but as a matter of practice go home at a set time. If

he responds angrily, reassure him that you will tackle any project first thing in the morning. Get him to set the priorities, so you can decide which tasks can wait.

19   If you have good rapport with the boss, says Mardy Grothe, consider discussing the problem openly. Your goal is to convince him that just as he needs to meet deadlines, you have personal responsibilities that are equally important.

The Jellyfish

20   "My boss hires people with the assumption that we all know our jobs," says a woman who works for a small firm in New England. "Unfortunately, he hates conflict. If someone makes a mistake, we have to tiptoe around instead of moving to correct it, so we don't hurt anyone's feelings."

21   Her boss is a jellyfish. He has refused to establish even a basic pecking order in his office. As a result, a secretary sat on important correspondence for over a month, risking a client's tax write-offs. Because no one supervises the firm's support staff, the secretary never received a reprimand, and nobody was able to prevent such mishaps from recurring. The jellyfish simply can't take charge because he's afraid of creating conflicts.

22   So "*you* must take charge," suggests Lee Colby, a Minneapolis-based management consultant. "Tell the jellyfish: 'This is what I think I ought to be doing. What do you think?' You are taking the first step, without stepping on your boss's toes."

23   Building an indecisive supervisor's confidence is another good strategy. For example, if you can supply hard facts and figures, you can then use them to justify any course you recommend—and gently ease the jellyfish into taking a firmer position.

The Perfectionist

24   When Nancy Ahlrichs was fresh out of college, she landed her first full-time job, supervising the advertising design and layout of a small-town newspaper. On deadline day, the paper's irritable general manager would suddenly appear over her shoulder, inspecting her work for errors. Then he'd ask a barrage of questions, ending with the one Ahlrichs dreaded most: "Are you sure you'll make deadline?"

25   "I never missed a single deadline," Ahlrichs says, "yet every week he'd ask that same question. I felt belittled by his lack of confidence in me."

26   Ironically, the general manager was lowering the staff's productivity. To paraphrase Voltaire, the perfect is the enemy of the good. According to psychiatrist Allan Mallinger, co-author with Jeannette DeWyze of *Too Perfect: When Being in Control Gets Out of Control*, "The perfectionist's overconcern for thoroughness slows down everyone's work. When everything has to be done perfectly, tasks loom larger." The nit-picking boss who is behind schedule becomes even more difficult, making subordinates ever more miserable.

27   "Remember," says Leonard Felder, "the perfectionist *needs* to find something to worry about." To improve your lot with a perfectionist boss, get her to focus on the big picture. If she demands that you redo a task you've just completed, mention your other assignments, and ask her to prioritize. Often, a boss will let the work you've completed stand—especially when she realizes another project may be put on hold. If your boss is nervous about a particular project, offer regular reports. By keeping the perfectionist posted, you might circumvent constant supervision.

28   Finally, protect yourself emotionally. "You can't depend on the perfectionist for encouragement," says Mallinger. "You owe it to yourself to get a second opinion of your work by asking others."

The Aloof Boss

29   When Gene Bergoffen, now CEO of the National Private Truck Council, worked for another trade association and asked to be included in the decision-making process, his boss was brusque and inattentive. The boss made decisions alone, and very quickly. "We used to call him 'Ready, Fire, Aim,'" says Bergoffen.

30   Many workers feel frozen out by their boss in subtle ways. Perhaps he doesn't invite them to key meetings or he might never be available to discuss projects. "At the core of every good boss is the ability to communicate expectations clearly," says Gerard Roche, chairman of Heidrick & Struggles, an executive search firm. "Employees should never have to wonder what's on a boss's mind."

31   If your boss fails to give you direction, Roche says, "the worst thing you can do is nothing. Determine the best course of action, then say to your boss: 'Unless I hear otherwise, here's what I'm going to do.'"

32   Other strategies: When your boss does not invite you to meetings or include you in decision making, speak up. "Tell her you have information that might prove to be valuable," suggests Lee Colby. If that approach doesn't work, find an intermediary who respects your work and can persuade the boss to listen to your views.

33   To understand your boss's inability to communicate, it's vital to examine his work style. "Some like hard data, logically arranged in writing," says Colby. "Others prefer face-to-face meetings. Find out what makes your boss tick—and speak in his or her language."

34   Understanding your boss can make your job more bearable in a number of ways. For instance, try offering the boss two solutions to a problem—one that will make him happy, and one that will help you to reach your goals. Even the most difficult boss will usually allow you to solve problems in your own way—as long as he's convinced of your loyalty to him.

35   No matter which type of bad boss you have, think twice before going over his head. Try forming a committee with your colleagues and approaching the boss all together. The difficult boss is usually unaware of the problem and often is eager to make amends.

36   Before embarking on any course of action, engage in some self-analysis. Chances are, no matter how difficult your job is, you are also contributing to the conflict. "Talk to people who know you both, and get some honest feedback," suggests Mardy Grothe. "If you can fix the ways in which you're contributing to the problem, you'll be more likely to get your boss to change."

37   Even if you can't, there's a silver lining: the worst bosses often have the most to teach you. Bullies, for example, are frequently masters at reaching difficult goals. Perfectionists can often prod you into exceeding your own expectations.

38   As a young resident psychologist at the Menninger psychiatric hospital in Topeka, Kansas, Harry Levinson was initially overwhelmed by the high standards of founder Karl Menninger. "I felt I was never going to be able to diagnose patients as well as he did or perform to such high academic requirements," Levinson recalls. He even considered quitting. But in the end, he rose to the challenge, and today he believes he owes much of his success to what he learned during that critical period.

39   Dealing with a difficult boss forces you to set priorities, to overcome fears, to stay calm under the gun, and to negotiate for better working conditions. And the skills you sharpen to ease a tense relationship will stand you in good stead throughout your career. "Employees who are able to survive a trying boss often earn the respect of higher-ups for their ability to manage a situation," says Levin-

son. "And because a difficult boss can cause rapid turnover, those who stick it out often advance quickly."

40   Your bad boss can also teach you what *not* to do with subordinates as you move up—and one day enable you to be a better boss yourself.

EXERCISE 9

Vocabulary Highlights

Write a short definition of each word as it is used in the essay. (Paragraph numbers are given in parentheses.) Be prepared to use the words in your own sentences.

modus operandi (6)	invades (17)
cower (8)	rapport (19)
browbeating (8)	recurring (21)
litmus test (10)	paraphrase (26)
subservient (12)	prioritize (27)
vulnerable (14)	brusque (29)

EXERCISE 10

Discussion and Critical Thinking

1. What is being classified?

2. What is the purpose of the classification?

3. What are the five classes of bad bosses?

4. Of the five classes, which is the most difficult for most people to deal with? for you to deal with? Can you give any examples?

5. Hogarty suggests that sometimes the boss's behavior is caused to some extent by the behavior of the workers. How would you explain that? Provide examples, if possible.

6. Which of the five types of behavior are sometimes found in combination?

Student Writers

For all the years he could remember, Boris Belinsky has observed doctors from up close and at a distance. It was only natural, therefore, that when asked to classify a group of people according to their behavior, he chose doctors.

His Writing Process Worksheet shows you how this writing evolved from idea to final draft. To conserve space here, the freewriting and two rough drafts have been omitted. The balance of his worksheet has been lengthened for you to be able to see his other work in its entirety.

You will find a full-size blank worksheet on page 6, which can be photocopied, filled in, and submitted with each assignment if your instructor directs you to do so.

Writing Process Worksheet

Title Doctors Have Their Symptoms, Too

Name Boris Belinsky   Due Date Friday, March 20, 8 a.m.

ASSIGNMENT   In the space below, write whatever you need to know about your assignment, including information about the topic, audience, pattern of writing, length, whether to include a rough draft or revised drafts, and whether your paper must be typed.

Write a paragraph of classification in which you group people according to their behavior in a particular vocation area. Your audience—your instructor and your peers—will be somewhat aware of the career field you select but will lack your insights. Submit a completed worksheet, a rough draft marked for revision, and a typed final draft of about 250 words.

STAGE ONE   Explore   Freewrite, brainstorm (list), cluster, or take notes as directed by your instructor. Use the back of this page or separate paper if you need more space.

Clustering

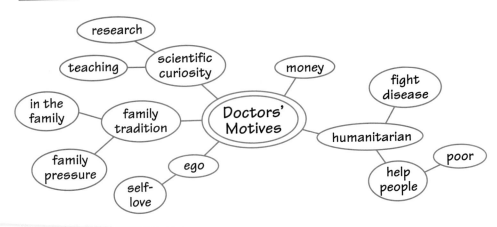

STAGE TWO   Organize   Write a topic sentence or thesis; label the subject and the treatment parts.

Doctors can be classified according to their motives for choosing their field
    ___subject___   ___treatment___

of work.

Write an outline or an outline alternative.

   I. Motive: to make money
      A. Slow with patients
      B. Fast with bills
  II. Motive: to pursue scientific interests
      A. Work in labs
      B. Teach in medical schools
 III. Motive: to help people
      A. Spend much time with patients
      B. Have good standards
         1. May locate in poor areas
         2. Advocate preventative methods
         3. Do volunteer work

STAGE THREE

Write   On separate paper, write and then revise your paragraph or essay as many times as necessary for **c**oherence, **l**anguage (usage, tone, and diction), **u**nity, **e**mphasis, **s**upport, and **s**entences (**CLUESS**). Read your work aloud to hear and correct any grammatical errors or awkward-sounding sentences.

Edit any problems in fundamentals, such as **c**apitalization, **o**missions, **p**unctuation, and **s**pelling (**COPS**).

Final Draft

Doctors Have Their Symptoms, Too
Boris Belinsky

Because I come from a large family that unfortunately has had a lot of illnesses, I have learned to classify doctors according to why they became doctors.

Topic sentence As doctors can diagnose illnesses by the symptoms they identify, I can figure out doctors' motives by their symptoms, by which I mean behavior. Some doctors

Support (class) have chosen the field of medicine because they want to make money. They hurry their patients (customers) through their multiple office spaces, answering few questions and never sitting down. Although slow to answer the desperate phone

Support (class) calls, they're fast with the bills. The second class is the group with scientific interests. Not as much concerned about money, they're often found in university hospitals, where they teach and work on special medical problems. They may be a bit remote and explain symptoms in technical terms. The third group is my fa-

Support (class) vorite: those who became doctors to help people. They spend much time with patients, often practice in areas that are not affluent, advocate preventative

Concluding sentence methods, and do volunteer work. Not all doctors easily fall into these three groups, but virtually every one has a tendency to do so.

EXERCISE 11   ## Discussion and Critical Thinking

1. What is the principle on which Belinsky's classification is based?

2. How does Belinsky protect himself against a charge that some doctors are not easily classified?

3. Why has Belinsky had occasion to make the observations on which this paragraph is based?

Types of Hepatitis

ANNIE CHEN

While volunteering to donate blood, Annie Chen discovered that she had hepatitis. After going to the doctor, she went to the library in search of medical information. Propelling her was one of the strongest motives she had ever had for doing research: concern about her health. She soon became a lay "expert" and was able to write about three different kinds of hepatitis.

1   Two years ago when I stopped at a hospital to donate blood, a simple screening procedure determined that I had hepatitis, a disease that involves the inflammation of the liver. After going to my doctor, who gave me information, instructions, and a shot of gamma globulin, I immediately went to the library. Nothing could stop me from learning what I could about this disease I thought only other people had. What I found there confirmed in more detail what the doctor had told me. Hepatitis has distinct early symptoms: jaundice, vomiting, nausea, poor
Subject   appetite, and general weakness. Nevertheless, hepatitis is not a single disease
Principle   coming from the same source; instead it takes mainly three forms based on
Thesis   transmission and effect, which are known as A, B, and C.

Topic Sentence 2   Hepatitis A is the seventh most commonly reported infectious disease in the
Class 1   United States (behind gonorrhea, chicken pox, syphilis, AIDS, salmonellosis, and shigellosis). The least harmful, Hepatitis A is a highly contagious liver disease commonly transmitted by human waste. It is also acquired by the ingestion of contaminated food, milk, or water; therefore, this type is said to be toxic. Outbreaks of Hepatitis A are often traced to eating seafood from polluted water. The highest incidence is in children, about 30 percent of them younger than fifteen. Fortunately, when treated with medicines such as gamma globulin, symptoms are usually gone in less than six weeks.

Topic Sentence 3   Unlike Hepatitis A, Hepatitis B is caused by a virus. Though it can also be trans-
Class 2   mitted by contact with human secretions and feces, it is most frequently spread during intimate sexual contact and the sharing of needles by drug abusers.

Nurses, doctors, laboratory technicians, and dentists are often exposed to Hepatitis B. A common infectious disease in Southeast Asian countries, Hepatitis B is much more serious than A. Although most patients recover completely, some with weak immune systems may suffer lifelong infection, cirrhosis, liver failure, or even death.

Topic Sentence 4

Class 3

In 1990 the Hepatitis C virus was identified. It is spread by blood-to-blood contact. Therefore, any way that one person's blood may be in contact with an infected person's blood can spread the Hepatitis C virus. Two of the most common means of transmission are blood transfusions and intravenous drug use. Long-range effects include chronic infection and liver disease. Hepatitis C now accounts for about 20 percent of all viral hepatitis cases.

5   In most hepatitis patients, the liver cells will eventually regenerate with little or no residual damage. I feel perfectly fine. But with its numerous virulent forms, hepatitis is an extremely troublesome and dangerous disease. To some extent, blood screening for transfusions, effective medicines, and good health practices have reduced the effects, at least for the informed and careful public.

EXERCISE 12

Discussion and Critical Thinking

1. What is the subject?

2. What is the principle on which the classification is based?

3. Double underline the thesis.

4. Underline the topic sentences (which also indicate the classes by name) of paragraphs 2, 3 and 4.

Topics for Writing Classification

You will find a blank Writing Process Worksheet on page 6, which can be photocopied, filled in, and submitted with each assignment if your instructor directs you to do so.

Reading-Related Topics

"Styles of Leadership"

1. Using the basic definition by Pride, Hughes, and Kapoor, write a longer piece in which you use at least one example from your experience to explain each class.

2. Write about these classes of leadership as they apply to leading outside the workplace area. Consider family, sports, politics, and religion for another area where leadership is important. You may want to argue that one style is better in a situation you define.

"Nobles, Peasants, and Clergy"

3. In a paragraph or an essay, discuss contemporary social classes in a particular community, region, or country.

4. Using the Wallbank paragraph as a model, write about the divisions within a particular company (such as management, sales, manufacturing, distribution) or within a particular school (such as administration, faculty, certified support staff). Name the company or school.

"Which Stooge Are You?"

5. Using this essay as a model, write about the members of any group (of at least three members). Discuss how each member represents a recognizable type of person you are familiar with. You might write about a musical group such as the Beatles, a basketball team such as the Lakers, or a leadership group of politicians.

6. Write about three people you know (friends or associates) or know about (celebrities or other show-business characters) who resemble Moe (control freaks), Larry (passive, or passive-aggressive, but agreeable), and Curly (attention-seeking, but secretly ashamed).

"The Different Ways of Being Smart"

7. Write about each of the four types of being smart, giving examples from your own experience.

"How to Deal with a Difficult Boss"

8. Write about each of the five types of bad bosses, giving examples from your own experience.

9. Discuss a subdivision of the bully bosses (such as those who use words, threats of job loss, and physical threats) and explain how each functions.

10. Using this essay as a framework, write a classification of good bosses.

11. Hogarty mentions that bad bosses are often made worse by bad employees. Write a classification of bad employees, perhaps from a good boss's perspective.

"Doctors Have Their Symptoms, Too"

12. Classify another vocational group (clergy, teachers, lawyers, police officers, shop owners) according to their reasons for selecting their field.

"Types of Hepatitis"

13. Write an essay in which you discuss the various types of another disease, such as diabetes, skin cancer, arthritis, herpes, pneumonia, leukemia, or lupus. Some of these diseases not only have classes but also have subclasses. Medical books and encyclopedias can provide you with basic information.

General Topics

Write a paragraph or an essay using one of the topics listed here. Divide your topic into groups according to a single principle.

14. Intelligence
15. Waitresses
16. Dates
17. Smokers
18. Smiles
19. Liars
20. Gossips
21. TV watchers
22. Styles in clothing
23. Sports

24. Dopers
25. Sports fans
26. Churchgoers
27. Laughs
28. Bus drivers
29. Riders on buses or airplanes
30. Junk food
31. Graffiti
32. Home computers

33. Mothers or fathers
34. Rock music
35. Talkers on the telephone
36. Pick-up lines (as in a bar)
37. Chicken eaters
38. Surfers (Internet or ocean)
39. Beards
40. Pet owners

Cross-Curricular Topics

41. Write a paragraph or an essay on one of the following terms.

    • Business: Types of real estate sales, banking, management styles, interviews, evaluations.

    • Geology: Types of rocks, earthquakes, mountains, rivers, erosion, faults.

    • Biology: Types of cells, viruses, proteins, plants (working mainly with subgroups).

    • Psychology: Types of stressors, aggression, adjustments, love.

    • Sociology: Types of families, parents, deviants.

    • Music: Types of instruments, singers, symphonies, operas, folk songs, rock, rap.

Career-Related Topics

42. Discuss the different types of employees you have observed.

43. Discuss the different qualities of products or services in a particular field.

44. Discuss different types of customers with whom you have dealt (perhaps according to their purpose for seeking your services or products).

Writer's Guidelines: Classification

1. Follow this procedure for writing paragraphs and essays of classification:

   - Select a plural subject.

   - Decide on a principle for grouping the units of your subject.

   - Establish the groups, or classes.

   - Write about the classes.

2. Avoid uninteresting phrases for your classes, such as *good/average/bad, fast/medium/slow*, and *beautiful/ordinary/ugly.*

3. Avoid overlapping classes.

4. The Roman-numeral parts of your outline will probably indicate your classes.

   I. Class one
   II. Class two
   III. Class three

5. If you use subclasses, clearly indicate the different levels.

6. Following your outline, give somewhat equal (however much is appropriate) space to each class.

7. Use the writing process.

   - Write and then revise your paragraph or essay as many times as necessary for coherence, language (usage, tone, and diction), unity, emphasis, support, and sentences (**CLUESS**).

   - Read your work aloud to hear and correct any grammatical errors or awkward-sounding sentences.

   - Edit any problems in fundamentals, such as capitalization, omissions, punctuation, and spelling (**COPS**).

Chapter 14

Comparison and Contrast: Showing Similarities and Differences

FLOW OF WRITING

Comparison and Contrast Defined   266

Generating Topics and Working with
the 4 *P*s   266

   Purpose   266

   Points   267

   Patterns   268

   Presentation   269

Analogy   271

Practicing Patterns of Comparison and
Contrast   271

Connecting Reading and Writing   274

   Professional Writers   274

   "Business Battle Tactics"   274

   "Pink Kittens and Blue Spaceships"   276

   "The Small Town and the Big City"   277

   "Los Chinos Discover el Barrio"   278

   **Paired Essays on Orderly and Disorderly
People**   281

   "Neat People vs. Sloppy People"   282

   "The Messy Are in Denial"   284

   Student Writers   287

   "Disneyland or Magic Mountain: Fantasy or
Thrills?" (demonstration with stages)   289

   "The Piper Cherokee and the Cessna 172"   290

Topics for Writing Comparison and
Contrast   291

Writer's Guidelines   294

"My first draft usually has only a few elements worth keeping. I have to find what they are and build from them and throw out what doesn't work."

SUSAN SONTAG

THE QUIGMANS　　　　　　　　by Buddy Hickerson

"I hate to use the words 'You're fired . . .' so just get up and move to the other side of the desk."

B. Hickerson, copyright Los Angeles Times Syndicate. Reprinted by permission.

Comparison and Contrast Defined

Comparison and contrast is a method of showing similarities and differences between subjects. **Comparison** is concerned with organizing and developing points of similarity; **contrast** serves the same function for differences. In some instances, a writing assignment may require that you cover only similarities or only differences. Occasionally, an instructor may ask you to separate one from the other. Usually, you will combine them within the larger design of your paragraph or essay. For convenience, the term *comparison* is often used to refer to both comparison and contrast, because both use the same techniques and are regularly combined into one operation.

This chapter will help you deal with topics and choose strategies for developing comparison and contrast.

Generating Topics and Working with the 4 *Ps*

Comparison and contrast are basic to your thinking. In your daily activities, you consider similarities and differences between persons, things, concepts, political leaders, doctors, friends, instructors, schools, nations, classes, movies, and so on. You naturally turn to comparison and contrast to solve problems and make decisions in your life and in your writing. Because you have had so much experience with comparing, finding a topic to write about is likely to be easy and interesting. Freewriting, brainstorming, and listing will help you generate topics that are especially workable and appropriate for particular assignments.

Many college writing assignments will specify a topic or direct you to choose one from a list. Regardless of the source of your topic, the procedure for developing your ideas by comparison and contrast is the same. That procedure can appropriately be called the 4 *Ps*: **p**urpose, **p**oints, **p**atterns, and **p**resentation.

Purpose

In most of your writing, the main purpose will be either to inform or to persuade.

Informative Writing

If you want to explain something about a topic by showing each subject in relationship with others, then your purpose is informative. For example, you might be comparing two composers, Beethoven and Mozart. Both were musical geniuses, so you might decide that it would be senseless to argue that one is superior to the other. Instead, you choose to reveal interesting information about both by showing them in relation to each other. The emphasis of your writing would be on insights into their characteristics, the insights heightened because the characteristics are placed alongside each other.

Persuasive Writing

If you want to show that one actor, one movie, one writer, one president, one product, or one idea is better than another, your purpose is persuasive. Your argument will take shape as you write, beginning with emphasis in the topic sentence or thesis and reinforcement by repetition throughout your paper, in each case indicating that one side is superior.

Let's say, as an extended illustration, that you are taking a course in twentieth-century European history and you are asked to write about two leaders. You choose to write about Mussolini and Hitler as dictators. In freewriting, you discover that you know quite a bit about the two leaders. By brainstorming, you come up with some specific information.

Who?	Mussolini and Hitler
What?	fascist leaders, racists—with Hitler being more extreme
Where?	in Italy and Germany, respectively
When?	the decade before and during World War II
Why?	greed, morals, possible psychological problems—with Hitler being more extreme
How?	setting up totalitarian states

You tentatively decide that your purpose will be to persuade readers that, although both men were fascists, Hitler was more extreme in all important respects. If you need more information, you will have to consult your textbooks, your lecture notes, or sources in the library or on the Internet.

Points

The points are the ideas that will be applied somewhat equally to both sides of your comparison and contrast. They begin to emerge in freewriting, take on more precision in brainstorming, acquire a main position in listing, and assume the major part of the framework in the outline.

When writing on an assigned topic based on lectures and reading, you will probably be able to select these points quickly. The subject material itself may dictate the points. For example, if you were comparing the governments of the United States and Great Britain, you would probably use these three points: executive, legislative, and judicial.

Using listing as a technique for finding points is simple. Follow this procedure:

1. Select one side of your two-part subject (the side you know better) and compose a list in relation to a basic treatment you expect to extend to your comparative study.

> Hitler was a fascist dictator with racist views.
> subject   treatment

2. Make a list of points (about Hitler as a fascist dictator).

commitment
racial views
beliefs
fascism
flexibility
militaristic designs

3. Decide which points can also be applied in a useful way to the other subject, in this case, Mussolini. (You can also reverse the approach.) In this instance, all of the points can be applied in a useful way.

4. Select the points for your topic sentence or thesis.

racial views
commitment
militaristic designs

5. Incorporate these points into a topic sentence or thesis. (Your final topic sentence or thesis need not specify the points.)

<u>Although Mussolini and Hitler were both fascist dictators,</u> they
subject

<u>were significantly different in their racial views, commitment, and</u>
treatment (with points)

<u>militaristic designs.</u>

You now have a purpose and points. An outline or outline alternative will help you select and develop a pattern for your comparison.

Patterns

Now you will choose between two basic patterns of organization: (1) subject by subject (opposing) or (2) point by point (alternating). In long papers you may mix the two patterns, but in most college assignments, you will probably select just one and make it your basic organizational plan.

In comparison and contrast, the outline works especially well in indicating relationships and sequence. As with most other writing forms we have worked with, the sequence of a comparison-and-contrast paragraph or essay can be based on time, space, or emphasis. Emphasis is the most likely order.

Figures 14.1 and 14.2 show the two patterns as they are applied to both the paragraph (on the left) and the essay (on the right).

Figure 14.1
Subject-by-Subject Organization

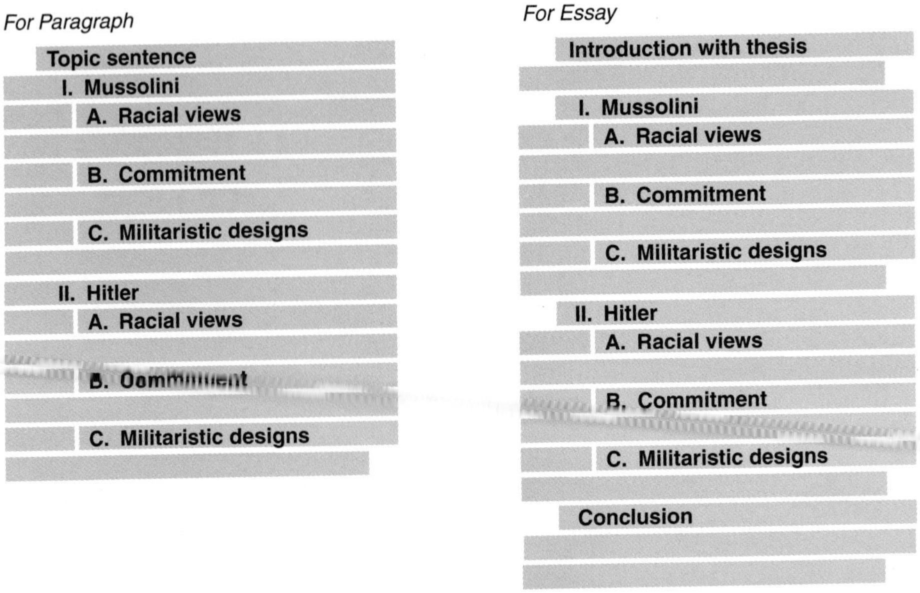

For Paragraph

Topic sentence
I. Mussolini
    A. Racial views
    B. Commitment
    C. Militaristic designs
II. Hitler
    A. Racial views
    B. Commitment
    C. Militaristic designs

For Essay

Introduction with thesis
I. Mussolini
    A. Racial views
    B. Commitment
    C. Militaristic designs
II. Hitler
    A. Racial views
    B. Commitment
    C. Militaristic designs
Conclusion

Figure 14.2
Point-by-Point Organization

For Paragraph

Topic sentence
I. Racial views
   A. Mussolini

   B. Hitler

II. Commitment
   A. Mussolini

   B. Hitler

III. Militaristic designs
   A. Mussolini

   B. Hitler

For Essay

Introduction with thesis

I. Racial views
   A. Mussolini

   B. Hitler

II. Commitment
   A. Mussolini

   B. Hitler

III. Militaristic designs
   A. Mussolini

   B. Hitler

Conclusion

In the subject-by-subject approach, organize your material around the subjects—the sides of the comparative study, as shown in Figure 14.1. In the point-by-point approach, organize your paper mainly around the points that you apply to the two subjects, as shown in Figure 14.2.

Presentation

The two patterns of organization—subject by subject and point by point—are equally valid, and each has its strengths for presentation of ideas.

As shown in Figure 14.1, the subject-by-subject pattern presents materials in large blocks, which means the reader can see a body of material that is complete. However, if the material is also complex, the reader has the burden of remembering ideas in going from one part to the next. Parallel development of ideas and cross-references in the second portion of the paragraph or essay can often offset that problem. Transitional words and phrases also help to establish coherence.

The point-by-point pattern shown in Figure 14.2 provides an immediate and direct relationship of points to subject. Therefore, it is especially useful in arguing that one side is superior to the other, in dealing with complex topics, and in working with longer compositions. But because of its systematic nature, if development is not sufficient, it can appear mechanical and monotonous. You can avoid that appearance by developing each idea thoroughly.

Some writers believe that the subject-by-subject form works best for short (paragraph-length) assignments, and the point-by-point form works best for longer pieces (essays).

In the following examples, the topic of Mussolini and Hitler is presented in the final draft stage of the paragraph form and then in the essay form. Note that the paragraph (often, as here, an essay in miniature) is expanded into an essay by developing the topic sentence, the supporting points, and the restated topic sentence into separate paragraphs: introduction, middle paragraph, middle paragraph, middle paragraph, and conclusion. Although both the paragraph and the essay make good observations and illustrate the use of pattern, for this topic the full essay would probably be more suitable in fulfilling the writer's purpose. Both the paragraph and the essay use a point-by-point arrangement.

Here is the paragraph:

Topic sentence

Point 1: Racism

Transition

Point 2: Commitment

Transition

Point 3: Militaristic designs

Transition

Restated topic sentence

Hitler and Mussolini often have been thought of as twin dictators, but there was considerable difference between the two men and their regimes, and Hitler was more extreme. Racism is justly associated with all fascism at that time; therefore, Mussolini is implicated. It should be pointed out, however, that the Italians' blatant racism occurred after Mussolini's deep association with Hitler. *But* Hitler had held racist views from the beginning of his political movement, and it was a main motive in the Nazi movement. Their degree of commitment to act also varied. Mussolini merely talked and strutted for the most part. He had few fixed doctrines and increasingly accommodated himself to circumstances. *But* Hitler meant every bit of his bellicosity, and he was willing to wage the most frightful war of all time. A study of their involvement in that war, however, reveals striking differences. Italian fascism was comparatively restrained and conservative until the Nazi example spurred it to new activity. *In contrast,* Hitler's radical and dynamic pace hardly flagged from January 1933 to April 1945. In the process, anti-Semitism, concentration camps, and total war produced a febrile and sadistic nightmare without any parallel in the Italian experience. Though both Hitler and Mussolini were fascist, history shows them to be different in all of these respects, and in each one Hitler was more radical.

Here is the essay:

Introduction with thesis

Topic sentence

(Middle paragraph)

Topic sentence

(Middle paragraph)

Topic sentence

(Middle paragraph)

Hitler and Mussolini have often been thought of as twin dictators, but there were considerable differences between the two men and their regimes, and Hitler was more extreme. These differences become apparent when one considers their racial views, their commitment, and their militaristic designs.

Racism is justly associated with all fascism at that time: therefore, Mussolini, along with Hitler, is implicated. It should be pointed out, however, that the Italians' blatant racism occurred after Mussolini's deep association with Hitler. Prior to that, for many years there had been no racial doctrine in Italian fascist ideology. But Hitler held racist views from the beginning of his political movement, and it was a main motive in the Nazi movement. To resolve the "Jewish problem," he eventually slaughtered at least six million people.

Their degree of commitment to act also varied. From a distance toward the end of the war, they may have seemed quite similar, but over the span of their reigns, they were different. Mussolini merely talked and strutted for the most part. He had few fixed doctrines and increasingly accommodated himself to circumstances. But Hitler meant every bit of his bellicosity and was willing to wage the most frightful war of all time.

A study of their involvement in that war, however, reveals striking differences. Italian fascism was comparatively restrained and conservative until the Nazi example spurred it to new activity. Mussolini talked of a militaristic policy, but he followed a more temperate course in practice and kept the peace for thirteen years, knowing that Italy could not gain from a major war. In contrast, Hitler's radical and dynamic pace hardly flagged from January 1933 to April 1945. In the process, anti-Semitism, concentration camps, and total war produced a febrile and sadistic nightmare without any parallel in the Italian experience.

Conclusion

Thus, though both were fascist, history shows the two men to be different in both ideas and actions. Only at the end of their relationship, when Mussolini succumbed to Hitler's domination, do the two leaders appear as twin dictators, but beneath appearances it is Hitler who was the true believer, the fascist dictator.

Analogy

Analogy is a method of organizing and developing ideas by comparison. In an analogy, a writer explains or clarifies an unfamiliar subject by likening it to a familiar but strikingly different subject. Writers use analogy to make the new, the different, the complex, or the difficult more understandable for the reader. Analogy, therefore, explains, clarifies, illustrates, and simplifies; it does not prove anything.

In the following model analogy, Emerson compares society to a wave. Most analogies, like this model, are part of a larger piece of writing.

Ralph Waldo Emerson, "Self-Reliance"

> Society is a wave. The wave moves onward, but the water of which it is composed does not. The same particle does not rise from the valley to the ridge. Its unity is only phenomenal. The persons who make up a nation today, next year die, and their experience dies with them.

Writers usually announce the analogy and then develop it. In addition, analogies, as a rule, rise spontaneously from the material as the writer's thoughts flow. Study the following model. Notice that the writer announces the comparison in the first sentence. To make the meaning clear, he compares the atmosphere of the earth to a window.

> The atmosphere of Earth acts like any window in serving two very important functions. It lets light in and it permits us to look out. It also serves as a shield to keep out dangerous or uncomfortable things. A normal glazed window lets us keep our house warm by keeping out cold air, and it prevents rain, dirt, and unwelcome insects and animals from coming in. As we have already seen, Earth's atmospheric window also helps to keep our planet to a comfortable temperature by holding back radiated heat and protecting us from dangerous levels of ultraviolet light.

Lester Del Ray, *The Mysterious Sky*

> Lately, we have discovered that space is full of a great many very dangerous things against which our atmosphere guards us. It is not a perfect shield, and sometimes one of these dangerous objects does get through. There is even some evidence that a few of these messengers from space contain life, though this has by no means been proven yet.

The steps for writing the analogy are identical to those of writing comparison and contrast.

Practicing Patterns of Comparison and Contrast

Shorter compositions such as paragraphs are likely to be arranged subject by subject, and longer compositions such as essays are likely to be arranged point by point, although either pattern can work in either length. In longer works, especially in published writing, the two patterns may be mixed. Being able to organize your material quickly and effectively according to the pattern that is best for your material is important to your success as a writer. Even in a timed assignment, make a simple scratch outline that will guide you in writing a piece that is unified and coherent.

EXERCISE 1

Completing Patterns of Comparison and Contrast

Fill in the blanks to complete the following outlines.

A. Point-by-Point Outline

John: Before and after marriage

I. Way of talking (content and manner)

    A. _____

    B. John: After

II. _____

    A. John: Before

    B. John: After

III. _____

    A. John: Before

    B. _____

B. Subject-by-Subject Outline

Two vans: Nissan Quest and Dodge Caravan (would be more specific if for a particular year)

I. Quest

    A. Horsepower and gears

    B. _____

    C. Cargo area

II. Caravan

    A. _____

    B. Safety

    C. _____

C. Point-by-Point Outline

Topic: Neighborhoods

I. _____ (point)

   A. _____ (subject)

   B. _____ (subject)

II. _____ (point)

   A. _____ (subject)

   B. _____ (subject)

III. _____ (point)

   A. _____ (subject)

   B. _____ (subject)

D. Subject-by-Subject Outline

Topic: Two friends you have had (or another approved topic)

I. _____ (friend)

   A. _____ (point)

   B. _____ (point)

   C. _____ (point)

II. _____ (friend)

   A. _____ (point)

   B. _____ (point)

   C. _____ (point)

Connecting Reading and Writing

Professional Writers

Business Battle Tactics

ROBERT McGARVEY

Analogies are used frequently in discussions of business. Here, Robert McGarvey interviews Brian Tracy, author and corporate sales consultant. McGarvey is a frequent contributor to Selling Power *magazine and writes often about selling and success. This article was first published in* American Way *magazine.*

1   Quick now, what's The Principle of the Mass and why do winners know it? How about The Principle of Maneuver? Or Concerted Action? No bells of familiarity ringing in your skull? Brian Tracy, who's made a career out of training salespeople and managers to succeed, wants to change that. His new idea is that grasping these concepts—and nine others outlined in his new book, *Victory!* (Amacom)—is key to business achievement. That's because all twelve are ideas that fueled breakthrough military victories, and, says Tracy, today's corporate leaders need military thinking to manage through topsy-turvy, economically unsettled times.

2   He backs up this belief in *Victory!* with a point-by-point exploration of how generals win their battles. Who better to inspire success than victorious military leaders, from Alexander the Great to George S. Patton?

3   The author and well-known business coach recently shared the high points of his military-meets-business scenario.

4   *AMERICAN WAY:* **What's the relevance of military thinking to today's business executive?**

5   **BRIAN TRACY:** Military thinking may be more important than ever to executives. The same kind of thinking that enables a person to function in the chaos and confusion of war will help a businessperson make good decisions in a turbulent business economy. The principles that great military leaders used to make effective decisions in high-stakes situations are ideas you can use today to run a business effectively.

6   *AMERICAN WAY:* **Your book covers twelve principles of military success. If you had to pinpoint one as the most critical, which would it be?**

7   **TRACY:** Let me rephrase that. One people find very helpful to know is "The Principle of the Objective." Great generals don't enter battle without knowing their objectives. Everywhere in life, lack of clarity with regard to goals is 89 percent of failure, and clarity is 89 percent of success. A for-instance: When General [Dwight D.] Eisenhower was sent to London to take command in World War II, his orders were, "Invade Europe. Defeat the Germans." Any meaningful objective has to be as clear as this one. Make sure that everyone who is involved in pursuing a goal is crystal-clear about the objective. What are the company's goals? What are this department's goals? What is each individual's goal? The clearer everybody is, the more likely success.

8   *AMERICAN WAY:* Once the goal is identified, what military lesson comes into play?

9   **TRACY:** The next principle is concentration—focus all your energy on your objectives. Napoleon shows this in the Battle of Austerlitz, where his army, although outnumbered by Austrian and Russian troops, charged to victory because he ordered his troops to throw their energies into winning the highest point on the battlefield, the Pratzen Heights. From there, they were able to dominate the fight. Executives can do likewise. There have been a whole lot of books on focus lately, and what they basically come down to is that the natural tendency in any organization is to diffuse its efforts over a wider and wider range of activities. But success comes to those who know how to concentrate, how to focus.

10 *AMERICAN WAY:* Focus on what? Isn't that a common complaint: "Sure, we know focus matters, but we don't know where to put our energy?"

11 **TRACY:** That's why you want to know "The Principle of the Mass." It tells us to concentrate combat power at the decisive place and time.

12 *AMERICAN WAY:* To illustrate that, you point to the Battle of Islandhlwana in the Zulu wars of 1879, when the British General Chemlsford scattered his 1,800 troops across a wide swath of land and suffered one of the worst defeats in history. That makes sense for a military principle—but how could an executive put this idea to use?

13 **TRACY:** In fact, it's more important now than ever, precisely because resources are limited. You cannot afford to scatter your efforts. Companies have to fall back on what I call the citadel. They have to fall back on their most important products and services and most important customers and markets. Focus single-mindedly on them. That's how to succeed in hard times.

14 *AMERICAN WAY:* Another principle that you say seems especially suited to today's business environment is your Principle of Maneuver. Why?

15 **TRACY:** Maneuver tells us to remain flexible at all times. George Washington won the decisive Battle of Trenton because his troops rowed across the Delaware River on December 26, in the middle of the night. He caught the British when they were still sleepy from their Christmas celebrations. That's showing how to maneuver, how to think outside the box. All originality and progress comes from doing things differently than they were done in the past—that's the plain fact, and it works in business as well as in the military.

16 *AMERICAN WAY:* Good as these ideas may be, can an executive expect his or her boss to buy into any of them?

17 **TRACY:** Here's how to win approval from your boss. Go to your manager and get clear about your priorities. Whatever you boss considers most important, work on it all day long—and that will bring immediate gratification both to you and your boss. How can this not please him or her?

18 *AMERICAN WAY:* Sounds good, but isn't that kind of single-mindedness a pipe dream in today's hectic, multitasking work world?

19 **TRACY:** My advice here is basic. Focus on results, and on making your actions count. That sounds simple but know this: It's a mindset possessed by the top 3 percent of movers and shakers in American corporations. Make that kind of commitment and you are taking big steps toward becoming a standout in any organization.

Discussion and Critical Thinking

1. Like other forms of comparison and contrast, this analogy can be analyzed by using the four *P*s. Fill in the blanks.

   Purpose (to inform or to persuade):

   Points (ideas that can be applied to both subjects):

   I. _____

   II. _____

   III. _____

   IV. _____

   Pattern (subject by subject or point by point):

   Presentation:

2. In this analogy, what is equivalent to winning a battle or war?

Pink Kittens and Blue Spaceships

ALISON LURIE

What are the sources of gender identity? In this passage from her book
The Language of Clothes, *Alison Lurie shows that people condition children from birth.*

1   Sex-typing in dress begins at birth with the assignment of pale-pink layettes, toys, bedding and furniture to girl babies, and pale-blue ones to boy babies. Pink, in this culture, is associated with sentiment; blue with service. The implication is that the little girl's future concern will be the life of the affections; the boy's, earning a living. As they grow older, light blue becomes a popular color for girls' clothes—after all, women must work as well as weep—but pink is rare on boys'; the emotional life is never quite manly.

2   In early childhood girls' and boys' clothes are often identical in cut and fabric, as if in recognition of the fact that their bodies are much alike. But the T-shirts, pull-on slacks and zip jackets intended for boys are usually made in darker colors (especially forest green, navy, red and brown) and printed with designs involving sports, transportation and cute wild animals. Girls' clothes are made in paler colors (especially pink, yellow and green) and decorated with flowers and cute domestic animals. The suggestion is that the boy will play vigorously and travel over long distances; the girl will stay home and nurture plants and small mammals. Alternatively, these designs may symbolize their wearers: the boy is a cuddly bear or a

smiling tiger, the girl a flower or a kitten. There is also a tendency for boys' clothes to be fullest at the shoulders and girls' at the hips, anticipating their adult figures. Boys' and men's garments also emphasize the shoulders with horizontal stripes, epaulets or yokes of contrasting color. Girls' and women's garments emphasize the hips and rear through the strategic placement of gathers and trimmings.

EXERCISE 3

Discussion and Critical Thinking

1. Does this selection stress comparison or contrast?

2. Is the purpose mainly to inform, to persuade, or to do both?

3. What are the two main points used for comparing and contrasting girls' and boys' clothes?

4. Is the pattern of the piece point by point or subject by subject?

5. Fill in the parts of this outline of the piece.

   I. Color
      A. _____
      B. _____

   II. Design
      A. _____
         1. _____
         2. _____
      B. _____
         1. _____
         2. _____

6. Now that most mothers work outside the home, do you think the preferred colors and designs will change?

The Small Town and the Big City
CRAIG CALHOUN

Presentations of comparison and contrast are used frequently in college textbooks. In this paragraph from Sociology, *sixth edition, Craig Calhoun discusses human behavior and the reasons for that behavior in a small community and in a large one.*

In almost every way, Diagonal [Iowa] and the Upper West Side of Manhattan appear to be opposites. In Diagonal, everyone knows everyone else personally; people are involved in a continual round of community-centered activities (the few who do not participate are thought aloof and antisocial); and everyone's activities are subject to close scrutiny. Gossip keeps most Diagonal residents from stepping very far out of line. Of course, sexual transgressions, public drunkenness, and teenage vandalism occasionally take place, but serious crime is rare. On the Upper West Side most people know only a few of the people who live in their apartment building; everyone has his or her own circle of friends; and community-based activities are rare (such as the occasional block party). Neighborliness is often considered nosiness. Anonymity is the norm, and widely different lifestyles are tolerated or simply ignored. At the same time, crime is common: most Upper West Side residents either have been the victim of a mugging or robbery or know someone who has been.

EXERCISE 4

Discussion and Critical Thinking

1. Underline the topic sentence of the paragraph.

2. Is the paragraph pattern subject by subject or point by point?

3. Fill in the parts of this basic outline:

   I. Diagonal

      A. People involved

      B. _____

      C. Serious crime rare

   II. _____

      A. _____

      B. Mostly anonymous

      C. _____

4. Could the paragraph be improved by using some transitional words such as *on the other hand*, *unlike*, or *to the contrary*? If so, where would you put them?

Los Chinos Discover el Barrio

LUIS TORRES

Blending nostalgic recollections and astute insights, Luis Torres chronicles the cultural changes of a Northeast Los Angeles neighborhood. Note how the concluding scene parallels the introductory scene. If, after you have finished reading the piece, you are not certain whether it is optimistic or pessimistic, reread the first and last paragraphs.

1   There's a colorful mural on the asphalt playground of Hillside Elementary School, in the neighborhood called Lincoln Heights. Painted on the beige handball wall, the mural is of life-sized youngsters holding hands. Depicted are Asian and Latino kids with bright faces and ear-to-ear smiles.

2   The mural is a mirror of the makeup of the neighborhood today: Latinos living side-by-side with Asians. But it's not all smiles and happy faces in the Northeast Los Angeles community, located just a couple of miles up Broadway from City Hall. On the surface there's harmony between Latinos and Asians. But there are indications of simmering ethnic-based tensions.

3   That became clear to me recently when I took a walk through the old neighborhood—the one where I grew up. As I walked along North Broadway, I thought of a joke that comic Paul Rodriguez often tells on the stage. He paints the picture of a young Chicano walking down a street on L.A.'s Eastside. He comes upon two Asians having an animated conversation in what sounds like babble. "Hey, you guys, knock off that foreign talk. This is America—speak Spanish!"

4   When I was growing up in Lincoln Heights 30 years ago most of us spoke Spanish—and English. There was a sometimes uneasy coexistence in the neighborhood between brown and white. Back then we Latinos were moving in and essentially displacing the working-class Italians (to us, they were just *los gringos*) who had moved there and thrived after World War II.

5   Because I was an extremely fair-skinned Latino kid I would often overhear remarks by gringos in Lincoln Heights that were not intended for Latino ears, disparaging comments about "smelly wetbacks," and worse. The transition was, for the most part, a gradual process. And as I recall—except for the slurs that sometimes stung me directly—a process marked only occasionally by outright hostility.

6   A trend that began about ten years ago in Lincoln Heights seems to have hit a critical point now. It's similar to the ethnic tug-of-war of yesteryear, but different colors, different words are involved. Today Chinese and Vietnamese are displacing the Latinos who, by choice or circumstance, had Lincoln Heights virtually to themselves for two solid generations.

7   Evidence of the transition is clear.

8   The bank where I opened my first meager savings account in the late 1950s has changed hands. It's now the East-West Federal Bank, an Asian-owned enterprise.

9   The public library on Workman Street, where I checked out *Charlotte's Web* with my first library card, abounds with signs of the new times: It's called "La Biblioteca del Pueblo de Lincoln Heights," and on the door there's a notice advising that the building is closed because of the Oct. 1 earthquake; it's written in Chinese.

10   The white, wood-frame house on Griffin Avenue that I once lived in is now owned by a Chinese family.

11   What used to be a Latino-run mortuary at the corner of Sichel Street and North Broadway is now the Chung Wah Funeral Home.

12   A block down the street from the funeral home is a *panaderia*, a bakery. As I would listen to radio reports of the U.S. war in faraway Indochina while walking from class at Lincoln High School, I often used to drop in the *panaderia* for a snack.

13   The word *panaderia*, now faded and chipped, is still painted on the shop window that fronts North Broadway. But another sign, a gleaming plastic one, hangs above the window. The sign proclaims that it is a Vietnamese-Chinese bakery. The proprietor, Sam Lee, bought the business less than a year ago. With a wave of his arm, he indicates that *La Opinion*, the Spanish-language daily newspaper, is still for sale on the counter. Two signs hang side by side behind the counter announcing in Spanish and in Chinese that cakes are made to order for all occasions.

14   Out on North Broadway, Fidel Farrillas sells *raspadas* (snow-cones) from his pushcart. He has lived and worked in Lincoln Heights "for 30 years and a pinch more," he says, his voice nearly whistling through two gold-framed teeth. He has seen the neighborhood change. Twice.

15   Like many older Latinos he remembers the tension felt between *los gringos y la raza* years ago—even though most people went about their business ostensibly co-existing politely. And others who have been around as long will tell an inquiring reporter scratching away in his notebook, "We're going out of our way to treat the *chinos* nice—better than the *gringos* sometimes treated us back then." But when the notebook is closed, they're likely to whisper, "But you know, the thing is, they smell funny, and they talk behind your back, and they are so arrogant—the way they're buying up everything in our neighborhood."

16   Neighborhood transitions can be tough to reconcile.

17   It isn't easy for the blue-collar Latinos of Lincoln Heights. They haven't possessed much. But they had the barrio, "a little chunk of the world where we belonged," as one described it. There may be some hard times and hard feelings ahead as *los chinos* continue to make inroads into what had been an exclusively Latino enclave. But there are hopeful signs as well.

18   On one recent Saturday afternoon a Latino fifth-grader, wearing the same type of hightop tennis shoes I wore as a 10-year-old on that same street corner, strode up to Señor Farrillas' snow-cone pushcart. The kid pulled out a pocketful of dimes and bought two *raspadas*. One for himself, and one for his school chum—a Vietnamese kid. He was wearing hightops, too. They both ordered strawberry, as I recall.

EXERCISE 5   ## Vocabulary Highlights

Write a short definition of each word as it is used in the essay. (Paragraph numbers are given in parentheses.) Be prepared to use the words in your own sentences.

depicted (1)   *los gringos y la raza* (15)

simmering (2)   ostensibly (15)

Chicano (3)   *chinos* (15)

animated (3)   barrio (17)

disparaging (5)   enclave (17)

EXERCISE 6   ## Discussion and Critical Thinking

1. Although this essay is not a highly structured comparative study, Torres is mainly concerned with Lincoln Heights then and Lincoln Heights now, thirty years later. What are the main points he uses to show the similarities?

2. What are some of the similarities?

3. What are some of the differences?

4. What is the implied comparison between the first and the last paragraphs?

5. What is Torres's main message? Specifically, is he mostly optimistic or pessimistic? What evidence do you find? Do you agree with him?

Paired Essays on Orderly and Disorderly People

Are you fundamentally orderly or disorderly? We all have tendencies toward one or the other extreme. Some of us are hardcore, to our shame or pride. If we lean toward the disorderly, we may scoff at the opposite, referring to them as "uptight" or "anal retentive." If we are in the orderly camp, we may pity the disorderly for failures in work ethic, analytical power, self-discipline, even personal hygiene.

As we read Suzanne Britt's essay, we are probably first surprised and then charmed by her wit and satirical jibes. She insists that the neat (orderly) people are the bad guys and that the sloppy (disorderly) people are the good guys. Moreover, to her, the distinction is not even close. She says, "Neat people are lazier and meaner than sloppy people." She doesn't use the slang term "neat freaks," but she makes it clear that the neat are twisted, self-centered individuals who "cut a clean swath through the organic as well as the inorganic world."

THE QUIGMANS   **by Buddy Hickerson**

"AAUGH! It'll take me weeks to clean this place up! *Dirt everywhere!!* And as for you, my friend, I have two words: public restroom!"

B. Hickerson, copyright Los Angeles Times Syndicate. Reprinted by permission.

Joyce Gallagher, author of "The Messy Are in Denial," is one of those people whom she characterizes as the organized. Her group has a preordained mission—to save and sustain the less fortunate, the disorganized, the sloppy. A bemused and grudgingly forgiving participant (after all, the disorganized can't help themselves), she traces the history of the organized and disorganized from a recent yard sale back to cave dwellers, saying that human nature hasn't changed much. The disorganized flounder, often in endearing ways, and the organized come to their rescue because of a genetic imperative.

Neat People vs. Sloppy People

SUZANNE BRITT

In this essay from her book Show and Tell, *Suzanne Britt discusses two kinds of people, the neat and the sloppy. Wouldn't the world be a better place if we were all a bit neater? If you think so, prepare to argue with Suzanne Britt.*

1   I've finally figured out the difference between neat people and sloppy people. The distinction is, as always, moral. Neat people are lazier and meaner than sloppy people.

2   Sloppy people, you see, are not really sloppy. Their sloppiness is merely the unfortunate consequence of their extreme moral rectitude. Sloppy people carry in their mind's eye a heavenly vision, a precise plan, that is so stupendous, so perfect, it can't be achieved in this world or the next.

3   Sloppy people live in Never-Never Land. Someday is their métier. Someday they are planning to alphabetize all their books and set up home catalogs. Someday they will go through their wardrobes and mark certain items for tentative mending and certain items for passing on to relatives of similar shape and size. Someday sloppy people will make family scrapbooks into which they will put newspaper clippings, postcards, locks of hair, and the dried corsage from their senior prom. Someday they will file everything on the surface of their desk, including the cash receipts from coffee purchases at the snack shop. Someday they will sit down and read all the back issues of *The New Yorker*.

4   For all these noble reasons and more, sloppy people never get neat. They aim too high and wide. They save everything, planning someday to file, order, and straighten out the world. But while these ambitious plans take clearer and clearer shape in their heads, the books spill from the shelves onto the floor, the clothes pile up in the hamper and closet, the family mementos accumulate in every drawer, the surface of the desk is buried under mounds of paper and the unread magazines threaten to reach the ceiling.

5   Sloppy people can't bear to part with anything. They give loving attention to every detail. When sloppy people say they're going to tackle the surface of the desk, they really mean it. Not a paper will go unturned; not a rubber band will go unboxed. Four hours or two weeks into their excavation, the desk looks exactly the same, primarily because the sloppy person is meticulously creating new piles of papers with new headings and scrupulously stopping to read all the old book catalogs before he throws them away. A neat person would just bulldoze the desk.

6   Neat people are bums and clods at heart. They have cavalier attitudes toward possessions, including family heirlooms. Everything is just another dust-catcher to

them. If anything collects dust, it's got to go and that's that. Neat people will toy with the idea of throwing the children out of the house just to cut down on the clutter.

7   Neat people don't care about process. They like results. What they want to do is get the whole thing over with so they can sit down and watch the rasslin' on TV. Neat people operate on two unvarying principles: Never handle any item twice, and throw everything away.

8   The only thing messy in a neat person's house is the trash can. The minute something comes to a neat person's hand, he will look at it, try to decide if it has immediate use and, finding none, throw it in the trash.

9   Neat people are especially vicious with mail. They never go through their mail unless they are standing directly over a trash can. If the trash can is beside the mailbox, even better. All ads, catalogs, pleas for charitable contributions, church bulletins and money-saving coupons go straight into the trash can without being opened. All letters from home, postcards from Europe, bills and paychecks are opened, immediately responded to, then dropped in the trash can. Neat people keep their receipts only for tax purposes. That's it. No sentimental salvaging of birthday cards or the last letter a dying relative ever wrote. Into the trash it goes.

10   Neat people place neatness above everything, even economics. They are incredibly wasteful. Neat people throw away several toys every time they walk through the den. I knew a neat person once who threw away a perfectly good dish drainer because it had mold on it. The drainer was too much trouble to wash. And neat people sell their furniture when they move. They will sell a La-Z-Boy recliner while you are reclining in it.

11   Neat people are no good to borrow from. Neat people buy everything in expensive little single portions. They get their flour and sugar in two-pound bags. They wouldn't consider clipping a coupon, saving a leftover, reusing plastic nondairy whipped cream containers or rinsing off tin foil and draping it over the unmoldy dish drainer. You can never borrow a neat person's newspaper to see what's playing at the movies. Neat people have the paper all wadded up and in the trash by 7:05 A.M.

12   Neat people cut a clean swath through the organic as well as the inorganic world. People, animals, and things are all one to them. They are so insensitive. After they've finished with the pantry, the medicine cabinet, and the attic, they will throw out the red geranium (too many leaves), sell the dog (too many fleas), and send the children off to boarding school (too many scuff marks on the hardwood floors).

EXERCISE 7

Vocabulary Highlights

Write a short definition of each word as it is used in the essay. (Paragraph numbers are given in parentheses.) Be prepared to use the words in your own sentences.

rectitude (2)	meticulously (5)
stupendous (2)	scrupulously (5)
métier (3)	cavalier (6)
tentative (3)	heirlooms (6)
excavation (5)	swath (12)

| EXERCISE 8 | # Discussion and Critical Thinking |

1. Is this essay mainly comparison or contrast?

2. Is Britt trying mainly to inform or to persuade?

3. What are the main points for this study?

4. Is the pattern mainly point by point or subject by subject?

5. What is the moral distinction between the neat and the sloppy?

6. Britt says that sloppy people are morally superior to neat people. How does that idea differ from common assumptions?

7. To what extent is Britt serious, and to what extent is she just being humorous?

8. Britt presents two extremes. What qualities would a person in the middle have?

The Messy Are in Denial

JOYCE GALLAGHER

Freelance journalist Joyce Gallagher gives us some insights into why the disorganized often marry the organized. She says it's all part of a design in Nature. Reasoning and her personal experience tell her so.

1   Others may see the disorganized as carefree people wallowing happily in the cluttered chaos of their own making. I see their conduct for what it so obviously is—a crying out for help. If they are so contented, then why are so many of them latching onto and becoming entirely dependent on those of us who are organized? Complaining all the while about being controlled, they, nevertheless, behave like mistletoe nailing itself to oaks, fleas colonizing St. Bernards, and funguses invading feet.

2   That tendency is easy to document and understand. Anyone can see why the disorganized (the messy, the sloppy, the disorderly, the Pisces, the idealist, the daydreamer) need the organized (the orderly, the systematic, the tidy, the Virgo, the neat, the realistic, the practical). But that leaves the more complicated question: Why would the organized even tolerate the disorganized? Or to use our figures of speech, why would oaks, St. Bernards, and feet be so submissive? I say the answer to all such connections can be found in the phrase "balance in nature." Every creature type occupies a niche or plunges into extinction. One role of those who are neat (while they are enjoying their own practical and artistic triumphs) is to provide a secure directive system so the sloppy can experience their measure of fulfillment. Like a stoical whale with a barnacle, the organized hang in there while the disorganized hang on.

3   Of course, hanging on, or even hanging around, doesn't mean the disorganized are always complete parasites. Far from it. In fact, the disorganized are often writers, artists, musicians, pop philosophers, and lovable flakes. They may even be fun to be around, even to get married to—even stay married to, if you can get past their messiness.

4   If you will just listen, the disorganized will explain *ad nauseam* their lives as works in progress. And in a sense their lives are works like writing in progress, not in advanced stages such as revision or editing, but in freewriting, brainstorming, and clustering. Without a thesis, they freewrite through the material world, not yet knowing what to keep or discard. They brainstorm through life, jumping from one acquisition to another, clustering their "treasures" in attics, work rooms, garages, and other handy, unprotected spaces. Finally, if not directed by an organized person, they run the risk of inundating themselves with their own junk.

5   Fortunately, when Nature has its way, an organizer comes to the rescue—as a friend, a relative, or, perhaps, an official. In my situation, I'm the organized spouse, sometimes succumbing to my disorganized companion's pathetic romanticism, but more often, saving him from himself.

6   I do what I can. As he busily accumulates, I busily distribute. It's not easy. Toil as I might, I look around and see him effortlessly acquiring, like a tornado sucking in stuff faster than I can throw it away. I especially donate to thrift stores. Hapless children, the disabled of all kinds, and veterans of all wars depend mightily on us organized people to provide merchandise to their benefactors. Unfortunately for the organized, the thrift industry also depends on the disorganized as customers to cart home items such as scratchy vinyl records, manual typewriters, vintage clothing, and myriad unspeakable artifacts called "collectibles."

7   And if it's not a thrift store providing a game preserve for the disorganized, it's a yard sale. Organized people conduct yard sales. The disorganized attend them. As slack-jawed, hollow-eyed hulks, they drive compulsively from one location to another, not knowing what they are looking for. I suppose it's an ancient yearning for the hunt, even when the belly, larder, and garage are full. I've known my significant disorganized other to stake out a promising sale site a full hour before opening time, peering through the windshield of his motorized blind, stalking the forlorn, unwanted inanimate prey. Way back in the distance, I shovel out junk, knowing it is the burden of the neat to offset every shopping binge of the sloppy.

8   Despite my taking credit for rescuing and sustaining my disorganized mate, pride didn't prompt me to write this. In fact, I don't particularly relish my lot as an organized person with a directive mission. My behavior is quite beyond my control. As mentioned previously, it's probably instinctive, genetic. Tens of thousands of evolutionary years have made my opposite and me what we are.

9   My spouse's counterpart was perhaps an ancient daydreaming troglodyte, who decorated sandstone cave walls with drawings of hunts, imagining the glories of bringing down that mammoth with one club whomp. If so, there was a well-groomed organizer in the background, arranging his clubs all in a row and his life generally. If she hadn't done so, he couldn't have contributed to the diverse gene pool into which we now dip.

10   Reason tells me that's what happened to the Neanderthals—there was too much inbreeding among the disorganized. Consider the artists' uniform depictions of these creatures: messy to the max, with grubby fingers and tousled hair, their privates barely concealed by scrappy animal-hide clothing. It's no wonder science has failed to establish kinship between them and the surviving relatively neat- and tidy-looking *homo sapiens*.

EXERCISE 9

Vocabulary Highlights

Write a short definition of each word as it is used in the essay. (Paragraph numbers are given in parentheses.) Be prepared to use the words in your own sentences.

stoical (2)

parasites (3)

ad nauseam (4)

inundating (4)

artifacts (6)

inanimate (7)

sustaining (8)

troglodyte (9)

Neanderthals (10)

homo sapiens (10)

EXERCISE 10

Discussion and Critical Thinking

1. Is this essay mainly comparison or contrast?

2. Is Gallagher trying mainly to inform or to persuade?

3. What points of contrast are applied to the two types?

4. How much truth do you find amid the humor? Explain.

5. Do you agree that disorganized people need organized people? Why or why not?

6. Can one also make the point that organized people need disorganized people?

7. Can the high rate of divorce be partly traced to how organized people and disorganized people do or do not pair up? Why or why not?

EXERCISE 11

Connecting the Paired Essays

1. In comparing the two essays, what subjects are equivalent?

2. Britt says that neat people are lazy and mean. Does Gallagher say anything similar about the disorganized? If Gallagher doesn't go that far, then how far does she go in characterizing the disorganized?

3. Are the differences mainly in the types (neat and messy) being discussed or in the interpretation of the two types?

4. Both authors use humor to exaggerate traits. Which author distorts reality more?

5. Which author seems more flexible? Explain.

6. With which side of which comparison do you identify, if at all?

Student Writers

As Omar Zayas skimmed through the topic list for his summer-session class, one phrase caught his eye: "Two Amusement Parks." Within recent months he had gone to three in his Southern California area. He liked all of them, and he knew them well. Without giving focused thought to the subject, in his mind he had ranked them.

Zayas's Writing Process Worksheet shows you how his writing evolved from idea to final draft. To conserve space here, his three rough drafts marked for revision have been omitted.

You will find a full-size blank worksheet on page 6, which can be photocopied, filled in, and submitted with each assignment if your instructor directs you to do so.

Writing Process Worksheet

Title Disneyland or Magic Mountain: Fantasy or Thrills?

Name Omar Zayas   Due Date March 21, 9 a.m.

ASSIGNMENT

In the space below, write whatever you need to know about your assignment, including information about the topic, audience, pattern of writing, length, whether to include a rough draft or revised drafts, and whether your paper must be typed.

Compare and contrast two amusement parks in a paragraph with the appropriate pattern. Write for a general audience who will have at least some experience with your topic. Include some specific information such as names of attractions. Submit this completed worksheet, a rough draft marked for revision, and a typed final draft of about 300 words.

STAGE ONE

Explore   Freewrite, brainstorm (list), cluster, or take notes as directed by your instructor. Use the back of this page or separate paper if you need more space.

Freewriting

I have been to three amusement parks in Southern California. I like them all. Each one has something special that the others do not have. I like Knott's Berry Farm for its good food and its informal country setting and the animals. I like Disneyland for the atmosphere and the characters. Also the bands and the rides that I can remember so well from being a kid there. Then there is Magic Mountain, where I go for the fantastic rides. The price is always an issue and so is the hassle in getting there. Right now my ranking is Magic Mountain, Disneyland, and Knott's Berry Farm.

Listing

Rides
Food
Entertainment
Admission price
Parking
Driving
Atmosphere
Rules of behavior and dress

STAGE TWO

Organize   Write a topic sentence or thesis; label the subject and the treatment parts.

For most visitors a <u>decision on which amusement park to attend</u> is likely to be
subject
based on the price of admission and the <u>kinds of attractions offered by the parks.</u>
treatment

Write an outline or an outline alternative.

  I. Price
    A. Disneyland
      1. Specials
      2. $38
    B. Magic Mountain
      1. Specials
      2. $25.95
  II. The fantasy factor
    A. Disneyland
      1. "Pinocchio"
      2. "Cinderella"
      3. "Peter Pan"
      4. "Snow White"
    B. Magic Mountain
      1. "Tweety's Escape"
      2. "Pepe Le Pew's Tea Party"
 III. The thrill factor
    A. Disneyland
      1. "Space Mountain"
      2. "The Matterhorn"
      3. "Big Thunder Mountain"
    B. Magic Mountain
      1. "Goliath"
      2. "X"
      3. "Scream"
      4. "Déjà Vu"

STAGE THREE

Write   On separate paper, write and then revise your paragraph or essay as many times as necessary for **c**oherence, **l**anguage (usage, tone, and diction), **u**nity, **e**mphasis, **s**upport, and **s**entences (**CLUESS**). Read your work aloud to hear and correct any grammatical errors or awkward-sounding sentences.

Edit any problems in fundamentals, such as **c**apitalization, **o**missions, **p**unctuation, and **s**pelling (**COPS**).

Final Draft

Disneyland or Magic Mountain: Fantasy or Thrills?

Omar Zayas

Here in Southern California, we are fortunate to have two famous amusement parks: Disneyland and Six Flags Magic Mountain. For most visitors a decision on which park to attend is likely to be based mainly on the price of admission and the kinds of attractions offered by the parks. Disneyland carries the greater reputation for its storybook atmosphere, but a higher admission price comes with that reputation. The basic price is about $38 (excluding the California Adventure). At Six Flags, a current online ticket special is only $25.99. Once inside, the attractions may seem similar, but overall the differences are as noticeable as Mickey's ears. The Magic Kingdom is especially known for fantasy, which takes shape as gentle kiddie excursions into the imaginary worlds of "Pinocchio," "Cinderella," "Peter Pan," and "Snow White." At the next age group of maybe 8 through 12 are other relaxing rides: "The Haunted Mansion," "Pirates of the Caribbean," and "It's a Small World." Competing, but not too well, for the fantasy factor, Magic Mountain offers Looney Toons themes featuring "Tweety's Escape and "Pepe Le Pew's Tea Party" yet has no memorable rides for the 8 through 12 crowd. Then we come to the thrill factor, the determining issue for many of us. Disneyland has three such attractions, all vintage, all mountains: "Space Mountain," "The Matterhorn," and "Big Thunder Mountain." For thrill-seekers there's only one mountain—Magic Mountain. It's in a different category, having recently developed four of the tallest, fastest, and most innovative roller coasters in the world: "Goliath" (2000), "X" (2002), "Déjà vu" (2001), and "Scream" (2003). The choice is yours. For fantasy, and maybe a Christmas season date, no park can touch Disneyland. But for price and thrills, Six Flags Magic Mountain is the first choice for me—and for anyone else who gets kicks out of pulling G's.

EXERCISE 12

Discussion and Critical Thinking

1. Circle the topic sentence.

2. Underline the points applied to the two subjects.

3. If the writer had written an essay (perhaps with a bit more development), he would have divided the passage into paragraphs of introduction, development (three), and conclusion. Mark each of those places with an "X."

The Piper Cherokee and the Cessna 172

BRITTANY MARKOVIC

As a student pilot and a student in a community college, Brittany Markovic leads a life rich in variety and excitement. She rides to school in an automobile, but her mind is in the skies where she flies training aircraft. This comparison-and-contrast assignment provided her with an opportunity to compare and contrast two aircraft often used in training student pilots.

1   When most people think of an airplane, the picture that comes to mind is likely that of a large aircraft such as a Boeing 747. Commercial airlines are what the public is most familiar with, for that is what travelers ordinarily use for long-distance transportation. However, most business handled by airplanes—in fact about 80 percent of all flights—is done by small planes in what is called general aviation. When a student pilot thinks of an airplane, it is probably a small training plane, the Cessna 172. Later, the student's attention may turn to another small aircraft, the Piper Cherokee. Although either can be used for training, I believe that certain features make the Cessna 172 the better aircraft for the student.

2   For the student at the controls, two key characteristics probably come to mind, all related to movement, namely the power for thrust and the landing speed. In all those respects, the two aircraft are similar. The Piper Cherokee must have enough thrust to lift a maximum of 2,350 pounds at takeoff, for which it has 150 horsepower. Then in landing, the Cherokee should come in at 63 knots. The Cessna 172 has quite similar ratings: it can lift 2,400 pounds, has 160 horsepower, and lands at a speed between 60 and 70 knots. All of those factors should be considered in relation to the particular flight. The maximum weight matters little in training flights because they are made without extra passengers and baggage. The landing speeds for the two are also about the same and nonconsequential. The only significant matter is found in the power plant, which favors the Cessna 172 by 10 horsepower, small but in some situations crucial.

3   That power and speed, of course, must be seen in relation to the design of the aircraft, especially the wing placement. For the Piper Cherokee, the wing is mounted below the cockpit. That design allows for great visibility above the aircraft, which, in turn, is better for observing other aircraft and certain weather conditions. The big problem for the student pilot is that the wing-under arrangement partially blocks the pilot's view of the runway. On the contrary, the Cessna 172 features a wing over the fuselage, providing the new pilot with a much appreciated better view of the runway. That design allows the student pilot to more easily master the two most difficult maneuvers: taking off and landing.

4   Another point to consider seriously is the fuel system, for the new pilot has enough things to take care of without having to worry about getting gas to the carburetor. In the wing-under Piper Cherokee, the tanks are in the wing, but because the wings are lower than the engine, the fuel must be pushed to the engine by a fuel pump, and a fuel pump may not work. But that possible problem does

not exist in the high-wing Cessna 172. It also has its gas tank in the wing; however, because the wing is above the engine, gravity delivers fuel to the carburetor without need of a pump. When it comes to airplanes, less may be more. We all know that gravity is more reliable than a fuel pump.

5   The first features, the power for thrust and the landing speed, give the Cessna 172 only a slight edge over the Piper Cherokee. But the other two factors are decisive. Better visibility for takeoffs and landings afforded by the high wing and gas delivered by gravity make the Cessna 172 the better aircraft for student pilots.

EXERCISE 13

Discussion and Critical Thinking

1. Is Markovic's purpose to inform or to persuade?

2. Markovic is writing for an audience that knows little about aerodynamics. How does her writing reflect her understanding of her audience?

3. Double underline the thesis of the essay and underline the topic sentence of paragraphs 2, 3, and 4.

4. Does Markovic use the subject-by-subject or point-by-point pattern?

5. Circle the words that provide a smooth transition between paragraphs 2 and 3 and between paragraphs 3 and 4.

Topics for Writing Comparison and Contrast

You will find a blank Writing Process Worksheet on page 6, which can be photocopied, filled in, and submitted with each assignment if your instructor directs you to do so.

Reading-Related Topics

"Business Battle Tactics"

1. Paraphrase this reading; that is, put it mostly into your own words. Use quotation marks for the phrases you borrow.

2. Write an analogy in paragraph or essay form about another activity. Here are some suggestions:
   * Riding the merry-go-round and dating
   * Juggling and paying bills
   * Driving on the freeway and pursuing a career
   * Going fishing and looking for a job
   * Shopping in a supermarket and getting an education
   * Caring for a child and for a dog
   * Driving in traffic and fighting on a battlefield
   * Sleeping and watching television

- Learning a new culture from an immigrant's viewpoint and learning an environment from an infant's viewpoint
- Looking for Elvis and looking for truth (or for the Holy Grail, an honest person, a unicorn, the Loch Ness monster, Big Foot, or the Abominable Snowman)

"Pink Kittens and Blue Spaceships"

3. Compare and contrast the toys traditionally given to boys and to girls.

4. Compare and contrast the games or recreation generally made available to girls and to boys.

"The Small Town and the Big City"

5. Compare and contrast two communities (for example, urban and suburban, city and country) that you have lived in, showing that one is more safe, friendly, or charitable than the other.

6. Compare and contrast two schools (small and large, city and rural) to show that one is different from the other in some respect, such as school spirit, seriousness about education, safety, and so on.

"Los Chinos Discover el Barrio"

7. Compare and contrast a neighborhood, a community, or a school as it once was and now is. Consider such points as change, lack of change, behavior, appearance, attitudes, and convictions. Use specific examples.

"Neat People vs. Sloppy People"

8. Using ideas and points from this essay, discuss two people you know or have read about to argue that Britt's conclusions are valid.

9. Using ideas and points from this essay, discuss two people you know or have read about to argue that Britt's ideas are not valid.

10. Write a comparative study on people with good table manners and those with bad table manners. Explain the causes and effects of their behavior.

11. Using Britt's essay as a model of exaggerated humor, write a comparative study of one of the following:

- People who exercise a lot and those who hardly exercise
- People who diet and those who do not
- Men with beards and those without
- Women with extremely long fingernails and those with short fingernails
- People who dye their hair and those who do not
- People who take care of their yards and those who do not
- People who take care of their children (or pets) and those who do not

"The Messy Are in Denial"

12. Using Gallagher's points and insights, discuss two people you know or have read about to argue that her conclusions are valid.

13. Using Gallagher's points and insights, discuss two people you know or have read about to argue that her ideas are not valid.

Paired Essays on Orderly and Disorderly People

14. Compare and contrast Britt's sloppy person with Gallagher's disorganized person.

15. Compare and contrast Britt's neat person with Gallagher's organized person.

"Disneyland or Magic Mountain: Fantasy or Thrills?"

16. Using this selection as a model, write a paragaph or an essay of comparison and contrast about two amusement parks, theaters, clubs, or athletic venues.

"The Piper Cherokee and the Cessna 172"

17. Compare and contrast two pickup trucks to show that one is better than the other for particular needs or purposes (everyday driving, certain kinds of work or recreation, making a good impression on peers). If you have a computer, use the Internet to collect specific information. Give credit to your source(s).

18. Compare any other two products to show that one is better or more useful for a particular need or purpose.

General Topics

Compare and contrast one or more of the following topics. After you limit your topic, personalize it or do some research so that you will have specific support.

19. Two generations of college students

20. Two automobiles, bicycles, motorcycles, or snowmobiles

21. Two types of (or specific) police officers, doctors, teachers, preachers, students, or athletes

22. Two famous persons—authors, generals, actors, or athletes

23. Two philosophies, religions, or ideologies

24. Cross-country skiing and downhill skiing

25. Living at college and living at home

26. A small college and a large college or a four-year college and a community college

27. Two gangs or two kinds of gangs

28. Two roommates, neighbors, friends, or dates

29. Two movies, television shows, commercials, songs, or singers

30. Dating and going steady, living together and being married, or a person before and after marriage

31. Shopping malls and neighborhood stores

32. Two political candidates or officeholders

Cross-Curricular Topics

33. In the fields of nutritional science and health, compare and contrast two diets, two exercise programs, or two pieces of exercise equipment.

34. Compare and contrast your field of study (or one aspect of it) as it existed some time ago (specify the years) and as it is now. Refer to new developments and discoveries, such as scientific breakthroughs and technological advances.

Career-Related Topics

35. Compare and contrast two pieces of office equipment or two services with the purpose of showing that one is better.

36. Compare and contrast two management styles or two working styles.

37. Compare and contrast two career fields to argue that one is better for you.

38. Compare and contrast a public school with a business.

39. Compare and contrast two computers or two software programs.

Writer's Guidelines: Comparison and Contrast

1. *Purpose:* During the exploration of your topic, define your purpose clearly.

   • Decide whether you are writing a work that is primarily comparison, primarily contrast, or balanced.

   • Determine whether your main purpose is to inform or to persuade.

2. *Points*

   • Indicate your points of comparison or contrast, perhaps by listing.

   • Eliminate irrelevant points.

3. *Pattern*

   • Select the subject-by-subject or the point-by-point pattern after considering your topic and planned treatment. The point-by-point pattern is usually preferred in essays. Only in long papers is there likely to be a mixture of patterns.

   • Compose an outline reflecting the pattern you select.

   • Use this basic subject-by-subject pattern:

        I. Subject X
            A. Point 1
            B. Point 2
        II. Subject Y
            A. Point 1
            B. Point 2

- Use this basic point-by-point pattern:

    I. Point 1
       A. Subject 1
       B. Subject 2
   II. Point 2
       A. Subject X
       B. Subject Y

4. *Presentation*

- Give each point more or less equal treatment. Attention to each part of the outline will usually ensure balanced development.

- Use transitional words and phrases to indicate comparison and contrast and to establish coherence.

- Use a carefully stated topic sentence for a paragraph and a clear thesis for an essay. Each developmental paragraph should have a topic sentence broad enough to embrace its content.

5. Use the writing process.

- Write and then revise your paragraph or essay as many times as necessary for coherence, language (usage, tone, and diction), unity, emphasis, support, and sentences (**CLUESS**).

- Read your work aloud to hear and correct any grammatical errors or awkward-sounding sentences.

- Edit any problems in fundamentals, such as capitalization, omissions, punctuation, and spelling (**COPS**).

Chapter

15

Definition: Clarifying Terms

FLOW OF WRITING

Writing Definition   297

   Techniques for Writing Simple Definitions   297

   Techniques for Writing Extended
   Definitions   300

Practicing Patterns of Definition   302

Connecting Reading and Writing   305

   Professional Writers   305

   "Burnout"   305

   "Georgia on My Mind"   306

   "Tortillas"   307

   "A Working Community"   308

   "Is It Sexual Harassment?"   311

   Student Writers   315

   "Going Too Far" (demonstration with stages)   317

   "Prison Slang"   318

Topics for Writing Definition   319

Writer's Guidelines   322

"A definition is the enclosing of a wilderness of ideas within a wall of words."

SAMUEL BUTLER

THE QUIGMANS   by **Buddy Hickerson**

B. Hickerson, copyright Los Angeles Times Syndicate. Reprinted by permission.

Writing Definition

Most definitions are short; they consist of a **synonym** (a word or phrase that has about the same meaning as the term to be defined), a phrase, or a sentence. For example, we might say that a hypocrite is a person "professing beliefs or virtues he or she does not possess." Terms can also be defined by **etymology,** or word history. *Hypocrite* once meant "actor" (*hypocrites*) in Greek because an actor was pretending to be someone else. We may find this information interesting and revealing, but the history of a word may be of no use because the meaning has changed drastically over the years. Sometimes definitions occupy a paragraph or an entire essay. The short definition is called a **simple definition;** the longer one is known as an **extended definition.**

Techniques for Writing Simple Definitions

If you want to define a term without being abrupt and mechanical, you have several alternatives. All of the following techniques allow you to blend the definition into your developing thought.

- *Basic dictionary meaning.* You can quote the dictionary's definition, but if you do, you are obliged to indicate your source, which you should do directly and explicitly. Always give the complete title of the dictionary, such as "*The American Heritage Dictionary* says," not simply "Webster says." Dozens of dictionaries use the "Webster" designation.
- *Synonyms.* Although no two words have exactly the same meaning, synonyms often follow as if in parentheses.

    He was guilty of the ancient sin of *hubris,* of excessive pride.

- *Direct explanation.* You can state the definition.

James Harvey Robinson, "On Various Kinds of Thinking"

    This spontaneous and loyal support of our preconception—this process of finding "good" reasons to justify our routine beliefs—is known to modern psychologists as *rationalizing*—clearly a new name for a very ancient thing.

- *Indirect explanation.* You can imply the definition.

Ruth Benedict, *Patterns of Culture*

    Trance is a similar abnormality in our society. Even a mild mystic is *aberrant* in Western civilization.

- *Analytical or formal definition.* In using this method, you define by placing the term (the subject) in a class (genus) and then identifying it with characteristics that show how it differs from other members of the same class, as the following examples show:

Subject	Class	Characteristics
A democracy	is a form of government	in which voters elect representatives to manage society.
A wolf	is a dog-like mammal	that is large and carnivorous, with coarse fur, erect, pointed ears, and a bushy tail.

| Jazz | is a style of music | that features improvisation and performance. |

Writing Simple Definitions

Complete the following formal definitions.

Subject	Class	Characteristics
1. A workaholic	is a person	
2. Dreadlocks	is a natural hairstyle	
3. A hawk		that has a short, hooked bill and strong claws.
4. Hay fever		affecting the mucous membranes of the upper respiratory tract and the eyes, causing sneezing, running nose, and itchy, watery eyes.
5. A muumuu	is a dress	
6. Bongos	are two connected drums	
7. A patriot		
8. A desert	is a large land area	
9. Jealousy	is a state of mind	
10. Sociology		

Dictionary Entries—Which One to Use

Suppose that you do not know the meaning of the term in italics in the following sentence:

That kind of cactus is *indigenous* to the Mojave Desert.

As you consider the term in context, you look at the dictionary definitions.

in•dig•e•nous \ ĭn-dĭj´ə-nəs \ *adj.* **1.** Originating and living or occurring naturally in an area or environment. See synonyms at **native. 2.** Intrinsic; innate. [From Latin *indigena,* a native. See INDIGEN.]

The first definition seems to fit the context of *indigneous.* It is followed by a reference: "See synonyms at **native.**" Then you look at the second set of definitions: "Intrinsic; innate." The words are synonyms. You can see that only *native* fits. To provide more information for the reader, the dictionary also presents *native* with a special treatment of synonyms as indicated by the reference.

Looking under the word *native,* you find this definition:

Synonyms   native, indigenous, endemic, autochthonous, aboriginal
These adjectives mean of, belonging to, or connected with a specific place or country by virtue of birth or origin. *Native* implies birth or origin in the specified place: *a native New Yorker; the native North American sugar maple. Indigenous* specifies that something or someone is native rather than coming or being brought in from elsewhere: *an indigenous crop; the Ainu, a people indigenous to the northernmost islands of Japan.* Something *endemic* is prevalent in or peculiar to a particular locality or people: *endemic disease. Autochthonous* applies to what is native and unchanged by outside sources: *autochthonous folk melodies. Aboriginal* describes what has existed from the beginning; it is often applied to the earliest known inhabitants of a place: *the aboriginal population; aboriginal nature.* See also synonyms at **crude.**

Usage Note   When used in reference to a member of an indigenous people, the noun *native,* like its synonym *aborigine,* can evoke unwelcome stereotypes of primitiveness or cultural backwardness that many people now seek to avoid. As is often the case with words that categorize people, the use of the noun is more problematic than the use of the corresponding adjective. Thus a phrase such as *the peoples native to northern Europe* or *the aboriginal inhabitants of the South Pacific* is generally much preferable to *the natives of northern Europe* or *the aborigines of the South Pacific.* • Despite its potentially negative connotations, *native* is enjoying increasing popularity in ethnonyms such as *native Australian* and *Alaska native,* perhaps due to the wide acceptance of *Native American* as a term of ethnic pride and respect. These compounds have the further benefit of being equally acceptable when used alone as nouns (*a native Australian*) or in an adjectival construction (*a member of a native Australian people*). Of terms formed on this model, those referring to peoples indigenous to the United States generally capitalize *native,* as in *Alaska Native* (or the less common *Native Alaskan*) and *Native Hawaiian,* while others usually style it lowercase.

In the synonyms at the close of the entry, did you observe the various shades of meaning, especially the meaning of *indigenous* and *native*? A dictionary is an invaluable aid to definition, but it must be used with care if you want to express yourself clearly and precisely. No two words have exactly the same meaning, and a word may have many meanings, some that extend to very different concepts.

Avoiding Common Problems

- Do not use the expression *is where* or *is when* in beginning the main part of a definition. The verb *is* (a linking verb) should be followed by a noun, a pronoun, or an adjective.

Weak:	A stadium is where they hold sports spectaculars.
Better:	A stadium is a structure in which sports spectaculars are held.
Weak:	Socialism is when the ownership and operation of the means of production and distribution are vested in the community as a whole.
Better:	Socialism is a theory or system of community organization that advocates that the ownership and control of the means of production, capital, land, and so forth, be vested in the community as a whole.

- Do not use the **circular definition,** a practice of defining a term with the term itself.

Circular:	An aristocracy is a form of government based on rule by the aristocrats.
Direct:	An aristocracy is a form of government in which the power resides in the hands of the best individuals or a small privileged class.

- Do not define the subject in more complicated language than the original.

Murky:	*Surreptitious* means "clandestine."
Clear:	*Surreptitious* means "secret."

- Do not substitute the example for the definition; the example may be excellent for clarification, but it does not completely define.

Weak:	Political conservatives are people like William F. Buckley Jr. and Pat Robertson.
Better:	Political conservatives are people who are dedicated to preserving existing conditions. Examples of conservatives are William F. Buckley Jr. and Pat Robertson.

Techniques for Writing Extended Definitions

Essays of definition can take many forms. Among the more common techniques for writing a paragraph or short essay of definition are the patterns we have worked with in previous chapters. Consider each of those patterns when you need to write an extended definition. For a particular term, some forms will be more useful than others; use the pattern or patterns that best fulfill your purpose.

Each of the following questions takes a pattern of writing and directs it toward definition.

- *Narration:* Can I tell an anecdote or story to define this subject (such as *jerk, humanitarian,* or *citizen*)? This form may overlap with description and exemplification.
- *Description:* Can I describe this subject (such as *a whale* or *the moon*)?
- *Exemplification:* Can I give examples of this subject (such as naming individuals, to provide examples of *actors, diplomats,* or *satirists*)?

- *Analysis by Division:* Can I divide this subject into parts (for example, the parts of a *heart, a cell,* or *a carburetor*)?
- *Process Analysis:* Can I define this subject (such as *lasagna, tornado, hurricane, blood pressure,* or any number of scientific processes) by describing how to make it or how it occurs? (Common to the methodology of communicating in science, this approach is sometimes called the "operational definition.")
- *Cause and Effect:* Can I define this subject (such as *a flood, a drought, a riot,* or *a cancer*) by its causes and effects?
- *Classification:* Can I group this subject (such as kinds of *families, cultures, religions,* or *governments*) into classes?

Subject	Class	Characteristics
A republic	is a form of government	in which power resides in the people (the electorate).

- *Comparison and Contrast:* Can I define this subject (such as *extremist* or *patriot*) by explaining what it is similar to and different from? If you are defining *orangutan* to a person who has never heard of one but is familiar with the gorilla, then you could make comparison-and-contrast statements. If you want to define *patriot,* then you might want to stress what it is not (the contrast) before you explain what it is: a patriot is not a one-dimensional flag waver, not someone who hates "foreigners" because America is always right and always best.

When you use prewriting strategies to develop ideas for a definition, you can effectively consider all the patterns you have learned by using a modified clustering form (Figure 15.1). Put a double bubble around the subject to be defined. Then put a single bubble around each pattern and add appropriate words. If a pattern is not relevant to what you are defining, leave it blank. If you want to expand your range of information, you could add a bubble for a simple dictionary definition and another for an etymological definition.

Order

The organization of your extended definition is likely to be one of emphasis, but it may be space or time, depending on the subject material. You may use just one pattern of development for the overall sequence. If so, you would use the principles of organization discussed in previous chapters.

Introduction and Development

Consider these ways of introducing a definition: with a question, with a statement of what it is not, with a statement of what it originally meant, or with a discussion of why a clear definition is important. You may use a combination of these ways or all of them before you continue with your definition.

Development is likely to represent one or more of the patterns of narration, description, exposition (with its own subdivisions), and argumentation.

Whether you personalize a definition depends on your purpose and your audience. Your instructor may ask you to write about a word from a subjective or an objective viewpoint.

Figure 15.1
Bubble cluster showing how a term could be defined using different essay patterns.

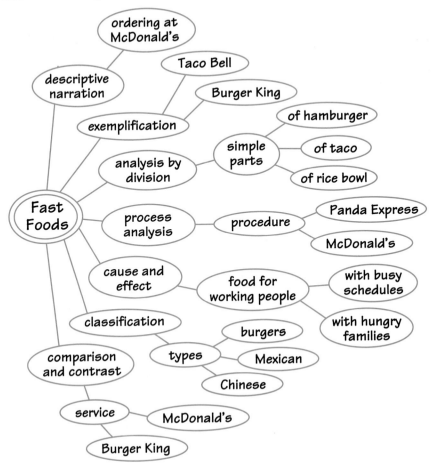

Practicing Patterns of Definition

Doing the following exercise will help you remember the patterns of writing used in extended definitions.

Completing Patterns of Definition

Fill in the double bubble with a term to be defined. You might want to define *culturally diverse society, educated person, leader, role model, friend, infatuation, true love, success,* or *intelligence.* Then complete a bubble on the right for each paragraph or essay pattern. If the pattern does not apply (that is, if it would not provide useful information for your definition), mark it NA ("not applicable").

A. Using Patterns in Definitions

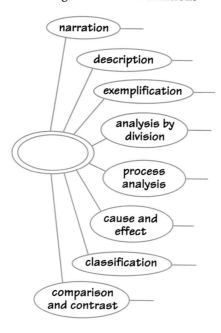

B. Using Patterns in Definitions

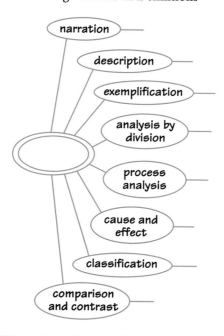

EXERCISE 3   # Techniques for Introducing and Developing Definitions

Pick one of the topics you selected for Exercise 2: _____.

A. Place an "X" beside each of the following techniques that might be useful in introducing the topic.

_____ A question calling for a definition.

_____ A statement about what the term does not mean.

_____ A statement about what the term meant originally (etymology).

_____ A statement about why a definition would help clarify an ongoing public debate.

B. Place an "X" beside each of the patterns that might be used in developing the topic.

_____ Exemplification

_____ Process Analysis

_____ Analysis by Division

_____ Cause and Effect

_____ Comparison and Contrast

Connecting Reading and Writing

Professional Writers

Burnout

GREGORY MOORHEAD AND RICKY W. GRIFFIN

Occupational sociologists Gregory Moorhead and Ricky W. Griffin provide the following definition of burnout *adapted from their book* Organizational Behavior *(2001). Their definition pertains mainly to vocational work, but burnout can occur in any organization—church, government, recreation, even marriage and family.*

Burnout, a consequence of stress, has clear implications for both people and organizations. Burnout is a general feeling of exhaustion that develops when a person simultaneously experiences too much pressure and has too few sources of satisfaction. Burnout usually develops in the following way. First, people with high aspirations and strong motivation to get things done are prime candidates for burnout under certain conditions. They are especially vulnerable when the organization suppresses or limits their initiative while constantly demanding that they serve the organization's own ends. In such a situation, the individual is likely to put too much of himself or herself into the job. In other words, the person may well keep trying to meet his or her own agenda while simultaneously trying to fulfill the organization's expectations. The most likely effects of this situation are prolonged stress, fatigue, frustration, and helplessness under the burden of overwhelming demands. The person literally exhausts his or her aspiration and motivation, much as a candle burns itself out. Loss of self-confidence and psychological withdrawal follow. Ultimately, burnout results. At this point, the individual may start dreading going to work in the morning, may put in longer hours but accomplish less than before, and may generally display mental and physical exhaustion.

EXERCISE 4 | ## Discussion and Critical Thinking

1. Underline the sentence that best conveys the basic definition.

2. What other pattern—comparison and contrast, classification, cause and effect, or narration—provides structure for this definition.

3. If you were going to personalize this definition, what other pattern would you use?

Georgia on My Mind

RAY JENKINS

What was it like to be a poor white Southerner in the Old South? Ray Jenkins knows. As you read this selection, anticipate a reading-related writing topic asking you to indicate what it is like to live in your neighborhood or in the neighborhood where your parents grew up.

Unless a man has picked cotton all day in August; has sat in an outhouse in 20 degrees in January and passed this time of necessity by reading last year's Sears Roebuck catalogue; has eaten a possum and liked it; has castrated a live pig with a dull pocket knife and has wrung a chicken's neck with his own hands; has learned at least a few chords on a fiddle and guitar; has tried to lure a sharecropper's daughter into the woods for mischievous purposes; has watched a man who had succeeded in doing just that have his sins washed away in the Blood of the Lamb in a baptism in a muddy creek; has been kicked by a mean milch cow and kicked her back; has drunk busthead likker knowing full well it might kill him; has wished the next day it had killed him; has watched a neighbor's house burn down; has drawn a knife on an adversary in fear and anger; has half-soled his one pair of shoes with a tire repair kit; has gone into a deep dark well to get out a dead chicken that had fallen in; has waited beside a dusty road in the midday heat, hoping the R.F.D. postman would bring some long-coveted item ordered from the catalogue; has been in close quarters with a snake; has, in thirsty desperation, drunk water that worked alive with mosquito larvae called wiggletails; has eaten sardines out of a can with a stick; has killed a cat just for the hell of it; . . . has stepped in the droppings of a chicken and not really cared; has been cheated by someone he worked hard for; has gone to bed at sundown because he could no longer endure the crushing isolation; has ridden a bareback mule three miles to visit a pretty girl who waited in a clean, flimsy cotton dress—unless he has done these things, then he cannot understand what it was like in my South.

EXERCISE 5   Discussion and Critical Thinking

1. This unconventional definition has no stated topic sentence. What is the unstated topic sentence?

2. What is the effect of using one exceedingly long sentence to develop the definition?

3. What pattern of development is featured in this definition?

4. Is there any overall pattern to Jenkins's use of examples?

Tortillas

JOSÉ ANTONIO BURCIAGA

A distinguished publisher and writer, José Antonio Burciaga died in 1996, leaving a rich legacy of poems, short stories, and essays. His essay here defines one of the most basic Hispanic foods, tortillas. Much more than a mere recipe, this definition is colorfully layered with historical, regional, and personal context.

1   My earliest memory of *tortillas* is my *Mamá* telling me not to play with them. I had bitten eyeholes in one and was wearing it as a mask at the dinner table.

2   As a child, I also used *tortillas* as hand warmers on cold days, and my family claims that I owe my career as an artist to my early experiments with *tortillas*. According to them, my clowning around helped me develop a strong artistic foundation. I'm not so sure, though. Sometimes I wore a *tortilla* on my head, like a *yarmulke,* and yet I never had any great urge to convert from Catholicism to Judaism. But who knows? They may be right.

3   For Mexicans over the centuries, the *tortilla* has served as the spoon and the fork, the plate and the napkin. *Tortillas* originated before the Mayan civilizations, perhaps predating Europe's wheat bread. According to Mayan mythology, the great god Quetzalcoatl, realizing that the red ants knew the secret of using maize as food, transformed himself into a black ant, infiltrated the colony of red ants, and absconded with a grain of corn. (Is it any wonder that to this day, black ants and red ants do not get along?) Quetzalcoatl then put maize on the lips of the first man and woman, Oxomoco and Cipactonal, so that they would become strong. Maize festivals are still celebrated by many Indian cultures of the Americas.

4   When I was growing up in El Paso, *tortillas* were part of my daily life. I used to visit a tortilla factory in an ancient adobe building near the open *mercado* in Ciudad Juárez. As I approached, I could hear the rhythmic slapping of the *masa* as the skilled vendors outside the factory formed it into balls and patted them into perfectly round corn cakes between the palms of their hands. The wonderful aroma and the speed with which the women counted so many dozens of *tortillas* out of warm wicker baskets still linger in my mind. Watching them at work convinced me that the most handsome and *deliciosas tortillas* are handmade. Although machines are faster, they can never adequately replace generation-to-generation experience. There's no place in the factory assembly line for the tender slaps that give each *tortilla* character. The best thing that can be said about mass-producing *tortillas* is that it makes it possible for many people to enjoy them.

5   In the *mercado* where my mother shopped, we frequently bought *taquitos de nopalitos,* small tacos filled with diced cactus, onions, tomatoes, and *jalapeños*. Our friend Don Toribio showed us how to make delicious, crunchy *taquitos* with dried, salted pumpkin seeds. When you had no money for the filling, a poor man's *taco* could be made by placing a warm *tortilla* on the left palm, applying a sprinkle of salt, then rolling the *tortilla* up quickly with the fingertips of the right hand. My own kids put peanut butter and jelly on *tortillas*, which I think is truly bicultural. And speaking of fast food for kids, nothing beats a *quesadilla*, a *tortilla* grilled-cheese sandwich.

6   Depending on what you intend to use them for, *tortillas* may be made in various ways. Even a run-of-the-mill *tortilla* is more than a flat corn cake. A skillfully cooked homemade *tortilla* has a bottom and a top; the top skin forms a pocket in

which you put the filling that folds your *tortilla* into a taco. Paper-thin *tortillas* are used specifically for *flautas,* a type of taco that is filled, rolled, and then fried until crisp. The name *flauta* means *flute,* which probably refers to the Mayan bamboo flute; however, the only sound that comes from an edible *flauta* is a delicious crunch that is music to the palate. In México *flautas* are sometimes made as long as two feet and then cut into manageable segments. The opposite of *flautas* is *gorditas,* meaning *little fat ones.* These are very thick small *tortillas.*

7   The versatility of *tortillas* and corn does not end here. Besides being tasty and nourishing, they have spiritual and artistic qualities as well. The Tarahumara Indians of Chihuahua, for example, concocted a corn-based beer called *tesgüino,* which their descendants still make today. And everyone has read about the woman in New Mexico who was cooking her husband a *tortilla* one morning when the image of Jesus Christ miraculously appeared on it. Before they knew what was happening, the man's breakfast had become a local shrine.

8   Then there is *tortilla* art. Various Chicano artists throughout the Southwest have, when short of materials or just in a whimsical mood, used a dry *tortilla* as a small, round canvas. And a few years back, at the height of the Chicano movement, a priest in Arizona got into trouble with the Church after he was discovered celebrating mass using a *tortilla* as the host. All of which only goes to show that while the *tortilla* may be a lowly corn cake, when the necessity arises, it can reach unexpected distinction.

EXERCISE 6   Discussion and Critical Thinking

1. Does the author assume his audience already knows what a *tortilla* is?

2. Where is the simplest, most direct definition?

3. Which of these patterns of development—description, narration, process analysis, classification, and exemplification—does Burciaga use?

4. What does Burciaga's use of personal experience add to his extended definition?

5. What different aspects of life does Burciaga bring into his definition?

A Working Community

ELLEN GOODMAN

Nationally syndicated columnist and associate editor of the Boston Globe, *Ellen Goodman often writes about topical concerns and social movements. Here she says it is time for a new definition of "community," because our basic patterns of life have changed.*

1   I have a friend who is a member of the medical community. It does not say that, of course, on the stationery that bears her home address. This membership comes from her hospital work.

2   I have another friend who is a member of the computer community. This is a fairly new subdivision of our economy, and yet he finds his sense of place in it.

3   Other friends and acquaintances of mine are members of the academic community, or the business community, or the journalistic community.

4   Though you cannot find these on any map, we know where we belong.

5   None of us, mind you, was born into these communities. Nor did we move into them, U-Hauling our possessions along with us. None has papers to prove we are card-carrying members of one such group or another. Yet it seems that more and more of us are identified by work these days, rather than by street.

6   In the past, most Americans lived in neighborhoods. We were members of precincts or parishes or school districts. My dictionary still defines community, first of all in geographic terms, as "a body of people who live in one place."

7   But today fewer of us do our living in that one place; more of us just use it for sleeping. Now we call our towns "bedroom suburbs," and many of us, without small children as icebreakers, would have trouble naming all the people on our street.

8   It's not that we are more isolated today. It's that many of us have transferred a chunk of our friendships, a major portion of our everyday social lives, from home to office. As more of our neighbors work away from home, the workplace becomes our neighborhood.

9   The kaffeeklatsch of the fifties is the coffee break of the eighties. The water cooler, the hall, the elevator, and the parking lot are the back fences of these neighborhoods. The people we have lunch with day after day are those who know the running saga of our mother's operations, our child's math grades, our frozen pipes, and faulty transmissions.

10 We may be strangers at the supermarket that replaced the corner grocer, but we are known at the coffee shop in the lobby. We share with each other a cast of characters from the boss in the corner office to the crazy lady in Shipping, to the lovers in Marketing. It's not surprising that when researchers ask Americans what they like best about work, they say it is "the shmoose factor." When they ask young mothers at home what they miss most about work, it is the people.

11 Not all the neighborhoods are empty, nor is every workplace a friendly playground. Most of us have had mixed experiences in these environments. Yet as one woman told me recently, she knows more about the people she passes on the way to her desk than on her way around the block. Our new sense of community hasn't just moved from house to office building. The labels that we wear connect us with members from distant companies, cities, and states. We assume that we have something "in common" with other teachers, nurses, city planners.

12 It's not unlike the experience of our immigrant grandparents. Many who came to this country still identified themselves as members of the Italian community, the Irish community, the Polish community. They sought out and assumed connections with people from the old country. Many of us have updated that experience. We have replaced ethnic identity with professional identity, the way we replaced neighborhoods with the workplace.

13 This whole realignment of community is surely most obvious among the mobile professions. People who move from city to city seem to put roots down into their professions. In an age of specialists, they may have to search harder to find people who speak the same language.

14   I don't think that there is anything massively disruptive about this shifting sense of community. The continuing search for connection and shared enterprise is very human. But I do feel uncomfortable with our shifting identity. The balance has tipped, and we seem increasingly dependent on work for our sense of self.

15   If our offices are our new neighborhoods, if our professional titles are our new ethnic tags, then how do we separate our selves from our jobs? Self-worth isn't just something to measure in the marketplace. But in these new communities, it becomes harder to tell who we are without saying what we do.

Discussion and Critical Thinking

1. In paragraph 6, Goodman says her "dictionary still defines community first of all in geographic terms, as 'a body of people who live in one place.'" What one word would you change to make this into her basic definition of a community?

2. Before the rise in working communities, were there only the geographical communities, or neighborhoods?

3. Goodman begins with what form (classification, cause and effect, or example) to advance her definition?

4. What do the communities listed in paragraph 3 have in common?

5. What form, or pattern, does Goodman use in paragraphs 8 and 9?

6. What bothers Goodman about the current sense of community?

7. If the average person changes jobs every four years, what implications does that have for people who see work as a community?

8. In this electronic age, more people are doing their work from remote locations. Does that development shift the location of community back to the neighborhood?

9. Can one make a case for other communities located at the sites of other activities? If so, what are they?

Is It Sexual Harassment?

ELLEN BRAVO AND ELLEN CASSEDY

From the mailroom to Senate chambers, the debate goes on. It's still not always clear how to define harassment or how to stop it. Here, the authors attempt to show the difference between what's merely annoying and what's illegal. First published in Redbook, *July 1992, the article is excerpted from Bravo and Cassedy's* The 1995 Guide to Combating Sexual Harassment: Candid Advice from the National Association of Working Women. *The authors credit the consulting firm Jane C. Edmonds and Associates for additional information.*

1   Who decides what constitutes offensive behavior in the workplace? You—the recipient. Try testing your instincts about whether the following scenarios are examples of sexual harassment. Then read the authors' expert analyses.

Is This Abuse?

2   *Scenario 1:* Justine works in a predominantly male department at Company XYZ. She has tried to fit in, and occasionally even laughs at the frequent, off-color sex jokes. But she gets more irritated every day. It's well-known in the department that Justine has an out-of-town boyfriend she sees most weekends. It's also known that one of her coworkers, Scott, has the hots for her. Boyfriend or not, he's willing to do almost anything to get a date with Justine. Recently, one of Justine's coworkers overheard their boss talking to Scott in the hallway. "If you get her into bed," the boss said, "I owe you a dinner. Good luck!" They chuckled and went their separate ways.

3   *Analysis:* The boss is out of line. He probably didn't intend anyone to overhear him—but he shouldn't have been having such a conversation at all. The boss is responsible for keeping the workplace free of harassment and telling employees the consequences of violating the law. Instead, he gave Scott an incentive to make sexual advances toward a coworker. Some may argue that whether Scott and Justine get together socially is a personal matter—but public workplace boasting or dares clearly is not. The law doesn't require Justine to be tough enough to speak up on her own; it says her company must provide an atmosphere free of offensive or hostile behavior. Instead of making Scott think the way to win favor with a supervisor is to pressure a coworker into bed, the boss might arrange for a department-wide seminar on sexual harassment.

4   *Scenario 2:* Freda has been working for Bruce for three years. She has never complained about anything and appears to be happy in her job. Bruce regularly compliments Freda on her outfits; in his opinion, she has a good figure and excellent taste in clothes. Typically, he'll remark, "You sure look good today." Last week, Freda was having a bad day and told Bruce she was "sick and tired of being treated like a sex object." Bruce was stunned at the angry comment. He had always thought they had a good working relationship.

5   *Analysis:* Context and delivery are everything in examining a case like this. When Bruce says, "You sure look good today," does Freda usually answer, "So do you"? Or does Bruce murmur suggestively, "Mmm, you sure look g-o-o-o-o-d," and stare at her chest while she crosses her arms? Does Bruce ever compliment other women? Men? Does he praise Freda's work performance as well?

6   Freda might have been upset earlier about Bruce's comments but failed to speak up because he is her boss. It's not uncommon for someone in her situation to keep quiet for fear of looking foolish or appearing to be a "bad sport." Even if she were just having a bad day, Freda probably wouldn't say she was tired of being treated like a sex object unless she'd felt that way before.

7   Since Bruce was "stunned" that Freda blew up at him, he needs to consider whether she may have sent him signals he ignored. He may be guilty only of not being tuned in. Or perhaps Freda doesn't really mind the personal praise, but wants more attention paid to her work.

8   Bruce and Freda should sit down and talk. He should listen to what she has to say, then let her know that he values her work *and* her feelings. He should also encourage her to speak up promptly in the future about issues that concern her rather than let them fester.

9   *Scenario 3:* Barbara is a receptionist for a printing company. Surrounding her desk are five ads printed by the company for a beer distributor. The posters feature provocatively posed women holding cans of beer and the slogan, What'll you have? Many times male customers have walked in, looked at the posters, and commented, "I'll have *you,* honey." When Barbara tells her boss she wants the posters removed, he replies that they represent the company's work, and he's proud to display them. He claims no one but Barbara is bothered by the posters, so what's her problem?

10   *Analysis:* The standard here is not how the boss feels but whether a "reasonable woman" might object to being surrounded by such posters, especially since the company has other products it could display. Because women are disproportionately victims of rape and sexual assault, women have a stronger incentive to be concerned with sexual behavior.

11   Barbara did not insist that the company refuse the account or exclude the posters from its portfolio. She merely said she didn't want them displayed around *her* desk. Barbara's view certainly is substantiated by how she's been treated; the posters seem to prompt customers to make suggestive remarks to her.

12   *Scenario 4:* Therese tells Andrew, her subordinate, that she needs him to escort her to a party. She says she's selecting him because he's the most handsome guy on her staff. Andrew says he's busy. Therese responds that she expects people on her staff to be team players.

13   *Analysis:* Therese may have wanted Andrew merely to accompany her to the party, not to have a sexual relationship with her. And Andrew might have been willing to go along if he hadn't been busy. Nevertheless, a reasonable employee may worry about what the boss means by such a request, particularly when it's coupled with remarks about personal appearance.

14   Andrew might not mind that Therese finds him handsome. But most people would object to having their job tied to their willingness to make a social appearance with the boss outside of work. The implicit threat also makes Therese's request unacceptable. The company should prohibit managers from requiring subordinates to escort them to social engagements.

15   *Scenario 5:* Darlene asks her coworker Dan out on a date. Their romance lasts several months before Darlene ends it. Dan is crushed and wants to keep seeing her. During the workday he frequently buzzes her on the intercom and stops by her desk to chat. Darlene tries to brush him off, with no success. She asks her manager to intervene. The manager says he doesn't get involved in personal matters.

[Analysis omitted. See Question 9 under "Discussion and Critical Thinking."]

16   *Scenario 6:* Someone has posted an explicit magazine centerfold in the men's rest room. No women, obviously, ever go in there.

[Analysis omitted. See Question 10 under "Discussion and Critical Thinking."]

Exploding the Myths

17   MYTH: Sexual harassment doesn't deserve all this attention. It happens rarely, and it's done by a few dumb—or sick—men.

18   FACT: Studies suggest that at least 50 percent of women experience harassment at some point in their work or academic careers. And though only a small percentage of men are considered "chronic harassers," most who engage in the abuse are not psychopaths. Many other men, intentionally or not, end up condoning or encouraging the harassers even if only by remaining silent.

19   MYTH: Boys will be boys. Sexual harassment is so widespread it's pointless to try to stamp it out.

20   FACT: Yes, sexual harassment is widespread. So is littering. So is stealing. The answer is to stop it, not accept it. To suggest that men aren't capable of controlling their behavior insults men's intelligence. Besides, like other forms of sexual abuse, harassment is usually a means of exerting power, not expressing passion.

21   MYTH: Most men accused of harassment are just kidding around or trying to flatter.

22   FACT: Chronic harassers *know* their behavior makes women uncomfortable; that's why they do it. Even if women tell them no again and again, this resistance is simply ignored. Other men are genuinely surprised to find that what they intend as innocent teasing isn't perceived that way. In the workplace, a man should assume a female coworker *won't* like sexual comments or gestures until he learns otherwise. And if he is told that he has offended someone, he should apologize at once.

23   MYTH: If women want to be treated as equals on the job, they can't expect special treatment.

24   FACT: A harassment-free workplace doesn't "coddle" women—it simply provides them with the same respectful treatment that men want. Rather than demanding that women adjust to a workplace that's comfortable only for men, management ought to provide an environment that reflects the sensitivities of *all* workers.

25   MYTH: All this talk about harassment will make women hypersensitive, causing them to imagine problems where there are none.

26   FACT: In the short run, defining sexual harassment and providing women with ways to speak up probably *will* lead to an increase in the number of reports filed—most of them regarding real, not imagined, offenses. In the long run, however, public discussion will cut down on unwelcome sexual attention on the job, resulting in fewer harassment complaints and a more productive workplace for everybody.

27   MYTH: You can't blame a guy for looking. Women invite attention by the way they dress.

28   FACT: If a woman's clothes are truly inappropriate for the job, management should tell her so. But a woman's dress *doesn't* give a male employee license to say or do whatever he likes. Once a woman tells him she doesn't like his comments about her clothing, he should back off—or be made to do so.

Harassment by Any Other Name . . .

29   Most cases of illegal sexual harassment fall into three categories:

30   1. *Quid pro quo*   This is Latin for "something in return for something." In other words, put out or else. A supervisor makes unwelcome sexual advances and either states or implies that the victim *must* submit if she wants to keep her job or receive a raise, promotion, or job assignment. These cases are the most clear-cut. The courts generally hold the employer liable for any such harassment whether he knew about it or not. That's because anyone who holds a supervisory position, with power over terms of employment, is considered to be an "agent" of the employer.

31   2. *Hostile environment*   An employee doesn't have to be fired, demoted, or denied a raise or promotion to be sexually harassed and to file a charge. Sexually explicit jokes, pinups, graffiti, vulgar statements, and abusive language and innuendos can poison the victim's work environment. The incidents generally must be shown to be repeated, pervasive, and harmful to the victim's emotional well-being. The employer is considered liable if he knew or should have known of the harassment and did nothing to stop it.

32   3. *Sexual favoritism*   In these situations, a supervisor rewards only those employees who submit to his sexual demands. The *other* employees—those who are denied raises or promotions—can claim that they're being penalized by the sexual attention directed at the favored coworkers.

EXERCISE 8 — Vocabulary Highlights

Write a short definition of each word as it is used in the essay. (Paragraph numbers are given in parentheses.) Be prepared to use the words in your own sentences.

constitutes (1)	unique (10)
incentive (3)	portfolio (11)
murmur (5)	substantiated (11)
fester (8)	intervene (15)
disproportionately (10)	quid pro quo (30)

EXERCISE 9 — Discussion and Critical Thinking

1. Which three paragraphs give a dictionary-like definition of sexual harassment?

2. The definition, divided into three parts, is a good example of the use of what other pattern of development?

3. Besides the three-part definition, what pattern of development is used most extensively in this article?

4. How are the causes and effects (as a pattern of development) relevant in this essay?

5. Do the authors go too far in defining sexual harassment?

6. Is having two female authors writing on this subject especially appropriate because the authors can reflect on personal experience? Or does it raise doubts about the objectivity of their observations? Does the gender of the authors matter at this time on this topic?

7. What kind of audience do the authors apparently expect?

8. In what way can men benefit from an enforcement of sexual harassment policies?

9. Analyze scenario 5 (paragraph 15).

10. Analyze scenario 6 (paragraph 16).

Student Writers

Linda Wong looked at a list of abstract terms for her assignment to write an extended definition and almost immediately found one that intrigued her. She had often heard people say things such as "I just can't love him [or her] enough," and "It was too much of a good thing," and she connected those ideas with one of the terms: *extremist*.

Wong's Writing Process Worksheet shows you how her writing evolved from idea to final draft. To conserve space here, the freewriting and the rough drafts marked for revision have been omitted. The balance of the worksheet has been lengthened for you to be able to see her other work in its entirety.

You will find a full-size blank worksheet on page 6, which can be photocopied, filled in, and submitted with each assignment if your instructor directs you to do so.

Writing Process Worksheet

Title Going Too Far

Name Linda Wong   Due Date Monday, December 3, 8 a.m.

ASSIGNMENT   In the space below, write whatever you need to know about your assignment, including information about the topic, audience, pattern of writing, length, whether to include a rough draft or revised drafts, and whether your paper must be typed.

Write a paragraph that defines an abstract word. Use at least three patterns of writing in your extended definition. Keep in mind that members of your audience may use your term in different ways, so using examples and clear explanations will be helpful for clarification. Submit your completed worksheet, one or more rough drafts marked for revision, and a typed final draft of about 300 words.

STAGE ONE   Explore   Freewrite, brainstorm (list), cluster, or take notes as directed by your instructor. Use the back of this page or separate paper if you need more space.

Clustering

STAGE TWO   **Organize**   Write a topic sentence or thesis; label the subject and the treatment parts.

<u>Extremists</u> are <u>involved people who lose their sense of balance and go too</u>
   subject   treatment

<u>far in concentrating on one thing</u>.

Write an outline or an outline alternative.

  I. Going too far
     A. Become preoccupied with one thing
     B. Lose sense of balance
 II. Produce bad effect
     A. Are unpleasant to be around
     B. Are often destructive
III. Become incomplete
     A. Are often thought of as one kind of person
        1. Workaholics
        2. Zealots
        3. Superpatriots
     B. Diminished by loss of perspective

STAGE THREE   **Write**   On separate paper, write and then revise your paragraph or essay as many times as necessary for **c**oherence, **l**anguage (usage, tone, and diction), **u**nity, **e**mphasis, **s**upport, and **s**entences (**CLUESS**). Read your work aloud to hear and correct any grammatical errors or awkward-sounding sentences.

Edit any problems in fundamentals, such as **c**apitalization, **o**missions, **p**unctuation, and **s**pelling (**COPS**).

Final Draft

Going Too Far
Linda Wong

What the term does not mean   Some people believe that it is good to be an extremist in some areas, but those people are actually changing the meaning of the word. According to the <u>Random House Dictionary of the English Language</u>, the word <u>extremism</u> itself means "excessively biased ideas, intemperate conduct." <u>The extremist goes too far; that means going too far in whatever the person is doing.</u> I once heard someone say that it is good for people to be extremists in love. But that is not true. <u>It is good to be enthusiastically and sincerely in love, but extremists in love love excessively and intemperately.</u> People who love well may be tender and sensitive and attentive, but extremists are possessive or smothering. The same can be said of parents. <u>We all want to be good parents, but parental extremists involve themselves too much in the lives of their children,</u> who, in turn, may find it difficult to develop as individuals and become independent. Even in patriotism, good patriots are to be distinguished from extreme patriots. <u>Good patriots love their country, but extreme patriots love their country so much that they think citizens from other countries are inferior and suspect.</u> Extreme patriots may have Hitlerlike tendencies. Just what is wrong with extremists then? It is the loss of perspective. <u>The extremists are so preoccupied with one concern that they lose their sense of balance.</u> They are the <u>workaholics</u>, the <u>zealots</u>, the <u>superpatriots</u> of the world.

Simple definition

Topic sentence

Example/contrast

Example/contrast

Example/contrast

Examples

Effect and concluding sentence

They may begin with a good objective, but they focus on it so much that they can become destructive, obnoxious, and often pitiful. <u>The worst effect is that these extremists lose their completeness as human beings.</u>

Discussion and Critical Thinking

1. Wong says that extremists "can become destructive, obnoxious, and often pitiful." Can you think of any good effects from people who were extremists? For example, what about a scientist who works fifteen hours a day to find a cure for a horrible disease? Is it possible that the scientist may succeed in his or her profession and fail in his or her personal life? But what if the scientist does not want a personal life? Discuss.

2. Why does Wong use contrast so much?

3. According to Wong, is it bad for a person to be an extremist in religion? Discuss.

Prison Slang

LOUISE RUBEC

Almost every subculture has certain words that are understandable only to people who live in that culture. American prison slang has been around for more than a hundred years. It is richly and colorfully complex, yet simple and direct. Prison student Louise Rubec presents a brief language lesson.

1   Prison slang is like other slang in that it is language used in a special way for special reasons. As with conventional slang, some words have unusual, nonstandard meanings, and some words are invented.

2   Most slang is used by people who want to conform to group language customs. In prison it is used both by people who don't want others to know what they are talking about and by those who are seeking group identity. As a variety of language, it is technically a dialect because it is an integral part of the culture of that group. Prison slang covers many areas, but it especially reflects prisoners' concerns such as violence, talking, and reputation.

3   The very idea of violence is strangely muted by the terms used to discuss brutal acts. If a person is attacked by a group of people who throw a blanket over her head before they beat her, she is said to be the recipient of a "blanket party" given by a "rat pack." If she "caught a cold" or they "took her wind," she died. They may have killed her with a sharp instrument called a "shank" or a "shiv." Perhaps she

didn't know there was a "raven" (contract) out on her; she thought they were only "putting on a floor show" (pretending) or "selling wolf tickets" (bluffing).

4   She should have listened with more care to what both her enemies and her friend were saying. Her foes claimed she had "snitched them off" (informed), but she didn't take the charge seriously enough. Then as a brave act of kindness, her friend "pulled her coat" (told her something she should know). Unfortunately a cop came by and she whispered to her friend, "Radio it," "Dog-face it," "Dummy up" (all meaning "shut up"). She actually thought about the danger and considered sending a "kite" (note) to a "homey" (close friend, perhaps someone from her neighborhood) asking for protection. But then she got distracted and "put the grapes on hold" (filed the bit of gossip away for future use).

5   That was her mistake because the woman out to get her was a "diehard" (will not conform to prison rules of conduct), "hard core" (career criminal), or "cold piece" (psychopath or sociopath) who was a "hog" (enforcer), "dancer" (fighter), and sometimes a "jive bitch" (agitator).

6   These are only a few of the hundreds of slang words used by women behind bars. They are part of prison life. All female convicts learn them—or else.

EXERCISE 11

Discussion and Critical Thinking

1. The essay begins with both a thesis and a definition. Which following sentence repeats that idea?

2. How are examples and causes used as patterns of development?

3. How is classification (meaning types of something) used?

4. How are comparison and contrast used as a pattern of development?

Topics for Writing Definition

You will find a blank Writing Process Worksheet on page 6, which can be photocopied, filled in, and submitted with each assignment if your instructor directs you to do so.

Reading-Related Topics

"Burnout"

1. Borrow the definition from this passage and develop it with an extended example of someone you know who is or was a burnout.

"Georgia on My Mind"

2. Ray Jenkins defines *traditional rural white southerner* by listing the unique and colorful experiences of such a person. Define a person (perhaps you or a parent) by listing his or her associations with a housing project, barrio, working-class neighborhood, streets, prison, affluent suburb, migrant worker camp, small town, reservation, or refugee camp. You may use the same form as Jenkins, but keep in mind that the extremely long sentence form he uses so well here is unconventional and should be used sparingly.

3. Using Jenkins's paragraph as a model, define a daycare worker, security guard, police officer, preacher, nurse, firefighter, parent, coach, or attendant in an extended-care facility.

"Tortillas"

4. Write a definition of one of the basic foods of your culture or your family. Consider dumplings, corn bread, biscuits, rice, potatoes, *pupusas,* beans, fry bread, bagels, muffins, spaghetti, and crumpets. Develop your paragraph or essay by relating the food to its cultural context and history and to your own experiences. Also consider classifying the main varieties of your basic food.

"A Working Community"

5. Using Goodman's basic concept, write about another out-of-neighborhood community. Consider writing about a school, place of worship, club, movement, or group connected through the Internet as a new community.

"Is It Sexual Harassment?"

6. Write a paragraph or an essay in response to scenario 5 or 6. Use the three categories of illegal sexual harassment in paragraphs 30 through 32 as guiding principles. Be sure your response has a clear definition.

7. Apply one of the three categories of illegal sexual harassment in paragraphs 30 through 32 to a situation with which you are familiar.

8. Discuss one of the myths in terms of its truth or accuracy. Use your own reasoning and experience as support for your views.

"Going Too Far"

9. Apply the definition of *extremist* from this paragraph to a situation with which you are familiar: an overprotective parent, a controlling companion, an over-controlling boss, a too-strict police officer or teacher, a too-virtuous friend or preacher, a too-clean housekeeper (companion, parent), a zealous patriot, a person fanatical about a diet, or a person concerned too much with good health or exercise. You might begin your paragraph or essay with the statement: "It is good to be _____, but when _____ is carried to the extreme, the result is _____."

"Prison Slang"

10. Define another term for language usage such as *jargon* ("shop talk" by a group of people in a restricted activity, especially vocational or recreational), regional slang, age-group slang, or sign-language slang.

11. Using Rubec's essay as a model, develop a definition of *body language.*

General Topics

The following topics are appropriate for extended development of definitions; most of them will also serve well for writing simple definitions.

12. Conservative	22. Educated	32. Feminist
13. Asian American	23. Gang	33. Chicano
14. Bonding	24. Freedom	34. Jock
15. Sexist	25. Body language	35. Hispanic American
16. Cult	26. Hero	36. African American
17. Liberal	27. Druggie	37. Macho
18. Workaholic	28. Convict	38. Cool
19. Surfer	29. Teen slang	39. Native American
20. Personal space	30. Psychopath	40. Jerk
21. Clotheshorse	31. School spirit	

Cross-Curricular Topics

Define one of the following terms in a paragraph or an essay.

41. History and government: socialism, democracy, patriotism, capitalism, communism.

42. Philosophy: existentialism, free will, determinism, ethics, stoicism.

43. Education: charter schools, school choice, gifted program, ESL, paired teaching, digital school.

44. Music: symphony, sonata, orchestra, tonic systems.

45. Health science: autism, circulatory system, respiratory system, thyroid, cancer, herbal remedies, acupuncture.

46. Marketing: depression, digitalization, discretionary income, electronic commerce, globalization, marketing channel, free trade, telemarketing, warehouse clubs.

Career-Related Topics

47. Define one of the following terms by using other patterns of development (such as exemplification, cause and effect, narration, comparison and contrast): total quality management, quality control, business ethics, customer satisfaction, cost effectiveness, Internet, temporary worker, union, outsource, or downsize.

48. Define a good boss, good employee, good workplace, good employer, or good job. Analysis by division is a useful form.

49. Define a term from computer technology such as Internet, World Wide Web, search engine, or chat room.

Writer's Guidelines: Definition

Simple Definition

1. No two words have exactly the same meaning.

2. Several forms of simple definitions can be blended into your discussion: basic dictionary definitions, synonyms, direct explanations, indirect explanations, and analytical definitions.

3. For a formal or an analytical definition, specify the term, class, and characteristic(s).

<u>Capitalism</u> <u>is an economic system</u> <u>characterized by investment</u>
    term   class

<u>of money, private ownership, and free enterprise.</u>
                  characteristics

4. Avoid "is where" and "is when" definitions, circular definitions, and the use of words in the definition that are more difficult than the word being defined.

Extended Definition

1. Use clustering to consider other patterns of development that may be used to define your term.

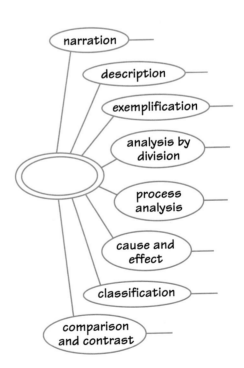

2. The organization of your extended definition is likely to be one of emphasis, but it may be space or time, depending on the subject material. You may use just one pattern of development for the overall organization.

3. Consider these ways of introducing a definition: with a question, with a statement of what it is not, with a statement of what it originally meant, or with a discus-

sion of why a clear definition is important. You may use a combination of these ways before you continue with your definition.

4. Whether you personalize a definition depends on your purpose and your audience. Your instructor may ask you to write about a word within the context of your own experience or to write about it from a detached, clinical viewpoint.

5. Use the writing process.

- Write and then revise your paragraph or essay as many times as necessary for coherence, language (usage, tone, and diction), unity, emphasis, support, and sentences (**CLUESS**).

- Read your work aloud to hear and correct any grammatical errors or awkward-sounding sentences.

- Edit any problems in fundamentals, such as capitalization, omissions, punctuation, and spelling (**COPS**).

Handbook

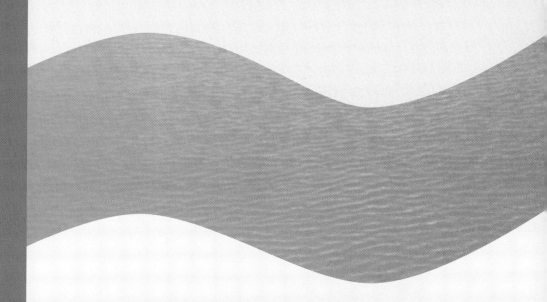

In your personal, cross-curricular, and career-related writing, almost all of your work will be in sentences. This part of your textbook will help you write correctly and effectively, enabling you to say what you want to say and even enhancing the flow of your message. Within the writing process, this handbook especially pertains to the "S" (sentences) part of CLUESS and all parts (capitalization, omissions, punctuation, and spelling) of COPS.

Handbook
Writing Effective Sentences

Subjects and Verbs 406

Kinds of Sentences 413

Combining Sentences 422

Omissions 431

Variety in Sentence Types, Order, Length,
  Beginnings 432

Correcting Fragments, Comma Splices, and
  Run-Ons 434

Verbs 444

Pronouns 467

Adjectives and Adverbs 481

Balancing Sentence Parts 491

Punctuation and Capitalization 496

Spelling 514

Avoiding Wordy Phrases 519

Brief Guide for ESL Students 521

*"I have rewritten—often several times—
every word I have ever published. My
pencils outlast their erasers."*

VLADIMIR NABOKOV

© Gary Larson, courtesy Chronicle Features

Subjects and Verbs

The two most important parts of any sentence are the subject and the verb. The **subject** is who or what causes the action or expresses a state of being. The **verb** indicates what the subject is doing or is being. Many times the subject and verb taken together carry the meaning of the sentence. Consider this example:

The <u>woman</u> <u>left</u> for work.
     subject verb

The subject *woman* and the verb *left* indicate the basic content of the sentence while providing structure.

Subjects

The simple subject of a sentence is usually a single noun or pronoun.

The judge's <u>reputation</u> for order in the courtroom is well known.
            simple subject

The complete subject is the simple subject with all its modifiers—that is, with all the words that describe or qualify it.

<u>The judge's reputation for order in the courtroom</u> is well known.
            complete subject

To more easily understand and identify simple subjects of sentences, you may want to review the following information about nouns and pronouns. (See Appendix A for more information about all eight parts of speech.)

Nouns

Nouns are naming words. Nouns may name persons, animals, plants, places, things, substances, qualities, or ideas—for example, *Bart, armadillo, Mayberry, tree, rock, cloud, love, ghost, music, virtue.*

Pronouns

A **pronoun** is a word that is used in place of a noun.

- Pronouns that can be used as subjects of sentences may represent specific persons or things and are called personal pronouns:

I   *we*
you   *you*
he, she, it *they*

Example: <u>They</u> recommended my sister for the coaching position.
         subject

- Indefinite pronouns refer to nouns (persons, places, things) in a general way:

each   *everyone*   *nobody*   *somebody*

Example: <u>Everyone</u> wants a copy of that paragraph.
         subject

- Other pronouns point out particular things:

  Singular: *this, that*   Plural: *these, those*

  This is my treasure.   *These* are my jewels.
  That is your junk.   *Those* are your trinkets.

- Still other pronouns introduce questions:

  > *Which* is the best CD player?
  > *What* are the main ingredients in a Twinkie?
  > *Who* understands this computer command?

Note: To be the subject of a sentence, a pronoun must stand alone.

> *This* is a treasure. [Subject is *this*; pronoun stands alone.]
> This *treasure* is mine. [Subject is *treasure*. *This* is an adjective—a word that describes a noun; *This* describes *treasure*.]

Compound Subjects

A subject may be compound. That is, it may consist of two or more subjects, usually joined by *and* or *or*, that function together.

> The *prosecutor* and the *attorney* for the defense made opening statements.
> *He* and his *friends* listened carefully.
> *Steven, Juan,* and *Alicia* attended the seminar. [Note the placement of commas for three or more subjects.]

Implied Subjects

A subject may be implied or understood. An imperative sentence—a sentence that gives a command—has *you* as the implied subject.

> (You) Sit in that chair, please.
> (You) Now take the oath.
> (You) Please read the notes carefully.

Trouble Spot: Prepositional Phrases

A **prepositional phrase** is made up of a preposition (a word such as *at, in, of, to, with*) and one or more nouns or pronouns with their modifiers: *at the time, by the jury, in the courtroom, to the judge and the media, with controlled anger.* Be careful not to confuse the subject of a sentence with the noun or pronoun (known as the object of the preposition) in a prepositional phrase. The object of a preposition cannot be the subject of a sentence.

> The <u>car</u> with the dents is mine.
>   subject   prepositional
>   phrase

The subject of the sentence is *car.* The word *dents* is the object of the preposition *with* and cannot be the subject of the sentence.

> <u>Most</u> of the pie has been eaten.
> subject prepositional
>   phrase

The <u>person in the middle of the crowd</u> has disappeared.
   subject   prepositional   prepositional
                phrase   phrase

Trouble Spot: The Words *Here* and *There*

The words *here* and *there* are adverbs (used as filler words) and cannot be subjects.

There is no <u>problem</u>.
            subject

Here is the <u>issue</u>.
           subject

Verbs

Verbs show action or express being in relation to the subject of a sentence.

Types of Verbs

Action verbs indicate movement or accomplishment in idea or deed. Someone can "consider the statement" or "hit the ball." Here are other examples:

She *sees* the arena.
He *bought* the book.
They *adopted* the child.
He *understood* her main theories.

Being verbs indicate existence. Few in number, they include *is, was, were, am,* and *are.*

The movie *is* sad.
The book *was* comprehensive.
They *were* responsible.
I *am* concerned.
We *are* organized.

Verb Phrases

Verbs may occur as single words or as phrases. A **verb phrase** is made up of a main verb and one or more helping verbs such as the following:

is	*was*	*can*	*have*	*do*	*may*	*shall*
are	*were*	*could*	*had*	*does*	*might*	*should*
am		*will*	*has*	*did*	*must*	
		would				

Here are some sentences that contain verb phrases:

The judge *has presided* over many capital cases.
His rulings seldom *are overturned* on appeal.

Trouble Spot: Words Such as *Never, Not,* and *Hardly*

Never, not, hardly, seldom, and so on, are modifiers, not verbs.

The attorney could *not* win the case without key witnesses.
[*Not* is an adverb. The verb phrase is *could win.*]

The jury could *hardly* hear the witness. [*Hardly* is an adverb; *could hear* is the verb phrase.]

Compound Verbs

Verbs that are joined by a word such as *and* or *or* are called **compound verbs.**

As a district attorney, Sumi *had presented* and *had won* famous cases.

She *prepared* carefully and *presented* her ideas with clarity.

We *will go* out for dinner or *skip* it entirely.

Trouble Spot: Verbals

Do not confuse verbs with verbals. **Verbals** are verblike words in certain respects, but they do not function as verbs. They function as other parts of speech. There are three kinds of verbals.

An **infinitive** is made up of the word *to* and a verb. An infinitive provides information, but, unlike the true verb, it is not tied to the subject of the sentence. It acts as a noun or describing unit.

He wanted *to get* a bachelor's degree.

To get a bachelor's degree was his main objective.

(In the first example, the word *wanted* is the verb for the subject *He.* The word *get* follows *to; to get* is an infinitive.)

A **gerund** is a verblike word ending in *-ing* that acts as a noun.

Retrieving her e-mail was always an exciting experience.

She thought about *retrieving* her e-mail.

Retrieving in each sentence acts as a noun.

A **participle** is a verblike word that usually has an *-ing* or an *-ed* ending.

Walking to town in the dark, he lost his way.

Wanted by the FBI, she was on the run.

The *starved* dog barked for food.

In the first example, the word *walking* answers the question *when.* In the second example, the word *wanted* answers the question *which one.* In the third example, *starved* describes the dog. *Walking, wanted,* and *starved* are describing words; they are not the true verbs in the sentences.

Location of Subjects and Verbs

Although the subject usually appears before the verb, it may follow the verb instead:

Into the court <u>stumbled</u> the <u>defendant</u>.
verb   subject

From tiny acorns <u>grow</u> mighty <u>oaks</u>.
verb   subject

There <u>was</u> little <u>support</u> for him in the audience.
verb   subject

Here <u>are</u> your <u>books</u> and your <u>papers</u>.
verb   subject   subject

Verb phrases are often broken up in a question. Do not overlook a part of the verb that is separated from another in a question such as "Where had the defendant gone on that fateful night?" If you have trouble finding the verb phrase, recast the question, making it into a statement: "The defendant *had gone* where on that fateful night." The result will not necessarily be a smooth or complete statement, but you will be able to see the basic elements more easily.

> *Can* the defense lawyer *control* the direction of the trial?

Change the question to a statement to find the verb phrase:

> The defense lawyer *can control* the direction of the trial.

EXERCISE 1

Finding Subjects and Verbs

Write the simple subject, without modifiers, in the first blank; write the verb in the second blank. Some sentences have compound subjects, compound verbs, or both; some sentences have an implied ("you") subject. (See Answer Key for answers.)

1. Every afternoon Joyce watches her favorite soap opera, *The Blameless and the Doomed.* _____ _____

2. Never again will José order the mystery meat stew. _____ _____

3. Jack and Jill should have been more careful on that hill. _____ _____

4. Maybe you and I will learn to tango. _____ _____

5. In Key West is the southernmost point of the United States. _____ _____

6. Several of the players are already stretching and warming up. _____ _____

7. Please knock three times on the window. _____ _____

8. Jesse Ventura, a former professional wrestler, was elected governor of Minnesota. _____ _____

9. Before long he will discover the sunken treasure and become famous. _____ _____

10. Whom can we persuade to clean the skunk's
    cage?   _____   _____

11. There is plenty of borscht for everyone.   _____   _____

12. How will you crack the code?   _____   _____

13. The boxers, just before the fight, touched gloves
    and returned to their corners of the ring.   _____   _____

14. In no time at all, Snow White had cleaned the
    whole cottage.   _____   _____

15. Many of the roller skaters were injured
    during the last race.   _____   _____

16. Has he ever wished upon a star?   _____   _____

17. Please bring me flies for my Venus fly trap. _____   _____

18. His response to her marriage proposal was to
    buy a single one-way ticket to Siberia.   _____   _____

19. In the jar floats a lone pickled egg.   _____   _____

20. Write you name on the paper.   _____   _____

EXERCISE 2

Finding Subjects and Verbs

Write the simple subject, without modifiers, in the first blank; write the verb in the second blank. Some sentences have compound subjects, compound verbs, or both; some sentences have an implied ("you") subject.

1. The earliest evidence of Chinese writing comes
   from the Shang dynasty.   _____   _____

2. Archaeologists have found and studied
   hundreds of animal bones and tortoise shells
   with written symbols on them.   _____   _____

3. These strange objects are known as oracle
   bones.   _____   _____

4. Priests used them in fortune telling.   _____   _____

5. People 3,500 years ago developed part of the culture existing in China today.   _____   _____

6. Some of the characters are very much like those in a modern Chinese newspaper.   _____   _____

7. In the Chinese method of writing, each character stands for an idea, not a sound.   _____   _____

8. On the other hand, many of the Egyptian hieroglyphs stood for sounds in their spoken language.   _____   _____

9. But there were practically no links between China's spoken language and its written language.   _____   _____

10. One might read Chinese and not speak it.   _____   _____

11. The Chinese system of writing had one great advantage.   _____   _____

12. People with different dialects in all parts of China could learn the same system of writing and communicate with it.   _____   _____

13. Thus, the Chinese written language aided the unification of a large and diverse land.   _____   _____

14. The disadvantage of the Chinese system is the enormous number of written characters.   _____   _____

15. A barely literate person needs at least 1,000 characters.   _____   _____

16. A true scholar needs about 10,000 characters.   _____   _____

17. For centuries, this requirement severely limited the number of literate, educated Chinese.   _____   _____

18. A noble's children learned to write.   _____   _____

19. A peasant's children did not.   _____   _____

20. Consider these ideas as a background to

    modern educational systems.   _____   _____

Kinds of Sentences

There are four kinds of basic sentences in English: simple, compound, complex, and compound-complex. The terms may be new to you, but if you can recognize subjects and verbs, with a little instruction and practice you should be able to identify and write any of the four kinds of sentences. The only new idea to master is the concept of the *clause*.

Clauses

A **clause** is a group of words with a subject and a verb that functions as a part or all of a complete sentence. There are two kinds of clauses: independent (main) and dependent (subordinate).

> Independent Clause: I have the money.

> Dependent Clause: When I have the money

Independent Clauses

An **independent (main) clause** is a group of words with a subject and a verb that can stand alone and make sense. An independent clause expresses a complete thought by itself and can be written as a separate sentence.

> She plays the bass guitar.
> The manager is not at fault.

Dependent Clauses

A **dependent clause** is a group of words with a subject and verb that depends on a main clause to give it meaning.

> since Shannon came home [no meaning alone]

> <u>Since Shannon came home,</u> <u>her mother has been happy</u>. [has meaning]
>   dependent clause   independent clause

> because she was needed [no meaning alone]

> <u>She stayed in the game</u> <u>because she was needed</u>. [has meaning]
>   independent clause   dependent clause

Relative Clauses

One type of dependent clause is called a relative clause. A **relative clause** begins with a relative pronoun, a pronoun such as *that, which,* or *who.* Relative pronouns *relate* the clause to another word in the sentence.

> that fell last night [no meaning alone]

> The snow <u>that fell last night</u> is nearly gone. [has meaning]
>   dependent clause

In the sentence above, the relative pronoun *that* relates the dependent clause to the subject of the sentence, *snow.*

who stayed in the game [no meaning alone]

<u>She was the only one</u> <u>who stayed in the game.</u>
     independent clause   dependent clause

In the sentence above, the relative pronoun *who* relates the dependent clause to the word *one.*

Trouble Spot: Phrases

A **phrase** is a group of words that go together. It differs from a clause in that a phrase does not have a subject and a verb. In the previous section, we discussed prepositional phrases (*in the house, beyond the horizon*) and saw some verbal phrases (infinitive phrase: *to go home;* participial phrase: *disconnected from the printer;* and gerund phrase: *running the computer*).

Types of Sentences

This section covers sentence types according to this principle: On the basis of the number and kinds of clauses it contains, a sentence may be classified as simple, compound, complex, or compound-complex. In the examples in the following list, the dependent clauses are italicized, and the independent clauses are underlined.

Type	Definition	Example
Simple	One independent clause	<u>She did the work well.</u>
Compound	Two or more independent clauses	<u>She did the work well</u>, and <u>she was paid well.</u>
Complex	One independent clause and one or more dependent clauses	*Because she did the work well,* <u>she was paid well.</u>
Compound-complex	Two or more independent clauses and one or more dependent clauses	*Because she did the work well,* <u>she was paid well,</u> and <u>she was satisfied.</u>

Simple Sentences

A **simple sentence** consists of one independent clause and no dependent clauses. It may contain phrases and have more than one subject and/or verb.

The *lake looks* beautiful in the moonlight. [one subject and one verb]

The *Army, Navy,* and *Marines sent* troops to the disaster area. [three subjects and one verb]

We sang the old songs and *danced* happily at their wedding. [one subject and two verbs]

My *father, mother,* and *sister came* to the school play, *applauded* the performers, and *attended* the party afterwards. [three subjects and three verbs]

EXERCISE 3

Writing Simple Sentences

Write six simple sentences. The first five have been started for you.

1. The mall _____

_____

2. The parking _____

_____

3. The sale _____

_____

4. After two hours _____

_____

5. Then _____

_____

6. _____

_____

Compound Sentences

A **compound sentence** consists of two or more independent clauses with no dependent clauses. Take, for example, the following two independent clauses:

He opened the drawer. He found his missing disk.

Here are two ways to join the independent clauses to form a compound sentence.

1. The two independent clauses can be connected by a connecting word called a coordinating conjunction. The coordinating conjunctions are *for, and, nor, but, or, yet, so*. (An easy way to remember them is to think of the acronym FANBOYS, which is made up of the first letter of each conjunction.)

He opened the drawer, *and* he found his missing disk.

He opened the drawer, *so* he found his missing disk.

Use a comma before the coordinating conjunction (FANBOYS) between two independent clauses (unless one of the clauses is extremely short).

2. Another way to join independent clauses to form a compound sentence is to put a semicolon between the clauses.

He opened the drawer; he found his missing disk.

EXERCISE 4

Writing Compound Sentences

Write five compound sentences using coordinating conjunctions. The sentences have been started for you. Then write the same five compound sentences without the co-ordinating conjunctions. Use a semicolon to join the independent clauses.

1. It was the car of her dreams, _____

   _____

2. She used the Internet to find the dealer's cost, _____

   _____

3. She now was ready to bargain, _____

   _____

4. Armed with facts, she went to the dealer, _____

   _____

5. The dealer made an offer, _____

   _____

6. _____

   _____

7. _____

   _____

8. _____

   _____

9. _____

   _____

10. _____

    _____

Complex Sentences

A **complex sentence** consists of one independent clause and one or more dependent clauses. In the following sentences, the dependent clauses are italicized.

> *When lilacs are in bloom,* we love to visit friends in the country. [one dependent clause and one independent clause]

> *Although it rained last night,* we decided to take the path *that led through the woods.* [one independent clause and two dependent clauses]

Punctuation tip: Use a comma after a dependent clause that appears before the main clause.

> *When the bus arrived,* we quickly boarded.

A relative clause (see page 413) can be the dependent clause in a complex sentence.

> I knew the actress *who played that part in the 1980s.*

EXERCISE 5

Writing Complex Sentences

Write six complex sentences. The first four have been started for you.

1. Although the job paid well, _____

   _____

2. Before she went to work each day, _____

   _____

3. When she returned home each night, _____

   _____

4. Because her social life was suffering, _____

   _____

5. _____

   _____

6. _____

   _____

Compound-Complex Sentences

A **compound-complex sentence** consists of two or more independent clauses and one or more dependent clauses.

Compound-Complex Sentence:	Albert enlisted in the Army, and Jason, who was his older brother, joined him a day later.
Independent Clauses:	Albert enlisted in the Army Jason joined him a day later
Dependent Clause:	who was his older brother
Compound-Complex Sentence:	Because Mr. Sanchez was a talented teacher, he was voted teacher of the year, and his students prospered.
Independent Clauses:	he was voted teacher of the year his students prospered
Dependent Clause:	Because Mr. Sanchez was a talented teacher

EXERCISE 6

Writing Compound-Complex Sentences

Write six compound-complex sentences. The first five have been started for you.

1. When he began his research paper, he was confident, but _____

_____

2. Although his college library offered good traditional sources, he wanted some online sources, so _____

_____

3. After he found sources for background information, he focused on one issue, and then _____

_____

4. When he discovered that an expert in his study lived nearby, he _____

_____

5. After he wrote his final draft on his word processor, he _____

_____

6. _____

_____

EXERCISE 7

Identifying Types of Sentences

Indicate the kind of sentence by writing the appropriate letter(s) in the blank. (See Answer Key for answers.)

S   simple
CP   compound
CX   complex
CC   compound-complex

_____ 1. The *Titanic*, a British passenger liner, began its maiden voyage from England to New York on April 10, 1912.

_____ 2. It was the largest and most luxurious ship ever built, and it carried 2,227 passengers and crew members.

_____ 3. The ship was described as a floating palace, and because its hull included a complicated system of watertight compartments, it was also declared to be "practically unsinkable."

_____ 4. After three days of calm, clear weather at sea, the captain received seven warnings of ice in the area.

_____ 5. At 11:40 P.M. on April 14, lookouts in the ship's crow's nest saw an iceberg directly in the vessel's path, but it was too late to change course.

_____ 6. The *Titanic* struck the iceberg in the North Atlantic Ocean.

_____ 7. Because the ship was supposedly unsinkable, it carried only twenty lifeboats.

_____ 8. Women and children were first to board the lifeboats, which offered room for only about half of the people aboard.

_____ 9. Water poured into the ship, and by 1:15 A.M., its bow sank.

_____ 10. At 2:17 A.M., as the stern rose almost vertically into the air, the lights finally flickered and went out.

_____ 11. At 2:18 A.M. on April 15, the sinking ship broke in two, and at 2:20 A.M., it disappeared beneath the waves.

_____ 12. Those who did not drown froze to death in the icy water.

_____ 13. The disaster claimed 1,522 lives; 705 people were rescued.

_____ 14. After this tragedy occurred, new agreements revised lifeboat standards and created the International Ice Patrol in North Atlantic sea lanes.

_____ 15. Immediately, people began talking about ways to find the *Titanic* and raise it to the surface.

_____ 16. Not until 1985, though, did a team of U.S. and French researchers locate the wreck off the coast of Newfoundland at a depth of two and a half miles.

_____ 17. Several subsequent expeditions sent cameras, lights, and manned submarines down to the eerie scene, where they explored and photographed the rusted wreckage and collected artifacts from it.

_____ 18. The photos revealed that the iceberg ripped a hole in six of the watertight compartments; the ship might have survived if only four of its compartments had been ruptured.

_____ 19. In 1996, when researchers tried to salvage a section of the ship's hull by raising it to the surface with balloons, a storm caused the lines to break, and the piece fell back to the bottom of the sea.

_____ 20. The ship is deteriorating rapidly in its saltwater grave, and it will eventually melt into the floor of the sea.

EXERCISE 8   ## Identifying Types of Sentences

Indicate the kind of sentence by writing the appropriate letter(s) in the blank.

S   simple
CP   compound
CX   complex
CC   compound-complex

_____ 1. Throughout history there have been truth tests for the innocent and the guilty.

———— 2. Many of these methods relied (unknowingly) on the basic physiological principles that also guided the creation of the polygraph.

———— 3. For example, one method of lie detection involved giving the suspect a handful of raw rice to chew.

———— 4. After the suspect chewed for some time, he or she was instructed to spit out the rice.

———— 5. An innocent person was expected to do this easily, but a guilty person was expected to have grains of rice sticking to the roof of the mouth and tongue.

———— 6. This technique relied on the increased sympathetic nervous system activity in the presumably fearful and guilty person.

———— 7. This activity would result in the drying up of saliva.

———— 8. That, in turn, would cause grains of rice to stick in the mouth.

———— 9. A similar but more frightening technique involved placing a heated knife blade briefly against the tongue.

———— 10. An innocent person would not be burned, but the guilty person would immediately feel pain, again because of the relative dryness of the mouth.

———— 11. A more primitive but functional technique for detecting liars was supposedly used by a Persian king.

———— 12. He was presumed to have a very special donkey, one that had the ability to tell an innocent person from a guilty one.

———— 13. When a crime was committed, the suspects would be gathered in a hall next to the room that held the donkey.

———— 14. According to directions, each suspect entered the room alone, found the donkey in the dark, and pulled its tail.

———— 15. The donkey did the rest.

_____ 16. If an innocent person pulled the tail, the donkey was said to remain

silent.

_____ 17. If a guilty person pulled the tail, the donkey would bray loudly.

_____ 18. In fact, the donkey's tail was dusted with graphite.

_____ 19. The guilty person emerged with clean hands because he or she

wanted to avoid detection.

_____ 20. The king knew that the person with clean hands was guilty, and he

proceeded with punishment.

Combining Sentences

The simple sentence, the most basic sentence in the English language, can be exceptionally useful and powerful. Some of the greatest statements in literature have been presented in the simple sentence. Its strength is in its singleness of purpose. However, a piece of writing made up of a long series of simple sentences is likely to be monotonous. Moreover, the form may suggest a separateness of ideas that does not serve your purpose well. If your ideas are closely related, some equal in importance and some not, you can combine sentences to show the relationships between your ideas.

Coordination: The Compound Sentence

If you intend to communicate two equally important and closely related ideas, you certainly will want to place them close together, probably in a compound sentence.

Suppose we take two simple sentences that we want to combine:

I am very tired. I worked very hard today.

We have already looked at coordinating conjunctions as a way of joining independent clauses to create compound sentences. Depending on which coordinating conjunction you use, you can show different kinds of relationships. (The following list is arranged according to the FANBOYS acronym discussed in the previous section. Only the first conjunction joins the original two sentences.)

For shows a reason:

I am very tired, *for* I worked very hard today.

And shows equal ideas:

I am very tired, *and* I want to rest for a few minutes.

Nor indicates a negative choice or alternative:

I am not tired, *nor* am I hungry right now.

But shows contrast:

I am very tired, *but* I have no time to rest now.

Or indicates a choice or an alternative:

> I will take a nap, *or* I will go out jogging.

Yet indicates contrast:

> I am tired, *yet* I am unable to relax.

So points to a result:

> I am tired, *so* I will take a nap.

Punctuation with Coordinating Conjunctions

When you combine two sentences by using a coordinating conjunction, drop the first period, change the capital letter that begins the second sentence to a small letter, and insert a comma before the coordinating conjunction.

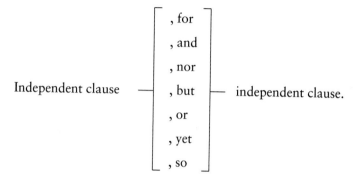

Independent clause — [, for / , and / , nor / , but / , or / , yet / , so] — independent clause.

Semicolons and Conjunctive Adverbs

In the previous section we saw that a semicolon can join independent clauses to make a compound sentence. Here are two more simple sentences to combine:

> We were late. We missed the first act.

We can make one compound sentence out of them by joining the two clauses with a semicolon:

> We were late; we missed the first act.

We can also use words called conjunctive adverbs after semicolons to make the relationship between the two clauses clearer. Look at how the conjunctive adverb *therefore* adds the idea of "as a result."

> We were late; *therefore,* we missed the first act.

Conjunctive adverbs include the following words and phrases: *also, consequently, furthermore, hence, however, in fact, moreover, nevertheless, now, on the other hand, otherwise, soon, therefore, similarly, then, thus.*

Consider the meaning you want when you use a conjunctive adverb to coordinate ideas.

> As a result of: *therefore, consequently, hence, thus, then*
>
> To the contrary or with reservation: *however, nevertheless, otherwise, on the other hand*
>
> In addition to: *moreover, also*

To emphasize or specify: *in fact, for example*

To compare: *similarly*

Punctuation with Semicolons and Conjunctive Adverbs

When you combine two sentences by using a semicolon, replace the first period with a semicolon and change the capital letter that begins the second sentence to a small letter. If you wish to use a conjunctive adverb, insert it after the semicolon and put a comma after it. (However, no comma follows *then, now, thus,* and *soon.*) The first letters of ten common conjunctive adverbs make up the acronym HOTSHOT CAT.

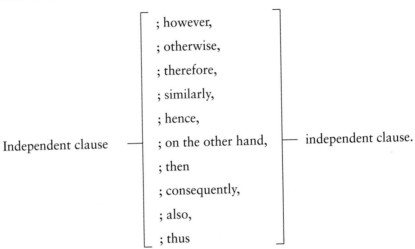

Independent clause — ; however,
; otherwise,
; therefore,
; similarly,
; hence,
; on the other hand,
; then
; consequently,
; also,
; thus — independent clause.

Subordination: The Complex Sentence

Whereas a compound sentence contains independent clauses that are equally important and closely related, a complex sentence combines ideas of unequal value. The following two sentences can be combined as either a compound sentence or a complex sentence, depending on whether the writer thinks the ideas are of equal value.

> My neighbors are considerate. They never play loud music.

Combined as a compound sentence, suggesting that the ideas are of equal value, the new sentence looks like this:

> My neighbors are considerate, and they never play loud music.
> independent clause   independent clause
> (main idea)   (main idea)

Here are the same two ideas combined as a complex sentence, suggesting that the ideas are of unequal value:

> Because my neighbors are considerate, they never play loud music.
> dependent clause   independent clause
> (less important idea)   (main idea)

Although both the compound and the complex forms are correct, the complex form conveys the ideas more precisely in this sentence because one idea does seem to be more important—one idea depends on the other.

Thus if you have two sentences with closely related ideas and one is clearly more important than the other, consider combining them in a complex sentence. Compare these two paragraphs:

1. Version 1 contains six simple sentences, implying that the ideas are of equal value:

   (1) I was very upset. (2) The Fourth of July fireworks were especially loud. (3) My dog ran away. (4) The animal control officer made his morning rounds. (5) He found my dog in another part of town. (6) I was relieved.

2. Version 2 consists of two simple sentences and two complex sentences, showing that some ideas are more important than others:

   (1) I was very upset. (2) Because the Fourth of July fireworks were especially loud, my dog ran away. (3) When the animal control officer made his morning rounds, he found my dog in another part of town. (4) I was relieved.

You will probably consider Version 2 superior to Version 1. In Version 1 sentences 2 and 3 are closely related, but 3 is more important. Sentences 4 and 5 are closely related, but 5 is more important. In Version 2 the revision made each pair into a complex sentence.

Although you could combine sentences 1 and 2, the result would be illogical because the wrong idea would be conveyed:

Illogical Combination: I was very upset because the Fourth of July fireworks were especially loud.

The person was very upset because the dog ran away, not because the fireworks were especially loud.

Subordinating Conjunctions

As you learned in the previous section, a complex sentence is composed of one independent clause and one or more dependent clauses. In combining two independent clauses to write a complex sentence, your first step is to decide on a word that will best show the relationship between the clauses. Words that show the relationship of a dependent clause to an independent one are called subordinating conjunctions. The italicized words in the following sentences are subordinating conjunctions. Consider the meaning as well as the placement of each one.

Because the storm hit, the game was canceled.

After the storm passed, the dogs began to bark.

When she read her poem, they were moved to fits of hysterics.

He did not volunteer to work on the holiday, *although* the pay was good.

No one has visited her *since* she moved into town.

They decided to wait *until* the cows came home.

They refused to work *unless* they were allowed to wear chef's hats.

Before the session ended, all the "hep cats" blew some sweet sounds.

Other subordinating conjunctions include the following:

as	*provided that*	*whereas*
as if	*rather than*	*wherever*
even if	*so that*	*whether*
even though	*than*	*while*
if	*whenever*	
in order that	*where*	

Punctuation with Subordinating Conjunctions

If the dependent clause comes *before* the main clause, set it off with a comma.

Before Mike wrote his final draft, he looked over his outline.

If the dependent clause comes *after* or *within* the main clause, set it off only if the clause is not necessary to the meaning of the main clause or if the dependent clause begins with the word *although, though,* or *even though.*

We went home *after* the concert had ended.

He continued painting, *although* he had repainted the cabinet twice.

Punctuation with Relative Pronouns

As you learned earlier, a relative clause begins with a relative pronoun, a pronoun such as *that, which,* or *who.*

The decision that I made is final.
                    relative clause

A student who uses a computer can save time in revising.
               relative clause

Set off the dependent (relative) clause with commas when it is not necessary to the sentence. Do not set off the clause if it is necessary for the meaning of the sentence.

Everyone *who tries* will pass this class. [The dependent clause is necessary because one would not say, "Everyone will pass this class."]

Rachel, *who tries,* will pass this class. [The dependent clause is not necessary because one can say, "Rachel will pass this class."]

The relative pronoun *which* usually refers to things. The word *which* almost always indicates that a clause is not necessary for the meaning of the sentence. Therefore, a clause beginning with *which* is almost always set off by commas.

My car, *which* is ten years old, has a flat tire.

The relative pronoun *that* also usually refers to things. However, the word *that* almost always indicates that the clause *is* necessary for the meaning of the sentence. Therefore, a clause beginning with *that* is almost always *not* set off by commas.

The car *that* has a flat tire is ten years old.

The relative pronouns *who* and *whom,* as well as *whoever* and *whomever,* usually refer to people. Clauses that begin with those relative pronouns are not set off by commas if they are necessary for the meaning of the sentence; if they are not necessary, they are set off.

A person *who* has a way with words is often quoted. [necessary for the meaning of the sentence]

My uncle, *whom* I quote often, has a way with words. [not necessary for the meaning of the sentence]

Coordination and Subordination: The Compound-Complex Sentence

At times you may want to show the relationship of three or more ideas within one sentence. If that relationship involves two or more main ideas and one or more supporting ideas, the combination can be stated in a compound-complex sentence (two or more independent clauses and one or more dependent clauses).

Before he learned how to operate a computer,
dependent clause

he had trouble with his typewritten assignments,
independent clause

but now he produces clean, attractive pages.
independent clause

In our previous discussion of the complex sentence, we presented this group of six sentences:

I was very upset. The Fourth of July fireworks were especially loud. My dog ran away. The animal control officer made his morning rounds. He found my dog in another part of town. I was relieved.

We then converted the group of six sentences to four:

I was very upset. Because the Fourth of July fireworks were especially loud, my dog ran away. When the animal control officer made his morning rounds, he found my dog in another part of town. I was relieved.

But what if we wanted to show an even closer relationship of ideas? One solution would be to combine the two complex sentences in this way (the italicized sentence is compound-complex):

I was very upset. *Because the Fourth of July fireworks were especially loud, my dog ran away; but when the animal control officer made his morning rounds, he found my dog in another part of town.* I was relieved.

Punctuation of Complicated Compound or Compound-Complex Sentences

If a compound or compound-complex sentence has one or more commas in the first clause, you may want to use a semicolon before the coordinating conjunction between the two clauses. Its purpose is to show the reader very clearly the division between the two independent clauses. The preceding example illustrates this use of the semicolon.

Other Ways to Combine Ideas

1. Use an appositive, a noun or a noun phrase that immediately follows a noun or pronoun and renames it.

   Garth Brooks claims Yukon, Oklahoma, as his home town. He is a famous singer.

   Garth Brooks, *a famous singer,* claims Yukon, Oklahoma, as his home town.

2. Use a prepositional phrase, a preposition followed by a noun or pronoun object.

   John Elway led the Denver Broncos to two Super Bowl victories. Both triumphs occurred in the 1990s.

   John Elway led the Denver Broncos to two Super Bowl victories *in the 1990s.*

3. Drop the subject in the sentence that follows and combine the sentences.

> Emily Dickinson's poetry went mostly unpublished during her lifetime. It was finally discovered and celebrated more than a half century later.

> Emily Dickinson's poetry went mostly unpublished during her lifetime but was finally discovered and celebrated more than a half century later.

4. Use a participial phrase, a group of words that includes a participle, which is a verbal that usually ends in -ing or -ed.

> Michael rowed smoothly. He reached the shore.

> *Rowing smoothly,* Michael reached the shore.

EXERCISE 9   # Combining Sentences

Combine each group of sentences into a single sentence. Use coordination, subordination, or one of the other ways of combining ideas. (See Answer Key for answers.)

1. Cobras are among the most feared of all snakes.
   They are not the deadliest of all snakes.

2. Cobras do not coil before they strike.
   They cannot strike for a long distance.

3. Cobras do not have a hood.
   They flatten their neck by moving their ribs when they are nervous or frightened.

4. Cobras use their poison in two ways.
   One way is by injecting venom with their fangs.
   Another way is by spitting venom at their victims.

5. Human beings will not die from the venom that has been spit.
   It can cause blindness if it is not washed from the eyes.

6. A person can die from a cobra bite.
   Death may come in only a few hours.

7. Snake charmers have long worked with cobras.
   They use only a snake, a basket, and a flute.

8. The snakes cannot hear the music.
   They respond to the rhythmic movements of the charmers.

9. The snake charmers are hardly ever in danger of being bitten.
   They defang the cobras or sew their mouths shut.

10. Most cobras flee from people.
    They attack if they are cornered or if they are guarding their eggs.

EXERCISE 10

Combining Sentences

Combine each group of sentences into a single sentence. Use coordination, subordination, or one of the other ways of combining ideas.

1. Henry David Thoreau grew tired of living in society.
   He wanted to face his essential self.

2. He built a cabin in the woods.
   He lived there for more than a year.

3. Gilligan had a plan.
   He would float in a shipping crate to Hawaii.

4. It would be a surprise.
   He would send help to his friends on the island.

5. A storm came up.
   Gilligan's craft sank in three feet of water in the lagoon.
   The skipper cried bitter tears over the loss of his little buddy.

6. The professor made a submarine out of coconut shells, Mrs. Howell's corset, Ginger's jewelry, and fish bones.
   Gilligan was rescued.

7. Captain Ahab set sail for the South Seas.
   Captain Ahab had an obsession.

8. He wanted to kill the great white whale.
   The name of the great white whale was Moby Dick.

9. The captain and the whale had their encounter. Moby Dick was easily the victor.

10. Hamlet was sad.
    His father was dead.
    His mother had married his uncle.

11. Hamlet believed that his uncle had killed his father.
    Hamlet plotted to kill his uncle.

12. Romeo and Juliet were young.
    They fell in love.

13. Their families were feuding.
    Romeo and Juliet decided to run away.

14. They tried to trick their families.
    Their plans turned sour.
    They both died.

15. The contestant spun the wheel one more time.
    Vanna White clapped her hands with glee.

16. Pat Sajak made a wry joke about greed.
    Only one letter remained.

17. The wheel stopped.
    The contestant lost his turn.

18. The audience groaned.
    Vanna White slumped, and Pat Sajak comforted her sad heart.

19. Several tabloids have reported that Elvis has not left us.
    He has been sighted in several parts of this country and even on other planets.

20. The tabloids report that the King is just tired and wants privacy.
    They give credit to unnamed reliable sources.

Omissions

Do not omit words that are needed to make your sentences clear and logical. Of the many types of undesirable constructions in which necessary words are omitted, the following are the most common.

1. **Subjects.** Do not omit a necessary subject in a sentence with two verbs.

   Illogical: The cost of the car was $12,000 but would easily last me through college. (subject of *last)*

   Logical: The cost of the car was $12,000, but the car would easily last me through college.

2. **Verbs.** Do not omit verbs that are needed because of a change in the number of the subject or a change of tense.

   Illogical: The bushes were trimmed and the grass mowed.

   Logical: The bushes were trimmed, and the grass was mowed.

   Illogical: True honesty always has and always will be admired by most people. (tense)

   Logical: True honesty always has been and always will be admired by most people.

3. *That* **as a conjunction.** The conjunction *that* should not be omitted from a dependent clause if there is danger of misreading the sentence.

   Misleading: We believed Eric, if not stopped, would hurt himself.

   Clear: We believed that Eric, if not stopped, would hurt himself.

4. **Prepositions.** Do not omit prepositions in idiomatic phrases, in expressions of time, and in parallel phrases.

   Illogical: Weekends the campus is deserted. (time)

   Logical: During weekends the campus is deserted.

   Illogical: I have neither love nor patience with untrained dogs. (parallel phrases)

   Logical: I have neither love for nor patience with untrained dogs.

   Illogical: Glenda's illness was something we heard only after her recovery.

   Logical: Glenda's illness was something we heard about only after her recovery.

Repairing Omissions

Identify the kinds of omissions by writing one of the following words in the blanks to the right: *preposition, verb, subject, that*. Insert the necessary words in the sentences.

1. Courage always has and always will be admired. _____

2. In the trees or the ground the squirrel is a fascinating animal. _____

3. Mornings they went to the coffee house to think. _____

4. I never have and never will like her. _____

5. He has neither love nor patience with children. _____

6. The price of the leather jacket was $763, but was something I'd always wanted. _____

7. The parking problem is getting worse, and already is unable to handle all the cars. _____

8. Doretta's prowess was something we heard from afar. _____

9. The puck was stopped by the goalie, and went down to defeat. _____

10. He discovered his feet were wet. _____

Variety in Sentence Types, Order, Length, Beginnings

Do not bother to look for formulas in this section. Variety may be desirable for its own sake, to avoid dullness. However, it is more likely you will revise your compositions for reasons that make good sense in the context of what you are writing. The following are some of the variations available to you.

Types

You have learned that all four types of sentences are sound. Your task as a writer is to decide which one to use for a particular thought. That decision may not be made until you revise your composition. Then you can choose on the basis of the relationship of ideas:

> **Simple:** a single idea
>
> **Compound:** two closely related ideas
>
> **Complex:** one idea more important than the other
>
> **Compound-Complex:** a combination of compound and complex

These types were all covered earlier in this handbook (pages 414–418). This section provides further practice, as you combine sentences.

Order

You will choose the order of parts and information according to what you want to emphasize. Typically the most emphatic location is at the end of any unit.

Length

Uncluttered and direct, short sentences commonly draw attention. But that focus occurs only when they stand out from longer sentences. Therefore, you would usually avoid a series of short sentences.

Beginnings

A long series of sentences with each beginning with a subject followed by a verb may become monotonous. Consider beginning sentences in different ways:

With a prepositional phase: *In the distance* a dog barked.

With a transitional connective (conjunctive adverb) such as *then, however,* or *therefore*: *Then* the game was over.

With a coordinating conjunction such as *and* or *but: But* no one moved for three minutes.

With a dependent clause: *Although he wanted a new Corvette,* he settled for a used Ford Taurus.

With an adverb: *Carefully* he removed the thorn from the lion's paw.

EXERCISE 12

Providing Sentence Variety

Revise the following passage to achieve better sentence variety by changing the types of sentences, order of information, length of sentences, and beginnings of sentences. Use the skills you have learned about combining sentences. Compare your revisions with those of others in your class. There is no single correct way of making these changes.

My School Nightmare
Anna Kuang

My first day of school in America was also my worst nightmare. I woke up early in the morning. My uncle took me to school. I sat in the classroom during the first period and listened. I couldn't understand what the teacher was talking about. Fifty minutes passed. I saw others walk out of the classroom. I didn't know what they were doing. I walked out with them. I still didn't realize that the school system in America was different from that in China. Students in China don't change classrooms every period. The teachers do. Students in America rather than teachers change classrooms. So I went back to the same classroom again. I stayed in that room until noon. Lunch hour was coming. In China, everybody goes home for lunch. I thought people did the same thing here. I left for home. A school security man stopped me outside the school. He talked to me. I didn't know what he was saying. I was frustrated and scared. I wanted to cry. Some of my schoolmates looked at me as if I were an alien. My face turned red. My heart was crying. I hid my tears. A Chinese girl came up and talked to me in Chinese. She told me we had to stay in school until the last period. I did not know she would become my best friend. I did know my worst nightmare had ended.

Correcting Fragments, Comma Splices, and Run-Ons

You have learned about subjects and verbs, and you have identified and written different kinds of sentences. With the information you now have, you will be able to spot and correct three problems that sometimes creep into what is otherwise good writing. Those problems are sentence fragments, comma splices, and run-on sentences.

Fragments

A correct sentence signals completeness. The structure and punctuation provide those signals. For example, if I say to you, "She left in a hurry," you do not necessarily expect me to say anything else, but if I say, "In a hurry," you do. If I say, "Tomorrow I will give you a quiz on the reading assignment," and I leave the room, you will merely take note of my words. But if I say, "Tomorrow when I give you a quiz on the reading assignment," and leave the room, you will probably be annoyed, and you may even chase after me and ask me to finish my sentence. Those examples illustrate the difference between completeness and incompleteness.

A **fragment** is a word or group of words without a subject ("Is going to town.") or without a verb ("He going to town.") or without both ("Going to town."). A fragment can also be a group of words with a subject and verb that cannot stand alone ("When he goes to town."). Although the punctuation signals a sentence (a capital letter at the beginning and a period at the end), the structure of a fragment signals incompleteness. If you said it or wrote it to someone, that person would expect you to go on and finish the idea.

Other specific examples of common unacceptable fragments are these:

- *Dependent clause only:* When she came.
- *Phrase(s) only:* Waiting there for some help.
- *No subject in main clause:* Went to the library.
- *No verb in main clause:* She being the only person there.

Acceptable Fragments

Sometimes fragments are used intentionally. When we speak, we often use the following fragments.

- *Interjections:* Great! Hooray! Whoa!
- *Exclamations:* What a day! How terrible! What a bother!

- *Greetings:* Hello. Good morning. Good night. Good evening.
- *Questions:* What for? Why not? Where to?
- *Informal conversation:* Eight o'clock. Really.

In novels, plays, and short stories, fragments are often used in conversation among characters. However, in your typical college assignments, you need to be able to identify fragments and turn them into complete sentences.

Dependent Clauses as Fragments: Clauses with Subordinating Conjunctions

You have learned that words such as *because, after, although, since, before* (see page 425 for a more complete list) are subordinating conjunctions, words that show the relationship of a dependent clause to an independent one. A dependent clause punctuated like a sentence (capital letter at the beginning; period at the end) is a sentence fragment.

> *While the ship was sinking.*

You can choose one of many ways to fix that kind of fragment.

Incorrect: They continued to dance. *While the ship was sinking.*

Correct: They continued to dance *while the ship was sinking.*

Correct: *While the ship was sinking,* they continued to dance.

Correct: The ship was sinking. They continued to dance.

Correct: The ship was sinking; they continued to dance.

In the first two correct sentences above, the dependent clause *while the ship was sinking* has been attached to an independent clause. Note that a comma is used when the dependent clause appears at the beginning of the sentence. In the next two sentences, the subordinating conjunction *while* has been omitted. The two independent clauses can then stand alone as sentences or as parts of a sentence joined by a semicolon.

Dependent Clauses as Fragments: Clauses with Relative Pronouns

You have also learned that words such as *that, which,* and *who* can function as relative pronouns, words that relate a clause back to a noun or pronoun in the sentence. Relative clauses are dependent. If they are punctuated as sentences (begin with a capital letter; end with a period), they are incorrect. They are really sentence fragments.

> *Which is lying on the floor.*

The best way to fix such a fragment is to attach it as closely as possible to the noun to which it refers.

Incorrect: That new red sweater is mine. *Which is lying on the floor.*

Correct: The new red sweater, *which is lying on the floor,* is mine.

Reminder: Some relative clauses are restrictive (necessary to the meaning of the sentence) and should not be set off with commas. Some are nonrestrictive (not necessary to the meaning of the sentence), as in the example above, and are set off by commas.

Phrases as Fragments

Although a phrase may carry an idea, a phrase is a fragment because it is incomplete in structure. It lacks both a subject and a verb. (See page 409 for verbal phrases, pages 407 and 529 for prepositional phrases, and page 427 for appositive phrases.)

Verbal Phrase

> **Incorrect:** *Having studied hard all evening*. John decided to retire.
>
> **Correct:** *Having studied hard all evening,* John decided to retire.

The italicized part of the incorrect example is a verbal phrase. As you have learned, a verbal is verblike without being a verb in sentence structure. Verbals include verb parts of speech ending in *-ed* and *-ing*. To correct a verbal phrase fragment, attach it to a complete sentence (independent clause). When the phrase begins the sentence, it is usually set off by a comma.

Prepositional Phrase

> **Incorrect:** *For the past ten hours*. I have been designing my home page.
>
> **Correct:** *For the past ten hours,* I have been designing my home page.

In this example, the fragment is a prepositional phrase—a group of words beginning with a preposition, such as *in, on, of, at,* and *with,* that connects a noun or pronoun object to the rest of the sentence. To correct a prepositional phrase fragment, attach it to a complete sentence (independent clause). If the prepositional phrase is long and begins the sentence, it is usually set off by a comma.

Appositive Phrase

> **Incorrect:** He lived in the small town of Whitman. *A busy industrial center near Boston.*
>
> **Correct:** He lived in the small town of Whitman, *a busy industrial center near Boston.*
>
> **Incorrect:** Many readers admire the work of the nineteenth-century American poet. *Emily Dickinson.*
>
> **Correct:** Many readers admire the work of the nineteenth-century American poet *Emily Dickinson.*

In these examples, the fragment is an appositive phrase—a group of words following a noun or pronoun and renaming it. To correct an appositive phrase fragment, connect it to a complete sentence (an independent clause). An appositive phrase fragment is set off by a comma or by commas only if it is not essential to the meaning of the sentence.

Fragments as Word Groups Without Subjects or Without Verbs

> **Incorrect:** Kristianna studied many long hours. And received the highest grade in the class. [without subject]
>
> **Correct:** Kristianna studied many long hours and received the highest grade in the class.
>
> **Incorrect:** Few children living in that section of the country. [without verb]
>
> **Correct:** Few children live in that section of the country

Each sentence must have an independent clause, a group of words that contains a subject and a verb and that can stand alone. As you may recall from the discussion of subjects, a command or direction sentence, such as "Think," has an understood subject of *you.*

Comma Splices and Run-Ons

The comma splice and the run-on are two other kinds of faulty "sentences" that give false signals to the reader. In each instance the punctuation suggests that there is only one sentence, but, in fact, there is material for two.

The **comma splice** consists of two independent clauses with only a comma between them:

> *The weather was disappointing, we canceled the picnic.* [A comma by itself cannot join two independent clauses.]

The **run-on** differs from the comma splice in only one respect: It has no comma between the independent clauses. Therefore, the run-on is two independent clauses with *nothing* between them:

> *The weather was disappointing we canceled the picnic.* [Independent clauses must be properly connected.]

Because an independent clause can stand by itself as a sentence and because two independent clauses must be properly linked, you can use a simple technique to identify the comma splice and the run-on. If you see a sentence that you think may contain one of these two errors, ask yourself this question: "Can I insert a period at some place in the word group and still have a sentence on either side?" If the answer is yes and there is no word such as *and* or *but* following the inserted period, then you have a comma splice or a run-on to correct. In our previous examples of the comma splice and the run-on, we could insert a period after the word *disappointing* in each case, and we would still have an independent clause—therefore, a sentence—on either side.

Four Ways to Correct Comma Splices and Run-Ons

Once you identify a comma splice or a run-on in your writing, you need to correct it. There are four different ways to fix these common sentence problems.

1. **Use a comma and a coordinating conjunction.**

   Incorrect: We canceled the picnic the weather was disappointing. [run-on]

   Correct: We canceled the picnic, *for* the weather was disappointing. [Here we inserted a comma and the coordinating conjunction *for.*]

Knowing the seven coordinating conjunctions will help you in writing sentences and correcting sentence problems. Remember the acronym FANBOYS: *for, and, nor, but, or, yet, so.*

2. **Use a subordinating conjunction.**

   Incorrect: The weather was disappointing, we canceled the picnic. [comma splice]

   Correct: *Because* the weather was disappointing, we canceled the picnic.

By inserting the subordinating conjunction *because,* you can transform the first independent clause into a dependent clause and correct the comma splice. Knowing the most common subordinating conjunctions will help you in writing sentences and correcting sentence problems. Here again is a list of frequently used subordinating conjunctions.

after	if	until
although	in order that	when
as	provided that	whenever
as if	rather than	where
because	since	whereas
before	so that	wherever
even if	than	whether
even though	unless	while

3. **Use a semicolon.**

   Incorrect: The weather was disappointing, we canceled the picnic.

   Correct: The weather was disappointing; we canceled the picnic.

   Correct: The weather was disappointing; *therefore*, we canceled the picnic.

This comma splice was corrected by a semicolon. The first correct example shows the semicolon alone. The second correct example shows a semicolon followed by the conjunctive adverb *therefore*. The conjunctive adverb is optional, but, as we have already seen, conjunctive adverbs can make the relationship between independent clauses stronger. Here is a list of conjunctive adverbs you saw on page 424.

however	on the other hand
otherwise	then
therefore	consequently
similarly	also
hence	thus

Consider using the acronym HOTSHOT CAT, made up of the first letter of each of these common conjunctive adverbs. The acronym will help you remember them. Other conjunctive adverbs include *in fact, for example, moreover, nevertheless, furthermore, now,* and *soon.*

4. **Make each clause a separate sentence.**

   Incorrect: The weather was disappointing, we canceled the picnic.

   Correct: The weather was disappointing. We canceled the picnic.

To correct the comma splice, replace the comma with a period and begin the second sentence (the second independent clause) with a capital letter. This method is at once the simplest and most common method of correcting comma splices and run-ons. For a run-on, insert a period between the two independent clauses and begin the second sentence with a capital letter.

Techniques for Spotting Problem Sentences

1. For the fragment, ask yourself: "If someone were to say or write this to me, would I expect the person to add to the statement or rephrase it?"

2. In checking for the comma splice or run-on, ask yourself: "Is there a point in this word group at which I can insert a period and create a sentence on either side?" (The question is not necessary if there is a coordinating conjunction—FANBOYS—at that point.)

3. If you have trouble with comma splices and run-ons, check these constructions as you revise:

   a. A comma preceded by a noun or pronoun followed by a noun or pronoun

   b. A sentence beginning with a subordinating conjunction

4. If you have trouble with fragments, look for these clues:

   a. A word group with a single verb ending in *-ing*

   b. A word group without both a subject and a verb

5. Use the grammar checker on your word processor to alert you to possible problem sentences. Then use instructions from this book to make necessary corrrections.

Correcting Fragments, Comma Splices, and Run-Ons

Write the appropriate identification in each blank. Correct the faulty sentences. (See Answer Key for answers.)

OK	correct
CS	comma splice
RO	run-on
FRAG	fragment

———— 1. King Henry VIII, who ruled England from 1509 to 1547, accomplished a number of important things.

———— 2. He separated the Church of England from Roman Catholicism, this act significantly altered his country's history.

———— 3. Credited with changing the king's role to that of head of state.

———— 4. However, Henry VIII's accomplishments are often overshadowed by the fact that he had six wives.

———— 5. Many people believe that he executed all six, but that is not true.

———— 6. He beheaded only two of them he divorced two of the others.

———— 7. Of the other two, one died in childbirth, and one outlived him.

———— 8. Wanting to divorce his first wife, Catherine of Aragon, who had not been able to give him an heir, and marry Anne Boleyn.

———— 9. Unfortunately, the pope refusing to annul his marriage to Catherine.

_____ 10. Anne, already pregnant with Henry's daughter Elizabeth, who would eventually rule England as Queen Elizabeth I for forty-five years.

_____ 11. Henry was forced to take drastic measures he declared that he was head of the Church of England and would decide whether or not he was still married to Catherine.

_____ 12. But then Anne, Henry's second wife, failed to produce a male heir, she was unpopular and made many enemies, Henry became interested in Jane Seymour, one of Anne's attendants.

_____ 13. Henry had Anne arrested and charged with treason and infidelity she was beheaded in 1536.

_____ 14. Within 24 hours of Anne's execution, Henry was engaged to Jane Seymour, they wed two weeks later.

_____ 15. Jane gave birth to a son but she died two weeks later.

_____ 16. For political reasons, Henry married Anne of Cleves next she was unattractive, and Henry was already smitten with young Kathryn Howard, cousin of Anne Boleyn.

_____ 17. Right after he annulled his marriage to Anne of Cleves, he married Kathryn.

_____ 18. She was nineteen, young, and vivacious, he was forty-nine, fat, and suffering from a painful leg ulcer.

_____ 19. Kathryn sought the company of handsome young men in 1542, she, too, was beheaded for infidelity.

_____ 20. Henry's last wife, Katherine Parr, who became his widow when he died in 1547.

EXERCISE 14

Correcting Fragments, Comma Splices, and Run-Ons

Write the appropriate identification in each blank. Correct the faulty sentences.

OK   correct
CS   comma splice
RO   run-on
FRAG   fragment

_____ 1. During the eighteenth and nineteenth centuries, many people developed an intense fear of being buried alive.

_____ 2. Doctors couldn't measure brainwaves and other vital signs, diagnosing death was an inexact science.

_____ 3. A person who was only in a coma could appear dead, lead poisoning, for example, led to a long state of unconciousness that mimicked death.

_____ 4. Premature burial was a real possibility people passed around hundreds of stories about re-opened caskets revealing lids with claw marks and corpses with bloodied fingers.

_____ 5. The horror stories of writer Edgar Allan Poe often included premature burials, in "The Fall of the House of Usher," a young woman breaks out of her tomb.

_____ 6. Poe's stories "The Premature Burial," "The Cask of Amontillado," and "The Black Cat."

_____ 7. Such stories contributed to the phobia, people developed customs designed to confirm that someone was actually dead.

_____ 8. The ceremony known as a "wake" allowed family and friends to sit with the deceased and give him or her time to wake up.

_____ 9. "Waiting mortuaries" were started in 1791 they were places where the deceased was kept for two weeks.

_____ 10. A system of cords and pulleys attached to the dead person's fingers, toes, and head that caused bells to ring if he or she made the slightest movement.

_____ 11. Although some people left instructions for their doctors to prod, poke, and pierce them in a variety of ways to confirm death.

_____ 12. In addition, numerous patents were issued for coffin escape devices.

_____ 13. One particular design gave the English langauge several phrases still in use today.

_____ 14. The deceased person's wrist was tied with a string attached to a bell above the ground, in the event of premature burial, he or she could ring the bell and be dug up by a person hired to keep watch.

_____ 15. Thus, the "dead ringer" "saved by the bell" by someone working the "graveyard shift."

_____ 16. An inventor named Herr Gusmuth, who invented a "security coffin" with a speaking tube.

_____ 17. Allowed the prematurely buried to yell for help.

_____ 18. The tube also permitted food and drink to be served to the awakened corpse while he or she was awaiting exhumation.

_____ 19. Some designs included flags or lights as signaling devices others were outfitted with heaters and stocked with food and beverages.

_____ 20. Today, of course, medical science is more advanced, we have more confidence in our doctors' abilities to recognize death.

EXERCISE 15

Correcting Fragments, Comma Splices, and Run-Ons

Write the appropriate identification in each blank. Correct the faulty sentences.

OK   correct
CS   comma splice
RO   run-on
FRAG   fragment

_____ 1. Piranhas live in freshwater streams and rivers of South America, they travel through the water in groups.

———— 2. These ferocious-looking fish have a protruding lower jaw revealing a mouthful of sharp teeth.

———— 3. Piranhas are meat-eaters they will eat just about any live or dead creature.

———— 4. A school of piranhas consuming an animal the size of a pig in just minutes.

———— 5. Like sharks, they are drawn toward the scent of blood in the water, movements such as splashing attract them, too.

———— 6. When a school of piranhas is in a feeding frenzy.

———— 7. The water appears to boil and become red with blood.

———— 8. The piranha owes its savage reputation, in part, to adventurer Theodore Roosevelt.

———— 9. Who wrote in a 1914 book that these ruthless predators would "devour alive any man or beast."

———— 10. Roosevelt had heard of a man who went out alone on a mule, the mule returned to camp without its rider.

———— 11. The man's skeleton was found in the water every bit of flesh had been stripped from his bones.

———— 12. Still, Americans intrigued by stories bought piranhas for aquarium pets.

———— 13. Fascinated by the fish's grisly reputation.

———— 14. Perhaps admiring the silver body and bright red belly of this handsome creature.

———— 15. As aquarium owners realized that their pets could be quite aggressive and dangerous.

———— 16. Piranhas dumped into ponds, lakes, and reservoirs across the United States.

———— 17. Fortunately, most of the waters were too cold for the piranhas to survive.

_____ 18. Truthfully, though, piranhas rarely attack humans, South Americans even bathe in piranha-infested waters.

_____ 19. South Americans also think piranhas are tasty and like to net, cook, and eat them.

_____ 20. However, U.S. officials are taking no chances, piranhas are illegal in many states.

Verbs

This section covers the use of standard verbs. To some, the word *standard* implies "correct." A more precise meaning is "that which is conventional among educated people." Therefore, a standard verb is the right choice in most school assignments, most published writing, and most important public speaking situations. We all change our language when we move from these formal occasions to informal ones: We don't talk to our families in the same way we would speak at a large gathering in public; we don't write letters to friends the same way we write a history report. But even with informal language we would seldom change from standard to nonstandard usage.

Regular and Irregular Verbs

Verbs can be divided into two categories, called *regular* and *irregular*. Regular verbs are predictable, but irregular verbs—as the term suggests—follow no definite pattern.

Verbs always show time. Present tense verbs show an action or a state of being that is occurring at the present time: I *like* your hat. He *is* at a hockey game right now. Present tense verbs can also imply a continuation from the past into the future: She *drives* to work every day.

Past tense verbs show an action or a state of being that occurred in the past: We *walked* to town yesterday. Tim *was* president of the club last year.

Regular Verbs

Present Tense
For *he, she,* and *it,* regular verbs in the present tense add an *-s* or an *-es* to the base word. The following chart shows the present tense of the base word *ask,* which is a regular verb.

	Singular	Plural
First Person:	I ask	we ask
Second Person:	you ask	you ask
Third Person:	he, she, it asks	they ask

If the verb ends in *-y,* you might have to drop the *-y* and add *-ies* for *he, she,* and *it.*

	Singular	Plural
First Person:	I try	we try
Second Person:	you try	you try
Third Person:	he, she, it tries	they try

Past Tense

For regular verbs in the past tense, add -*ed* to the base form:

Base Form (Present)	Past
walk	walked
answer	answered

If the base form already ends in -*e*, add just -*d*:

Base Form (Present)	Past
smile	smiled
decide	decided

If the base form ends in a consonant followed by -*y*, drop the -*y* and add -*ied*.

Base Form (Present)	Past
fry	fried
amplify	amplified

Regardless of how you form the past tense, regular verbs in the past tense do not change forms. The following chart shows the past tense of the base word *like*, which is a regular verb.

	Singular	Plural
First Person:	I liked	we liked
Second Person:	you liked	you liked
Third Person:	he, she, it liked	they liked

Past Participles

The past participle uses the helping verb *has*, *have*, or *had* along with the past tense of the verb. For regular verbs, the past participle form of the verb is the same as the past tense.

Base Form	Past	Past Participle
happen	happened	happened
hope	hoped	hoped
cry	cried	cried

Following is a list of some common regular verbs, showing the base form, the past tense, and the past participle. The base form can also be used with such helping verbs as *can, could, do, does, did, may, might, must, shall, should, will,* and *would*.

Regular Verbs

Base Form (Present)	Past	Past Participle
ask	asked	asked
answer	answered	answered
cry	cried	cried
decide	decided	decided
dive	dived (dove)	dived
finish	finished	finished
happen	happened	happened
learn	learned	learned
like	liked	liked
love	loved	loved
need	needed	needed
open	opened	opened
start	started	started
suppose	supposed	supposed
walk	walked	walked
want	wanted	wanted

Irregular Verbs

Irregular verbs do not follow any definite pattern.

Base Form (Present)	Past	Past Participle
shake	shook	shaken
make	made	made
begin	began	begun

Some irregular verbs that sound similar in the present tense don't follow the same pattern.

Base Form (Present)	Past	Past Participle
ring	rang	rung
swing	swung	swung
bring	brought	brought

Present Tense

For *he, she,* and *it,* irregular verbs in the present tense add an *-s* or an *-es* to the base word. The following chart shows the present tense of the base word *break,* which is an irregular verb.

	Singular	Plural
First Person:	I break	we break
Second Person:	you break	you break
Third Person:	he, she, it breaks	they break

If the irregular verb ends in *-y,* you might have to drop the *-y* and add *-ies* for *he, she,* and *it.*

	Singular	**Plural**
First Person:	I cry	we cry
Second Person:	you cry	you cry
Third Person:	he, she, it cries	they cry

Past Tense

Like past tense regular verbs, past tense irregular verbs do not change their forms. This chart shows the past tense of the irregular verb *do*.

	Singular	**Plural**
First Person:	I did	we did
Second Person:	you did	you did
Third Person:	he, she, it did	they did

The list below includes the past tense of many irregular verbs.

Past Participles

Use the past tense form with the helping verbs *has, have,* or *had.*

Here is a list of some common irregular verbs, showing the base form (present), the past tense, and the past participle. Like regular verbs, the base forms can be used with such helping verbs as *can, could, do, does, did, may, might, must, shall, should, will,* and *would.*

Irregular Verbs

Base Form (Present)	Past	Past Participle
arise	arose	arisen
awake	awoke (awaked)	awoken (awaked)
be	was, were	been
become	became	become
begin	began	begun
bend	bent	bent
blow	blew	blown
break	broke	broken
burst	burst	burst
buy	bought	bought
catch	caught	caught
choose	chose	chosen
cling	clung	clung
come	came	come
cost	cost	cost
creep	crept	crept
deal	dealt	dealt
do	did	done
drink	drank	drunk
drive	drove	driven
eat	ate	eaten
feel	felt	felt

Base Form (Present)	Past	Past Participle
fight	fought	fought
fling	flung	flung
fly	flew	flown
forget	forgot	forgotten
freeze	froze	frozen
get	got	got (gotten)
go	went	gone
grow	grew	grown
hang	hung	hung
have	had	had
hit	hit	hit
know	knew	known
lead	led	led
leave	left	left
lose	lost	lost
make	made	made
mean	meant	meant
put	put	put
read	read	read
ride	rode	ridden
ring	rang	rung
see	saw	seen
shine	shone	shone
shoot	shot	shot
sing	sang	sung
sink	sank	sunk
sleep	slept	slept
slink	slunk	slunk
speak	spoke	spoken
spend	spent	spent
spread	spread	spread
steal	stole	stolen
stink	stank (stunk)	stunk
sweep	swept	swept
swim	swam	swum
swing	swung	swung
take	took	taken
teach	taught	taught
tear	tore	torn
think	thought	thought
throw	threw	thrown
thrust	thrust	thrust
wake	woke (waked)	woken (waked)
weep	wept	wept
write	wrote	written

Selecting Verbs

Cross out the incorrect verb form.

1. Mark (knew/knowed) he could not finish the term paper that semester.

2. They (dragged, drug, drugged) the cart into the back yard.

3. I was sure that I hadn't (ate, eaten) the lobster.

4. When we arrived, the windows were (broke, broked, broken).

5. Vanessa (dive, dived) from the high board and swam over to us.

6. Imelda had (spread, spreaded) the maps out on the table before the meeting.

7. Have they (began, begun) to gather that material this early?

8. Shawna (swimmed, swam, swum) that distance twice last week.

9. The water pipes have (burst, busted, bursted) again.

10. I (ran, runned) over to Colleen's house for help.

"Problem" Verbs

The following pairs of verbs are especially troublesome and confusing: *lie* and *lay, sit* and *set,* and *rise* and *raise.* One way to tell them apart is to remember which word in each pair takes a direct object. A direct object answers the question *whom* or *what* in connection with a verb. The words *lay, raise,* and *set* take a direct object.

He *raised* the window. (He *raised* what?)

Lie, rise, and *sit,* however, cannot take a direct object. We cannot say, for example, "He rose the window." In the examples, the italicized words are objects.

Present Tense	Meaning	Past Tense	Past Participle	Example
lie	to rest	lay	lain	I lay down to rest.
lay	to place something	laid	laid	We laid the *books* on the table.
rise	to go up	rose	risen	The smoke rose quickly.
raise	to lift, bring forth	raised	raised	She raised the *question.*
sit	to rest	sat	sat	He sat in the chair.
set	to place something	set	set	They set the *basket* on the floor.

Selecting Verbs

Cross out the incorrect verb form.

1. The book is (lying, laying) on top of the bureau.

2. Will we (receive, received) your package soon?

3. His recent decision will certainly (change, changed) our policy.

4. When he heard Lenore call, he (rose, raised) and left the room.

5. That dog can (sit, set) in the yard for hours and bark constantly.

6. Marcia (done, did) many chores before she left for school.

7. Why are you (sitting, setting) those plants in the hot sun?

8. My mother (don't, doesn't) understand why Victor takes so long to come home from kindergarten.

9. A stray cat (drowned, drownded) in the river yesterday.

10. The spy (fool, fooled) his captor by disguising himself as a workman.

11. My cousins will (left, leave) Europe soon.

12. We (learn, learned) from his conversation that he did not wish to go again.

13. Kim hasn't been able to (taught, teach) those boys anything.

14. Have you (tryed, tried) to relax for a few minutes this evening?

15. The police officers could not (see, saw) us cross the bridge during the heavy rainstorm.

16. You (lie, lay) down here and rest for a few minutes before class.

17. The cost of those articles has (raised, risen) considerably since the first of the year.

18. Pam (rose, raised) the window and waved to me as I passed.

19. My brother (lay, laid) the money on the table and looked hopefully at Mother.

20. Please (sit, set) the shoes down on the rack and come over here.

Writing Sentences with Troublesome Verbs

Use each of these words in a sentence of ten words or more.

1. *lie, lay* (rest), *lain, laid* _____

_____

_____

_____

_____

_____

2. *sit, sat, set* _____

_____

_____

_____

_____

_____

3. *is, was, were* _____

_____

_____

_____

_____

_____

4. *do, does* (or *don't, doesn't*) _____

_____

_____

_____

The Twelve Verb Tenses

Some languages, such as Chinese and Navajo, have no verb tenses to indicate time. English has a fairly complicated system of tenses, but most verbs pattern in what are known as the simple tenses: present, past, and future. Altogether there are twelve tenses in English. The four sections that follow illustrate those tenses in sentences. The charts place each verb on a time line; they also explain what the different tenses mean and how to form them.

Simple Tenses

Present: I, we, you, they *drive*.
He, she, it *drives*.

Past: I, we, you, he, she, it, they *drove*.

Future: I, we, you, he, she, it, they *will drive*.

Perfect Tenses

Present Perfect: I, we, you, they *have driven*.
He, she, it *has driven*.

Past Perfect: I, we, you, he, she, it, they *had driven*.

Future Perfect: I, we, you, he, she, it, they *will have driven*.

Progressive Tenses

Present Progressive: I *am driving*.
He, she, it *is driving*.
We, you, they *are driving*.

Past Progressive: I, he, she, it *was driving*.
We, you, they *were driving*.

Future Progressive: I, we, you, he, she, it, they *will be driving*.

Perfect Progressive Tenses

Present Perfect Progressive: I, we, you, they *have been driving*.
He, she, it *has been driving*.

Past Perfect Progressive: I, we, you, he, she, it, they *had been driving*.

Future Perfect Progressive: I, we, you, he, she, it, they *will have been driving*.

Simple Tenses

Tense	Time Line	Time	Verb Form
Present I *drive* to work. She *drives* to work.	past —— XXX —— future Now	Present; may imply a continuation from past to future	Present: *drive* *drives*
Past I *drove* to work.	X Now	Past	Past: *drove*
Future I *will drive* to work.	X Now	Future	Present preceded by *will*: *will drive*

Perfect Tenses

Tense	Time Line	Time	Verb Form
Present Perfect I *have driven* to work.	past —— XXX —— future Now	Completed recently in past; may continue into the present	Past participle preceded by *have* or *has*: *have driven*
Past Perfect I *had driven* to work before I moved to the city [event].	Event XO Now	Prior to a specific time in the past	Past participle preceded by *had*: *had driven*
Future Perfect I *will have driven* to work thousands of times by December [event].	Event X O Now	At a time prior to a specific time in the future	Past participle preceded by *will have*: *will have driven*

Progressive Tenses

Tense	Time Line	Time	Verb Form
Present Progressive I *am driving* to work.	past ——XXX—— future **Now**	In progress now	Progressive (*-ing* ending) preceded by *is, am,* or *are:* *am driving*
Past Progressive I *was driving* to work.	XXX **Now**	In progress in the past	Progressive (*-ing* ending) preceded by *was* or *were:* *was driving*
Future Progressive I *will be driving* to work.	XXX **Now**	In progress in the future	Progressive (*-ing* ending) preceded by *will be:* *will be driving*

Perfect Progressive Tenses

Tense	Time Line	Time	Verb Form
Present Perfect Progressive I *have been driving* to work.	past ——XXX—— future **Now**	In progress before now or up to now	Progressive (*-ing* ending) preceded by *have been* or *has been:* *have been driving*
Past Perfect Progressive I *had been driving* when I began ride-sharing [event].	Event XXX O **Now**	In progress before another event in the past	Progressive (*-ing* ending) preceded by *had:* I *had been driving*
Future Perfect Progressive By May 1 [event], I *will have been driving* to work for six years.	Event XXX O **Now**	In progress before another event in the future	Progressive (*-ing* ending) preceded by *will have been:* *will have been driving*

EXERCISE 19

Selecting Verbs

Underline the correct verb form. (See Answer Key for answers.)

1. I wished I (stayed, had stayed) home.

2. I remembered that I (paid, had paid) him twice.

3. After parking their car, they (walk, walked) to the beach.

4. I (have, had) never encountered a genius until I met her.

5. I hoped that we (could have gone, went) to the big game.

6. They know that they (will complete, will have completed) the job before the first snow.

7. We (are considering, consider) the proposal.

8. He told us of the interesting life he (had led, led).

9. We went to the desert to see the cabin they (built, had built).

10. Tomorrow I (drive, will drive) to the supermarket for party items.

EXERCISE 20

Selecting Verbs

Underline the correct verb form.

1. The scholars (worked, had worked) many hours before they solved the problem.

2. The shipping clerks wished they (had sent, sent) the package.

3. We (study, are studying) the issue now.

4. We (decide, will decide) on the winner tomorrow.

5. They reminded us that we (made, had made) the same promise before.

6. Before she went to Mexico, Jill (had never been, never was) out of the country.

7. Jake (had been napping, napped) when the alarm sounded.

8. By the time he finished talking, he realized that he (said, had said) too much.

9. At the end of the semester, the course grade (depends, will depend) on your ability to write well.

10. After he retired, I realized how much I (had learned, learned) from working with him.

Subject-Verb Agreement

This section is concerned with number agreement between subjects and verbs. The basic principle of **subject-verb agreement** is that if the subject is singular, the verb should be singular, and if the subject is plural, the verb should be plural. There are ten major guidelines. In the examples under the following guidelines, the simple subjects and verbs are italicized.

1. Do not let words that come between the subject and verb affect agreement.

    - Modifying phrases and clauses frequently come between the subject and verb:

        The various *types* of drama *were* not *discussed*.

        Angela, who is hitting third, *is* the best player.

        The *price* of those shoes *is* too high.

    - Certain prepositions can cause trouble. The following words are prepositions, not conjunctions: *along with, as well as, besides, in addition to, including, together with*. The words that function as objects of prepositions cannot also be subjects of the sentence.

        The *coach*, along with the players, *protests* the decision.

    - When a negative phrase follows a positive subject, the verb agrees with the positive subject.

        Philip, not the other boys, *was* the culprit.

2. Do not let inversions (verb before subject, not the normal order) affect the agreement of subject and verb.

    - Verbs and other words may come before the subject. Do not let them affect the agreement. To understand subject-verb relationships, recast the sentence in normal word order.

        Are Juan and his *sister* at home? [question form]

        Juan and his *sister are* at home. [normal order]

    - A sentence filler is a word that is grammatically independent of other words in the sentence. The most common fillers are *there* and *here*. Even though a sentence filler precedes the verb, it should not be treated as the subject.

        There *are* many *reasons* for his poor work. [The verb *are* agrees with the subject *reasons*.]

3. A singular verb agrees with a singular indefinite pronoun.

    - Most indefinite pronouns are singular.

        Each of the women *is* ready at this time.

        Neither of the women *is* ready at this time.

        One of the children *is* not paying attention.

    - Certain indefinite pronouns do not clearly express either a singular or plural number. Agreement, therefore, depends on the meaning of the sentence. These pronouns are *all, any, none,* and *some*.

        All of the melon *was* good.

        All of the melons *were* good.

        None of the pie *is* acceptable.

        None of the pies *are* acceptable.

4. Two or more subjects joined by *and* usually take a plural verb.

> The *captain* and the *sailors were* happy to be ashore.

> The *trees* and *shrubs need* more care.

- If the parts of a compound subject mean one and the same person or thing, the verb is singular; if the parts mean more than one, the verb is plural.

> The *secretary* and *treasurer is* not present. [one]

> The *secretary* and the *treasurer are* not present. [more than one]

- When *each* or *every* precedes singular subjects joined by *and,* the verb is singular.

> Each *boy* and each *girl brings* a donation.

> Each *woman* and *man has asked* the same questions.

5. Alternative subjects—that is, subjects joined by *or, nor, either/or, neither/nor, not only/but also*—should be handled in the following manner:

- If the subjects are both singular, the verb is singular.

> *Rosa* or *Alicia is* responsible.

- If the subjects are plural, the verb is plural.

> Neither the *students* nor the *teachers were* impressed by his comments.

- If one of the subjects is singular and the other subject is plural, the verb agrees with the nearer subject.

> Either the Garcia *boys* or their *father goes* to the hospital each day.

> Either their *father* or the Garcia *boys go* to the hospital each day.

6. Collective nouns—*team, family, group, crew, gang, class, faculty,* and the like—take a singular verb if the verb is considered a unit, but they take a plural verb if the group is considered as a number of individuals.

> The *team is playing* well tonight.

> The *team are getting* dressed.

(In the second sentence the individuals are acting not as a unit but separately. If you don't like the way the sentence sounds, substitute "The members of the team are getting dressed.")

7. Titles of books, essays, short stories, and plays, a word spoken of as a word, and the names of businesses take a singular verb.

> *The Canterbury Tales was written* by Geoffrey Chaucer.

> *Ives is* my favorite name for a pet.

> *Markel Brothers has* a sale this week.

8. Sums of money, distances, and measurements are followed by a singular verb when a unit is meant. They are followed by a plural verb when the individual elements are considered separately.

> *Three dollars was* the price. [unit]

> *Three dollars were* lying there. [individual]

Five years is a long time. [unit]

The *first five years were* difficult ones. [individual]

9. Be careful of agreement with nouns ending in -*s*. Several nouns ending in -*s* take a singular verb—for example, *aeronautics, civics, economics, ethics, measles, mumps.*

Mumps is an unpleasant disease.

Economics is my major field of study.

10. Some nouns have only a plural form and so take only a plural verb—for example, *clothes, fireworks, scissors, pants.*

His *pants are* badly wrinkled.

Marv's *clothes were* stylish and expensive.

Making Subjects and Verbs Agree

Underline the correct verb form. (See Answer Key for answers.)

1. There (is, are) very little remote wilderness left in the world.

2. Neither the jungles, nor the oceans, nor the desert (has, have) gone unexplored.

3. Mount Everest, the world's highest mountain, (is, are) no exception.

4. Before 1953, though, many a thrill-seeker (was, were) hoping to be the first to stand on its summit.

5. Everyone (know, knows) that George Mallory died trying in 1924.

6. Although we can never be sure, some of us (believe, believes) Mallory was the first to make it to the top.

7. According to the record books, Sir Edmund Hillary, along with his partner Tenzing Norgay, (was, were) the first to reach the highest place on Earth on May 29, 1953.

8. There (is, are) many reasons why someone would want to climb Mount Everest.

9. (Is, Are) personal satisfaction or prestige more important to today's climbers?

10. (Is, Are) mountaineers driven by passion or by sport?

11. Now, $65,000 (is, are) the price anyone can pay for a guided hike to the summit.

12. Trips to the top of Mount Everest (is, are) now routine.

13. A 64-year-old man, a legally blind person, and an amputee (has, have) successfully climbed the mountain.

14. A solo climber or a group (take, takes) about eleven hours to ascend.

15. Everest has been climbed more than 1,300 times; however, not all of the attempts (was, were) successful.

16. Either falls or an avalanche (has, have) caused numerous deaths.

17. *Into Thin Air* (is, are) a riveting tale of one catastrophic expedition during which eight people died.

18. The majority of the 175 people who have died (is, are) still on the mountain.

19. The news (is, are) always bad when people make mistakes and lose their lives.

20. But adventurers like Sir Edmund Hillary (is, are) always willing to take the risk.

EXERCISE 22

Making Subjects and Verbs Agree

Underline the correct verb form.

1. Three varieties of poison ivy (grow, grows) in her garden.

2. Enrique, an executive with Sony Records, (is, are) looking for new talent.

3. Someone with psychic abilities (is, are) what you need.

4. My face, as well as my legs, (is, are) sunburned.

5. One B, not just A's, (was, were) on her report card.

6. (Is, Are) Bert and Ernie still roommates?

7. There (is, are) several skeletons in his particular closet.

8. Each of the bongo songs (sound, sounds) the same.

9. Neither of the girls (is, are) good at bagging groceries.

10. One of the Indians (shoot, shoots) better than the cowboys.

11. Some of the jelly (has, have) been stolen.

12. Some of the jelly beans (was, were) stuck together.

13. (Do, Does) your family or your friends know that you've joined the circus?

14. Neither the baton twirlers nor the band (like, likes) to march behind the horse-drawn carriages.

15. Every person, place, or thing (is, are) a noun.

16. My mentor and friend (advise, advises) me to read *The Wall Street Journal*.

17. *The Shell Seekers* (is, are) one of my favorite books.

18. McDonald's (stays, stay) open late.

19. My glasses (is, are) at the bottom of the pool.

20. Your thanks (is, are) much appreciated.

Consistency in Tense

Consider this paragraph:

> We (1) went downtown, and then we (2) watch a movie. Later we (3) met some friends from school, and we all (4) go to the mall. For most of the evening, we (5) play video games in arcades. It (6) was a typical but rather uneventful summer day.

Does the shifting verb tense bother you (to say nothing about the lack of development of ideas)? It should! The writer makes several unnecessary changes. Verbs 1, 3, and 6 are in the past tense, and verbs 2, 4, and 5 are in the present tense. Changing all verbs to past tense makes the paragraph much smoother.

> We went downtown, and then we watched a movie. Later we met some friends from school, and we all went to the mall. For most of the evening, we played video games in arcades. It was a typical but rather uneventful summer day.

In other instances you might want to maintain a consistent present tense. There are no inflexible rules about selecting a tense for certain kinds of writing, but you should be consistent, changing tense only for a good reason.

The present tense is ordinarily used in writing about literature, even if the literature was composed long in the past:

> *Moby Dick* is a novel about Captain Ahab's obsession with a great white whale. Ahab *sets* sail with a full crew of sailors who *think* they *are going* on merely another whaling voyage. Most of the crew *are* experienced seamen.

The past tense is likely to serve you best in writing about your personal experiences and about historical events (although the present tense can often be used effectively to establish the feeling of intimacy and immediacy):

In the summer of 1991, Hurricane Bob *hit* the Atlantic coast region. It *came* ashore near Cape Hatteras and *moved* north. The winds *reached* a speed of more than ninety miles per hour on Cape Cod but then *slackened* by the time Bob *reached* Maine.

EXERCISE 23   ## Making Verbs Consistent in Tense

In each sentence, the last verb is in the wrong tense. Cross it out and write the correct form above it. (See Answer Key for answers.)

1. Ralph Waldo Emerson said that a success was defined as leaving the world a better place.

2. After Lou graduated from college, he joins the Peace Corps.

3. She lost the game because she wasn't sure where the Galapagos Islands were.

4. Joe was determined to shed twenty pounds before he goes to his high school reunion.

5. I'd like to fight you in the Tough Man contest, but I had a pedicure appointment.

6. After having dated only losers for fifteen years, Roxanne decides to remain single.

7. Not everyone who tries out got to play on the team next year.

8. She hopes to be a star some day, but she was not going to give up her day job.

9. The guest did not realize that caviar was fish eggs.

10. Albert Einstein said that imagination was more important than knowledge.

11. The lawyer answered all of her questions; then he sends her a bill for $100.

12. She always claims to be on a diet, but she ordered dessert every time we go out to eat.

13. As Taloola cuts your hair, she gossiped about everyone in town.

14. Tanya takes her lunch to school because she disliked the smell of the cafeteria food.

15. When Rhonda pulled the gun from her purse, everyone in the room runs for cover.

16. Trixie wondered aloud if the 1930s were called The Great Depression because everyone is so depressed.

17. He did fifty sit-ups every morning before he takes a shower.

18. She regretted not telling him that she will always love him.

19. George thinks that he's in trouble when the police car pulled up behind him.

20. Tex and his bride chose a home site where the buffalo were roaming and the antelopes are playing.

EXERCISE 24

Making Verbs Consistent in Tense

Change the verbs in the following paragraph as necessary to maintain a mostly consistent past tense. (See Answer Key for answers.)

(1) Tarzan spoke to Jane in simple language. (2) His most famous words were "Me Tarzan, you Jane." (3) Before the arrival of Jane, there are only jungle friends for Tarzan. (4) Those animals seldom used the full eight parts of speech. (5) For example, lions seldom utter verbs. (6) Elephants had no patience with prepositions. (7) Chimps condemn conjunctions. (8) Their punctuation was replaced largely by snarls, growls, and breast-beating. (9) Their language is well suited to Tarzan. (10) To him, jungle language was like swinging on a vine. (11) A one-syllable yell is a full oration. (12) Jane never ridiculed his grammar or even his yelling. (13) She holds back criticism of the king of the apes. (14) Despite their difference in language skills, they establish hutkeeping. (15) They were very poor and wore simple garments made of skins. (16) Their main transportation is well-placed hanging vines. (17) Tarzan and Jane had a child. (18) They name him "Boy." (19) Fortunately, they did not have another male child. (20) Such an occurrence could have caused a language gridlock.

EXERCISE 25

Making Verbs Consistent in Tense

Change the verbs in the following paragraph as necessary to maintain a mostly consistent past tense.

(1) Once upon a time, a Professor Glen was very popular with his students. (2) He kept long office hours and always speaks nicely to his students on campus. (3) He even bought popcorn for them to munch on during tests. (4) Respecting their sensitivity, he marks with a soothing green ink instead of red. (5) He often told jokes and listened attentively to their complaints about assignments. (6) The leaders of student government elect him teacher of the century. (7) Who would not admire such a person? (8) Then late one semester, a strange and shocking thing happens. (9) Everywhere there were students in despair. (10) Professor Glen no longer speaks openly to students. (11) During his office hours, he locked his door and posted a pit bull. (12) He corrects student papers in flaming scarlet. (13) Instead of popcorn, he gave them hot scorn. (14) He told no more jokes and sneered at their complaints about assignments. (15) He sticks out his tongue at students on campus. (16) He offered good grades for cash. (17) Professor Glen even accepts Visa cards and validated parking. (18) One day the students heard a thumping sound in a classroom closet. (19) Looking inside, they find the true Professor Glen. (20) The other one was an evil twin professor.

Active and Passive Voice

Which of these sentences sounds better?

> Ken Griffey Jr. slammed a home run.

> A home run was slammed by Ken Griffey Jr.

Both sentences carry the same message, but the first expresses it more effectively. The subject (*Ken Griffey Jr.*) is the actor. The verb (*slammed*) is the action. The direct object (*home run*) is the receiver of the action. The second sentence lacks the vitality of the first because the receiver of the action is the subject; the one who performs the action is embedded in the prepositional phrase at the end of the sentence.

The first sentence demonstrates the active voice. It has an active verb (one that leads to the direct object), and the action moves from the beginning to the end of the sentence. The second exhibits the passive voice (with the action reflecting back on the subject). When given a choice, you should usually select the active voice. It promotes energy and directness.

The passive voice, though not usually the preferred form, does have its uses.

- When the doer of the action is unknown or unimportant:

  My car was stolen. [The doer, a thief, is unknown.]

- When the receiver of the action is more important than the doer:

  My neighbor was permanently disabled by an irresponsible drunk driver. [The neighbor's suffering is the focus, not the drunk driver.]

As you can see, the passive construction places the doer at the end of a prepositional phrase (as in the second example) or does not include the doer in the statement at all (as in the first example). In the first example the receiver of the action (the car) is in the subject position. The verb is preceded by the *to be* helper *was*. Here is another example:

Passive: The book was read by her.

Active: She read the book.

Weak sentences often involve the unnecessary and ineffective use of the passive form; Exercise 24 gives you practice in identifying the passive voice and changing it to active.

EXERCISE 26

Using Active and Passive Voice

Rewrite these sentences to convert the verbs from passive to active voice. (See Answer Key for answers to 1 through 5.)

1. A letter has been written by me to you.

2. An honest dollar was never made by his ancestors, and now he is following in their fingerprints.

3. The assignment was approved by the instructor.

4. The instructor was given a much-deserved medal of valor by the president of the student body.

5. Few people noticed that most of the work was done by the quiet students.

6. The ballgame was interrupted by bats catching flies in the outfield.

7. The commotion at the apathy convention was caused by a person who attended.

8. The air was filled with speeches by him.

9. He doesn't have an enemy, but he is hated by all his friends.

10. His lips are never passed by a lie—he talks through his nose.

Strong Verbs

Because the verb is an extremely important part of any sentence, it should be chosen with care. Some of the most widely used verbs are the *being* verbs: *is, was, were, are, am.* We couldn't get along in English without them, but writers often use them when more forceful and effective verbs are available. Consider these examples:

Weak Verb: He *is* the leader of the people.

Strong Verb: He *leads* the people.

Weak Verb: She *was* the first to finish.

Strong Verb: She *finished* first.

EXERCISE 27

Using Strong Verbs

Rewrite the following sentences to strengthen the weak verbs. (See Answer Key for answers to 1 through 5.)

1. He is the writer of that essay.

2. She was the driver of the speeding car.

3. He was the player of the guitar.

4. They were the leaders of the entire region in sales.

5. The medicine was a cure for the cold.

6. The last entertainer was the winner of the award.

7. The yowling cat was the cause of my waking up last night.

8. The mechanic is the fixer of my car.

9. He was in attendance at the computer seminar.

10. She is a shoe salesperson.

Subjunctive Mood

Mood refers to the intention of the verb. Three moods are relevant to our study: indicative, imperative, and subjunctive.

The **indicative mood** expresses a statement of fact.

> I considered the issue.

> I was tired.

The **imperative mood** expresses a command (and has a *you* understood subject).

> Go to the store.

The **subjunctive mood** expresses a statement as contrary to fact, conditional, desirable, possible, necessary, or doubtful. In current English the subjunctive form is distinguishable only in two forms: The verb *to be* uses *be* throughout the present tense and *were* throughout the past tense.

> He requires that we *be* [instead of *are*] on time.

> If she *were* [instead of *was*] the candidate, she would win.

In other verbs, the final *s* is dropped in the third person singular [*he, she, it*] of the present tense to make all forms the same in any one tense.

> I request that he *report* [instead of *reports*] today.

Here are examples of the common forms:

> If I *were* [instead of *was*] you, I wouldn't do that. [contrary to fact]

> She behaves as if she *were* [instead of *was*] not certain. [doubt]

> I wish I *were* [instead of *was*] in Texas. [wish]

EXERCISE 28   ## Selecting Subjunctive Verbs

Underline the subjunctive verbs. (See Answer Key for answers to 1 through 5.)

1. If I (was, were) going to work, I would give you a ride.
2. I wish I (were, was) on the beach.
3. I demand that you (will return, return) the deposit.
4. They act as if they (are, were) rich.
5. I require that my workers (are, be) on time.
6. You may wish you (are, were) an adult, but you must show your ID.
7. You talk as if winning (was, were) possible.
8. My manager insists that I (be, am) tactful with clients.
9. Suppose, for sake of argument, your statement (was, were) true.
10. Sometimes I wish I (were, was) of the younger generation.

Pronouns

Should you say, "Between you and *I*" or "Between you and *me*"? What about "Let's you and *I* do this" or "Let's you and *me* do this"? Are you confused about when to use *who* and *whom*? Is it "Everyone should wear *their* coat, or *his* coat, or *his or her* coat"? Is there anything wrong with saying, "When *you* walk down the streets of Laredo"?

The examples in the first paragraph represent the most common problems people have with pronouns. This section will help you identify the standard forms and understand why they are correct. The result should be expertise and confidence.

Pronoun Case

Case is the form a pronoun takes as it fills a position in a sentence. Words such as *you* and *it* do not change, but others do, and they change in predictable ways. For example, *I* is a subject word and *me* is an object word. As you refer to yourself, you will select a pronoun that fits a certain part of sentence structure. You say, "*I* will write the paper," not "*Me* will write the paper," because *I* is in the subject position. But you say, "She will give the apple to *me*," not "She will give the apple to *I*," because *me* is in the object position. These are the pronouns that change:

Subject	Object
I	me
he	him
she	her
we	us
they	them
who, whoever	whom, whomever

Subjective Case

	Singular	Plural
First Person:	I	we
Second Person:	you	you
Third Person:	he she it	they
	who	

Subjective-case pronouns can fill two positions in a sentence.

1. Pronouns in the subjective case fill subject positions.
   a. Some will be easy to identify because they are at the beginning of the sentence.

   I dance in the park.

   He dances in the park.

   She dances in the park.

We dance in the park.

They dance in the park.

Who is dancing in the park?

b. Others will be more difficult to identify because they are not at the beginning of a sentence and may not appear to be part of a clause. The words *than* and *as* are signals for these special arrangements, which can be called incompletely stated clauses.

He is taller than *I* (am).

She is younger than *we* (are).

We work as hard as *they* (do).

The words *am, are,* and *do,* which complete the clauses, have been omitted. We are actually saying, "He is taller than *I am,*" "She is younger than *we are,*" and "We work as hard as *they do.*" The italicized pronouns are subjects of "understood" verbs.

2. Pronouns in the subjective case refer back to the subject.

   a. They follow a form of the verb *to be,* such as *was, were, am, is,* and *are.*

   I believe it is *he.*

   It was *she* who spoke.

   The victims were *they.*

   b. Some nouns and pronouns refer back to an earlier noun without referring back through the verb.

   The leading candidates—Juan, Darnelle, Steve, Kimlieu, and *I*—made speeches.

Objective Case

	Singular	Plural
First Person:	me	us
Second Person:	you	you
Third Person:	him her it	them
	whom	

Objective-case pronouns can also fill two positions in sentences.

1. Pronouns in the objective case fill object positions.
   a. They may be objects after the verb.
      • A direct object answers the question *what* or *whom* in connection with the verb.

We brought *it* to your house. [*what* did we bring? *it*]

We saw *her* in the library. [*whom* did we see? *her*]

- An indirect object answers the question *to whom* in connection with the verb.

  I gave *him* the message. [*to whom* did I give the message? *to him*]

  The doctor told *us* the test results. [*to whom* did the doctor tell the results? *to us*]

b. Objective-case pronouns are objects after prepositions.

  The problem was clear to *us*.

  I went with Steve and *him*.

2. Objective-case pronouns may also refer back to object words.

  They had the costumes for us—Judy and *me*.

  The judge addressed the defendants—John and *her*.

Techniques for Determining Case

Here are three techniques that will help you decide which pronoun to use when the choice seems difficult.

1. If you have a compound element (such as a subject or an object of a preposition), consider only the pronoun part. The sound alone will probably tell you the answer.

  She gave the answer to Marie and (I, me).

  Marie and the pronoun make up a compound object of the preposition *to*. Disregard the noun, *Marie*, and ask yourself, "Would I say, 'She gave the answer *to me* or *to I*'?" The way the words sound would tell you the answer is *to me*. Of course, if you immediately notice that the pronoun is in an object position, you need not bother with sound.

2. If you are choosing between *who* (subject word) and *whom* (object word), look to the right to see if the next verb has a subject. If it does not, the pronoun probably *is* the subject, but if it does have a subject, the pronoun probably is an object.

  The person (*who*, whom) works hardest will win. [*Who* is the correct answer because it is the subject of the verb *works*.]

  The person (who, *whom*) we admire most is José. [*Whom* is the correct answer because the next verb, *admire*, already has a subject, *we*. *Whom* is an object.]

A related technique works the same way. If the next important word after *who* or *whom* in a statement is a noun or pronoun, the correct word will almost always be *whom*. However, if the next important word is not a noun or pronoun, the correct word will be *who*.

To apply this technique, you must disregard qualifier clauses such as "I think," "it seems," and "we hope."

  Tyrone is a natural leader (*who*, whom) has charisma. [*Who* is the correct answer; it is followed by something other than a noun or pronoun.]

Tyrone is a natural leader (*who*, whom), we think, has charisma. [*Who* is the correct answer; it is followed by the qualifier clause *we think*, which is then followed by something other than a noun or pronoun.]

Tyrone is a natural leader (who, *whom*) we supported. [*Whom* is the correct answer; it is followed by a pronoun.]

3. *Let's* is made up of the words *let* and *us* and means "you *let us*"; therefore, when you select a pronoun to follow it, consider the two original words and select another object word—*me*.

Let's you and (I, *me*) take a trip to Westwood. [Think of "You let us, you and me, take a trip to Westwood." *Us* and *me* are object words.]

EXERCISE 29   # Selecting Pronouns: Case

Underline the correct pronoun form. (See Answer Key for answers.)

Compounds

1. Sacagawea and (he, him) helped Lewis and Clark as they explored the West.

2. Did you and (she, her) practice throwing curve balls?

3. She insisted on setting up Roxanne and (them, they) with blind dates.

4. The fortune cookie revealed to (they, them) their destinies.

Appositives

5. Let's you and (I, me) order the crawfish platter.

6. Two of the dancers—Cheyenne and (she, her)—couldn't high-kick very well.

7. She has narrowed her suitors down to three—you, Bob, and (he, him).

8. (We, Us) know-it-alls consider it our duty to correct those who are wrong.

9. They frowned upon (we, us) women showing off our tattoos.

Comparisons

10. My friend Raj is a better rapper than (I, me).

11. Lucy has more freckles than (she, her).

12. He makes a lot more money than (they, them).

13. The chimpanzee knew as many words as (he, him).

Who/Whom

14. (Who, Whom) did you invite to the luau?

15. She is a person (who, whom) we can trust.

16. (Who, Whom) leaked the information to the press?

17. She is now dating the fellow (who, whom) she accidently ran over last month.

18. (Who, Whom) do you predict will be our first female president?

Refer Back to Subject

19. Was it (I, me) you hoped to find?

20. It is (she, her) for whom he sold his soul.

EXERCISE 30

Selecting Pronouns: Case

Cross out the incorrect pronoun form.

1. She did not realize that you and (I, me) would be asked to testify.

2. Give the award to (whoever, whomever) is voted most valuable player.

3. We need one person (who, whom) we can rely on.

4. Would you support (her, she) in the election?

5. Let's you and (I, me) take that trip next year.

6. Everybody but (he, him) was ready for the test.

7. Only two were chosen, Kathy and (he, him).

8. She thinks more clearly than (I, me).

9. Distribute the cards among John, Joe, and (he, him).

10. Gilligan knows the answer better than (we, us).

11. The person (which, who) came will call on you again.

12. You know that much better than (I, me).

13. The police believed (they, them) to be us.

14. The court found (us, we) to be responsible.

15. (Whoever, Whomever) they choose will receive the promotion.

16. I would have taken (she, her) to the meeting.

17. Is it (I, me) you are looking for?

18. Just between you and (I, me), I think we should go.

19. It could have been (he, him) whom you saw.

20. The soldiers (who, whom) they trained were sent to the front.

Pronoun-Antecedent Agreement

Every pronoun refers to an earlier noun, which is called the **antecedent** of the pronoun. The antecedent is the noun that the pronoun replaces. The pronoun brings the reader back to the earlier thought. Here are some examples:

I tried to buy *tickets* for the concert, but *they* were all sold.

Roger painted a *picture* of a pickup truck. *It* was so good that *he* entered *it* in an art show.

A **pronoun** agrees with its antecedent in person, number, and gender. **Person**—first, second, or third—indicates perspective, or point of view. **Number** indicates singular or plural. **Gender** indicates masculine, feminine, or neuter.

	Subject Words			Object Words	
	Singular	**Plural**		**Singular**	**Plural**
First Person:	I	we	**First Person:**	me	us
Second Person:	you	you	**Second Person:**	you	you
Third Person:	he, she, it	they	**Third Person:**	him, her, it	them
	who			whom	

Agreement in Person

Avoid needless shifting of person, which means shifting of point of view, such as from *I* to *you*. First person, second person, and third person indicate perspectives from which you can write. Select one point of view and maintain it, promoting continuity and consistency. Needless shifting of person, meaning changing perspectives without reasons important for your content and purpose, is distracting and awkward. Each point of view has its appropriate purposes.

First Person

Using the word *I* and its companion forms *we, me,* and *us,* the first-person point of view emphasizes the writer, who is an important part of the subject of the composition. Choose first person for friendly letters, accounts of personal experience, and, occasionally, business correspondence, such as a letter of application for a job, which requires self-analysis.

Observe the presence of the writer and the use of *I* in this example.

I could tell that the wedding would not go well when the caterers started serving drinks before the ceremony and the bride began arguing with her future mother-in-law. After the sound system crashed, the band canceled and I wished I hadn't come.

Second Person

Using or implying the word *you*, the second-person point of view is fine for informal conversation, advice, and directions. Although it is occasionally found in academic writing, most instructors prefer that you use it only in process analysis, directions in how to do something.

In this example, note that the word *you* is sometimes understood and not stated.

To juggle three balls, first you place two balls (A and B) in one hand and one ball (C) in the other. Then toss one of the two balls (A), and before you catch it with your other hand, toss the single ball (C) from that hand. Before that ball (C) lands in the other hand, toss the remaining inactive ball (B). Then pick up the balls and repeat the process until balls no longer fall to the ground.

Third Person

Referring to subject material, individuals, things, or ideas, the third-person point of view works best for most formal writing, be it academic or professional. Third-person pronouns include *he, she, it, they, him, her,* and *them*. Most of your college writing—essay exams, reports, compositions that explain and argue, critiques, and research papers—will be from this detached perspective with no references to yourself.

In this example, written in the third person, the name *Bartleby* is replaced by forms of *he*.

Bartleby, one of Herman Melville's most memorable characters, has befuddled critics for more than a century. At a point in *his* life chosen for no obvious reason, *he* decides not to work, not to cooperate with others, and not to leave the premises of *his* employer because *he* "prefers not to." Most readers do not know what to make of *him*.

Correcting Problems of Agreement in Person

Most problems with pronoun agreement in person occur with the use of *you* in a passage that should have been written in the first or third person. If your composition is not one of advice or directions, the word *you* is probably not appropriate and should be replaced with a first- or third-person pronoun.

If you are giving advice or directions, use *you* throughout the passage, but, if you are not, replace each *you* with a first- or third-person pronoun that is consistent with the perspective, purpose, and content of the passage.

Inconsistent: *I* love to travel, especially when *you* go to foreign countries.

Consistent: *I* love to travel, especially when *I* go to foreign countries.

Inconsistent: When *you* are about to merge with moving traffic on the freeway, *one* should not stop *his or her* car.

Consistent: When *you* are about to merge with moving traffic on the freeway, *you* should not stop *your* car.

> **Consistent:** When *one* is about to merge with moving traffic on the freeway, *one* should not stop *his or her* car. [using third-person pronouns, including the indefinite pronoun *one*]
>
> **Consistent:** When *drivers* are about to merge with moving traffic on the freeway, *they* should not stop *their* car. [using third-person plural pronouns to match plural noun]

Agreement in Number

Most problems with pronoun-antecedent agreement involve **number.** The principles are simple: If the antecedent (the word the pronoun refers back to) is singular, use a singular pronoun. If the antecedent is plural, use a plural pronoun.

1. A singular antecedent requires a singular pronoun.

   > *Vincent* forgot *his* notebook.

2. A plural antecedent requires a plural pronoun.

   > Many *students* cast *their* votes today.

3. A singular indefinite pronoun as an antecedent takes a singular pronoun. Most indefinite pronouns are singular. The following are common indefinite singular pronouns: *anybody, anyone, each, either, everybody, everyone, no one, nobody, one, somebody, someone.*

   > *Each* of the girls brought *her* book.
   >
   > When *one* makes a promise, *one* [or *he or she*] should keep it.

4. A plural indefinite pronoun as an antecedent takes a plural pronoun.

   > *Few* knew *their* assignments.

5. Certain indefinite pronouns do not clearly express either a singular or plural number. Agreement, therefore, depends on the meaning of the sentence. These pronouns are *all, any, none,* and *some.*

   > *All* of the apple *was* wormy.
   >
   > *All* of the apples *were* wormy.
   >
   > *None* of the cake *is* acceptable.
   >
   > *None* of the cakes *are* acceptable.

6. Two or more antecedents, singular or plural, take a plural pronoun. Such antecedents are usually joined by *and* or by commas and *and.*

   > *Howard* and his *parents* bought *their* presents early.
   >
   > *Students, instructors,* and the *administration* pooled *their* ideas at the forum.

7. Alternative antecedents—that is, antecedents joined by *or, nor, whether/or, either/or, neither/nor, not only/but also*—require a pronoun that agrees with the nearer antecedent.

   > Neither Alex nor his *friends* lost *their* way.
   >
   > Neither his friends nor *Alex* lost *his* way.

8. In a sentence with an expression such as *one of those _____ who,* the antecedent is usually the plural noun that follows the preposition *of.*

> He is one of those *people who* want *their* money now.

9. In a sentence with the expression *the only one of those_____ who,* the antecedent is usually the singular word *one.*

> She is the *only one* of the members *who* wants *her* money now.

10. When collective nouns such as *team, jury, committee,* and *band* are used as antecedents, they take a singular pronoun if they are considered as units.

> The *jury* is doing *its* best.

When individual behavior is suggested, antecedents take a plural form.

> The *jury* are putting on *their* coats.

11. The words *each, every,* and *many a(n)* before a noun make the noun singular.

> *Each child* and *adult* was *his* or *her* own authority.

> *Each* and *every person* doubted *himself* or *herself.*

> *Many* a person is capable of knowing *himself* or *herself.*

Agreement in Gender

The pronoun should agree with its antecedent in gender, if the gender of the antecedent is specific. Masculine and feminine pronouns are gender-specific: *he, him, she, her.* Others are neuter: *I, we, me, us, it, they, them, who, whom, that, which.* The words *who* and *whom* refer to people. *That* can refer to ideas, things, and people, but usually does not refer to individuals. *Which* refers to ideas and things, but never to people.

> My *girlfriend* gave me *her* best advice. [feminine]

> Mighty *Casey* tried *his* best. [masculine]

> The *people* with *whom* I work are loud. [neuter]

Indefinite singular pronouns used as antecedents require, of course, singular pronouns. Handling the gender of these singular pronouns is not as obvious; opinion is divided.

1. Traditionally, writers have used the masculine form of pronouns to refer to the indefinite singular pronouns when the gender is unknown.

> *Everyone* should work until *he* drops.

2. To avoid a perceived sex bias, use *he or she* or *his or her* instead of just *he* or *his.*

> *Everyone* should work until *he or she* drops.

3. Although option 1 is more direct, it is illogical to many listeners and readers, and option 2 used several times in a short passage can be awkward. To avoid those possible problems, writers often use plural forms.

> *All people* should work until *they* drop.

In any case, avoid using a plural pronoun with a singular indefinite pronoun; such usage violates the basic principle of number agreement.

Incorrect: *Everyone* should do *their* best.

Correct: *Everyone* should do *his* or *her* best.

Correct: *People* should do *their* best.

Making Pronouns Agree

Underline the correct pronoun form. (See Answer Key for answers.)

1. When someone does a favor for you, (he or she, they) must be thanked.

2. The audience clapped and cheered to communicate (their, its) approval.

3. No one in the maze could find (his or her, their) way out.

4. The corporation has decided to move (its, their) headquarters to Hawaii.

5. Everyone wearing high heels knew that (she, they) had made a bad shoe choice.

6. Ricardo is one of those people who like to do everything (himself, themselves).

7. Lynn's name was on the list of people (that, who) still owed money.

8. The drill sergeant required perfection from everyone and everything (who, that, which) was part of his platoon.

9. Ellen is the only one in the whole class who can laugh at (himself or herself, themselves, herself) after making a mistake.

10. Both of my parents are conscientious about (his or her, their) health.

11. The team faces (its, their) toughest challenge this Friday.

12. Neither of the men wanted to carry (his, their) wife's purse while she shopped.

13. Either John or Ralph will win the contest and see (his, their) hard work pay off.

14. A parent should read to (you, his or her, their) child every day.

15. Either of the mothers will be willing to tell you (her, their) story.

16. The writer and the artist have joined forces to produce (his or her, their) next book.

17. Neither George nor his brothers have been able to locate (his, their) grandmother's jewelry box.

18. Students must keep up with the reading if (he or she, they) want to pass the exam.

19. A babysitter should learn CPR in case (you, he or she, they) faces an emergency.

20. We assumed that everyone would take (his or her, their) time.

EXERCISE 32

Making Pronouns Agree

Underline the correct pronoun form.

1. I like to ride roller coasters, especially when (I, you) flip upside down.

2. He was the only one of the three judges who gave (his, their) honest opinion.

3. The music was lively and upbeat; (you, one) couldn't help tapping a foot in time with the rhythm.

4. Each of the men sucked in (his, their) stomach as the beautiful woman approached.

5. Neither Eric nor his brothers would take responsibility for (his, their) actions.

6. Todd is one of those people who like to get (his, their) own way all of the time.

7. She is the only one of the cast who did not flub (their, her) lines.

8. The members of the audience clapped (its, their) hands together.

9. Everybody should be treated as though (they, he or she) is a valued customer.

10. Only a few had brought (their, his or her) books to class.

11. Everyone likes to get discounts on (their, his or her) purchases.

12. To get ahead in life, (you need, one needs) a good education.

13. All too late, I realized that (you, one) should not eat a sloppy joe sandwich and drive at the same time.

14. Each of the rabbits had dug (its, his or her) way out of the pen.

15. She is the only one in her group of friends who is sure about (her, their) career path.

16. A fortune-teller should keep (his or her, their) crystal ball smudge-free and shiny.

17. Either of the tour guides will enlighten you with (his or her, their) vast knowledge.

18. The poet and the peasant declared (their, his) boundless love for her.

19. The committee submitted (their, its) recommendation to the president.

20. Every American must vote in order to do (his or her, their) civic duty.

Pronoun Reference

A pronoun must refer clearly to its antecedent. Because a pronoun is a substitute word, it can express meaning clearly and definitely only if its antecedent is easily identified.

In some sentence constructions, gender and number make the reference clear.

> Kevin and Latisha discussed *his* absences and *her* good attendance. [gender]

> If the three older boys in the *club* carry out those plans, *it* will break up. [number]

Avoid ambiguous reference. The following sentences illustrate the kind of confusion that results from structuring sentences with more than one possible antecedent for the pronoun.

> Unclear: Tyler gave Walt *his* money and clothes.

> Clear: Tyler gave his own money and clothes to Walt.

> Unclear: Lynette told her sister that *her* car had a flat tire.

> Clear: Lynette said to her sister, "Your car has a flat tire."

When using a pronoun to refer to a general idea, make sure that the reference is clear. The pronouns used frequently in this way are *this, that, which,* and *it.* The best solution may be to recast the sentence to omit the pronoun in question.

> Unclear: She whistled the same tune over and over, *which* irritated me.

> Clear: She whistled the same tune over and over, a *habit* that irritated me.

> Recast: Her whistling the same tune over and over irritated me.

Correcting Problems in Pronoun Reference

Some of the following sentences contain pronouns that are examples of faulty reference; cross out these pronouns and correct them. If the sentence is correct, write OK in the blank. (See Answer Key for answers.)

_____ 1. Tyrone said he would not be going on the trip, which worried his friends.

_____ 2. Yolanda criticized Monique because she was closed-minded and intolerant.

_____ 3. If that child doesn't get his own way, he has a temper tantrum.

_____ 4. During a recession, you find it harder to get a good job.

_____ 5. Fred told Barney that he may be laid off from his job at the quarry.

_____ 6. To cook sufficiently well, one must know how to read a cookbook.

_____ 7. That is Rachel's husband you met yesterday.

_____ 8. She loved to visit the Bahamas, but she didn't want to live there.

_____ 9. In that state, they don't require motorists to wear seatbelts.

_____ 10. Dottie asked her mother if she could wear her high heels to the dance.

_____ 11. Jolene gave her daughter her dinner.

_____ 12. Rita told her boss that she was sorry.

_____ 13. It was one of those days that we'd like to forget.

_____ 14. Robert hinted that he would love a new watch.

_____ 15. Julio was able to get a discount, which pleased him.

_____ 16. Most Americans admit to speeding, eating while driving, and running yellow or even red lights. This is what causes accidents.

_____ 17. My father made a fortune by dealing in real estate. I want that, too.

_____ 18. If a victim catches on fire, you should stop, drop, and roll.

_____ 19. In this brochure, it says that the hotel's pool has a waterslide.

_____ 20. Paul listens to his mother and follows her advice.

EXERCISE 34

Correcting Problems in Pronoun Reference

The following sentences contain pronouns that are examples of faulty reference. Correct the sentences.

1. They treated him like a child and that angered him.

2. Noel talked while he was eating, which annoyed his companions.

3. You could disagree with the idea, but it would not be easy.

4. Marcus handed Jim his keys.

5. Jannis told Jannel that her hair was too long.

6. We installed mud flaps, but some of it still got on the fenders.

7. The instructor told the student that his deadline was tomorrow.

8. This is my sister's house, whom you met yesterday.

9. They say unemployment is causing social problems.

10. Timothy never looked at me when he talked, which made me distrust him.

11. He often interrupted other people, which I found annoying.

12. They regarded him as incompetent, which embarrassed him.

13. You could come to her aid, but would it be appreciated?

14. Franklin told Jeff that his car needed to be repaired.

15. They say that the big bands are coming back.

16. In prison, you have little freedom.

17. This is my uncle's dog, who has a hundred-acre farm.

18. You could build a baseball field, but would it be worth the bother?

19. They say on television that anyone can buy a new car.

20. Hans put his finger into a hole in the dike at the edge of the ocean, but some of it still came in.

Adjectives and Adverbs

Adjectives modify (describe) nouns and pronouns and answer the questions *Which one? What kind?* and *How many?*

> *Which one?* The <u>new</u> <u>car</u> is mine.
>   adj n

> *What kind?* <u>Mexican</u> <u>food</u> is my favorite.
>   adj   n

> *How many?* A <u>few</u> <u>friends</u> are all one needs.
>   adj   n

Adverbs modify verbs, adjectives, or other adverbs and answer the questions *How? Where? When?* and *To what degree?* Most words ending in *-ly* are adverbs.

> *Where?* The cuckoo <u>flew</u> <u>south</u>.
>   v   adv

> *When?* The cuckoo <u>flew</u> <u>yesterday</u>.
>   v   adv

> *Why?* The cuckoo <u>flew</u> <u>because of the cold weather</u>.
>   v   adv phrase

> *How?* The cuckoo <u>flew</u> <u>swiftly</u>.
>   v   adv

> <u>Without adjectives and adverbs</u>, <u>even</u> John Steinbeck, the <u>famous</u>
>   adv phrase   adv   adj
>
> <u>Nobel Prize–winning</u> author, <u>surely</u> could <u>not</u> have described the
>   adj   adv   adv
>
> <u>crafty</u> octopus <u>very</u> <u>well</u>.
> adj   adv adv

We have two concerns regarding the use of adjectives and adverbs (modifiers) in writing. One is a matter of diction, or word choice—in this case, selecting adjectives and adverbs that will strengthen the writing. The other is how to identify and correct problems with modifiers.

Selecting Adjectives and Adverbs

If you want to finish the sentence "She was a(n) _____ speaker," you have many adjectives to select from, including these:

distinguished	dependable	effective	sly
influential	impressive	polished	astute
adequate	boring	abrasive	humorous

If you want to finish the sentence "She danced _____ ," you have another large selection, this time of adverbs such as the following:

bewitchingly	angelically	quaintly	zestfully
gracefully	grotesquely	carnally	smoothly
divinely	picturesquely	serenely	unevenly

Adjectives and adverbs can be used to enhance communication. If you have a thought, you know what it is, but when you deliver that thought to someone else, you may not say or write what you mean. Your thought may be eloquent and your word choice weak. Keep in mind that no two words mean exactly the same thing. Further, some words are vague and general. If you settle for a common word such as *good* or a slang word such as *neat* to characterize something that you like, you will be limiting your communication. Of course, those who know you best may understand fairly well; after all, certain people who are really close may be able to convey ideas using only grunts and gestures.

But what if you want to write to someone you hardly know to explain how you feel about an important issue? Then the more precise the word, the better the communication. By using modifiers, you may be able to add significant information. Keep in mind, however, that anything can be overdone; therefore, use adjectives and adverbs wisely and economically.

Your first resource in searching for more effective adjectives should be your own vocabulary storehouse. Another resource is a good thesaurus (book of synonyms), either in print form or on a computer.

Supply the appropriate modifiers in the following exercises, using a dictionary, a thesaurus, or the resources designated by your instructor.

EXERCISE 35

Supplying Adjectives

Provide adjectives to modify these nouns. Use only single words, not adjective phrases.

1. A(n) _____ cat

2. A(n) _____ politician

3. A(n) _____ echo

4. A(n) _____ friend

5. A(n) _____ waiter

6. A(n) _____ conference

7. A(n) _____ comedian

8. A(n) _____ street

9. A(n) _____ school

10. A(n) _____ vacation

Supplying Adverbs

Provide adverbs to modify these verbs. Use only single words, not adverb phrases.

1. stare   _____

2. flee   _____

3. yell   _____

4. approach _____

5. taste   _____

6. smile   _____

7. look   _____

8. leave   _____

9. cry   _____

10. eat   _____

Comparative and Superlative Forms

For making comparisons, most adjectives and adverbs have three different forms: the positive (one), the comparative (comparing two), and the superlative (comparing three or more).

Adjectives

1. Some adjectives follow a regular pattern:

Positive (one)	Comparative (two)	Superlative (three or more)
nice	nicer	nicest
rich	richer	richest
big	bigger	biggest
tall	taller	tallest
lonely	lonelier	loneliest
terrible	more terrible	most terrible
beautiful	more beautiful	most beautiful

These are the general rules:

a. Add -er to short adjectives (one or two syllables) to rank units of two.

Julian is *nicer* than Sam.

b. Add *-est* to short adjectives (one or two syllables) to rank units of three or more.

Of the fifty people I know, Julian is the *kindest*.

c. Add the word *more* to long adjectives (three or more syllables) to rank units of two.

My hometown is *more beautiful* than yours.

d. Add the word *most* to long adjectives (three or more syllables) to rank units of three or more.

My hometown is the *most beautiful* in all America.

2. Some adjectives are irregular in the way they change to show comparison:

Positive (one)	Comparative (two)	Superlative (three or more)
good	better	best
bad	worse	worst

Adverbs

1. Some adverbs follow a regular pattern.

Positive (one)	Comparative (two)	Superlative (three or more)
clearly	more clearly	most clearly
quickly	more quickly	most quickly
carefully	more carefully	most carefully
thoughtfully	more thoughtfully	most thoughtfully

a. Add *-er* to some one-syllable adverbs for the comparative form and add *-est* for the superlative form.

My piglet runs *fast*. [positive]

My piglet runs *faster* than your piglet. [comparative]

My piglet runs *fastest* of all known piglets. [superlative]

b. Add the word *more* to form longer comparisons and *most* to form longer superlative forms.

Judy reacted *happily* to the marriage proposal. [positive]

Judy reacted *more happily* to the marriage proposal than Nancy. [comparison]

Of all the women Clem proposed to, Judy reacted *most happily*. [superlative]

c. In some cases, the word *less* may be substituted for *more*, and *least* for *most*.

Mort's views were presented *less effectively* than Craig's. [comparative]

Of all the opinions that were shared, Mort's views were presented *least effectively*. [superlative]

2. Some adverbs are irregular in the way they change to show comparisons.

Positive (one)	Comparative (two)	Superlative (three or more)
well	better	best
far	farther (distance)	farthest (distance)
	further	furthest
badly	worse	worst

Using Adjectives and Adverbs Correctly

1. Avoid double negatives. Words such as *no, not, none, nothing, never, hardly, barely,* and *scarcely* should not be combined.

Double Negative: I do *not* have *no* time for recreation. [incorrect]

Single Negative: I have *no* time for recreation. [correct]

Double Negative: I've *hardly never* lied. [incorrect]

Single Negative: I've *hardly* ever lied. [correct]

2. Do not confuse adjectives with adverbs. Among the most commonly confused adjectives and adverbs are *good/well, bad/badly,* and *real/really.* The words *good, bad,* and *real* are always adjectives. *Well* is sometimes an adjective. The words *badly* and *really* are always adverbs. *Well* is usually an adverb.

To distinguish these words, consider what is being modified. Remember that adjectives modify nouns and pronouns and that adverbs modify verbs, adjectives, and other adverbs.

Incorrect: I feel *badly* today. [We're concerned with the condition of *I.*]

Correct: I feel *bad* today. [The adjective *bad* modifies the pronoun *I.*]

Incorrect: She feels *well* about that choice. [We're concerned with the condition of *she.*]

Correct: She feels *good* about that choice. [The adjective *good* modifies the pronoun *she.*]

Incorrect: Lazarro plays the piano *good.* [The adjective *good* modifies the verb *plays,* but adjectives should not modify verbs.]

Correct: Lazarro plays the piano *well.* [The adverb *well* modifies the verb *plays.*]

Incorrect: He did *real* well. [Here the adjective *real* modifies the adverb *well,* but adjectives should not modify adverbs.]

Correct: He did *really* well. [The adverb *really* modifies the adverb *well.*]

3. Do not use an adverb such as *very, more,* or *most* before adjectives such as *perfect, round, unique, square,* and *straight.*

Incorrect: It is more round.

Correct: It is round.

Correct: It is more nearly round.

4. Do not double forms, such as *more lonelier* or *most loneliest*.

> **Incorrect:** Julie was *more nicer* than Jake.

> **Correct:** Julie was *nicer* than Jake.

5. Do not confuse standard and nonstandard forms of adjectives and adverbs.

- **Accidently.** This is a substandard form of *accidentally*.

- **All ready, already.** *All ready* means "completely prepared." *Already* means "previously."

  > We are *all ready* to give the signal to move out. [prepared]

  > When he arrived at the station, we had *already* left. [previously]

- **All right, alright.** *All right* (two words) means "correct," "yes," "fine," "certainly." *Alright* is a substandard spelling of "all right."

  > Yes, I am *all right* now.

- **All together, altogether.** *All together* means "in a group." *Altogether* means "completely," "wholly," "entirely."

  > The boys were *all together* at the end of the field.

  > The manuscript is *altogether* too confusing.

Be careful to place such words as *also, almost, even, just, hardly, merely, only,* and *today* in the right position to convey the intended meaning. As these words change position in the sentence, they may also change the meaning of the sentence.

> I *only* advised him to act cautiously.
> I advised *only* him to act cautiously.
> *Only* I advised him to act cautiously.
> I advised him *only* to act cautiously.

EXERCISE 37

Selecting Adjectives and Adverbs

Cross out the mistake in each sentence and write in the correction above it. (See Answer Key for answers.)

1. Ping-Sim thought his teacher had a most unique method of lecturing.

2. Some jobs are done easier by blind people than by those with sight.

3. It was up to the parents to decide if this kind of movie is real bad for children.

4. The adventure of life is too impossible to discuss.

5. Oscar felt badly about rejection slips but worse about his bank account.

6. Victor was not the stronger of the pair, but he was the best boxer.

7. The whole class thought Kyoka's sunglasses the most perfect they had seen.

8. The suspect became violenter as the police drew nearer.

9. Of all the potential winners, the judges agreed that Miss Idaho was more beautiful.

10. The United States has no central educational authority, but overall it does good.

11. An unambiguous word only can mean one thing.

12. It is real easy to forget that "liquor" used to mean "liquid."

13. Hurtful experiences in childhood don't fade out easy.

14. She said he had all ready ruined his reputation by making her buy her own flowers.

15. A trembling voice may indicate that the speaker does not feel alright.

16. Julian had two ways of starting a speech: One way was with a definition, but the easiest way was with a joke.

17. Sherman choked as if the very words tasted badly to him.

18. Natasha made a real good decision.

19. Erika didn't say the food was terrible; only she said it was bad.

20. On controversial topics, he was all together too easily offended.

EXERCISE 38 — Selecting Adjectives and Adverbs

Cross out the mistake in each sentence and write in the correction above it.

1. I remember one real good experience.

2. It left me feeling alright.

3. Of the two cars I have owned, the '69 Camaro was best.

4. It was also the beautifulest car I have ever seen.

5. When I drove it, I felt like the most rich person in town.

6. For a year I didn't have no time for anything except polishing my car.

7. I had it painted green so it was real handsome.

8. My name for it was the "Hornet," and when people gave me glances as I drove it, I felt well.

9. I hardly never abused that vehicle.

10. When I finally traded it in, I didn't never look back for fear I would cry.

11. All I can say is that it was most perfect.

12. Later I went back to the dealer, but I was all ready too late.

13. The Hornet had been bought by a young man who thought it was the better of all the cars on the lot.

14. He said he couldn't find no better car anywhere.

15. I could see he felt real good.

16. He and his family were standing altogether.

17. It was no time for me to feel badly.

18. In fact, as I said, I felt alright about the transaction.

19. I didn't shed no tears.

20. That experience is a real happy memory for me.

Dangling and Misplaced Modifiers

Modifiers should clearly relate to the word or words they modify.

1. A modifier that fails to modify a word or group of words already in the sentence is called a **dangling modifier.**

   Dangling: *Walking down the street,* a snake startled him. [Who was walking down the street? The person isn't mentioned in the sentence.]

   Correct: *Walking down the street, Don* was startled by a snake.

   Correct: As *Don* walked down the street, *he* was startled by a snake.

   Dangling: *At the age of six,* my uncle died. [Who was six years old? The person isn't mentioned in the sentence.]

   Correct: *When I was six,* my uncle died.

2. A modifier that is placed so that it modifies the wrong word or words is called a **misplaced modifier.** The term also applies to words that are positioned so as to unnecessarily divide closely related parts of sentences such as infinitives (*to* plus verb) or subjects and verbs.

   Misplaced: The sick man went to a doctor *with a high fever.*

   Correct: The sick man *with a high fever* went to the doctor.

   Misplaced: I saw a great movie *sitting in my pickup.*

Correct: *Sitting in my pickup,* I saw a great movie.

Misplaced: Kim found many new graves *walking through the cemetery.*

Correct: *Walking through the cemetery,* Kim found many new graves.

Misplaced: I forgot all about my sick dog *kissing my girlfriend.*

Correct: *Kissing my girlfriend,* I forgot all about my sick dog.

Misplaced: They tried to *earnestly and sincerely* complete the task. [splitting of the infinitive *to complete*]

Correct: They tried *earnestly and sincerely* to complete the task.

Misplaced: My neighbor, *while walking to the store,* was mugged. [unnecessarily dividing the subject and verb]

Correct: *While walking to the store,* my neighbor was mugged.

Try this procedure in working through Exercises 39 and 40.

1. Circle the modifier.

2. Draw an arrow from the modifier to the word or words it modifies.

3. If the modifier does not relate directly to anything in the sentence, it is dangling, and you must recast the sentence.

4. If the modifier does not modify the nearest word or words, or if it interrupts related sentence parts, it is misplaced and you need to reposition it.

EXERCISE 39

Correcting Dangling and Misplaced Modifiers

In the blank, write D for dangling modifier, M for misplaced modifier, and OK for correct sentences. Correct the sentences with modifier problems. (See Answer Key for answers.)

_____ 1. Late again, there was no time for breakfast.

_____ 2. Racking up points, the video-game player was close to setting a new record.

_____ 3. Bath, clipped, and perfumed, she allowed the dog to enter the house again.

_____ 4. We guessed approximately that the jar contained 3,000 jelly beans.

_____ 5. Filling out the form, my pen ran out of ink.

_____ 6. With grim determination, the mountain had been conquered.

_____ 7. Rudely, the interrupting child burst into the room without knocking.

_____ 8. The student made an appointment to see the teacher with a complaint.

_____ 9. By brushing and flossing every day, cavities can be avoided.

_____ 10. Sitting in the back row, the speaker was hard to hear.

_____ 11. He asked her to marry him yesterday.

_____ 12. Right after buying it, the popcorn was spilled all over the floor.

_____ 13. Strolling through the garden, the hot sun beat down.

_____ 14. I only have one objection to your devious plan.

_____ 15. To be healthy, smoking must be given up.

_____ 16. To find the gold, the map was followed by the treasure hunters.

_____ 17. When I was two years old, my mother enrolled me in swimming lessons.

_____ 18. I only signed up for one class.

_____ 19. Bill tried to slowly and persistently worm his way into her heart.

_____ 20. As the mother of six children, her grocery bill is always high.

EXERCISE 40

Correcting Dangling and Misplaced Modifiers

In the blank, write D for dangling modifier, M for misplaced modifier, and OK for correct sentences. Correct the sentences with modifier problems.

_____ 1. When I was in the third grade, my family moved to Texas.

_____ 2. When ten years old, my father won the lottery.

_____ 3. During the summer, I worked at the mall.

_____ 4. Raynelle went after the game was over, to the banquet.

_____ 5. Traveling over the mountain road, the inn was reached.

_____ 6. To be a successful runner, one needs strength and stamina.

_____ 7. Driving through the forest, many deer were seen from our car.

_____ 8. After studying it for many weeks, the plan was discontinued.

_____ 9. Searching the computer screen, we found the answer.

_____ 10. After giving it considerable study, the plan of action was discontinued.

———— 11. After three hours of walking, they rested.

———— 12. The ring sparkled on her hand, which she had bought in Italy.

———— 13. Climbing the mountain, we stopped to admire the view.

———— 14. Ms. Prank wanted to buy a car for her husband with a large trunk.

———— 15. He found a wallet in the park that didn't belong to him.

———— 16. Standing on top of the hill, we could see Catalina Island.

———— 17. Ginny took, to miss the construction, a detour.

———— 18. To play basketball well, good coordination.

———— 19. After playing all the game, the coach knew that Jean was tired.

———— 20. It is desirable to usually avoid splitting an infinitive.

Balancing Sentence Parts

We are surrounded by balance. Watch a colorful cross-frame, or diamond, kite as it soars in the sky. If you draw an imaginary line from the top to the bottom of the kite, you will see corresponding parts on either side. If you were to replace one of the sides with a loose-fitting fabric, the kite would never fly. A similar lack of balance can also cause a sentence to crash.

Consider these statements:

"*To be* or *not to be*—that is the question." [dash added]

This line from *Hamlet,* by William Shakespeare, is one of the most famous lines in literature. Compare it to the well-balanced kite in a strong wind. Its parts are parallel and it "flies" well.

"*To be* or *not being*—that is the question."

It still vaguely resembles the sleek kite, but now the second phrase causes it to dip like an unbalanced kite. Lurching, the line begins to lose altitude.

"*To be* or *death is the other alternative*—that is the question."

The line slams to the floor. Words scatter across the carpet. We return to the revision board.

The first sentence is forceful and easy to read. The second is more difficult to follow. The third is almost impossible to understand. We understand it only because we know what it should look like from having read the original. The point is that perceptive readers are as critical of sentences as kite-watchers are of kites.

Basic Principles of Parallelism

Parallelism as it relates to sentence structure is usually achieved by joining words with similar words: nouns with nouns, adjectives (words that describe nouns and pronouns) with adjectives, adverbs (words that describe verbs, adjectives, and other adverbs) with adverbs, and so forth.

> *Men, women* and *children* enjoy the show. [nouns]
>
> The players are *excited, eager,* and *enthusiastic.* [adjectives]
>
> The author wrote *skillfully* and *quickly.* [adverbs]

You can create parallel structure by joining groups of words with similar groups of words: prepositional phrase with prepositional phrase, clause with clause, sentence with sentence.

> She fell *in love* and *out of love* in a few minutes. [prepositional phrases]
>
> *Who he was* and *where he came from* did not matter. [clauses]
>
> *He came in a hurry. He left in a hurry.* [sentences]

Parallelism means balancing one structure with another of the same kind. Faulty parallel structure is awkward and draws unfavorable attention to what is being said.

> Nonparallel: Gary Payton's reputation is based on his ability in *passing, shooting,* and *he is good at rebounds.*
>
> Parallel: Gary Payton's reputation is based on his ability in *passing, shooting,* and *rebounding.*

In the nonparallel sentence, the words *passing* and *shooting* are of the same kind (verblike words used as nouns), but the rest of the sentence is different. You don't have to know terms to realize that there is a problem in smoothness and emphasis. Just read the material aloud. Then compare it with the parallel statement; *he is good at rebounds* is changed to *rebounding* to make a sentence that's easy on the eye and ear.

Signal Words

Some words signal parallel structure. If you use *and,* the items joined by *and* should almost always be parallel. If they aren't, then *and* is probably inappropriate.

> The weather is hot *and* humid. [*and* joins adjectives]
>
> The car *and* the trailer are parked in front of the house. [*and* joins nouns]

The same principle is true for *but,* although it implies a direct contrast. Where contrasts are being drawn, parallel structure is essential to clarify those contrasts.

> He *purchased* a Dodger Dog, *but* I *chose* the Stadium Peanuts. [*but* joins contrasting clauses]
>
> She *earned* an A in math *but failed* her art class. [*but* joins contrasting verbs]

You should regard all the coordinating conjunctions (FANBOYS: *for, and, nor, but, or, yet, so*) as signals for parallel structure.

Combination Signal Words

The words *and* and *but* are the most common individual signal words used with parallel constructions. Sometimes, however, **combination words** signal the need for parallelism or balance. The most common ones are *either/or, neither/nor, not only/*

but also, both/and, and *whether/or.* Now consider this faulty sentence and two possible corrections:

Nonparallel: *Either we will* win this game, *or let's* go out fighting.

Parallel: *Either we will* win this game, *or we will* go out fighting.

The correction is made by changing *let's* to *we will* to parallel the *we will* in the first part of the sentence. The same construction should follow the *either* and the *or.*

Nonparallel: Flour is used *not only* to bake cakes *but also* in paste.

Parallel: Flour is used *not only to bake* cakes *but also to make* paste.

The correction is made by changing *in* (a preposition) to *to make* (an infinitive). Now an infinitive follows both *not only* and *but also.*

EXERCISE 41

Correcting Faulty Parallelism

Mark each sentence as P for parallel or NP for nonparallel. Correct the sentences with nonparallel structure. (See Answer Key for answers.)

_____ 1. Jacques Cousteau was an adventurer, explorer, and educated people.

_____ 2. He will be remembered not only as a pioneer but also he was an environmentalist of great influence.

_____ 3. His love for the sea led him to devote his life to research, protecting, photographing, and writing about it.

_____ 4. His passion for the world's oceans made him an environmentalist, inventive, and a romantic.

_____ 5. He is credited with co-inventing scuba gear, developing a bathyscaphe, and helped start the first human undersea colonies.

_____ 6. Cousteau also helped invent skin-diving gear that freed divers from air hoses and to allow them to float at will.

_____ 7. His famous boat, the *Calypso,* was not only his transportation but also giving him a marine laboratory for experiments.

_____ 8. He not only was a filmmaker who created many documentaries but also the author of countless books.

_____ 9. His famous adventures included unearthing an ancient Greek shipwreck and photography of Antarctica's underwater ice sculptures.

_____ 10. Millions recognized Cousteau, who was thin, bespectacled, and he wore a red cap.

_____ 11. Cousteau was born in 1910, and his death occurred in 1997.

_____ 12. Although he was a sickly child, he liked going to the beach, swimming, and to dive.

_____ 13. He started out aiming for the skies in naval aviation school but ending up in the water.

_____ 14. He was honored both with France's Legion of Honor for his military service and forty Emmy nominations for his documentaries.

_____ 15. In his eighties he gave up diving, but he did not give up his mission to protect the sea for future generations.

_____ 16. To preserve the oceans for future generations was as important to him as teaching people.

_____ 17. Not long before he died at age 87, Cousteau said that he was proudest of helping to save the environment and with informing people everywhere.

_____ 18. He was not only beloved in France but also the subject of American songs such as John Denver's "Calypso."

_____ 19. Cousteau's films and what he believed influenced people of all ages.

_____ 20. He brought the mystery and beauty of the sea into the lives of even those who were landlocked.

EXERCISE 42

Correcting Faulty Parallelism

Mark each sentence as P for parallel or NP for nonparallel. Correct the sentences with nonparallel structure.

_____ 1. Both children and people who are adults enjoy fairy tales.

_____ 2. You may be interested to know who wrote them and their origins.

————— 3. When asked to name authors of fairy tales, most people either say the Grimm brothers or Hans Christian Andersen.

————— 4. But these men didn't write the stories; they merely collected or retold them.

————— 5. Many originated hundreds of years ago as oral folk stories told by women who wanted to pass on their knowledge and what they had experienced.

————— 6. These women, who had no rights in their male-dominated society, had two other purposes: rebelling against their many restrictions and to make their opinions known.

————— 7. Their stories, which were imaginative, gruesome, and with frightening parts, were not meant for children.

————— 8. They included cannibalistic witches, murdeous parents, and animals that eat men.

————— 9. Their tales were filled not only with scary characters but also gory violence.

————— 10. In the original "Cinderella," one of Cinderella's greedy stepsisters cuts off her toe so it would fit into the slipper, and the other cutting off her heel.

————— 11. As blood oozes from their shoes, pigeons peck out their eyes to punish them for their wickedness and being liars.

————— 12. In Charles Perrault's seventeenth-century version of "Little Red Riding Hood," the heroine not only fails to outsmart the wolf but also to escape being devoured.

————— 13. In the Grimm brothers' version, a woodcutter is Red Riding Hood's rescuer and who slices open the wolf's belly to let her out.

————— 14. The original "Snow White" contained neither dwarves nor a magic mirror.

_____ 15. In that version, it is Snow White's natural mother and father who drive her cruelly and with malice out of the house and into the woods.

_____ 16. The Grimm brothers changed the story so that she is abandoned by a male servant, protected by male dwarves, and a male prince rescues her.

_____ 17. It is their version that adds the wicked stepmother, the poisoned apple, and putting the girl in the glass coffin.

_____ 18. The story "Sleeping Beauty" had to be stripped of cannibalism, sex crimes, and people being unfaithful to their spouses.

_____ 19. The old versions taught people what were punishable sins and those deserving rewards.

_____ 20. In today's versions, the good still win. The bad still are losers.

Punctuation and Capitalization

Understanding punctuation will help you to write better. If you aren't sure how to punctuate a compound or compound-complex sentence, then you probably will not write one. If you don't know how to show that some of your words come from other sources, you may mislead your reader. If you misuse punctuation, you will force your readers to struggle to get your message. So take the time to review and master the mechanics. Your efforts will be rewarded.

End Punctuation

Periods

1. Place a period after a statement.

   The weather is beautiful today.

2. Place a period after common abbreviations.

Dr.	Mr.	Mrs.	Dec.	a.m.
Exceptions:	FBI	UN	NAACP	FHA

3. Use an ellipsis—three periods within a sentence and four periods at the end of a sentence—to indicate that words have been omitted from quoted material.

James Thurber, "The Secret Life of Walter Mitty"

   He stopped walking and the buildings . . . rose up out of the misty courtroom. . . .

Question Marks

1. Place a question mark at the end of a direct question.

   Will you go to the country tomorrow?

2. Do *not* use a question mark after an indirect (reported) question.

   She asked me what caused that slide.

Exclamation Points

1. Place an exclamation point after a word or a group of words that expresses strong feeling.

   Oh!   What a night!   Help!   Gadzooks!

2. Do not overwork the exclamation point. Do not use double exclamation points. Use the period or comma for mild exclamatory words, phrases, or sentences.

   Oh, we can leave now.

Commas

Commas to Separate

1. Use a comma to separate main clauses joined by one of the coordinating conjunctions—*for, and, nor, but, or, yet, so*. The comma may be omitted if the clauses are brief and parallel.

   We traveled many miles to see the game, *but* it was canceled.

   Mary left and I remained. [brief and parallel clauses]

2. Use a comma after introductory dependent clauses and long introductory phrases [generally, four or more words is considered long].

   Before the arrival of the shipment, the boss had written a letter protesting the delay. [two prepositional phrases]

   If you don't hear from me, assume that I am lost. [introductory dependent clause, an adverbial modifier]

   In winter we skate on the river. [short prepositional phrase, no comma]

3. Use a comma to separate words, phrases, and clauses in a series.

   Red, white, and *blue* were her favorite colors. [words]

   He ran *down the street, across the park,* and *into the arms of his father.* [prepositional phrases]

   When John was asleep, when Mary was at work, and *when Bob was studying,* Mother had time to relax. [dependent clauses]

4. However, when coordinating conjunctions connect all the elements in a series, the commas are omitted.

   He bought apples and pears and grapes.

5. Use a comma to separate coordinate adjectives not joined by *and* that modify the same noun.

> I need a *sturdy, reliable* truck.

6. Do not use a comma to separate adjectives that are not coordinate. Try the following technique to determine whether the adjectives are coordinate: Put *and* between the adjectives. If it fits naturally, the adjectives are coordinate; if it does not, they are not, and you do not need a comma.

> She is a kind, beautiful person.
>
> kind *and* beautiful [natural, hence the comma]
>
> I built a red brick wall.
>
> red *and* brick wall [not natural, no comma]

7. Use a comma to separate sentence elements that might be misread.

> Inside the dog scratched his fleas.
>
> *Inside,* the dog scratched his fleas.

Without benefit of the comma, the reader might initially misunderstand the relationship among the first three words.

Commas to Set Off

1. Use commas to set off (enclose) adjectives in pairs that follow a noun.

> The scouts, *tired and hungry,* marched back to camp.

2. Use commas to set off nonessential (unnecessary for meaning of the sentence) words, phrases, and clauses.

> My brother, *a student at Ohio State University,* is visiting me. [If you drop the phrase, the basic meaning of the sentence remains intact.]
>
> Marla, *who studied hard,* will pass. [The clause is not essential to the basic meaning of the sentence.]
>
> All students *who studied hard* will pass. [Here the clause *is* essential. If you remove it, you would have *All students will pass,* which is not necessarily true.]
>
> I shall not stop searching *until I find the treasure.* [A dependent clause at the end of a sentence is usually not set off with a comma. However, a clause beginning with the word *though* or *although* will be set off regardless of where it is located.]
>
> I felt unsatisfied, *though we had won the game.*

3. Use commas to set off parenthetical elements such as mild interjections (*oh, well, yes, no,* and others), most conjunctive adverbs (*however, otherwise, therefore, similarly, hence, on the other hand,* and *consequently* but not *then, thus, soon, now,* and *also*), quotation indicators, and special abbreviations (*etc., i.e., e.g.,* and others).

> *Oh,* what a silly question! [mild interjection]
>
> It is necessary, *of course,* to leave now. [sentence modifier]

We left early; *however,* we missed the train anyway. [conjunctive adverb]

"When I was in school," *he said,* "I read widely." [quotation indicators]

Books, papers, pens, *etc.,* were scattered on the floor. [The abbreviation *etc.* should be used sparingly, however.]

4. Use commas to set off nouns used as direct address.

Play it again, *Sam.*

Please tell us the answer, *Jane,* so we can discuss it.

5. Use commas to separate the numbers in a date.

June 4, 1965, is a day I will remember.

6. Do not use commas if the day of the month is not specified, or if the day is given before the month.

June 1965 was my favorite time.

One day I will never forget is 4 June 1965.

7. Use commas to separate the city from the state. No comma is used between the state and the ZIP code.

Walnut, CA 91789

8. Use a comma after both the city and the state when they are used together in a sentence.

Our family visited Anchorage, Alaska, last summer.

9. Use a comma following the salutation of a friendly letter and the complimentary closing in any letter.

Dear John,

Sincerely,

10. Use a comma in numbers to set off groups of three digits. However, omit the comma in dates, serial numbers, page numbers, years, and street numbers.

The total assets were $2,000,000.

I look forward to the year 2050.

EXERCISE 43

Using Commas

Insert all necessary commas in the following sentences. (See Answer Key for answers.)

1. Commas are used to separate words phrases and clauses in a series.

2. A strong assertive comma separates coordinate adjectives.

3. After long introductory modifiers a comma is used.

4. A comma is used between independent clauses and a period is usually found at the end of a sentence.

5. After all the meaning of the sentence is often clarified by a comma.

6. Inside the car smelled new and clean.

7. In the beginning of the game there was nothing but noise and chaos.

8. The crazy-looking car was painted pink black green and lavender.

9. Cherise worked at her desk all night but the job was not finished in time.

10. The sharp burning rays of the sun would soon be hidden by the trees.

11. Having finished the banquet the diners moved to the living room.

12. Bach and Handel both born in 1685 were the two greatest baroque composers.

13. Motor racing not horse racing is the more popular sport.

14. "When I was a boy" Arturo said "one dollar a week was enough!"

15. Dwight Jones the salesperson will take your order now.

16. Well that's the way it's going to be!

17. The new car all sleek and shiny was nowhere to be found.

18. He arrived in Tribbey Oklahoma on February 21 1934.

19. The old boxer was only down not out.

20. The Eiffel Tower which is located in Paris is no longer the highest tower in the world.

EXERCISE 44

Using Commas

Insert all necessary commas in the following sentences.

1. Before most people were superstitious.

2. People now know that superstitions are silly but many of these beliefs are still alive and well.

3. I know you believe dear friend that blowing out all the candles on your birth-day cake will make your wish come true.

4. Do you knock on wood say "bless you" when someone sneezes and avoid opening your umbrella indoors?

5. When you knock on wood you're calling upon the good spirits that live in trees to protect you.

6. Pope Gregory passed a law requiring people of the sixth century to bless a sneezer who had probably contracted the deadly plague.

7. If you break a mirror you face seven years of bad luck.

8. The bird which had flown into the house was an omen of death.

9. Brides must wear something old something new something borrowed and something blue.

10. It is however bad luck for the groom to see his bride before the wedding.

11. "Don't step on a crack or you'll break your mother's back."

12. You've heard I'm sure that pulling out a gray hair causes ten more to grow back.

13. The young guy well schooled in superstition waited beneath the mistletoe for the object of his affection to happen by.

14. If you take a test with the same pencil you used when you studied the pencil will remember the answers.

15. He carried at all times a rabbit's foot a four-leaf clover and a horseshoe.

16. Throw a coin into the fountain and make a wish.

17. Edmund Burke said "Superstition is the religion of feeble minds."

18. But Johann Wolfgang von Goethe a German novelist said that "superstition is the poetry of life."

19. The wishbone clean and dry was ready to be pulled in two.

20. Don't harm a cricket or a ladybug for they both bring good luck.

Semicolons

The semicolon indicates a stronger division than the comma. It is used principally to separate independent clauses within a sentence.

1. Use a semicolon to separate independent clauses not joined by a coordinating conjunction.

    > You must buy that car today; tomorrow will be too late.

2. Use a semicolon between two independent clauses joined by a conjunctive adverb such as one of the HOTSHOT CAT words (*however, otherwise, therefore, similarly, hence, on the other hand, then, consequently, accordingly, thus*).

    > It was very late; therefore, I remained at the hotel.

3. Use a semicolon to separate main clauses joined by a coordinating conjunction if one or both of the clauses contain distracting commas.

    > Byron, the famous English poet, was buried in Greece; and Shelley, who was his friend and fellow poet, was buried in Italy.

4. Use a semicolon in a series between items that themselves contain commas.

    > He has lived in Covina, California; Reno, Nevada; Prague, Oklahoma; and Bangor, Maine.

EXERCISE 45

Using Commas and Semicolons

Each sentence needs one or more semicolons or commas. Insert the appropriate marks. (See Answer Key for answers.)

1. Each year many species of birds fly south for the winter for example ducks and geese migrate to warmer areas to find more abundant food.

2. Most insects cannot fly the distances that these birds can fly instead they time their development so that they are in eggs or cocoons during the winter.

3. There is one exception however the Monarch butterfly is different from other insects.

4. Birds avoid lethal cold by getting away from it the Monarch butterfly does the same thing.

5. The long, hot days begin to grow shorter the temperatures grow colder and the beautiful, black and orange Monarch butterflies know that it's time to make their amazing journey.

6. These butterflies have tiny insect brains however, those brains somehow guide them over thousands of miles they've never seen before.

7. On their way to central Mexico, eastern Monarch butterflies stop in places like San Angelo, Texas Bracketville, Texas and Eagle Pass, Texas.

8. Thousands of them travel together in the same "flyways" to see all of them flying together at once is truly awesome.

9. They don't mind crowds as a matter of fact a 10-acre colony can contain five to six million butterflies per acre.

10. Biologists estimate that 15,000 to 20,000 butterflies perch on a single tree bough as a result the trees appear to be covered with bright autumn leaves.

11. They arrive in their winter home in November and they remain until March of the next year.

12. The Monarch butterfly breeds four or five times per year in a cycle each generation migrates either north or south.

13. The generation of butterflies that migrates to Mexico returns to the Gulf Coast states of the South and this generation lays eggs on milkweed plants.

14. The next generation lives only four to six weeks its mission is to get to the northern states and southern Canada.

15. Milkweed is plentiful at north latitudes so the butterflies spend their summer there eating and increasing their numbers.

16. Milkweed is the only thing these butterflies eat and this plant has one additional benefit.

17. Milkweed contains toxins therefore the butterflies become poisonous to predators when they ingest these toxins.

18. These butterflies need no camouflage for their bright colors signal poison to animals looking for a snack.

19. The generation that makes the journey to Mexico is rewarded for its hard work with a longer life those butterflies live eight months instead of two.

20. The Monarch butterfly is a fascinating creature and its travels are one of the world's biological wonders.

EXERCISE 46

Using Commas and Semicolons

Each sentence needs one or more semicolons or commas. Insert the appropriate marks.

1. The oldest science is the study of the stars and planets even ancient peoples looked up at the night sky with wonder and awe.

2. Early scientists plotted the positions and changing brightness of the stars and people worshipped the Sun and the Moon as gods.

3. Modern scientific discoveries have led to new knowledge about our solar system but astronomers continue to gather more information every day.

4. We've learned that our Sun is a star it radiates heat and light because of nuclear reactions inside its core.

5. The mass of the universe, including our bodies, is made up of elements from stars that exploded billions of years ago therefore humans are the stuff of stars.

6. A galaxy is a huge collection of stars bound together by gravity our Sun and its satellites are part of the spiral-shaped Milky Way Galaxy.

7. The universe is unbelievably vast astronomers estimate that there are at least one *billion* different galaxies close enough to photograph.

8. Our own solar system is so big that it could take up to twelve years to journey from Earth to the outermost planet yet it occupies only a tiny area of this vast universe.

9. There are two types of planets Earth and the three planets like it (Mercury, Venus, and Mars) are known as the terrestrial planets.

10. The other group consists of the planets that resemble Jupiter these Jovian planets include Jupiter, Saturn, Uranus, and Neptune.

11. Pluto does not resemble either Earth or Jupiter so some atronomers suggest that it be classified as an asteroid rather than a planet.

12. The farthest planet from the sun is Pluto it orbits the Sun only once every 248 years.

13. Pluto is the only planet that has not been visited by a probe from Earth but scientists hope to launch one in the near future.

14. Venus is the closest planet to Earth as a result it is the brightest object in our nighttime sky.

15. Jupiter is the largest planet of our solar system also it has sixteen moons, more than any other planet.

16. One of Jupiter's moons, Europa, may have an ocean of liquid water if it does, it could contain life.

17. Saturn is distinctive because of its rings they are believed to be composed of ice and rocks.

18. Many scientists believe that Mars may have once supported life for a Martian asteroid contains what looks like fossils of tiny organisms.

19. Neptune and Uranus are twins both have rings like Saturn and a similar composition.

20. Mercury is closest to the sun thus its average surface temperature is 350 degrees F during the day.

Quotation Marks

Quotation marks are used principally to set off direct quotations. A direct quotation consists of material taken from the written work or the direct speech of others; it is set off by double quotation marks. Single quotation marks are used to set off a quotation within a quotation.

Double Quotation Marks: He said, "I don't remember."

Single Quotation Marks: He said, "I don't remember if she said, 'Wait for me.'"

1. Use double quotation marks to set off direct quotations.

> Erin said, "Give me the book."
>
> As Edward McNeil writes of the Greek achievement: "To an extent never before realized, mind was supreme over faith."

2. Use double quotation marks to set off titles of shorter pieces of writing such as magazine articles, essays, short stories, short poems, one-act plays, chapters in books, songs, and separate pieces of writing published as part of a larger work.

> The book *Literature: Structure, Sound, and Sense* contains a deeply moving poem titled "On Wenlock Edge."
>
> Have you read "The Use of Force," a short story by William Carlos Williams?
>
> My favorite Elvis song is "Don't Be Cruel."

3. Use double quotation marks to set off slang, technical terms, and special words.

> There are many aristocrats, but Elvis is the only true "King." [special word]

> The "platoon system" changed the game of football. [technical term]

4. Use double quotation marks in writing dialogue [conversation]. Write each speech unit as a separate paragraph and set it off with double quotation marks.

> "Will you go with me?" he asked.

> "Yes," she replied. "Are you ready now?"

5. Use single quotation marks to set off a quotation within a quotation.

> Professor Baxter said, "You should remember Shakespeare's words, 'Nothing will come of nothing.'"

6. Do *not* use quotation marks for indirect quotations.

> Incorrect: He said that "he would bring the supplies."

> Correct: He said that he would bring the supplies.

7. Do *not* use quotation marks for the title on your own written work. If you refer to that title in another piece of writing, however, you need the quotation marks.

Punctuation with Quotation Marks

1. A period or comma is always placed *inside* the quotation marks.

> Our assignment for Monday was to read Poe's poem "The Raven."

> "I will read you the story," he said. "It's a good one."

2. A semicolon or colon is always placed *outside* the quotation marks.

> He read Robert Frost's poem "Design"; then he gave the examination.

> He quoted Frost's "Stopping by Woods on a Snowy Evening": "But I have promises to keep."

3. A question mark, an exclamation point, or a dash (see page 507) is placed *outside* the quotation marks when it applies to the entire sentence and *inside* the quotation marks when it applies to the material in quotation marks.

> He asked, "Am I responsible for everything?" [quoted question within a statement]

> Did you hear him say, "I have the answer"? [statement within a question]

> Did she say, "Are you ready?" [question within a question]

> She shouted, "Impossible!" [exclamation]

> Roy screamed, "I'll flunk if I don't read Poe's short story "The Black Cat"! [exclamation that does not belong to the material inside the quotation marks]

> "I hope—that is, I—" he began. [dash]

> "Accept responsibility"—those were his words. [dash that does not belong to the material inside the quotation marks]

4. A single question mark is used in sentence constructions that contain a double question—that is, a quoted question following a question.

> Mr. Martin said, "Did he say, 'Are you going?'"

Italics

Italics (slanting type) is used to call special attention to certain words or groups of words. In handwriting, such words are <u>underlined;</u> however, computers provide italics.

1. Italicize (underline) foreign words and phrases that are still listed in the dictionary as foreign.

> *nouveau riche*
>
> *Weltschmerz*

2. Italicize (underline) titles of books (except the Bible); long poems; plays; magazines; motion pictures; musical compositions; newspapers; works of art; names of aircraft and ships; and letters, figures, and words.

> I think Hemingway's best novel is *A Farewell to Arms.*
>
> His source material was taken from *Time, Newsweek,* and the Los Angeles *Times.* [Sometimes the name of the city in titles of newspapers is italicized—for example, the *New York Times.*]
>
> The *Mona Lisa* is my favorite painting.

3. Italicize (underline) the names of ships, airplanes, spacecraft, and trains.

> Ships: *Queen Mary   Lurline   Stockholm*
>
> Spacecraft: *Challenger   Voyager 2*

4. Italicize (underline) to distinguish letters, figures, and words when they refer to themselves rather than to the ideas or things they usually represent.

> Do not leave the *o* out of *sophomore.*
>
> Your *3*'s look like *5*'s.

Dashes

The dash is used when a stronger break than the comma is needed. The dash is typed as two hyphens with no space before or after them (--).

1. Use a dash to indicate a sudden change in sentence construction or an abrupt break in thought.

> Here is the true reason—but maybe you don't care.

2. Use a dash after an introductory list. The words *these, those, all,* and occasionally *such* introduce the summarizing statement.

> English, French, history—these are the subjects I like.

Colons

The colon is a formal mark of punctuation used chiefly to introduce something that is to follow, such as a list, a quotation, or an explanation.

1. Use a colon after a main clause to introduce a formal list, an emphatic or long restatement (appositive), an explanation, an emphatic statement, or a summary.

> The following cars were in the General Motors show: Cadillac, Chevrolet, Buick, Oldsmobile, and Pontiac. [list]
>
> He worked toward one objective: a degree. [restatement or appositive]
>
> Let me emphasize one point: I do not accept late papers. [emphatic statement]

2. Use a colon to introduce a formal quotation or a formal question.

> Shakespeare's Polonius said: "Neither a borrower nor a lender be." [formal quotation]
>
> The question is this: Shall we surrender? [formal question]

3. Use a colon in the following conventional ways: to separate a title and subtitle, a chapter and verse in the Bible, and hours and minutes; after the salutation in a formal business letter; and between the act and the scene of a play.

Title and subtitle:	*Korea: A Country Divided*
Chapter and verse:	Genesis 4:12
Hour and minutes:	8:25 P.M.
Salutation:	Dear Ms. Johnson:
Act and scene:	*Hamlet* III:ii

Parentheses

Parentheses are used to set off material that is of relatively little importance to the main thought of the sentence. Such material—numbers, supplementary material, and sometimes explanatory details—merely amplifies the main thought.

1. Use parentheses to set off material that is not part of the main sentence but is too relevant to omit altogether. This category includes numbers that designate items in a series, amplifying references, explanations, directions, and qualifications.

> Jay offered two reasons for his losing: (1) he was tired, and (2) he was out of condition. [numbers]
>
> Review the chapters on the Civil War (6, 7, and 8) for the next class meeting. [references]
>
> Her husband (she had been married about a year) died last week. [explanation]

2. In business writing, use parentheses to enclose a numerical figure that repeats and confirms a spelled-out number.

> I paid twenty dollars ($20) for the book.

3. Use a comma, semicolon, and colon after the parentheses when the sentence punctuation requires their use.

> Although I have not lived here long (I arrived in 2003), this place feels like my only true home.

Use the period, question mark, and exclamation point in appropriate positions depending on whether they go with the material within the parentheses or with the entire sentence.

> The greatest English poet of the seventeenth century was John Milton (1608–1674).

> The greatest English poet of the seventeenth century was John Milton. (Some might not agree; I myself favor Andrew Marvell.)

Brackets

Brackets are used within a quotation to set off editorial additions or corrections made by the person who is quoting.

> Churchill said: "It [the Yalta Agreement] contained many mistakes."

Apostrophes

The apostrophe is used with nouns and indefinite pronouns to show possession; to show the omission of letters and figures in contractions; and to form the plurals of letters, figures, and words referred to as words.

1. A possessive shows that something is owned by someone. Use an apostrophe and -*s* to form the possessive of a noun, singular or plural, that does not end in -*s*.

   man's coat   women's suits

2. Use an apostrophe alone to form the possessive of a plural noun ending in -*s*.

   girls' clothes   the Browns' house

3. Use an apostrophe and -*s* or the apostrophe alone to form the possessive of singular nouns ending in -*s*. Use the apostrophe and -*s* only when you would pronounce the *s*.

   James' hat or (if you would pronounce the *s*) James's hat

4. Use an apostrophe and -*s* to form the possessive of certain indefinite pronouns.

   everybody's idea   one's meat   another's poison

5. Use an apostrophe to indicate that letters or figures have been omitted.

   o'clock (short for *of the clock*)   in the '90s (short for 1990s)

6. Use an apostrophe with pronouns only when you are making a contraction. A contraction is a combination of two words. The apostrophe in a contraction indicates where a letter has been omitted.

it is	=	it's
she has	=	she's
you are	=	you're

If no letters have been left out, don't use an apostrophe.

Incorrect: The dog bit it's tail.

Correct: The dog bit its tail. [not a contraction]

Incorrect: Whose the leader now?

Correct: Who's the leader now? [a contraction of *who is*]

Incorrect: Its a big problem.

Correct: It's a big problem. [a contraction of *it is*]

7. Use an apostrophe to indicate the plural of letters, figures, and words used as words.

Dot your *i*'s.   five *8*'s   *and*'s

Note that the letters, figures, and words are italicized, but the apostrophe and -*s* are not.

Hyphens

The hyphen brings two or more words together into a single compound word. Correct hyphenation, therefore, is essentially a spelling problem rather than one of punctuation. Because the hyphen is not used with any degree of consistency, consult your dictionary for current usage. Study the following as a beginning guide.

1. Use a hyphen to separate the parts of many compound words.

brother-in-law   go-between

2. Use a hyphen between prefixes and proper names.

all-American   mid-Atlantic

3. Use a hyphen to join two or more words used as a single adjective modifier before a noun.

bluish-gray eyes   first-class service

4. Use a hyphen with spelled-out compound numbers up to ninety-nine and with fractions.

twenty-six   two-thirds

Note: Dates, street addresses, numbers requiring more than two words, chapter and page numbers, time followed directly by A.M. or P.M., and figures after a dollar sign or before measurement abbreviations are usually written as figures, not words.

Capitalization

Following are some of the many conventions concerning the use of capital letters in English.

1. Capitalize the first word of a sentence.

2. Capitalize proper nouns and adjectives derived from proper nouns.

Names of persons
Edward Jones

Adjectives derived from proper nouns
a Shakespearean sonnet   a Miltonic sonnet

Countries, nationalities, races, languages
Germany   English   Spanish   Chinese

States, regions, localities, other geographical divisions
California   the Far East   the South

Oceans, lakes, mountains, deserts, streets, parks
Lake Superior   Fifth Avenue   Sahara Desert

Educational institutions, schools, courses
Santa Ana College   Spanish 3   Joe Hill School   Rowland High School

Organizations and their members
Boston Red Sox   Boy Scouts   Audubon Society

Corporations, governmental agencies or departments, trade names
U.S. Steel Corporation   Treasury Department
Coca-Cola   White Memorial Library

Calendar references such as holidays, days of the week, months
Easter   Tuesday   January

Historic eras, periods, documents, laws
Declaration of Independence   Geneva Convention
Romantic Age   First Crusade

3. Capitalize words denoting family relationships when they are used before a name or substituted for a name.

> He walked with his nephew and Aunt Grace.

> *but*

> He walked with his nephew and his aunt.

> Grandmother and Mother are away on vacation.

> *but*

> My grandmother and my mother are away on vacation.

4. Capitalize abbreviations after names.

Henry White Jr.   Juan Gomez, M.D.

5. Capitalize titles of essays, books, plays, movies, poems, magazines, newspapers, musical compositions, songs, and works of art. Do not capitalize short conjunctions and prepositions unless they come at the beginning or the end of the title.

Desire Under the Elms   *Terminator*
Last of the Mohicans   *Of Mice and Men*
"Blueberry Hill"

6. Capitalize any title preceding a name or used as a substitute for a name. Do not capitalize a title following a name.

Judge Wong   Alfred Wong, a judge
General Clark   Raymond Clark, a general
Professor Fuentes   Harry Fuentes, the biology professor

Using Punctuation and Capitalization

One punctuation mark, a capital letter, or italic type is omitted in each of the following sentences. Insert them as needed. Pairs of quotation marks or dashes are considered one unit. (See Answer Key for answers.)

1. Odyssey is a famous epic poem of Greek mythology.

2. The professor said, The poem tells of the wanderings and sufferings of Odysseus, who is also known as Ulysses.

3. This poem is a great classic of literature; its famous for its beautiful poetry as well as its exciting tales of adventure.

4. The author was Homer, who wrote this poem and the equally well-known Iliad in the ninth century B.C.

5. The story begins at the end of the Trojan war as Odysseus and his band of Greeks prepare to sail back to their home in Ithaca.

6. It would take Odysseus if you can believe it ten years to get back.

7. He and his companions encounter many obstacles people, creatures, and gods who seek to kill them.

8. A one-eyed giant called the Cyclops eats several of Odysseus men and imprisons the rest in his cave.

9. Odysseus blinds the giant, and his men must sneak out of the cave by tying themselves under the bellies of the Cyclops sheep.

10. The sea-god Neptune the Cyclops' father tries to sink the Greek ships in a storm.

11. Many of Odysseus' sailors are eaten by cannibals called lestrigonians.

12. For a year, Odysseus and his men remain captives of the beautiful sorceress circe on her enchanted island.

13. Circe turns Odysseus' twenty two companions into pigs but finally lets them go.

14. The Sirens half women and half birds enticed sailors to their doom with their sweet songs.

15. Odysseus evades their charms by putting wax in his mens ears and lashing himself to the mast of the ship, where he can enjoy the songs but resist temptation.

16. Next, he manages to get past two more monsters Scylla and Charybdis.

17. Scylla is a six headed female monster, with six mouths containing three rows of sharp teeth.

18. Did you know that Charybdis is a dangerous whirlpool.

19. This a great story! exclaimed the students.

20. It's amazing that a poem so old can be so action packed.

EXERCISE 48

Using Punctuation and Capitalization

Twenty punctuation marks are needed in the following paragraphs; the locations are indicated by the numbers. Pairs such as quotation marks and parentheses are considered one unit. Insert the marks as needed.

  1   2   3   4
Shakespeares age was like ours it was full of change and turmoil" the old gentle-
          5   6   7
man said. New ideas were not confined exclusively to one social class one religion or
                                                                        8
one political party. Outer space stirred the imaginations of most of the people not
                                                    9   10
just the astronomers. They went to see Hamlet for fun and they bought all the books
                                                              11
available on the strange customs of other cultures. And whos to say that when Ham-
  12   13 14   15   (14)
lets father says I am thy fathers spirit he is any less visible than the ghosts some
                              16   17   18
people say they see today. There wasnt much Shakespeare didnt know about us.
  19   20
Thats why we still quarrel about the meaning of his plays we are still discovering the
                                              (5)
truth about ourselves in them.

Spelling

Spelling Tips

The following tips will help you become a better speller.

1. **Do not omit letters.**

   Many errors occur because certain letters are omitted when the word is pronounced or spelled. Observe the omissions in the following words. Then concentrate on learning the correct spellings.

Incorrect	Correct	Incorrect	Correct
aquaintance	acquaintance	irigation	irrigation
ajourned	adjourned	libary	library
agravate	aggravate	paralell	parallel
aproved	approved	parlament	parliament
artic	arctic	paticulaly	particularly
comodity	commodity	readly	readily
efficent	efficient	sophmore	sophomore
envirnment	environment	stricly	strictly
familar	familiar	unconsious	unconscious

2. **Do not add letters.**

Incorrect	Correct	Incorrect	Correct
athelete	athlete	ommission	omission
comming	coming	pasttime	pastime
drownded	drowned	priviledge	privilege
folkes	folks	similiar	similar
occassionally	occasionally	tradgedy	tragedy

3. **Do not substitute incorrect letters for correct letters.**

Incorrect	Correct	Incorrect	Correct
benefisial	beneficial	offence	offense
bullitins	bulletins	peculier	peculiar
sensus	census	resitation	recitation
discription	description	screach	screech
desease	disease	substansial	substantial
dissention	dissension	surprize	surprise
itims	items	technacal	technical

4. **Do not transpose letters.**

Incorrect	Correct	Incorrect	Correct
alunmi	alumni	prehaps	perhaps
childern	children	perfer	prefer
dupilcate	duplicate	perscription	prescription
irrevelant	irrelevant	principels	principles
kindel	kindle	yeild	yield

Note: Whenever you notice other words that fall into any one of these categories, add them to the list.

5. **Apply the spelling rules for spelling *ei* and *ie* words correctly.**
   Remember this poem?

   > Use *i* before *e*
   > Except after *c*
   > Or when sounded like *a*
   > As in *neighbor* and *weigh.*

   i before e

achieve	chief	niece	relieve
belief	field	piece	shield
believe	grief	pierce	siege
brief	hygiene	relief	variety

   Except after c

ceiling	conceive	deceive	receipt
conceit	deceit	perceive	receive

   Exceptions: either, financier, height, leisure, neither, seize, species, weird

   When sounded like a

deign	freight	neighbor	sleigh
eight	heinous	rein	veil
feign	heir	reign	vein
feint	neigh	skein	weigh

6. **Apply the rules for dropping the final *e* or retaining the final *e* when a suffix is added.**
   Words ending in a silent *e* usually drop the *e* before a suffix beginning with a vowel; for example, *accuse + -ing = accusing.* Here are some common suffixes beginning with a vowel: *-able, -al, -age, -ary, -ation, -ence, -ing, -ion, -ous, -ure.*

admire + *-able* = admirable	imagine + *-ary* = imaginary
arrive + *-al* = arrival	locate + *-ion* = location
come + *-ing* = coming	please + *-ure* = pleasure
explore + *-ation* = exploration	plume + *-age* = plumage
fame + *-ous* = famous	precede + *-ence* = precedence

   Exceptions: *dye + -ing = dyeing* (to distinguish it from *dying*), *acreage, mileage.*

   Words ending in a silent *-e* usually retain the *e* before a suffix beginning with a consonant; for example: *arrange + -ment = arrangement.* Here are some common suffixes beginning with a consonant: *-craft, -ful, -less, -ly, -mate, -ment, -ness, -ty.*

entire + *-ty* = entirety	manage + *-ment* = management
hate + *-ful* = hateful	safe + *-ly* = safely
hope + *-less* = hopeless	stale + *-mate* = stalemate
like + *-ness* = likeness	state + *-craft* = statecraft

   Exceptions: Some words taking the *-ful* or *-ly* suffixes drop the final *e*:

awe + *-ful* = awful	true + *-ly* = truly
due + *-ly* = duly	whole + *-ly* = wholly

   Some words taking the suffix *-ment* drop the final *e*; for example:

acknowledgment	argument	judgment

Words ending in silent -*e* after *c* or *g* retain the *e* when the suffix begins with the vowel *a* or *o*. The final -*e* is retained to keep the *c* or *g* soft before the suffixes.

advantageous	noticeable
courageous	peaceable

7. **Apply the rules for doubling a final consonant before a suffix beginning with a vowel.**

Words of one syllable:

blot	blotted	get	getting	rob	robbed
brag	bragging	hop	hopped	run	running
cut	cutting	hot	hottest	sit	sitting
drag	dragged	man	mannish	stop	stopped
drop	dropped	plan	planned	swim	swimming

Words accented on the last syllable:

acquit	acquitted	equip	equipped
admit	admittance	occur	occurrence
allot	allotted	omit	omitting
begin	beginning	prefer	preferred
commit	committee	refer	referred
concur	concurring	submit	submitted
confer	conferring	transfer	transferred
defer	deferring		

Words that are not accented on the last syllable and words that do not end in a single consonant preceded by a vowel do not double the final consonant (whether or not the suffix begins with a vowel).

Frequently Misspelled Words

a lot	committee	etc.	independent
absence	competition	exaggerate	intelligence
across	complete	excellent	interest
actually	consider	exercise	interfere
all right	criticism	existence	involved
among	definitely	experience	knowledge
analyze	dependent	explanation	laboratory
appearance	develop	extremely	leisure
appreciate	development	familiar	length
argument	difference	February	library
athlete	disastrous	finally	likely
athletics	discipline	foreign	lying
awkward	discussed	government	marriage
becoming	disease	grammar	mathematics
beginning	divide	grateful	meant
belief	dying	guarantee	medicine
benefit	eighth	guard	neither
buried	eligible	guidance	ninety
business	eliminate	height	ninth
certain	embarrassed	hoping	nuclear
college	environment	humorous	occasionally
coming	especially	immediately	opinion

opportunity	pursue	sense	though
parallel	receipt	separate	tragedy
particular	receive	severely	tried
persuade	recommend	shining	tries
physically	reference	significant	truly
planned	relieve	similar	unfortunately
pleasant	religious	sincerely	unnecessary
possible	repetition	sophomore	until
practical	rhythm	speech	unusual
preferred	ridiculous	straight	using
prejudice	sacrifice	studying	usually
privilege	safety	succeed	Wednesday
probably	scene	success	writing
professor	schedule	suggest	written
prove	secretary	surprise	
psychology	senior	thoroughly	

Confused Spelling and Confusing Words

The following are more words that are commonly misspelled or confused with one another. Some have similar sounds, some are often mispronounced, and some are only misunderstood.

a	An adjective (called an article) used before a word beginning with a consonant or a consonant sound, as in "I ate *a* donut."
an	An adjective (called an article) used before a word beginning with a vowel (*a, e, i, o, u*) or with a silent *h*, as in "I ate an artichoke."
and	A coordinating conjunction, as in "Sara *and* I like Alison Krauss."
accept	A verb meaning "to receive," as in "I *accept* your explanation."
except	A preposition meaning "to exclude," as in "I paid everyone *except* you."
advice	A noun meaning "guidance," as in "Thanks for the *advice*."
advise	A verb meaning "to give guidance," as in "Will you please *advise* me of my rights?"
all right	An adjective meaning "correct" or "acceptable," as in "It's *all right* to cry."
alright	Not used in formal writing.
all ready	An adjective that can be used interchangeably with *ready*, as in "I am *all ready* to go to town."
already	An adverb meaning "before," which cannot be used in place of *ready*, as in "I have *already* finished."
a lot	An adverb meaning "much," as in "She liked him *a lot*," or a noun meaning "several," as in "I had *a lot* of suggestions."
alot	Misspelling.
altogether	An adverb meaning "completely," as in "He is *altogether* happy."
all together	An adverb meaning "as one," which can be used interchangeably with *together*, as in "The group left *all together*."
choose	A present tense verb meaning "to select," as in "Do whatever you *choose*."

chose	The past tense form of the verb *choose*, as in "They *chose* to take action yesterday."
could of	A misspelled phrase caused by confusing *could've*, meaning *could have*, with *could of*.
could have	Correctly spelled phrase, as in "I could have left."
could've	Correctly spelled contraction of *could have*, as in "He could've succeeded."
affect	Usually a verb meaning "change," as in "Ideas *affect* me."
effect	Usually a noun meaning "result," as in "That *effect* was unexpected."
hear	A verb indicating the receiving of sound, as in "I *hear* thunder."
here	An adverb meaning "present location," as in "I live *here*."
it's	A contraction of *it is*, as in "*It's* time to dance."
its	Possessive pronoun, as in "Each dog has *its* day."
know	A verb usually meaning "to comprehend" or "to recognize," as in "I *know* the answer."
no	An adjective meaning "negative," as in "I have *no* potatoes."
lead	A present tense verb, as in "I *lead* a stable life now," or a noun referring to a substance, such as "I sharpened the *lead* in my pencil."
led	The past tense form of the verb *lead*, as in "I *led* a wild life in my youth."
loose	An adjective meaning "without restraint," as in "He is a *loose* cannon."
lose	A present tense verb from the pattern *lose, lost, lost*, as in "I thought I would *lose* my senses."
paid	The past tense form of *pay*, as in "He *paid* his dues."
payed	Misspelling.
passed	The past tense form of the verb *pass*, meaning "went by," as in "He *passed* me on the curve."
past	An adjective meaning "former," as in "That's *past* history," or a noun, meaning "a time gone by," as in "He lived in the *past*."
patience	A noun meaning "willingness to wait," as in "Job was a man of much *patience*."
patients	A noun meaning "people under care," as in "The doctor had fifty *patients*."
peace	A noun meaning "a quality of calmness" or "absence of strife," as in "The guru was at *peace* with the world."
piece	A noun meaning "part," as in "I gave him a *piece* of my mind."
quiet	An adjective meaning "silent," as in "She was a *quiet* child."
quit	A verb meaning "to cease" or "to withdraw," as in "I *quit* my job."
quite	An adverb meaning "very," as in "The clam is *quite* happy."
receive	A verb meaning "to accept," as in "I will *receive* visitors now."
recieve	Misspelling.
stationary	An adjective meaning "not moving," as in "Try to avoid running into *stationary* objects."
stationery	A noun meaning "paper material to write on," as in "I bought a box of *stationery* for Sue's birthday present."
than	A conjunction, as in "He is taller *than* I am."
then	An adverb, as in "She *then* left town."
their	An adjective (possessive pronoun), as in "They read *their* books."

there	An adverb, as in "He left it *there*," or a filler word, as in "*There* is no time left."
they're	A contraction of *they are,* as in "*They're* happy."
thorough	An adjective, as in "He did a *thorough* job."
through	A preposition, as in "She went *through* the yard."
to	A preposition, as in "I went *to* town."
too	An adverb meaning "exceeding or going beyond what is acceptable," as in "You are *too* late to qualify for the discount," or "also," as in "I have feelings, *too*."
two	An adjective of number, as in "I have *two* jobs."
truely	Misspelling.
truly	An adverb meaning "sincerely" or "completely," as in "He was *truly* happy."
weather	A noun meaning "condition of the atmosphere," as in "The *weather* is pleasant today."
whether	A conjunction, as in "*Whether* he would go was of no consequence."
write	A present tense verb, as in "Watch me as I *write* this letter."
writen	Misspelling.
written	A past participle verb, as in "I have *written* the letter."
you're	A contraction of *you are,* as in "*You're* my friend."
your	A possessive pronoun, as in "I like *your* looks."

Your Spell Checker

Your computer spell checker is an important tool with many benefits and some limitations. With about 100,000 words in a typical database, the spell checker alerts you to problem words in your text that should be verified. If you agree that the spelling of a word should be checked, you can then select from a list of words with similar spellings. A likely substitute word will be highlighted. With a keystroke, you can correct a problem, add your own word to the database, or ignore the alert. With a few more keystrokes, you can type in your own correction, and you can add an unusual spelling or word to the database. You will be amazed at how many times your computer will catch misspellings that your eye did not see.

However, the spell checker has limitations. If you intended to type *he* and instead typed *me,* the spell checker will not alert you to a possible problem because the word you typed is spelled correctly. If you use the wrong word, such as *herd* instead of *heard,* the spell checker will not detect a problem. Thus, you should always proofread your writing after you have spell checked it.

Avoiding Wordy Phrases

Be More Concise

Certain phrases clutter sentences, consuming our time in writing and our readers' time in reading. Be on the lookout for wordy phrases as you revise and edit.

> **Wordy:** *Due to the fact that* he was unemployed, he had to use public transportation.

> **Concise:** *Because* he was unemployed, he had to use public transportation.

Wordy: *Deep down inside* he believed that the Red Sox would win.

Concise: He believed that the Red Sox would win.

Wordy	Concise
at the present time	now
basic essentials	essentials
blend together	blend
it is clear that	(delete)
due to the fact that	because
for the reason that	because
I felt inside	I felt
in most cases	usually
as a matter of fact	in fact
in the event that	if
until such time as	until
I personally feel	I feel
in this modern world	today
in order to	to
most of the people	most people
along the lines of	like
past experience	experience
at that point in time	then
in the final analysis	finally
in the near future	soon
have a need for	need
in this day and age	now

EXERCISE 48 ## Wordy Phrasing

Circle the wordy phrases and write in concise phrases.

1. Past experience tells me I should read the fine print.

2. In the final analysis, I feel inside that the college courses will blend together.

3. It is clear that most of the people can be fooled.

4. For the reason that I am too young, I must say no to your marriage proposal.

5. In most cases I would agree with you.

6. I am learning the basic essentials in this class.

7. In the near future I will have some investment money.

8. I personally feel that success is within my grasp.

9. I have no other comment at the present time.

10. I don't have a need for a pocket tool kit.

Brief Guide for ESL Students

If you came to this country knowing little English, you probably acquired vocabulary first. Then you began using that vocabulary within the basic patterns of your own language. If your native language had no articles, you probably used no articles; if your language had no verb tenses, you probably used no verb tenses, and so on. Using the grammar of your own language with your new vocabulary may initially have enabled you to make longer and more complex statements in English, but eventually you learned that your native grammar and your adopted grammar were different. You may even have learned that no two grammars are the same, and that English has a bewildering set of rules and an even longer set of exceptions to those rules. The Handbook presents grammar (the way we put words together) and rhetoric (the way we use language effectively) that can be applied to your writing. The following are some definitions, rules, and references that are of special help to writers who are learning English as a second language (ESL).

Using Articles in Relation to Nouns

Articles

Articles are either indefinite (*an, a*) or definite (*the*). Because they point out nouns, they are often called *noun determiners*.

Nouns

Nouns can be either singular (*book*) or plural (*books*) and are either count nouns (things that can be counted, such as "book") or noncount nouns (things that cannot be counted, such as "homework"). If you are not certain whether a noun is a count noun or a noncount noun, try placing the word *much* before the word. You can say, "much homework," so *homework* is a noncount noun.

Rules

- **Use an indefinite article (*a* or *an*) before singular count nouns and not before noncount nouns.** The indefinite article means "one," so you would not use it before plural count nouns.

    Correct: I saw a book. [count noun]

    Correct: I ate an apple. [count noun]

    Incorrect: I fell in a love. [noncount noun]

    Correct: I fell in love. [noncount noun]

    Incorrect: I was in a good health. [noncount noun]

    Correct: I was in good health. [noncount noun]

- **Use the definite article (*the*) before both singular and plural count nouns that have specific reference.**

    Correct: I read the book. [a specific one]

    Correct: I read the books. [specific ones]

Correct: I like to read a good book. [nonspecific, therefore the indefinite article]

Correct: A student who works hard will pass. [any student, therefore non-specific]

Correct: The student on my left is falling asleep. [a specific student]

- **Use the definite article with noncount nouns only when they are specifically identified.**

Correct: Honesty (as an idea) is a rare commodity.

Correct: The honesty of my friend has inspired me. [specifically identified]

Incorrect: I was in trouble and needed the assistance. [not specifically identified]

Correct: The assistance offered by the paramedics was appreciated. [specifically identified]

- **Place the definite article before proper nouns (names) of**

oceans, rivers, and deserts (for example, *the* Pacific Ocean and *the* Red River).
countries, if the first part of the name indicates a division (*the* United States of America).
regions (*the* South).
plural islands (*the* Hawaiian Islands).
museums and libraries (*the* Los Angeles County Museum).
colleges and universities when the word *college* or *university* comes before the name (*the* University of Oklahoma).

These are the main rules. For a more detailed account of rules for articles, see a comprehensive ESL book in your library.

Sentence Patterns

The Kinds of Sentences section in this Handbook defines and illustrates the patterns of English sentences. Some languages include patterns not used in standard English. The following principles are well worth remembering:

- **The conventional English sentence is based on one or more clauses, each of which must have a subject (sometimes the implied "you") and a verb.**

Incorrect: Saw the book. (subject needed even if it is obvious)

Correct: I saw the book.

- **English does not repeat a subject, even for emphasis.**

Incorrect: The book that I read it was interesting.

Correct: The book that I read was interesting.

Verb Endings

- **English indicates time through verbs.** Learn the different forms of verb tenses and the combinations of main verbs and helping verbs.

Incorrect: He watching the game. [A verb-like word ending in -*ing* cannot be a verb all by itself.]

Correct: He is watching the game. [Note that a helping verb such as *is, has, has been, will,* or *will be* always occurs before a main verb ending in -*ing*.]

- **Take special care in maintaining consistency in tense.**

Incorrect: I went to the mall. I watch a movie there. (verb tenses inconsistent)

Correct: I went to the mall. I watched a movie there.

All twelve verb tenses are covered with explanations, examples, and exercises in the Verbs section of the Handbook, pages 444–466.

Idioms

Some of your initial problems with writing English are likely to arise from trying to adjust to a different and difficult grammar. If the English language used an entirely systematic grammar, your learning would be easier, but English has patterns that are both complex and irregular. Among them are idioms, word groups that often defy grammatical rules and mean something other than what they appear to mean on the surface.

The expression "He kicked the bucket" does not mean that someone struck a cylindrical container with his foot; instead, it means that someone died. That example is one kind of idiom. Because the expression suggests a certain irreverence, it would not be the choice of most people who want to make a statement about death; but if it is used, it must be used with its own precise wording, not "He struck the long cylindrical container with his foot," or "He did some bucket-kicking." Like other languages, the English language has thousands of these idioms. Expressions such as "the more the merrier" and "on the outs" are ungrammatical. They are also very informal expressions and therefore seldom used in college writing, although they are an indispensable part of a flexible, effective, all-purpose vocabulary. Because of their twisted meanings and illogic, idioms are likely to be among the last parts of language that a new speaker learns well. A speaker must know the culture thoroughly to understand when, where, and how to use slang and other idiomatic expressions.

If you listen carefully and read extensively, you will learn English idioms. Your library will have dictionaries that explain them.

More Suggestions for ESL Writers

1. Read your material aloud and try to detect inconsistencies and awkward phrasing.

2. Have others read your material aloud for the same purposes.

3. If you have severe problems with grammatical awkwardness, try composing shorter, more direct sentences until you become more proficient in phrasing.

4. On your Self-Evaluation Chart, list the problems you have (such as articles, verb endings, clause patterns), review relevant parts of the Handbook, and concentrate on your own problem areas as you draft, revise, and edit.

Correcting ESL Problems

Make corrections in the use of articles, verbs, and phrasing. (See Answer Key for answers.)

George Washington at Trenton

One of most famous battles during the War of Independence occur at Trenton, New Jersey, on Christmas Eve of the 1776. The colonists outmatched in supplies and finances and were outnumbered in troop strength. Most observers in other countries think rebellion would be put down soon. British overconfident and believe there would be no more battles until spring. But George Washington decide to fight one more time. That Christmas, while large army of Britishers having party and thinking about the holiday season, Americans set out for surprise raid. They loaded onto boats used for carrying ore and rowed across Delaware River. George Washington stood tall in lead boat. According to legend, drummer boy floated across river on his drum, pulled by rope tied to boat. Because British did not feel threatened by the rag-tag colonist forces, they unprepared to do battle. The colonists stormed living quarters and the general assembly hall and achieved victory. It was good for the colonists' morale, something they needed, for they would endure long, hard winter before fighting again.

Appendixes

FLOW OF WRITING

Appendix A: Parts of Speech   526
Appendix B: Taking Tests   535
Appendix C: Writing a Job-Application Letter
 and a Résumé   537
Answer Key   540

"For excellence, the presence of others is always required."

HANNAH ARENDT

THE QUIGMANS   by Buddy Hickerson

"We're not exactly on the cutting edge of surgical techniques here. We're mostly into licking the wounds clean."

Appendix A   Parts of Speech

To classify a word as a part of speech, we observe two simple principles:

- The word must be in the context of communication, usually in a sentence.
- We must be able to identify the word with others that have similar characteristics—the eight parts of speech: nouns, pronouns, adjectives, verbs, adverbs, prepositions, conjunctions, or interjections.

The first principle is important because some words can be any of several parts of speech. The word *round,* for example, can function as five:

1. I watched the potter *round* the block of clay. [verb]

2. I saw her go *round* the corner. [preposition]

3. She has a *round* head. [adjective]

4. The astronauts watched the world go *round.* [adverb]

5. The champ knocked him out in one *round.* [noun]

Nouns

- **Nouns** are naming words. Nouns may name persons, animals, plants, places, things, substances, qualities, or ideas—for example, *Bart, armadillo, Mayberry, tree, rock, cloud, love, ghost, music, virtue.*
- Nouns are often pointed out by noun indicators. These noun indicators—*the, a, an*—signal that a noun is ahead, although there may be words between the indicator and the noun itself.

  the slime   *a* werewolf   *an* aardvark
  the green slime   *a* hungry werewolf   *an* angry aardvark

Pronouns

A **pronoun** is a word that is used in place of a noun.

- Some pronouns may represent specific persons or things:

I	she	they	you
me	her	them	yourself
myself	herself	themselves	yourselves
it	he	we	who
itself	him	us	whom
that	himself	ourselves	

- Indefinite pronouns refer to nouns (persons, places, things) in a general way:

  each   everyone   nobody   somebody

- Other pronouns point out particular things:

Singular	Plural
this, that	*these, those*
This is my treasure.	*These* are my jewels.
That is your junk.	*Those* are your trinkets.

- Still other pronouns introduce questions.

    Which is the best CD player?

    What are the main ingredients of a Twinkie?

Verbs

Verbs show action or express being in relation to the subject of a sentence. They customarily occur in set positions in sentences.

- **Action verbs** are usually easy to identify.

    The aardvark *ate* the crisp, tasty ants. [action verb]

    The aardvark *washed* them down with a snoutful of water. [action verb]

- The *being* **verbs** are few in number and are also easy to identify. The most common *being* verbs are *is, was, were, are,* and *am.*

    Gilligan *is* on an island in the South Pacific. [being verb]

    I *am* his enthusiastic fan. [being verb]

- The form of a verb expresses its tense, that is, the time of the action or being. The time may be in the present or past.

    Roseanne *sings* "The Star-Spangled Banner." [present]

    Roseanne *sang* "The Star-Spangled Banner." [past]

- One or more **helping verbs** may be used with the main verb to form other tenses. The combination is called a *verb phrase.*

    She *had sung* the song many times in the shower. [Helping verb and main verb indicate a time in the past.)

    She *will be singing* the song no more in San Diego. [Helping verbs and main verb indicate a time in the future.]

- Some helping verbs can be used alone as main verbs: *has, have, had, is, was, were, are, am.* Certain other helping verbs function only as helpers: *will, shall, should, could.*

The most common position for the verb is directly after the subject or after the subject and its modifiers.

    At high noon only two men [subject] *were* on Main Street.

    The man with the faster draw [subject and modifiers] *walked* away alone.

Adjectives

Adjectives modify nouns and pronouns. Most adjectives answer the questions *What kind? Which one?* and *How many?*

- Adjectives answering the *What kind?* question are descriptive. They tell the quality, kind, or condition of the nouns or pronouns they modify.

  red convertible   *dirty* fork
  noisy muffler   *wild* roses
  The rain is *gentle.*   Bob was *tired.*

- Adjectives answering the *Which one?* question narrow or restrict the meaning of a noun. Some of these are pronouns that become adjectives by function.

  my money   *our* ideas   the *other* house
  this reason *these* apples

- Adjectives answering the *How many?* question are, of course, numbering words.

  some people   *each* pet   *few* goals
  three dollars *one* glove

- The words *a, an,* and *the* are adjectives called *articles.* As "noun indicators," they point out persons, places, and things.

Adverbs

Adverbs modify verbs, adjectives, and other adverbs. Adverbs answer the questions *How? Where? When?* and *To what degree?*

  Modifying Verbs: They <u>did</u> their work <u>quickly</u>.
                         v   adv

  Modifying Adjectives: They were <u>somewhat</u> <u>happy.</u>
                                    adv   adj

- Adverbs that answer the *How?* question are concerned with manner or way.

  She ate the snails *hungrily.*

  He snored *noisily.*

- Adverbs that answer the *Where?* question show location.

  They drove *downtown.*

  He stayed *behind.*

  She climbed *upstairs.*

- Adverbs that answer the *When?* question indicate time.

  The ship sailed *yesterday.*

  I expect an answer *soon.*

- Adverbs that answer the *To what degree?* question express extent.

  She is *entirely* correct.

  He was *somewhat* annoyed.

Most words ending in *-ly* are adverbs.

  He completed the task *skillfully.* [adverb]

  She answered him *courteously.* [adverb]

However, there are a few exceptions.

The house provided a *lovely* view of the valley. [adjective]

Your goblin mask is *ugly*. [adjective]

Prepositions

A **preposition** is a word or group of words that function as a connective. The preposition connects its object(s) to some other word(s) in the sentence. A preposition and its object(s)—usually a noun or pronoun—with modifiers make up a **prepositional phrase,** which will function as an adjective or adverb.

Bart worked <u>against</u> great <u>odds.</u>

Everyone <u>in</u> his <u>household</u> cheered his effort.

A storm is forming <u>on</u> the <u>horizon</u>.
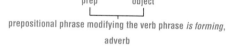

Some of the most common prepositions are the following:

about	before	but	into	past
above	behind	by	like	to
across	below	despite	near	toward
after	beneath	down	of	under
against	beside	for	off	until
among	between	from	on	upon
around	beyond	in	over	with

Some prepositions are composed of more than one word and are made up from other parts of speech:

according to	as far as	because of	in spite of
ahead of	as well as	in back of	instead of
along with	aside from	in front of	together with

Caution: Do not confuse adverbs with prepositions.

I went *across* slowly. [without an object—adverb]

I went *across* the field. [with an object—preposition]

We walked *behind* silently. [without an object—adverb]

We walked *behind* the mall. [with an object—preposition]

Conjunctions

A **conjunction** connects and shows a relationship between words, phrases, or clauses. A phrase is two or more words acting as a part of speech. A clause is a group of words with a subject and a verb. An independent clause can stand by itself: *She plays bass guitar.* A dependent clause cannot stand by itself: *when she plays bass guitar.*

There are two kinds of conjunctions: coordinating and subordinating.

Coordinating conjunctions connect words, phrases, and clauses of equal rank: noun with noun, adjective with adjective, verb with verb, phrase with phrase, main clause with main clause, and subordinate clause with subordinate clause. The seven common coordinating conjunctions are *for, and, nor, but, or, yet,* and *so.* (They form the acronym FANBOYS.)

Two Nouns: Bring a <u>pencil</u> <u>and</u> some <u>paper</u>.
              noun   conj   noun

Two Phrases: Did she go <u>to the store</u> <u>or</u> <u>to the game?</u>
              prep phase   conj   prep phrase

Paired conjunctions such as *either/or, neither/nor,* or *both/and* are usually classed as coordinating conjunctions.

<u>Neither</u> the coach <u>nor</u> the manager was at fault.
 conj   conj

Subordinating conjunctions connect dependent clauses with main clauses. The most common subordinating conjunctions include the following:

after	because	provided	whenever
although	before	since	where
as	but that	so that	whereas
as if	if	till	wherever
as long as	in order that	until	
as soon as	notwithstanding	when	

Sometimes the dependent clause comes *before* the main clause where it is set off by a comma.

<u>Although</u> <u>she</u> <u>was</u> in pain, she stayed in the game.
 conj   subj   v
     └────────┬────────┘
        dependent clause

Sometimes the dependent clause comes *after* the main clause, where it usually is *not* set off by a comma.

She stayed in the game <u>because</u> <u>she</u> <u>was needed</u>.
                        conj   subj   v
                            └────────┬────────┘
                               dependent clause

Caution: Certain words can function as either conjunctions or prepositions. It is necessary to look ahead to see if the word introduces a clause with a subject and verb—conjunction function—or takes an object—preposition function. Some of the words with two functions are these: *after, for, since, until.*

After the concert was over, we went home. [clause follows—conjunction]

After the concert, we went home. [object follows—preposition]

Interjections

An **interjection** conveys strong emotion or surprise. When an interjection appears alone, it is usually punctuated with an exclamation mark.

Awesome!   Curses!   Cowabunga!   Yaba dabba doo!

When it appears as part of a sentence, an interjection is usually followed by a comma.

Oh, I did not consider that problem.

The interjection may sound exciting, but it is seldom appropriate for college writing.

EXERCISE 1

Identifying Parts of Speech

Identify the part of speech of each italicized word or group of words by placing the appropriate abbreviations in the blanks. (See Answer Key for answers.)

n	noun	pro	pronoun
v	verb	adj	adjective
adv	adverb	prep	preposition
conj	conjunction		

1. I could *never* do *that* hard work at my age. _____ _____

2. We *must leave* for the seashore at once *before* the shower. _____ _____

3. *Until* Steve signs the checks, *we* must remain here. _____ _____

4. *These* men are anxiously awaiting your *instructions*. _____ _____

5. What is the *price* of those new *foreign* cars? _____ _____

6. Your *sister* is later than *you* this time. _____ _____

7. The coach is always *nervous before* the game begins. _____ _____

8. The *Norwegian* people protested the visit *of* the alleged terrorist. _____ _____

9. *I* shall have been absent a week *tomorrow*. _____ _____

10. That *reckless* driver hurt only *himself* in the accident. _____ _____

11. Her attitude *toward* the suspension of the

students was *somewhat* cool.   _____   _____

12. We *found* the answer to those difficulties *since*

he was last present.   _____   _____

13. Joan is much *wiser* now, *and* she will never

forget the lesson.   _____   _____

14. We saw the ship *that* was in the *collision*.   _____   _____

15. *Behind* the store is a *winding* road that leads

to the farms.   _____   _____

16. *If* you wish, I *will take* down his message for

you.   _____   _____

17. A *group* of students *asked* to see those new

paintings earlier.   _____   _____

18. When Kristin had finished talking, she came

over to *my* side of the room.   _____   _____

19. *Certainly,* you may see *his* answers.   _____   _____

20. I will *not* agree to *your* criticism.   _____   _____

EXERCISE 2   Identifying Parts of Speech

Identify the part of speech of each italicized word or group of words by placing the appropriate abbreviations in the blanks.

n	noun	pro	pronoun
v	verb	adj	adjective
adv	adverb	prep	preposition
conj	conjunction		

1. *According to* legend, silk *was discovered* by

Empress Hsi Ling-shi.   _____   _____

2. Empress Hsi Ling-shi *lived around* 2500 B.C.   _____   _____

3. *One* day while walking, *she* saw a mulberry tree
    covered with caterpillars.   _____   _____

4. The *caterpillars* were eating the *mulberry*
    leaves.   _____   _____

5. A few days *later* she saw the branches filled
    with the caterpillars' cocoons.   _____   _____

6. She plucked a cocoon *from* a branch and *took*
    it home.   _____   _____

7. *There* she placed *it* in a pot of water.   _____   _____

8. She *watched as* it loosened into a web.   _____   _____

9. She picked the *web apart*.   _____   _____

10. She discovered that *it* was a *long* thread of silk.   _____   _____

11. The process of making silk *became* China's
    special secret.   _____   _____

12. The *secret lasted* for the next 3,000 years.   _____   _____

13. Foreign gold poured *into* China from the *silk*
    trade.   _____   _____

14. To pass on the secret of silk-making *to* the
    outside world was forbidden.   _____   _____

15. Betraying the secret was punishable *by death*.   _____   _____

16. *Anyone* who has ever seen or worn a garment
    of pure silk knows why the Chinese had to guard
    their invention so jealously.   _____   _____

17. Silk is *petal* soft and lighter than the *sheerest*
    cotton.   _____   _____

18. It is *stronger* than *some* kinds of steel thread
    of equal thickness.   _____   _____

19. Silk *drapes* and flows *gracefully*.   _____   _____

20. It can be dyed to *richer* hues than any other

    natural *fabric*.   _____   _____

Supplying and Identifying Words in Context

Bubba and Lisa LaRue made a handsome couple at their wedding. Everyone had said so. But now, after seven years of marriage, they are not always happy with each other. After one heated argument, Lisa left, and Bubba sat down with his guitar to write a song describing their situation.

Fill in the blanks with words that you think would fit the context of the song. Then identify the part of speech of each of your choices by placing the appropriate abbreviation in the blanks at the left. The lines from the songs have been converted to sentences and may seem a bit less lyrical than Bubba's inspired original creation, "You Hurt My Feelings."

_____   You always burn my (1) _____ TV dinners.

_____   You (2) _____ my brand-new station-wagon car.

_____   You said (3) _____ didn't like to do housekeeping.

_____   By accident you broke my best (4) _____.

_____ _____   You went (5) _____ and spent my hard-earned (6) _____.

_____ _____   Then you (7) _____ a dozen bouncing (8) _____.

_____ _____   And then (9) _____ had to go and hurt my (10) _____

_____   when you ran (11) _____ with my best friend named Tex.

Chorus:

_____ _____   You (12) _____ my feelings, and I'm feeling (13) _____.

_____ _____   You hurt my (14) _____ (15) _____ I'm feeling sad. You

    hurt my feelings, ran away with my friend.

_____ _____   (16) _____ hurt my feelings, and (17) _____ is the end.

_____   You went out drinking on my (18) _____.

_____ _____   Then you (19) _____ my mother is a (20) _____.

_____   You made (21) _____ of my special mustache.

_____   You (22) _____ it gives you a funny itch.

———— You broke all my Dolly Parton (23) ————.

———— Then you went (24) ———— dancing with your ex.

———— And then you had to go and (25) ———— my feelings

———— when you ran away with my best (26) ———— named Tex.

Chorus:

You hurt my feelings, and I'm feeling sad.

———— ———— You hurt my (27) ————, and I'm feeling (28) ————.

———— You (29) ———— my feelings, and I'm feeling sad

———— because Tex was the best (30) ———— I ever had.

Scale for correctly labeled parts of speech (have your instructor check your answers):

  0–10 = need help with grammar
11–20 = starting to catch on to parts of speech
21–25 = becoming highly capable with parts of speech
26–30 = excellent knowledge of parts of speech

Scale for correct answers (exact matches or close enough, as determined by your instructor) of word selections.

  0–10 = need help with basic song writing
11–20 = ready for simple ditties
21–25 = becoming highly capable in dealing with sentimentality
26–30 = ready for advanced country song writing

Appendix B   Taking Tests

Good test-taking begins with good study techniques. These techniques involve, among other things, how to read, think, and write effectively. Those skills have been covered in this book. Here we will discuss only a few principles that apply directly and immediately to the test situation.

At the beginning of the semester, you should discover how you will be tested in each course. Match your note-taking and underlining of texts to the kind or kinds of tests you will take. Objective tests will usually require somewhat more attention to details than will subjective, or essay, tests.

For both types of tests—and you will probably have a combination—you should carefully apportion your time, deciding how much to spend on each section or essay and allowing a few minutes for a quick review of answers. For both, you should also read the directions carefully, marking key words (if you are permitted to do so) as a reminder to you for concentration.

Objective Tests

Here are some tips on taking objective tests.

- Find out whether you will be graded on the basis of the number of correct answers or on the basis of right-minus-wrong answers. This is the difference: If you are graded on the basis of the number of correct answers, there is no penalty for guessing; therefore, if you want the highest possible score, you should leave no blanks. But if you are graded on the basis of right-minus-wrong (meaning one or a fraction of one is subtracted from your correct answers for every miss), then answer only if the odds of being right are in your favor. For example, if you know an answer is one of two possibilities, you have a 50 percent chance of getting it right; consequently, guess if the penalty is less than one because you could gain one by getting it right and lose less than one by getting it wrong. Ask your teacher to explain if there is a right-minus-wrong factor.
- If you are going to guess and you want to get some answers correct, you should pick one column and fill in the bubbles. By doing that, you will almost certainly get some correct.
- Studies show that in a typical four-part multiple-choice test section, more answers are B and C than A and D.
- Statements with absolutes such as *always* and *never* are likely to be false, whereas statements with qualifications such as *usually* and *probably* are likely to be true.
- If you don't know an answer, instead of fixating on it and getting frustrated, mark it with what seems right, put a dot alongside your answer, and go back later for a second look if time permits.
- When (and if) you go back to check your work, do not make changes unless you discover that you obviously marked one incorrectly. Studies have shown that first hunches are usually more accurate.

Subjective, or Essay, Tests

Here are some tips on taking subjective tests.

- Consider the text, the approach taken by the instructor in lectures, and the overall approach in the course outline and try to anticipate essay questions. Then, in your preparation, jot down and memorize simple outlines that will jog your memory during the test if you have anticipated correctly.
- Remember to keep track of time. A time-consuming A+ essay that does not allow you to finish the second half of the exam will result in a failing grade.
- Study the essay questions carefully. Underline key words. Each essay question will have two parts: the subject part and the treatment part. It may also have a limiting part. If you are required, for example, to compare and contrast President Jimmy Carter and President George H.W. Bush on their environmental programs, you should be able to analyze the topic immediately in this fashion:

    The *subject* is President Carter and President Bush.

    The *limitation* is their environmental programs.

    The *treatment* is comparison and contrast.

    Hence, you might mark the question in this fashion:

<u>Compare and contrast</u> the <u>environmental programs</u> of
treatment   limitation

<u>President Carter and President Bush</u>
subject

The treatment part (here "compare and contrast") may very well be one of the forms of discourse such as definition, classification, or analysis, or it may be something like "evaluate" or "discuss," in which a certain form or forms would be used. Regardless of what the treatment word is, the first step is to determine the natural points of division and to prepare a simple outline or outline alternative for organization.

- In writing the essay, be sure to include specific information as support for your generalizations.

Appendix C   Writing a Job-Application Letter and a Résumé

Two forms of practical writing that you may need even before you finish your college work are the job-application letter and the résumé. They will often go together as requirements by an employer. In some instances, the employer will suggest the form and content of the letter and résumé; in others, you will receive no directions and should adjust your letter and résumé to match the requirements and expectations as you perceive them. The models on pages 538 and 539 are typical of what job applicants commonly submit.

Job-Application Letter

The following basic guidelines will serve you well:

- Use standard letter-size paper and type.
- Do not apologize, and do not brag.
- Do not go into tedious detail, but do relate your education, work experience, and career goals to the available job.
- Begin your letter with a statement indicating why you are writing the letter and how you heard about the job opening.
- End the letter by stating how you can be contacted for an interview.

Résumé

Employers are especially concerned about your most recent work experiences and education, so include them first, as indicated in the example on page 539. The heading "College Activities" can be replaced with "Interests and Activities." Your main concern is presenting relevant information in a highly readable form. Always end with a list of references.

See the *Paragraphs and Essays* Website for additional examples and instructions for writing letters of application and résumés.

203 Village Center Avenue
Glendora, CA 91740
July 11, 2003

Mr. Roy Ritter
Computers Unlimited
1849 N. Granada Avenue
Walnut, CA 91789

Dear Mr. Ritter:

I am responding to your advertisement in the Los Angeles *Times* for the position of salesperson for used computers. Please consider me as a candidate.

In one more semester I will have completed my Associate in Arts degree at Mt. San Antonio College with a major in business management and a minor in computer technology.

My experience relates directly to the job you offer. As a result of my part-time work for two years as lab technician at my college, I have come to know the operations of several different computers. I have also learned to explain the operations to people who have very little knowledge of computers. In my business classes, I have studied the practical approaches to advertising and sales while also learning theory. Each semester for the past two years, I have worked in the college bookstore, where I helped customers who were buying various products, including computers.

This job would coincide perfectly with my work at school, my work experience, and even my goal of being a salesperson with a large company.

Enclosed is my résumé with several references to people who know me well. Please contact them if you want information or if you would like a written evaluation.

I am available for an interview at your request.

Sincerely yours,

Benjamin Johanson

Benjamin Johanson

Benjamin Johanson
203 Village Center Avenue
Glendora, CA 91740
(626) 987-5555

WORK EXPERIENCE
Lab Assistant in the Mt. San Antonio College Computer Lab   2001–03
Sales Clerk in the Mt. San Antonio College Bookstore   2001–03

EDUCATION
Full-time student at Mt. San Antonio College   2001–03
High school diploma from Glendora High School   2001

COLLEGE ACTIVITIES
Hackers' Club (2000–02)
Chess Club (2000–02)
Forensics Club (2001–03)—twice a regional debate champion

REFERENCES   Howard McGraw
Stewart Hamlen   Coach, Forensics Team
Chairperson, Business Department   Mt. San Antonio College
Mt. San Antonio College   Walnut, CA 91789
Walnut, CA 91789   (909) 594-5611, ext. 4575
(909) 594-5611, ext. 4707

Bart Grassmont
Human Resources Director, Bookstore
Mt. San Antonio College
Walnut, CA 91789
(909) 594-5611, ext. 4706

Answer Key

Chapter 3

Exercise 1

1. <u>Students who cheat in school</u> <u>may be trying to relieve certain emotional</u>
   _S _T

   <u>pressures.</u> (E)

2. <u>Shakespeare</u> <u>was an Elizabethan writer.</u> (I)
   _S _T

3. <u>The quarterback in football and the general of an army</u> <u>are alike in significant</u>
   _S _T

   <u>ways.</u> (E)

4. <u>Animals</u> <u>use color chiefly for protection.</u> (E)
   _S _T

5. <u>Portland</u> <u>is a city in Oregon.</u> (I)
   _S _T

6. <u>Life in the ocean</u> <u>has distinct realms.</u> (E)
   _S _T

7. <u>Rome</u> <u>has had a glorious and tragic history.</u> (I)
   _S _T

8. <u>Boston</u> <u>is the capital of Massachusetts.</u> (I)
   _S _T

9. <u>The word *macho*</u> <u>has a special meaning to the Hispanic community.</u> (E)
   _S _T

10. <u>The history of plastics</u> <u>is exciting.</u> (I)
    _S _T

Chapter 4

Exercise 2

Pain Unforgettable
James Hutchison

One evening in 1968 while I was working the swing shift at the General Tire Recapping Plant, I ~~came up with~~ experienced the greatest pain of my life because of a terrible accident. Raw rubber was heated up in a large tank. ~~Pryor~~ prior to its being fed into an
extruder. I was recapping large off-road tires. When The lowering platform was in the up

position the chain snapped/ ~~It sent~~ *sending* the heavy platform crashing down into the tank.

This caused a huge wave of steaming water to surge out of the tank. Unfortunately, I was in its path *T* the wave hit my back just above my waist. The sudden pain ~~shook~~ *took my* ~~me up.~~ *breath away.* I could not move. My clothes were steaming *and I could only stand there and scream.* ~~I freaked out.~~ Co-workers ran to my aid and striped *p* the hot clothing from my body, taking skin as they did. I lay face down on the plant floor, naked and shaking for ~~a long time.~~ *what seemed like eternity.* The paramedics *arrived to transport me to the hospital.* ~~came to pick me up.~~ The painful experence *i* is still ~~scary when I think about it~~ *with me as a nightmare memory.*

Handbook

Exercise 1

1. Joyce, watches
2. José, will order
3. Jack/Jill, should have been
4. you/I, will learn
5. point, is
6. Several, was stretching/warming
7. (You), knock
8. Jesse Ventura, was elected
9. he, will discover/become
10. we, can persuade
11. plenty, is
12. you, will crack
13. boxers, touched/returned
14. Snow White, had cleaned
15. Many, were injured
16. he, has wished
17. (You), bring
18. response, was
19. egg, floats
20. (You), write

Exercise 7

1. S	5. CP	9. CP	13. CP	17. CX
2. CP	6. S	10. CX	14. CX	18. CC
3. CC	7. CX	11. CP	15. S	19. CC
4. S	8. CX	12. CX	16. S	20. CP

Exercise 9

1. Although cobras are among the most feared of all snakes, they are not the deadliest of all snakes.

2. Cobras do not coil before they strike; therefore, they cannot strike for a long distance.

3. Cobras do not have a hood, but they flatten their neck by moving their ribs when they are nervous or frightened.

4. Cobras use their poison by injecting venom with their fangs and by spitting venom at their victims.

5. Although human beings will not die from the venom that has been spit, it can cause blindness if it is not washed from their eyes.

6. A person can die from a cobra bite, and death may come in only a few hours.

7. Snake charmers have long worked with cobras; they use only a snake, a basket, and a flute.

8. The snakes cannot hear the music, but they respond to the rhythmic movements of the charmers.

9. The snake charmers are hardly ever in danger of being bitten because they de-fang the cobras or sew their mouths shut.

10. Most cobras flee from people, but they attack if they are cornered or if they are guarding their eggs.

Exercise 13

1. OK
2. CS;   Catholicism; this
3. FRAG; He is also credited
4. OK
5. OK
6. RO;   them, and he
7. OK
8. FRAG; Henry wanted to divorce
9. FRAG; pope refused
10. FRAG; Anne was already

11. RO;   measures; he
12. CS;   enemies, and Henry
13. RO;   infidelity. She
14. CS;   Seymour, and they
15. OK
16. RO;   next, but she
17. OK
18. CS;   vivacious; in contrast, he
19. RO;   men, and in 1542
20. FRAG; Parr became

Exercise 19

1. had stayed
2. had paid
3. walked
4. had
5. could have gone
6. will have completed
7. are considering
8. had led
9. had built
10. will drive

Exercise 21

1. is
2. has
3. is
4. was
5. knows
6. believe
7. was
8. are
9. Is
10. Are
11. is
12. are
13. have
14. takes
15. were
16. has
17. is
18. are
19. is
20. are

Exercise 23

1. is
2. joined
3. are
4. went
5. have
6. decided
7. will get
8. is
9. is
10. is
11. sent
12. orders
13. gossips
14. dislikes
15. ran
16. was
17. took
18. would
19. pulls
20. were

Exercise 24

From	To		From	To
1. OK			7. condemn	condemned
2. OK			8. OK	
3. are	were		9. is	was
4. OK			10. OK	
5. utter	uttered		11. is	was
6. OK			12. OK	

From	To	From	To
13. holds	held	17. OK	
14. establish	established	18. name	named
15. OK		19. OK	
16. is	was	20. OK	

Exercise 26

1. I have written a letter to you.

2. His ancestors never made an honest dollar, and now he is following in their fingerprints.

3. The instructor approved the assignment.

4. The president of the student body gave the instructor a much-deserved medal of valor.

5. Few people noticed that the quiet students did most of the work.

Exercise 27

1. He wrote that essay.

2. She drove the speeding car.

3. He played the guitar.

4. They led the entire region in sales.

5. The medicine cured the cold.

Exercise 28

1. were

2. were

3. return

4. were

5. be

Exercise 29

1. he	5. me	9. us	13. he	17. whom
2. she	6. she	10. I	14. Whom	18. Whom
3. them	7. him	11. she	15. whom	19. I
4. them	8. We	12. they	16. Who	20. she

Exercise 31

1. he or she	5. she	9. herself	13. his	17. their
2. its	6. themselves	10. their	14. his or her	18. they
3. his or her	7. who	11. its	15. her	19. he or she
4. its	8. that	12. his	16. their	20. his or her

Exercise 33

	From	To
1.	Which	a decision that
2.	because she was	for being
3.	OK	
4.	you find	one finds
5.	told Barney that he . . . his	said to Barney, "You . . . your. . . ."
6.	OK	
7.	That . . . yesterday.	That is the husband of Rachel, whom you met yesterday
8.	OK	
9.	In that state, they don't	That state does not
10.	if she could wear her . . . dance	, "Can I wear your . . . dance?"
11.	her dinner	the dinner she had prepared
12.	that she was	, "I'm
13.	OK	
14.	OK	
15.	was able to get a discount, which pleased him	was pleased that he was able to get a discount
16.	This is what causes	These behaviors cause
17.	that	to buy and sell real estate
18.	you	he or she
19.	In this brochure, it	This brochure says
20.	OK	

Exercise 37

	From	To
1.	most unique	unique
2.	easier	more easily
3.	real	really
4.	too impossible	impossible
5.	badly	bad
6.	best	better
7.	most perfect	most nearly perfect
8.	violenter	more violent
9.	more beautiful	the most beautiful
10.	good	well
11.	only can mean	can mean only
12.	real	really
13.	easy	easily
14.	all ready	already
15.	alright	all right
16.	easiest	easier
17.	badly	bad
18.	real	really
19.	only she	she only
20.	all together	altogether

Exercise 39

1. D; Late again, I had no time
2. OK
3. M; perfumed, the dog was allowed to enter
4. M; guessed that the jar contained approximately 3,000
5. D; While I was filling
6. D; With grim determination, the climbers conquered the mountain.
7. M; Rudely interrupting, the child
8. M; student with a complaint made an appointment to see the teacher.
9. D; every day, one can avoid cavities.
10. D; row, we couldn't hear the speaker.
11. M; Yesterday, he asked her to marry him.
12. D; it, they spilled the popcorn all
13. D; As we were strolling
14. M; I have only one
15. D; healthy, one must give up smoking.
16. M; gold, the treasure hunters followed the map.
17. OK
18. M; I signed up for only one class.
19. M; tried slowly and persistently to worm
20. D; children, she has a high grocery bill.

Exercise 41

1. NP; and educator.
2. NP; also as a major figure
3. NP; to researching, protecting,
4. NP; an inventor, and
5. NP; and helping to start
6. NP; and allowed them
7. NP; also a floating laboratory
8. NP; He was not only a filmmaker
9. NP; and photographing Antarctica's
10. NP; and clad in a trademark
11. NP; in 1910 and died in
12. NP; and diving.
13. NP; but ended up
14. NP; honored with both France's
15. P
16. NP; Preserving the
17. NP; and of awakening
18. NP; but also celebrated in American
19. NP; and beliefs
20. P

Exercise 43

1. words, phrases,
2. strong,
3. modifiers,
4. clauses,
5. all,
6. Inside,
7. game,
8. pink, black, green,
9. night,
10. sharp,
11. banquet,
12. Handel, both born in 1685,
13. Motor racing, not horse racing,
14. boy," Arturo said,
15. Jones, the salesperson,
16. Well,
17. car, all sleek and shiny,
18. Tribbey, Oklahoma, on February 21, 1934.
19. down,
20. Tower, which is located in Paris,

Exercise 45

1. winter; for example,
2. fly; instead
3. exception, however;
4. it;
5. shorter; the temperatures grow colder;
6. brains;
7. San Angelo, Texas; Bracketville, Texas;
8. "flyways";
9. crowds; as a matter of fact,
10. bough; as a result,
11. November,
12. cycle;
13. South,
14. weeks;
15. latitudes,
16. eat,
17. toxins; therefore
18. camouflage,
19. life;
20. creature,

Exercise 47

1. <u>Odyssey</u>
2. "The poem . . . Ulysses."
3. it's famous
4. <u>Iliad</u>
5. War
6. Odysseus—if you can believe it—ten
7. obstacles: people
8. Odysseus'
9. Cyclops'
10. (the Cyclops' father)
11. Lestrigonians
12. Circe
13. twenty-two
14. Sirens—half women and half birds—enticed
15. men's
16. monsters: Scylla
17. six-headed
18. whirlpool?
19. "This is a great story!"
20. action-packed.

Exercise 49

George Washington at Trenton

One of ^the most famous battles during the War of Independence ~~occur~~ occurred at Trenton, New Jersey, on Christmas Eve of ~~the~~ 1776. The colonists ^were outmatched in supplies and finances and ~~were~~ outnumbered in troop strength. Most observers in other countries ~~think~~ thought the rebellion would be put down soon. The ^British overconfident and ^were ~~believe~~ believed there would be no more battles until spring. But George Washington ~~decide~~ decided to fight one more time. That Christmas, while ^a large army of Britishers ^were having ^a party and thinking about the holiday season, ^the Americans set out for ^a surprise raid. They loaded onto boats used for carrying ore and rowed across ^the Delaware River. George Washington stood tall in ^the lead boat. According to legend, ^the drummer boy floated across ^the river on his drum, pulled by ^a rope tied to ^a boat. Because ^the British did not feel threatened by the rag- tag colonist forces, they ^were unprepared to do battle. The colonists stormed ^the living quarters and the general assembly hall and achieved victory. It was good for the colonists'

morale, something they needed, for they would endure $\overset{a}{\underset{\wedge}{}}$ long, hard winter before

fighting again.

Appendix A

Exercise 1

1. adv, adj
2. v, prep
3. conj, pro
4. adj, n
5. n, adj
6. n, pro
7. adj, conj
8. adj, prep
9. pro, adv
10. adj, pro
11. prep, adv
12. v, conj
13. adj, conj
14. pro, n
15. prep, adj
16. conj, v
17. n, v
18. adv, adj
19. adv, adj
20. adv, adj

Text Credits

Author/Title Index

"Alley, The" (Tan), 135

Angell, Roger, "On the Ball," 126

Angelou, Maya, "Cotton-Picking Time," 104

"Assembly Line Adventure" (Hazelton), 111–114

"B. B. King Live!" (Lee), 108–109

"Babe Ruth" (Gallico), 126–127

Balleau, Michael
"A Summary of 'Total Institutions'," 16
"Total Institutions: A Summary and a Reaction," 17–18

Belinsky, Boris, "Doctors Have Their Symptoms, Too," 259

Benedict, Ruth, *Patterns of Culture*, 297

"Ben Franklin, Renaissance Man" (Udell), 185–186

"Birth of an Island, The" (Carson), 196

Blaylock, Richard, "More Than the Classroom," 230

Bradley, Karen, "A Moment in the Sun" 117–118

Bravo, Ellen, "Is It Sexual Harassment?" 311–314

Brehm, Sharon S., "How Low-Balling Works on Your Mind," 199–200

Britt, Suzanne, "Neat People vs. Sloppy People," 281–283

Brock, Will, "Zen and the Art of Pomegranate Eating," 197–198

Browning, Robert, "My Last Duchess," 339–341

Burciaga, José Antonio, "Tortillas," 307–308

"Burnout" (Moorhead, Griffin), 305

"Business Battle Tactics" (McGarvey), 274–275

Calhoun, Craig, "The Small Town and the Big City," 277–278

Campos, Maria, "A Divorce with Reasons," 87

Capp, Glenn R., "Listen Up!" 238

Carson, Rachel, "The Birth of an Island," 196

Cassedy, Ellen, "Is It Sexual Harassment?" 311–314

Catcher in the Rye, The (Salinger), 326

"Cheating Is Not Worth the Bother" (Olivas), 161–162

Chen, Annie, "Types of Hepatitis," 260–261

Chopin, Kate, "The Story of an Hour," 334–336

Chung, Michael, "Zoos—An Endangered Species?" 395–401

Clark, Ross, "Hefty Burger," 127–128

Cofer, Judith Ortiz, "More," 136–137

"Colorado Springs—Every Which Way" (Schlosser), 154–155

"Conserving Energy as You Ski" (Wingus), 87

"Cotton-Picking Time" (Angelou), 104

Cousins, Norman, "Who Killed Benny Paret?" 87

"Customers Are Like Canines" (Harris), 79–80

Del Ray, Lester, "The Mysterious Sky," 271

DeSarro, Angela, "My Life to Live—or Not," 370

"Different Ways of Being Smart, The" (Gilbert), 249–252

"Disneyland or Magic Mountain: Fantasy or Thrills" (Zayas), 288–289

"Divorce with Reasons, A" (Campos), 87

"Doctors Have Their Symptoms, Too" (Belinsky), 259

"Drag, The" (Kavanagh), 143

Durning, Alan Thein, "The Seven Sustainable Wonders of the World," 226–227

Eardley, A. J., "Glaciers: Types and Subtypes," 239

Edelman, Marian Wright, "Family Heroes and Role Models," 219

Edwards, Tamala M., "I Surrender, Dear," 362–364

"Effective E-Mail Practices" (Ober), 13

Emerson, Ralph Waldo, "Self-Reliance," 271

Engel, Leonard, "The Zones of the Sea," 171

"Fall of the House of Usher, The" (Poe), 325–326

"Family and Its Parts, The" (Robertson), 170–171

"Family Heroes and Role Models" (Edelman), 219

"Fast, Sleek, and Shiny: Using the Internet to Help Buy New Cars" (Gralla), 201–203

Fein, Steven, "How Low-Balling Works on Your Mind," 199–200

Feshbach, Seymour
"Pity, Anger, and Achievement Performance," 73–74

"Primitive Methods of Lie Detection," 74

"Total Institutions," 11–12

"Fighting, Founding Mothers, The" (Johnson), 75

Finley, Craig, "The Mousetrap," 134, 135

"Forever Elvis" (Miller), 84

Fox, Michael W., "What Is Your Pet Trying to Tell You?" 60–61

"Frankie and Johnny" (anonymous), 337–338

"From Survival to Living" (Sewell), 118–120

Gallagher, Joyce, "The Messy Are in Denial," 284–285

Gallico, Paul, "Babe Ruth," 126–127

"Georgia on My Mind" (Jenkins), 306

Geraci, Ron, "Which Stooge Are You?" 245–248

"Get a Knife, Get a Dog, But Get Rid of Guns" (Ivins), 360–361

"Get Them Off the Road" (Humphries), 88

"Getting High and Living Low" (Ramos), 230–231

Gilbert, Sara, "The Different Ways of Being Smart," 249–252

"Girls in Their Summer Dresses, The" (Shaw), 330–333

"Glaciers: Types and Subtypes" (Eardley), 239

"Going Too Far" (Wong), 317

Goodman, Ellen, "A Working Community," 308–310

"Graffiti: Taking a Closer Look" (Grant), 365–368

Gralla, Preston, "Fast, Sleek, and Shiny: Using the Internet to Help Buy New Cars," 201–203

Grant, Christopher, "Graffiti: Taking a Closer Look," 365–368

Greenlee, Gina, "No Tears for Frankie," 109–110

Griffin, Ricky W.
"Burnout," 305
"Working in a Chicken-Processing Plant," 155–156

"Growing Up Asian in America" (Noda), 177–182

Hamlet (Shakespeare), 491

Harris, Vera, "Customers Are Like Canines," 79–80

Hazelton, Lesley, "Assembly Line Adventure," 111–114

"Hefty Burger" (Clark), 127–128

Hogarty, Donna Brown, "How to Deal with a Difficult Boss," 253–257

"How Do I Love Thee?" (Trotter), 328–329

"How Low-Balling Works on Your Mind" (Brehm, Kassin, Fein), 199–200

"How to Deal with a Difficult Boss" (Hogarty), 253–257

Hoyer, Wayne D., "Novelty Sells," 153

Hughes, Robert J., "Styles of Leadership," 242–243

Humphries, Daniel, "Get Them Off the Road," 88

Hutchison, James, "Pain Unforgettable," 68

"If I Were a Traffic Cop" (Jackson), 67

"Institutions Always Win" (Morris), 16–17

"In the Land of 'Coke-Cola'" (Least Heat-Moon), 138–140

"Is It Sexual Harassment?" (Bravo, Cassedy), 311–314

"I Surrender, Dear" (Edwards), 362–364

Ivins, Molly, "Get a Knife, Get a Dog, But Get Rid of Guns," 360–361

Jackson, Betsy, "If I Were a Traffic Cop," 67

Jackson, Shirley, "The Lottery," 326

Jenkins, Ray, "Georgia on My Mind," 306

Johnson, Maxine, "The Fighting, Founding Mothers," 75

Kapoor, Jack R., "Styles of Leadership," 242–243

Kassin, Saul M., "How Low-Balling Works on Your Mind," 199–200

Kavanagh, Mike, "The Drag," 143

Keller, Helen
    The Story of My Life, 103
    "W-A-T-E-R," 107–108

Kong, Deborah, "Spanglish Creeps into Mainstream," 157–159

Leah, "Razor Wire Sweat Lodge," 95

Least Heat-Moon, William, "In the Land of 'Coke-Cola'," 138–140

"Leaving Los Angeles" (Maxwell), 87–88

Lee, Andrea, "B. B. King Live!," 108–109

"Listen Up!" (Capp), 238

Little Soldier, Lee, "Native American Core Values and Cooperative Learning," 23–24

"Living in Sin" (Yochim), 221–225

Lopez, Jerry, "Types of Nightclubbers," 74–75

"Los Chinos Discover el Barrio" (Torres), 104, 278–280

"Lottery, The" (Jackson), 326

"Low Wages, High Skills" (Newman), 172–176

Lurie, Alison, "Pink Kittens and Blue Spaceships," 276–277

MacInnis, Deborah J., "Novelty Sells," 153

Malone, Jackie, "Sexist Men as Victims," 20

Markovic, Brittany, "The Piper Cherokee and the Cessna 172," 289–290

Maxwell, Brian, "Leaving Los Angeles," 87–88

McGarvey, Robert, "Business Battle Tactics," 274–275

McLain, Doretta, "Quitting School," 68–69

Mendez, Gloria, "The Use of Self-Analysis," 346–347

"Messy Are in Denial, The" (Gallagher), 284–285

Miller, Jim, "Forever Elvis," 84

"Moment in the Sun, A" (Bradley), 117–118

Mondegaran, Maysim, "Sabzi Polo Mahi," 206

Moorhead, Gregory
    "Burnout," 305
    "Working in a Chicken-Processing Plant," 155–156

"More" (Cofer), 136–137

"More Than Just a House Call" (Mylonas), 345–346

"More Than the Classroom" (Blaylock), 230

Morris, Tanya, "Institutions Always Win," 16–17

"Mousetrap, The" (Finley), 134, 135

"My Aircraft Carrier 'Bedroom'" (Werner), 144–145

"My Last Duchess" (Browning), 339–341

"My Life to Live—or Not" (DeSarro), 370

Mylonas, Ajax, "More Than Just a House Call," 345–346

"Mysterious Sky, The" (Del Ray), 271

"Native American Core Values and Cooperative Learning" (Little Soldier), 23–24

"Neat People vs. Sloppy People" (Britt), 281–283

Newman, Katherine S., "Low Wages, High Skills," 172–176

"Nobles, Peasants, and Clergy" (Wallbank), 244

Noda, Kesaya E., "Growing Up Asian in America," 177–182

"No Tears for Frankie" (Greenlee), 109–110

"Novelty Sells" (Hoyer, MacInnis), 153

Ober, Scot, "Effective E-Mail Practices," 13

Olivas, Lara, "Cheating Is Not Worth the Bother," 161–162

"On the Ball" (Angell), 126

"On Various Kinds of Thinking" (Robinson), 297

"Pain Unforgettable" (Hutchison), 68

Patterns of Culture (Benedict), 297

"Pink Kittens and Blue Spaceships" (Lurie), 276–277

"Piper Cherokee and the Cessna 172, The" (Markovic), 289–290

"Pity, Anger, and Achievement Performance" (Feshbach, Weiner), 73–74

Poe, Edgar Allan, "The Fall of the House of Usher," 325–326

Pride, William M., "Styles of Leadership," 242–243

"Primitive Methods of Lie Detection" (Feshbach, Weiner), 74

"Prison Slang" (Rubec), 318–319

"Purpose of Shopping, The" (Rose), 220

"Quitting School" (McLain), 68–69

Ramos, Sergio, "Getting High and Living Low," 230–231

"Razor Wire Sweat Lodge" (Leah), 95

Robertson, Ian, "The Family and Its Parts," 170–171

Robinson, James Harvey, "On Various Kinds of Thinking," 297

Rose, Phyllis, "The Purpose of Shopping," 220

Rubec, Louise, "Prison Slang," 318–319

"Sabzi Polo Mahi" (Mondegaran), 206

Salinger, J. D., *The Catcher in the Rye*, 326

Schlosser, Eric, "Colorado Springs—Every Which Way," 154–155

"Secret Life of Walter Mitty, The" (Thurber), 496

"Self-Reliance" (Emerson), 271

Sergio, Tina, "Teaching Our Kids to Shoot 'Em Up," 371–372

"Seven Sustainable Wonders of the World, The" (Durning), 226–227

Sewell, Jeanne, "From Survival to Living," 118–120

"Sexist Men as Victims" (Malone), 20

Shakespeare, William, *Hamlet*, 491

Shaw, Irwin, "The Girls in Their Summer Dresses," 330–333

Simon, Selin, "Skin," 184

"Skin" (Simon), 184

"Small Town and the Big City, The" (Calhoun), 277–278

"Spanglish Creeps into Mainstream" (Kong), 157–159

"Story of an Hour, The" (Chopin), 334–336

Story of My Life, The (Keller), 103

"Struggle to Be an All-American Girl, The" (Wong), 20–22, 105

"Styles of Leadership" (Pride, Hughes, Kapoor), 242–243

"Summary of 'Total Institutions', A" (Balleau), 16

Tan, Amy, "The Alley," 135

"Teaching Our Kids to Shoot 'Em Up" (Sergio), 371–372

Thurber, James, "The Secret Life of Walter Mitty," 496

Torres, Luis, "Los Chinos Discover el Barrio," 104, 278–280

"Tortillas" (Burciaga), 307–308

"Total Institutions" (Feshbach, Weiner), 11–12

"Total Institutions: A Summary and a Reaction" (Balleau), 17–18

Toufexis, Anastasia, "What Happens to Steroid Studs?" 218

"Traveling the World at Home" (Yegavian), 162–163

Trotter, Robert J., "How Do I Love Thee?" 328–329
"Types of Hepatitis" (Chen), 260–261
"Types of Nightclubbers" (Lopez), 74–75

Udell, Allison, "Ben Franklin, Renaissance Man," 185–186
"Use of Force, The" (Williams), 343
"Use of Self-Analysis, The" (Mendez), 346–347

"W-A-T-E-R" (Keller), 107–108
Wallbank, T. Walter, "Nobles, Peasants, and Clergy," 244
Weiner, Bernard
    "Pity, Anger, and Achievement Performance," 73–74
    "Primitive Methods of Lie Detection," 74
    "Total Institutions," 11–12

Werner, Chanya
    "My Aircraft Carrier 'Bedroom'," 144–145
    "What's Behind a Brilliant Smile," 207–208
"What Happens to Steroid Studs?" (Toufexis), 218
"What Is Your Pet Trying to Tell You?" (Fox), 60–61
"What's Behind a Brilliant Smile" (Werner), 207–208
"Which Stooge Are You?" (Geraci), 245–248
"Who Killed Benny Paret?" (Cousins), 87
Williams, William Carlos, "The Use of Force," 343
Wingus, Carl, "Conserving Energy as You Ski," 87

Wong, Elizabeth, "The Struggle to Be an All-American Girl," 20–22, 105
Wong, Linda, "Going Too Far," 317
"Working Community, A" (Goodman), 308–310
"Working in a Chicken-Processing Plant" (Moorhead, Griffin), 155–156

Yegavian, Garabed, "Traveling the World at Home," 162–163
Yochim, Dayana, "Living in Sin," 221–225

Zayas, Omar, "Disneyland or Magic Mountain: Fantasy or Thrills," 288–289
"Zen and the Art of Pomegranate Eating" (Brock), 197–198
"Zones of the Sea, The" (Engel), 171
"Zoos—An Endangered Species?" (Chung), 395-401

Subject Index

a, an, and, 517
abbreviations
  capitalization of, 511
  punctuation for, 496, 498, 499
abstract words, 128
accept, except, 517
accidently, accidentally, 486
action verbs, 408, 527
active learning, 3
  and analytical reading, 10–12
active voice, 463–464
adjectives
  articles as, 528
  comma usage with, 498
  common problems with, 485–486
  comparative and superlative forms of,
    483–484
  confused with adverbs, 485
  coordinate, 498
  defined, 481, 527–528
  hyphenating, 510
  irregular, 484
  pronouns as, 528
  proper nouns as, 510, 511
  selecting, 481–482
  See also modifiers
adverbs
  common problems with, 485–486
  comparative and superlative forms of,
    484–485
  confused with adjectives, 485
  confused with prepositions, 529
  defined, 481, 528–529
  irregular, 484–485
  selecting, 481–482
  sentences beginning with, 433
  See also conjunctive adverbs;
    modifiers
advice, advise, 517
affect, effect, 518
afterthought, concluding with, 88
agreement
  pronoun-antecedent, 472–476
  subject-verb, 453–458
all ready, already, 486, 517
all right, alright, 486, 517
all together, altogether, 486, 517
a lot, alot, 517
Alta Vista, 383
alternative subjects
  agreement with verb, 457
  and pronoun-antecedent agreement,
    474

analogy
  as comparison, 271
  false, 355
analysis by division, 168–169
  defined, 150
  for definition, 301
  guidelines for writing, 188–189
  organization for, 48, 168
  procedure for writing, 168, 188–189
  professional writings, 170–182
  roman numeral headings in, 169
  sequence of parts in, 168–169
  student writings, 182–186
  topics for writing, 186–188
analytical approach, to literary analysis,
    347–348
analytical definitions, 297, 322
anecdote, concluding with, 87–88
angry tone, 57
annotating
  after freewriting, 33
  for effective reading, 11–12, 25
  for gathering information, 38
antagonist, 326
antecedent
  agreement with pronoun, 472–476
  clear references to, 478
  defined, 55
anthologies
  documenting, 384, 385
  parenthetical references to, 392
apostrophes, 509–510
appositive phrases
  for combining sentences, 427
  as fragments, 436
  punctuation for, 508
argument, 353–356
  considering audience in, 354
  defined, 353
  guidelines for writing, 376
  kinds of evidence in, 354–355
  and logical fallacies, 355–356
  organization for, 353–354, 376
  professional writings, 360–368
  student writings, 369–372
  techniques for developing, 353–354
  topics for writing, 373–375
argumentum ad hominem, 356
articles. *See* periodicals
articles (parts of speech), 528
  definite and indefinite, 521–522
  as noun determiners, 521, 526
  in relation to nouns, 521–522

assignments
  recording details about, 5, 30–31, 64
  types of, 31–32
audience
  for writing argument, 354
  writing for, 31, 56, 57
authoritative sources, in argument, 354–355
author tags, in summaries, 15

background
  in argument, 353, 354, 376
  in introductory paragraph, 85
  in narratives, 102
  in process analysis, 191
bad, badly, 485
begging the question, 356
being verbs, 408, 465, 527
bibliography
  preliminary, 383
  for research paper, 381
  See also documentation of sources
big six questions, 34, 38, 65, 77, 90
block quotations, 393
books
  documenting, 383–384, 387
  library search for, 381–382
  parenthetical references to, 392
brackets, 509
brainstorming, 34–35, 38
  big six questions, 34
  for comparison and contrast, 267
  examples of, 65, 77, 90
  for exemplification, 166
  listing, 34–35
  See also listing

capitalization
  in editing process, 63
  general rules for, 510–512
  self-evaluation of, 4
career-related topics
  for analysis by division, 188
  for argument, 375
  for cause and effect analysis, 234
  for classification, 263
  for comparison and contrast, 293
  for definition, 321
  for description, 148
  for exemplification, 165–166
  gathering ideas for, 18
  for literary analysis, 350
  for narratives, 123
  for process analysis, 210

careers
  job-application letter for, 537, 538
  résumé writing for, 537, 539
case studies, 102
cause and effect analysis, 213–216
  for argument, 354
  composing topic sentence/thesis for, 213–214
  defined, 150, 213
  for definition, 301
  guidelines for writing, 234–235
  immediate and remote, 214–215
  introducing subject in, 215–216
  organizing ideas in, 47
  outline for, 214
  patterns for, 216
  prewriting strategies for, 213
  primary and secondary, 214
  professional writings, 218–227
  sequence and order in, 215
  student writings, 228–231
  topics for writing, 232–234
CD-ROMs, documenting, 388–389
characters, in literature, 326, 347
choose, chose, 517–518
chronological order. *See* time organizational pattern
circular definitions, 300, 322
circular reasoning, 356
classification, 237–239
  avoiding overlapping in, 237, 264
  controlling principle in, 237
  defined, 150, 237
  for definition, 301
  diction for, 237, 264
  establishing classes for, 237–238
  guidelines for writing, 263–264
  outlines for, 241, 264
  professional writings, 242–257
  selecting subject for, 237
  simple and complex forms of, 238–239
  student writings, 257–261
  topics for writing, 261–263
clauses, 413–414
  defined, 413, 530
  dependent, 413
  incompletely stated, 468
  independent, 413
  modifying, and subject-verb agreement, 456
  vs. phrases, 414
  relative, 413–414
  See also specific clauses
clichés, avoiding, 58
climax, in literature, 326
CLUESS acronym, 54. *See also* revision process
clustering
  for analysis by division, 183
  for classification, 258
  defined, 36, 38
  for definition, 301, 302, 316, 322
  for description, 142
  examples of, 65, 78, 91
  for exemplification, 151
  for literary analysis, 344

for organizing support, 44, 45, 51
for process analysis, 204
coherence
  and overall pattern, 55
  and point of view, 56
  and pronouns, 55
  repetition of key words for, 55
  in revision process, 54–56, 70
  transitional terms for, 55, 192, 211, 269
collective nouns
  agreement with verb, 457
  and pronoun-antecedent agreement, 475
colons, 342
  common usage for, 508
  with parentheses, 509
  with quotation marks, 506
combination words, for parallel structure, 492–493
command sentences, 436
commas, 497–499
  with coordinating conjunctions, 415, 423, 497
  with dependent clauses, 417, 426, 435, 530
  for introductory clauses, 435, 497
  for nonessential elements, 498
  with parentheses, 509
  with quotation marks, 506
  to separate, 497–498
  to set off, 498–499
  with subordinating conjunctions, 426
comma splices, 63, 437–438
comparative modifiers, 483–485
comparison and contrast, 266–272
  analogy as, 271
  for argument, 354
  defined, 150, 266
  for definition, 301
  generating topics for, 266
  guidelines for writing, 294–295
  patterns for organizing, 268–269, 271–272
  points in, 267–268
  presentation of, 269–271
  prewriting strategies for, 267
  professional writings, 274–285
  purpose in, 266–267
  student writings, 286–290
  topics for writing, 291–293
complaint, concluding with, 88
complex classification, 238–239
complex sentences, 62, 414, 417
  punctuation for, 417, 426
  relative clauses in, 426
  subordinating conjunctions in, 425–426
  for subordination of ideas, 424–426
compound-complex sentences, 62, 414, 418
  coordination and subordination in, 426–427
  punctuation for, 427
compound sentences, 62, 414, 415
  conjunctive adverbs in, 423–424
  coordinating conjunctions in, 415, 422–423
  for coordination of ideas, 422–424
  punctuation for, 415, 423–424

compound subjects, 407
  agreement with verb, 457
  and pronoun-antecedent agreement, 474
  and pronoun case, 469
compound verbs, 409
compound words, hyphenating, 510
computers
  advantages of, 5
  grammar checkers, 63, 439
  spell checkers, 63, 519
  thesaurus on, 56
  See also electronic sources
concentration, techniques for developing, 10–12
concluding paragraphs
  defined, 72, 83, 96
  ineffective, 88
  types of, 87–88
concluding sentence, 73
concrete particulars, 128
concrete words, 128
conference proceedings, documenting, 385
conflict
  in literature, 326, 347
  in narratives, 102, 123
conjunctions
  confused with prepositions, 530
  defined, 530
  See also coordinating conjunctions; subordinating conjunctions
conjunctive adverbs
  for comma splices and run-ons, 438
  in compound sentences, 423–424
  list of common, 423, 424, 438
  punctuation with, 424, 498, 499, 502
  sentences beginning with, 62, 433
content, self-evaluation of, 4
contractions, 509–510
contrast. *See* comparison and contrast
controlling idea
  in classification, 237
  defining, 40
  generating with prewriting strategies, 43
  guidelines for writing, 50–51
  in outlines, 46–47
  placement of, 53
  revising, 44
  as thesis or topic sentence, 40–44
  and unity, 58–59
  See also thesis; topic sentence
conversation, as acceptable fragment, 435. *See also* dialogue
coordinating conjunctions
  for comma splices and run-ons, 437
  in compound sentences, 415, 422–423
  confused with prepositions, 530
  defined, 530
  list of common, 415, 422–423
  and parallel structure, 492
  punctuation with, 415, 423, 497, 502
  sentences beginning with, 433
coordination, for combining sentences, 422–424, 426–427
COPS acronym, 63. *See also* editing
Correction Chart, 3

correspondence
    point of view in, 472
    punctuation for, 499, 508
could of, could have, could've, 518
cross-curricular topics
    for analysis by division, 188
    for argument, 375
    for cause and effect analysis, 234
    for classification, 263
    for comparison and contrast, 293
    for definition, 321
    for description, 147–148
    for exemplification, 165
    for narratives, 123
    for process analysis, 210

dangling modifiers, 488–489
dashes, 506, 507
dates, punctuation for, 499
definitions
    circular, 300, 322
    common problems with, 300
    defined, 150, 297
    dictionary, 298–299
    extended, 297, 300–302
    guidelines for writing, 322–323
    introduction and development of, 301
    in introductory paragraph, 86
    "is where" and "is when," 300, 322
    order for, 301
    prewriting strategies for, 301, 302
    professional writings, 305–314
    simple, 297–300
    student writings, 315–319
    topics for writing, 319–321
    using different patterns for, 300–301, 302, 303
dependent clauses
    commas with, 417, 426, 435, 530
    in complex sentences, 417, 426
    in compound-complex sentences, 418
    defined, 413, 530
    as fragments, 62, 434, 435
    introductory, 435, 497
    sentences beginning with, 62, 433
description, 126–130
    defined, 126
    for definition, 300
    dominant impression in, 127–128, 129
    guidelines for writing, 148
    in narratives, 104
    objective, 126
    order in, 129
    point of view in, 129
    professional writings, 134–140
    student writings, 141–145
    subjective, 126–127, 128
    techniques for writing, 127–130
    topics for writing, 146–148
    word choice in, 128–129
detached perspective, 103, 129, 327
details
    in description, 129
    in narratives, 104, 123, 124
development
    for definitions, 301
    in literary analysis, 342

self-evaluation of, 4
    See also support
developmental paragraphs
    basic patterns for, 72–74, 80
    defined, 72, 80, 83
    in essays, 83, 85
    See also paragraphs
dialogue
    as acceptable fragment, 435
    in narratives, 104–105, 123
    quotation marks for, 506
diction
    abstract vs. concrete words, 128
    avoiding clichés, 58
    in descriptive writing, 128–129
    general vs. specific words, 58, 128
    idioms, 523
    impact of modifiers on, 481–482
    importance of, 57–58
    self-evaluation of, 4
    and tone, 57
    See also language
dictionary definitions, 297, 298–299
directive process analysis, 191, 192, 193, 211
direct references. *See* references
discussion lists (electronic), documenting, 388
documentation of sources, 10, 26
    for avoiding plagiarism, 390–391
    basic guidelines for, 19–20
    for career-related writing, 18
    for electronic sources, 383, 386–389, 393
    example of, 20, 400–401
    MLA style for, 383–389, 391–393
    parenthetical references, 391–393
    preliminary bibliography, 383
    for printed sources, 384–385, 392–393
    for quotations and references, 18–19, 391–393
    for research paper, 380
    for unknown authorship, 392–393
    works cited list, 383
dominant impression, 127–128, 129
double negatives, 485

-e, silent, spelling rules for, 515–516
EBSCOhost, 386
editing, 54, 63, 70, 79
ei words, spelling, 515
Elbow, Peter, 31
electronic sources
    documenting, 386–389, 393
    parenthetical references to, 393
    searching, 381–383
ellipsis, 496
e-mail messages, documenting, 389
emotional description, 126
emphasis
    and placement of ideas, 59
    punctuation for, 508
    and repetition of key words and ideas, 59–60
    in revision process, 59–60, 70
emphasis organizational pattern
    in analysis by division, 169
    in cause and effect analysis, 215

for coherence, 55
    in comparison and contrast, 268
    in definition, 301, 322
    in description, 129
    in exemplification, 152
    words indicating, 55
encyclopedias, documenting, 385, 389
end punctuation, 496–497
English as second language (ESL) skills, 521–523
    articles in relation to nouns, 521–522
    idioms, 523
    other suggestions, 523
    sentence patterns, 522
    verb tenses, 522–523
essays
    applying writing process to, 88–96
    compared with paragraphs, 83–85
    concluding paragraphs in, 87–88
    defined, 83
    guidelines for writing, 96–97
    introductory paragraphs in, 85–86
    main parts of, 83
    patterns for, 84
essay tests, 536–537
etymology, 297
evidence, in argument, 354–355
examples
    in argument, 354
    in definitions, 300
    types of, 150
    See also exemplification
exclamation points, 497, 506, 509, 531
exclamations, as acceptable fragment, 434
exemplification, 150–152
    characteristics of good, 150
    defined, 150
    for definition, 300
    guidelines for writing, 166
    number and order in, 152
    organizing ideas in, 47
    prewriting strategies for, 151
    professional writings, 153–159
    student writings, 159–163
    topics for writing, 164–166
explanations
    direct and indirect, 297, 322
    parentheses for, 508
    supporting ideas with, 18, 26
exposition
    defined, 150
    in literature, 326
    types of, 150
extended definitions, 297, 300–302, 322–323

facts, in argument, 354
false analogy, 355
false dilemma, 355
FANBOYS acronym, 415, 422–423, 437, 530. *See also* coordinating conjunctions
Faulkner, William, 3
fictional point, 326
field-trip reports, 102
figures of speech, in descriptive writing, 127–128
filler words, 408, 456

films, documenting, 385
first draft
    examples of, 66–67, 79, 93–94, 344–345
    guidelines for writing, 53–54, 69–70
    for research paper, 390–393
first person perspective, 56, 472–473
    in description, 129
    in literature, 326–327
    in narratives, 103
    See also point of view
foreign words, italics for, 507
formal definitions, 297, 322
fragments, 62–63, 434–436
    acceptable, 434–435
    dependent clauses as, 435
    missing subject or verb, 436
    phrases as, 435–436
freewriting
    for comparison and contrast, 267, 287
    defined, 31–33, 37–38
    examples of, 64, 77, 89–90

gathering information, 37, 38
gender agreement, 472, 475–476
general words, 58, 128, 482
gerunds, 409, 414
good, well, 485
Google, 383
gopher, documenting, 388
government publications
    documenting, 385
    searching for, 383
grammar
    self-evaluation of, 4
    and standard usage, 56
grammar checkers, 5, 63, 439
greetings, as acceptable fragment, 435

hasty generalization, 355
hear, here, 518
helping verbs, 408, 445, 447, 527
here, there, 408, 456
historical events
    point of view in, 56, 103, 129, 460–461
    verb tense for, 103
HOTSHOT acronym, 424, 438, 502. *See also* conjunctive adverbs
humorous tone, 57
hyphens, 510

idioms, 523
ie words, spelling, 515
imagery
    in descriptive writing, 127–128
    in narratives, 104, 123
immediate cause and effect, 214–215
imperative mood, 466
imperative sentences, 407, 436
implied subject, 407
indefinite pronouns, 406
    agreement with antecedent, 474, 475–476
    agreement with verb, 456
    defined, 526
    possessive form of, 509
independent clauses
    as comma splices and run-ons, 437–438
    in complex sentences, 417

in compound-complex sentences, 418
in compound sentences, 415, 502
defined, 62, 413, 530
in simple sentences, 414
indicative mood, 466
infinitives, 409, 414, 488
informative process analysis, 191, 192, 193, 211
informative purpose, 213, 266
InfoTrac, 382
interjections
    as acceptable fragment, 434
    defined, 531
    punctuation for, 498
Internet, 5
    documenting sources from, 386–389, 393
    finding sources on, 381, 383
    for gathering information, 37
interviews, documenting, 385
introductory paragraphs
    defined, 72, 83, 96
    length of, 86
    methods used in, 85–86
inversions, and subject-verb agreement, 456
involved perspective, 103, 129
irregular verbs, 444, 446–448
italics, 507
it's, its, 518

job-application letter, 537, 538
Johnson, Samuel, 3
journal writing
    as reading-related writing, 18
    for self-improvement, 3

key words and ideas
    emphasizing, 59–60
    repetition of, 55, 59, 216, 235
    underlining, 10
know, no, 518

language, 56–58, 70
    diction, 57–58
    tone, 56–57
    usage, 56, 444
    wordy vs. concise, 519–520
    See also diction
lead, led, 518
lectures, documenting, 385
letters. *See* correspondence
letters (alphabet)
    italics for, 507
    plural form of, 510
LexisNexis, 383, 386
library sources
    books, 381–382
    computerized indexes, 382–383
    periodicals, 381, 382–383
    printout forms for, 383–384
    subscription services, 386
lie, lay, 449
listing
    for argument, 369
    in brainstorming, 34–35, 38
    for cause and effect analysis, 213, 229, 234
    for comparison and contrast, 267, 287

examples of, 77, 90
for exemplification, 151, 160
for narratives, 116
for organizing support, 44, 45, 51
for process analysis, 193, 205, 211
lists, punctuation for, 507, 508
literary analysis
    analytical approach to, 347–348
    defined, 150, 327
    development in, 342
    and elements of literature, 325–327
    guidelines for writing, 350–351
    quotations in, 342
    speculative approach to, 348
    student writings, 342–347
    topics for writing, 348–350
    verb tense in, 342
literature
    characters in, 326, 347
    conflict in, 326, 347
    importance of, 325
    interpreting, 325
    plot in, 326, 347–348
    point of view in, 129, 326–327, 348, 460
    professional writings, 327–341
    setting in, 325–326, 347
    theme in, 326, 348
    verb tense for, 103
    writing about, 325–327
logical fallacies, 215, 355–356
loose, lose, 518

magazines
    documenting, 384–385, 386–387, 388
    library search for, 382, 386
main ideas
    in summaries, 15
    underlining, 10
    See also controlling idea
major support, in outlines, 46, 51. *See also* support
meaning, in narratives, 103, 123
metaphors, in descriptive writing, 128
minor support, in outlines, 46, 51. *See also* support
misplaced modifiers, 488–489
MLA (Modern Language Association) style, 19, 380, 383–389
    for electronic sources, 386–389
    for parenthetical references, 391–393
    for printed sources, 383–385
modifiers
    comparative and superlative forms of, 483–485
    dangling and misplaced, 488–489
    defined, 481
    and subject-verb agreement, 456
    See also adjectives; adverbs
mood, of verb, 466

names and titles, capitalization of, 511, 512
narrative literature. *See* literature
narrative poems, 325. *See also* literature
narratives, 102–105
    defined, 102
    for definition, 300
    description in, 104

dialogue in, 104–105
guidelines for writing, 123–124
organizing ideas in, 47
point of view in, 103
professional writings, 107–114
properties of, 102–103
student writings, 115–120
topics for writing, 121–123
verb tense in, 103
never, not, hardly, 408–409
Newspaper Abstracts Ondisc, 382
newspapers
documenting, 385, 386–387, 388
library search for, 382, 386
nonessential elements, punctuating, 498, 508
non sequitur, 356
note taking
for gathering information, 37
for research paper, 389
for taking tests, 535
noun indicators, 521, 526, 528
noun phrases, 427
nouns
articles in relation to, 521–522
collective, 457, 475
count and noncount, 521–522
defined, 406, 526
direct address, 499
plural, and verb agreement, 458
possessive form of, 509
See also proper nouns
number agreement
consistency in, 56
pronoun-antecedent, 472, 474–475
subject-verb, 453–458
and verb omissions, 431
numbers
hyphens with spelled-out, 510
italics for, 507
parentheses for, 508
plural form of, 510
punctuation with, 499
verb agreement with, 457–458

objective-case pronouns, 468–469
objective description, 126, 147
objective tests, 535, 536
objective tone, 57
observations, 102
omissions
apostrophes for indicating, 509
in editing process, 63
ellipsis for indicating, 496
and sentence clarity, 431
opinion column, 353
opinions
in argument, 354
in summaries, 15
order
in analysis by division, 168–169
in cause and effect analysis, 215, 235
and coherence, 55
in comparison and contrast, 268
for definition, 301, 322
in description, 129
in exemplification, 152
in process analysis, 192, 211

organization
for analysis by division, 168
for argument, 353–354, 376
common patterns for, 47–48
for comparison and contrast, 268–269, 294
for definitions, 300–301, 302, 303
for literary analysis, 350
self-evaluation of, 4
of supporting material, 44–48, 51
outcome, in narratives, 102, 123
outlines
for analysis by division, 168, 184, 189
for argument, 370
for cause and effect analysis, 214, 229, 235
for classification, 241, 259, 264
for comparison and contrast, 268–269, 288
for definition, 317
for description, 142
for developmental paragraph, 81
for effective reading, 12, 25
examples of, 65–66, 78, 92
for exemplification, 161
for gathering information, 37
for literary analysis, 344
for narratives, 117
for organizing support, 44, 45–48, 51
for process analysis, 205
for research paper, 380, 381, 390, 394, 396–397
for test taking, 536, 537
types of, 46
writing first draft from, 53–54
overbearing tone, 57

paid, payed, 518
paired conjunctions, 530
paragraphs
applying writing process to, 75–80
basic patterns for, 72–74
compared with essays, 83–85
defined, 72, 83
guidelines for writing, 80–81
introductory, 85–86
structure of model, 61
types of, 72
paragraph unit, 73
parallelism, 491–493
signal words for, 492–493
paraphrasing
and avoiding plagiarism, 390–391
documentation of, 19
parentheses, 508–509
parenthetical elements, punctuation for, 498–499
parenthetical references, 391–393
participial phrases, 414
for combining sentences, 428
participles, 409
parts, in analysis by division, 168–169
parts of speech, 526–531. *See also specific parts of speech*
passed, past, 518
passive voice, 463–464
past participles

of irregular verbs, 447–448
of regular verbs, 445–446
past tense
for historical events/personal experience, 103, 460–461
of irregular verbs, 447
of regular verbs, 445
patience, patients, 518
peace, piece, 518
perfect progressive verb tenses, 452, 455
perfect verb tenses, 452, 454
Periodical Abstracts, 382
periodicals
documenting, 384–385, 386, 387–388
library search for, 381, 382–383, 386
parenthetical references to, 392
periods, 496, 506, 509
person, agreement in, 472–474
personalized account
in cause and effect analysis, 214
for definition, 301, 323
in literary analysis, 348
point of view in, 56, 103, 129, 460, 472
in process analysis, 193
using examples for, 152
verb tense for, 103
persuasion, 353. *See also* argument
persuasive purpose, 213, 266–267
phrases
vs. clauses, 414
defined, 530
as fragments, 434, 435–436
modifying, and subject-verb agreement, 456
wordy, 519–520
plagiarism, 19, 390–391
plot, in literature, 326, 347–348
poems
documenting, 387
narrative, 325
point-by-point pattern, for comparison and contrast, 269, 271–272
point of view
consistency in, 56, 472–474
in description, 129
in literary analysis, 350
in literature, 326–327, 348
in narratives, 103, 124
in process analysis, 191, 210
points, in comparison and contrast, 267–268, 294
positive attitude, for writing, 5
possessives, apostrophes for, 509
post hoc fallacy, 215, 355
practice, in writing process, 2–3
preparation, in process analysis, 191
prepositional phrases, 414
for combining sentences, 427
confused as subject, 407–408
defined, 529
as fragments, 436
illogical omissions in, 431
sentences beginning with, 62, 433
prepositions
confused with adverbs, 529
confused with conjunctions, 530
defined, 436, 529

prepositions (*cont.*)
  list of common, 529
  object of, 407, 529
  and subject-verb agreement, 456
presentation, in comparison and contrast, 269–271, 294
present tense
  of irregular verbs, 446–447
  for literature, 103, 460
  of regular verbs, 444–445
prewriting strategies, 31–37
  brainstorming, 34–35
  for cause and effect analysis, 213
  clustering, 36
  for comparison and contrast, 267
  defining controlling idea with, 43
  for definition, 301, 302
  for exemplification, 151
  freewriting, 31–33
  gathering information, 37
  guidelines for, 37–38
  for organizing support, 44–48
  for process analysis, 193
  See also writing process
primary cause and effect, 214
principles
  in analysis by division, 168
  in classification, 237, 264
  in writing process, 2–3
printed sources, documenting, 383–385, 392–393. *See also* books; periodicals
process analysis, 191–193
  basic forms for, 192
  combination, 193
  defined, 150, 191
  for definition, 301
  diction for, 192
  directive, 191
  guidelines for writing, 210–211
  informative, 191
  order in, 192
  organizing ideas in, 47
  point of view in, 191, 210, 473
  preparation/background in, 191
  prewriting procedure for, 193
  professional writings, 196–203
  steps/sequence in, 192
  student writings, 203–208
  topics for writing, 209–210
progressive verb tenses, 452, 455
pronouns
  as adjectives, 528
  agreement with antecedent, 472–476
  case of, 467–470
  and coherence, 55
  defined, 406–407, 526–527
  and gender agreement, 475–476
  indefinite, 406, 456, 474, 526
  and number agreement, 474–475
  objective case, 468–469
  and person agreement, 472–474
  personal, 406
  possessive form of, 509
  references, avoiding unclear, 478
  relative, 413–414, 426
  singular and plural, 407, 527
  standard usage of, 467

subjective case, 467–468
  See also indefinite pronouns
proofreading, 63, 519
proper nouns
  capitalization of, 510, 511
  definite articles with, 522
  hyphenating, 510
  See also nouns
proposition, in argument, 353, 376
ProQuest Direct, 386
protagonist, 326
punctuation
  apostrophes, 509–510
  brackets, 509
  colons, 508
  commas, 497–499
  for complex sentences, 417, 426
  for compound-complex sentences, 427
  for compound sentences, 415, 423–424
  dashes, 507
  in editing process, 63
  end, 496–497
  hyphens, 510
  italics, 507
  parentheses, 508–509
  for quotations, 342–343, 505–507
  self-evaluation of, 4
  semicolons, 502
purpose
  for comparison and contrast, 266–267, 294
  informative vs. persuasive, 213, 266–267

question marks, 497, 506, 509
questions
  as acceptable fragment, 435
  direct and indirect, 497
  formal, introducing, 508
  in introductory paragraph, 86
  pronouns introducing, 407, 527
  punctuation for, 497
  underlining answers to, 10
  verb location in, 410
quiet, quit, quite, 518
quotation indicators, punctuating, 498, 499
quotation marks
  common usage for, 19, 505–506
  punctuation with, 506–507
quotations
  block, 393
  concluding with, 88
  direct and indirect, 19, 342, 505, 506
  documenting, 19, 390–391, 393
  formal, introducing, 508
  in introductory paragraph, 86
  in literary analysis, 342, 350
  punctuation for, 342–343, 505–507
  within quotations, 505, 506
  in research paper, 380
  in summaries, 15
  supporting ideas with, 18–19, 26
  using brackets with, 509

reaction statement, 10, 16–17, 26
  in two-part response, 17–18
Readers' Guide to Periodical Literature, 382

reading
  annotating, 11–12
  importance of, 3
  outlining, 12
  techniques for effective, 10–12, 25
  underlining, 10–11
  for writing, 10–12
reading-related writing
  applying to essays, 20–24
  career-related, 18
  defined, 10
  documentation of sources in, 19–20
  gathering information for, 37
  guidelines for, 25–26
  journal writing, 18
  quotations and references in, 18–19
  reaction statement, 16–17
  summaries, 15–16
  supporting ideas in, 18–19, 26
  two-part response, 17–18
  types of, 14–18
real, really, 485
receive, recieve, 518
"recipe language," 192
recursive writing, 2, 30, 44
reference databases, documenting, 389
references
  documenting, 19
  parenthetical, 391–393
  in research paper, 380
  supporting ideas with, 18–19, 26
  See also documentation of sources
refutation, in argument, 353, 354, 376
regular verbs, 444–446
relative clauses
  in complex sentences, 417, 426
  defined, 413–414
  restrictive and nonrestrictive, 435
relative pronouns, 413–414, 426
remote cause and effect, 214–215
repetition
  for coherence, 55
  for emphasis, 59–60, 216, 235
  misuse of, 60
representative examples, 150, 166
research paper
  avoiding plagiarism in, 390–391
  defined, 380
  documentation of sources for, 383–389, 391–393
  example of, 394–401
  finding sources for, 381–383
  guidelines for writing, 402
  note taking for, 389
  parenthetical references in, 391–393
  preparing works cited list, 393
  refining thesis and outline for, 390
  selecting topic for, 380–381
  submitting required materials with, 394
  writing final draft, 393–394
  writing first draft, 390–393
resolution, in literature, 326
restatement, punctuation for, 508
résumé writing, 537, 539
reviews, documenting, 388

revision process, 54–63
 CLUESS acronym for, 54
 coherence in, 54–56
 and controlling idea, 44
 defined, 54
 emphasis in, 59–60
 evaluating support in, 60–61
 examples of, 66–67, 78–79, 93–94,
  344–345
 guidelines for, 70
 language in, 56–58
 for research paper, 393
 sentence patterns and structure in, 61–63
 unity in, 58–59
rise, raise, 449
rough draft. *See* first draft
run-on sentences, 63, 437–438

sarcastic tone, 57
scholarly projects, documenting, 388
search engines, 383
secondary cause and effect, 214
second person perspective, 56, 472, 473. *See
  also* point of view
Self-Evaluation Chart, 3–4
self-improvement strategies, 3–5
semicolons
 for comma splices and run-ons, 438
 common usage for, 502
 in compound-complex sentences, 427
 in compound sentences, 415, 423–424,
  435
 with conjunctive adverbs, 423–424
 with parentheses, 509
 with quotation marks, 506
sensory impressions, in descriptive writing,
  127–128
sentence outline, 46
sentences
 balance in, 491–493
 basic patterns for, 61–62
 basics for ESL students, 522
 beginnings for, 62, 433
 clauses in, 413–414
 comma splices, 63, 437–438
 complex, 62, 417, 424–426
 compound, 62, 415, 422–424
 compound-complex, 62, 418
 fragments, 62–63, 434–436
 illogical omissions in, 431
 length of, 61, 433
 order in, 433
 parallel structure in, 491–493
 and revision process, 61–63, 70
 run-on, 63, 437–438
 self-evaluation of, 4
 simple, 62, 414
 techniques for spotting problem,
  438–439
 trouble spots with, 62–63, 414
 types of, 413, 414–418, 432
 using variety, 61–62, 432–433
 weak, 464
 and wordy phrases, 519–520
sentences, combining, 422–428
 coordination, 422–424
 coordination and subordination, 426–427

other methods for, 427–428
 subordination, 424–426
series, punctuation for, 497, 502
servile tone, 57
setting, in literature, 325–326, 347
sex bias, avoiding, 475
shocking statement, in introductory paragraph, 86
short stories, 325. *See also* literature
similes, in descriptive writing, 128
simple classification, 238–239
simple definitions, 297–300, 322
simple sentences, 62, 414
simple verb tenses, 452, 454
sit, set, 449
situation, in narratives, 102, 123
slang
 and ESL students, 523
 quotation marks for, 506
 using, 56, 482
slide programs, documenting, 385
sources
 credibility of, 383
 for research paper, 380, 381–383
 types of, 381
 using, in argument, 354–355
 See also documentation of sources; library
  sources
space organizational pattern
 in analysis by division, 168–169
 in cause and effect analysis, 215
 for coherence, 55
 in description, 129
 in exemplification, 152
 words indicating, 55, 129, 152
specific examples, 150, 166
specific words, 58, 128
speculative approach, to literary analysis, 348
speeches, documenting, 385
spell checkers, 5, 63, 519
spelling
 commonly confused and misspelled words,
  517–519
 in editing process, 63
 frequently misspelled words, 516–517
 general rules for, 514–516
 self-evaluation of, 4
stationary, stationery, 518
statistics, in argument, 354
struggle, in narratives, 102, 123
style checkers, 5
subject (of sentence)
 agreement with verb, 453–458
 alternative, 457, 474
 compound, 407, 457, 474
 defined, 406
 illogical omission of, 431
 implied, 407
 location of, 409–410
 missing, as fragment, 434, 436
 nouns as, 406
 and prepositional phrases, 407–408
 pronouns as, 406–407, 467–468
 trouble spots with, 407–408
subject (paragraph/essay)
 defined, 40–41, 51
 in developmental paragraph, 72, 80

in outlines, 47
 in research paper, 380
 See also controlling idea
subject-by-subject pattern, for comparison
  and contrast, 268–269, 271–272
subjective-case pronouns, 467–468
subjective description, 126–127, 128, 147
subjective tests, 536–537
subjunctive mood, 466
subordinating conjunctions
 for comma splices and run-ons, 437
 in complex sentences, 425–426
 confused with prepositions, 530
 defined, 530
 fragments with, 435
 list of common, 425, 438, 530
 punctuation with, 426
subordination, for combining sentences,
  424–427
suffixes, spelling rules for adding, 516
summary
 concluding with, 87, 88
 documentation of sources in, 19
 for gathering information, 37
 guidelines for writing, 15, 25–26
 as reading-related writing, 10, 15–16
 in two-part response, 17
superlative modifiers, 483–485
support
 in argument, 353, 354, 376
 concluding with, 87
 in developmental paragraph, 72, 73–74, 80
 in essays, 83
 evaluating, in revision process, 60–61, 70
 organizing, 44–48, 51
 in outlines, 46–47, 53
 relating to controlling idea, 58–59
 in research paper, 380
 underlining, 10
 using quotations and references for, 18–19
symbolism, in literature, 326
synchronous communications, documenting,
  388
synonyms, 322
 in definitions, 60, 297, 299
systematic learning, 3

tagged conclusion, 88
technical terms, quotation marks for, 506
test taking, 535–537
than, then, 518
that, 431
their, there, they're, 518–519
theme, in literature, 326, 348
there, here, 408, 456
thesaurus, 5
 electronic, 56
 for selecting modifiers, 482
thesis
 in cause and effect analysis, 213–214, 215
 compared with topic sentence, 83, 84–85
 in comparison and contrast, 268
 defined, 40, 84, 96
 direct statement of, 85
 methods for introducing, 85–86
 in outlines, 46–47
 placement of, 59, 84

thesis (*cont.*)
  relating examples to, 150, 166
  in research paper, 380, 390, 394, 396
  restating in conclusion, 59, 87
  revising, 44
  and unity, 58–59
  writing effective, 40–44, 50–51
  See also controlling idea
third person objective perspective, 327
third person omniscient perspective, 327
third person perspective, 56, 472, 473
  in description, 129
  in literature, 327
  in narratives, 103
  See also point of view
thorough, through, 519
time organizational pattern
  in analysis by division, 168
  in cause and effect analysis, 215
  for coherence, 55
  in description, 129
  in exemplification, 152
  in narratives, 103, 124
  in process analysis, 192, 211
  words indicating, 55, 124, 129, 152, 192
title page, in research paper, 380, 394, 395
titles. *See* names and titles
titles of works
  agreement with verb, 457
  capitalization of, 511
  italics for, 507
  quotation marks for, 505
to, too, two, 519
tone, of language, 56–57
topic outline, 46, 81
topics
  for analysis by division, 186–188
  for argument, 373–375
  for cause and effect analysis, 232–234
  for classification, 261–263
  for comparison and contrast, 291–293
  for definition, 319–321
  for description, 146–148
  for exemplification, 164–166
  for literary analysis, 347–350
  for narratives, 121–123
  prescribed, 32
  for process analysis, 209–210
  for research paper, 380–381
  restricted list, 31–32
  topic of your choice, 31
topic sentence
  in cause and effect analysis, 213–214, 215
  compared with thesis, 83, 84–85
  in comparison and contrast, 268
  defined, 40
  in developmental paragraph, 72, 73–74, 80
  in outlines, 46–47
  placement of, 59
  restating in conclusion, 59
  revising, 44
  underlining, 10
  and unity, 58–59
  writing effective, 40–44, 50–51
  See also controlling idea

transitional paragraphs, 72, 83, 85
transitional terms
  for coherence, 55, 192, 211, 269
  sentences beginning with, 433
  for time order, 124
treatment
  defined, 40–41, 51
  in outlines, 47
  in research paper, 380
  in topic sentence, 80
  See also support
truely, truly, 519
two-part response, 10, 17–18, 26

underlining
  after freewriting, 33
  for effective reading, 10–11, 25
  for gathering information, 38
  and test taking, 535, 536
units
  in analysis by division, 168
  in classification, 237
unity, in revision process, 58–59, 70
usage, of language, 56, 444
usage notes, 299

verbals
  defined, 409
  as fragments, 436
  phrases, 414
verb phrases, 408, 527
  in questions, 410
verbs
  action, 408, 527
  active and passive voice of, 463–464
  agreement with subject, 453–458
  being, 408, 465, 527
  compound, 409
  confused with verbals, 409
  defined, 406, 408, 527
  helping, 408, 445, 447, 527
  illogical omission of, 431
  inverted, 456
  location of, 409–410, 527
  missing, as fragment, 434, 436
  regular and irregular, 444–449
  standard usage of, 444
  strong, 465
  subjunctive mood of, 466
  trouble spots with, 408–409, 449
verb tenses
  basics for ESL students, 522–523
  consistency in, 56, 103, 460–461, 523
  defined, 527
  for irregular verbs, 446–448
  kinds of, 452, 454–455
  for literary analysis, 342
  in narratives, 103, 124
  of regular verbs, 444–446
  and verb omissions, 431
videotapes, documenting, 385
vivid examples, 150, 166
vocabulary, self-evaluation of, 4. *See also*
  spelling; words

vocabulary highlights, 114, 138, 140, 176, 248, 252, 280, 283, 285, 314

Warren, Robert Penn, 325
weather, whether, 519
Web sites, documenting, 387
who, whom, 469–470
word choice, and tone, 57. *See also* diction
word histories, 297
word processors, 5
words
  abstract vs. concrete, 128
  commonly confused and misspelled, 517–519
  filler, 408, 456
  frequently misspelled, 516–517
  general vs. specific, 58, 128
  misuse of repetition of, 60
  signaling parallel structure, 492–493
words used as words
  agreement with verb, 457
  italics for, 507
  plural form of, 510
wordy phrases, 519–520
workplace reports, 102
works cited list, 383–389, 393, 400–401.
    See also documentation of sources
write, writen, written, 519
writing in margins. *See* annotating
writing process
  applying to essays, 88–96
  applying to paragraphs, 75–80
  considering audience in, 31
  defined, 30
  editing, 54, 63
  example of stages of, 64–67
  organizing support in, 44–48
  positive attitude in, 5
  practice and principles in, 2–3
  prewriting strategies, 31–37
  as recursive, 2, 30, 44
  revising, 54–63
  self-improvement strategies for, 3–5
  stating controlling idea, 40–44
  understanding assignment, 30–31
  writing first draft, 53–54
  See also prewriting strategies; revision process
Writing Process Worksheet, 5, 6, 30
  for analysis by division, 183–184
  for argument, 369–370
  for cause and effect analysis, 228–229
  for classification, 258–259
  for comparison and contrast, 287–288
  for definitions, 316–317
  for description, 141–142
  examples of, 64–67, 76–80, 89–92
  for exemplification, 160–161
  for literary analysis, 343–345
  for narratives, 116–117
  for process analysis, 204–205

Yahoo!, 383
you're, your, 519